The Marshall Attack

The Marshall Attack

John Nunn and Tim Harding

Collier Books
Macmillan Publishing Company
New York

Collier Books
Macmillan Publishing Company
866 Third Avenue, New York, NY 10022
Collier Macmillan Canada, Inc.

Library of Congress Cataloging-in-Publication Data
Nunn, John
    The Marshall attack / John Nunn and Tim Harding.—1st Collier
Books ed.
        p.   cm.
    ISBN 0–02–035530–0
    1. Chess—Openings. I. Harding, T. D.   II. Title.
    GV1450.2.N88   1990   90–31103   CIP
794.1'22—dc20

Macmillan books are available at special discounts for bulk purchases for sales promotions, premiums, fund-raising, or educational use. For details contact:
Special Sales Director
Macmillan Publishing Company
866 Third Avenue
New York, NY 10022

First Collier Books Edition 1990

10 9 8 7 6 5 4 3 2 1

Printed in Great Britain

Contents

1 Introduction and Layout

This chapter is devoted to a little history and a layout index, showing what is in the book and where it can be found. In addition, a few minor variations which do not fit into any of the other chapters have found their way into this one. Readers should note that Chapters 1–12 inclusive were written by JN, and the rest of the book by TDH. The manuscript was handed in on 29th March 1989, and all important games up to that date are included. In particular, *Informator 45, Tournament Chess 31* and *ChessBase Magazine 11* were consulted, so readers keeping their own updates will know where to start! (Important developments up to and including Skelleftea 1989, which ended on 4th September, were added in proof.)

1	e4	e5
2	♘f3	♘c6
3	♗b5	a6
4	♗a4	♘f6
5	0-0	♗e7
6	♖e1	b5
7	♗b3	0-0 *(1)*

1
W

If Black intends to play the Marshall Attack then this move is essential, but it is interesting to note that some players adopt 7 ... 0-0 as a bluff, even when they have no intention of playing the Marshall. The reason is that many White players are reluctant to enter the main lines of the Marshall, and therefore they adopt an anti-Marshall system (usually 8 a4) against 7 ... 0-0. If a Black player believes that 7 ... 0-0 8 a4 causes Black fewer problems than the main 7 ... d6 lines of the Spanish, then there is no disadvantage to playing 7 ... 0-0; if White plays 8 a4 Black is happy, while after 8 c3 d6 Black has transposed back to the usual lines, having lost nothing. The independent Trajkovic Variation 7 ... ♗b7 is briefly mentioned in Chapter 15.

8 c3

The main anti-Marshall system is 8 a4, but other moves are possible. After 8 d4 Black has a choice between the gambit continuation 8 ... ♘xd4 and the solid 8 ... d6, when White has nothing better than 9 c3. The latter transposes to the line 7 ... d6 8 c3 0-0 9 d4, which has experienced occasional surges of popularity (Chandler, van der Wiel and I have all dabbled with it), but without making any permanent breakthrough. This line is covered in Chapter 21. Less important anti-Marshall systems, such as 8 h3 and 8 d3, may be found in Chapter 22. 8 a4 is normally met by 8 ... ♗b7, but a number of Grandmasters, including Karpov, have tried 8 ... b4. This is in Chapter 18, and the less important lines after 8 a4 are in Chapter 17. The main line of the anti-Marshall is 8 a4 ♗b7 9 d3 d6 10 ♘c3 ♘a5 11 ♗a2 b4 12 ♘e2 and there has been a great deal of top-class experience with this position in the last few years. This main line is in Chapter 19, while deviations on moves 9–12 will be found in Chapter 20.

8 ... d5

This is the characteristic move of the Marshall Attack, named after the American player Frank J. Marshall (1877–1944), who was one of the world's top players for the first quarter of the 20th century. Marshall introduced the gambit in his game against Capablanca at New York 1918 and although he lost this game Marshall continued to experiment with the gambit for the rest of his life. He played 11 ... ♘f6 against Capablanca and to begin with he adopted either this or 11 ... ♗b7, but later he discovered the merits of 11 ... c6, now considered the main line.

9 ed

The alternatives 9 d3 and 9 d4 may be found in Chapter 15, while 9 a4 will normally transpose to line C3 of Chapter 15 after 9 ... ♗b7, or to line B of Chapter 18 after 9 ... b4.

9 ... ♘xd5

The Herman Steiner variation, 9 ... e4, has suffered a decline in popularity so has been cut down to one chapter, namely Chapter 16.

10 ♘xe5

10 h3, 10 d3, 10 d4 and 10 a4 are the other possibilities, analysed in line C of Chapter 15.

10 ... ♘xe5

11 ♖xe5 *(2)*

The first major decision point

2
B

for Black in the Marshall Attack. 11 ... ♘f6, Marshall's original choice, is still occasionally played today even though the tide has been flowing in favour of 11 ... c6 for at least forty years! For 11 ... ♘f6 see Chapter 13. Of the other moves 11 ... ♘b6, 11 ... ♘f4 and 11 ... ♗b7, the first two are distinctly dubious, but the third has recently found favour with some players as a realistic alternative to 11 ... c6. It is too early to say if 11 ... ♗b7 will become a major line in the Marshall, but it is certainly a tricky move for a poorly prepared White player to meet.

11 ... c6
12 d4

At one time this was an almost automatic response, but the merits of other 12th moves are now better appreciated and the important alternatives 12 g3, 12 ♖e1 and 12 d3 may be found in Chapter 12. After the first two alternatives White will usually

continue with d3 rather than d4, in order to support the e4 square. 12 ♕f1 is also in Chapter 12, but this move has nothing to recommend it. Chapter 11 deals with 12 ♗xd5, the so-called Kevitz Variation, aiming to retreat the rook to e3 when Black attacks it, supporting the third rank so that ... ♕h4 may be met by h3 instead of g3. Finally 12 ♗c2 is bad because of 12 ... ♗d6 13 ♖e1 ♗xh2+! 14 ♔xh2 ♕h4+ 15 ♔g1 ♗g4 16 f3 ♗xf3 17 gf (17 ♕xf3 ♕xe1+ 18 ♕f1 ♖ae8 19 d4 ♕g3 20 ♗d2 ♘e3! is good for Black) ♕g3+ 18 ♔f1 (18 ♔h1 ♖ae8!) ♘f4! 19 ♖e2 ♕xf3+ 20 ♔e1 ♖ae8 21 ♖xe8 ♘g2 mate (Bronstein).

12 ... ♗d6
13 ♖e1

Not 13 ♗g5? ♕c7 14 f4 h6 and Black wins. The main alternative here is 13 ♖e2, which has developed over the past five years to become one of the most important lines in the Marshall. It may be found in Chapter 10.

13 ... ♕h4
14 g3

Not 14 h3 ♗xh3 15 gh ♕xh3 16 ♖e5 (16 f4 ♖ae8 is also unpleasant) ♗xe5 17 de ♖fe8 with advantage for Black.

14 ... ♕h3(3)
15 ♗e3

The alternative 15th moves 15 ♗c2, 15 ♕f3, 15 a4, 15 ♕d3, 15

♗xd5 and 15 ♖e4 are in Chapter 9. Of these only the last two have any real importance.

    15 ...   ♗g4

Practically the only move played today, although other ideas have been tested in the past. See Chapter 8.

    16 ♕d3   ♖ae8

There are two significant alternatives, 16 . . . f5 and 16 . . . ♘xe3, both dealt with in Chapter 7. The former attempts to gain flexibility by missing out . . . ♖ae8, so as to play the rook directly to f8 in some lines. There are many transpositional possibilities, but the only independent line is rather risky for Black. 16 . . . ♘xe3 aims for positional compensation based on the two bishops, but it does not equalize.

    17 ♘d2

At almost any stage White may exchange on d5, but playing this too soon gives Black extra options and the best White can hope for is a transposition to normal lines.

    17 ...   ♖e6(4)

This is the most important branch in the Marshall Attack. We call 17 . . . ♖e6 the Main Line, while the alternative 17 . . . f5, the Pawn Push, is the subject of Chapter 6. This book comes to no conclusion as to which line is better.

    18 a4

There are four other playable moves. 18 ♗d1, 18 ♕f1 and 18 c4 are in Chapter 5, while 18 ♗xd5 is in Chapter 4. Lines in which ♗xd5 is played earlier may well transpose into Chapter 4.

    18 ...   f5

This may not be the best move. Of the two alternatives covered in Chapter 3, 18 . . . ba is often just a transposition, but the important Spassky Variation 18 . . . ♕h5 leads to completely independent lines. This relatively positional continuation is probably Black's best option in the Main Line.

After 18 . . . f5 we are in Chapter 2.

2 Main Line: 17 ... ♜e6 18 a4 f5

1 e4 e5 2 ♘f3 ♘c6 3 ♗b5 a6 4
♗a4 ♘f6 5 0-0 ♗e7 6 ♖e1 b5 7
♗b3 0-0 8 c3 d5 9 ed ♘xd5 10
♘xe5 ♘xe5 11 ♖xe5 c6 12 d4
♗d6 13 ♖e1 ♛h4 14 g3 ♛h3 15
♗e3 ♗g4 16 ♛d3 ♖ae8 17 ♘d2
♖e6 18 a4 f5*(5)*

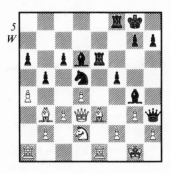

This may be considered the
main line of the Marshall Attack
and, despite numerous games and
analyses, a definite verdict has still
not been reached. Opinion has
swayed first one way and then the
other, but most recent games give
white the upper hand in the
theoretical argument. Black combines his usual ... f5–f4 attack
with the possibility of doubling
rooks on the e-file, while White
will slow down the attack by playing f4 himself and then hope to
break through on the queenside
before he is mated on the other
wing. As usual in the Marshall,
White should not voluntarily take
on d5 without a good reason (e.g.
if he can follow up with an immediate ♛xb5).

19   ♛f1

19 f4 is simply wrong; Henkin
gives 19 ... ♖fe8! 20 ab (Shamkovich and Schiller suggest 20 ♗f2,
but what is the reply to 20 ... ♗e2
21 ♛c2 ♗xf4?) ♗xf4! 21 bc (21 gf
♖g6) ♖xe3 22 ♗xd5+ ♚h8 23
♖xe3 ♗xe3+ 24 ♚h1 ♗xd2 25
♛xd2 ♖e2 26 ♛xe2 ♗xe2 27 c7
f4 winning as the refutation, while
the alternative line 19 ... ♖h6 20
♘f1 ♗f3 21 ♛d2 ba! 22 ♖xa4
♖b8 23 ♗xd5+ ♗xd5 24 ♖xa6
♖e6 25 ♖a7 ♗xf4 26 c4 ♖xe3+
27 ♘xe3 ♗e4 28 d5 ♖g6 29 ♖e7
♖xg3+ 30 hg ♛h1+ 31 ♚f2
♛h2+ 32 ♘g2 ♛xg2+ 33 ♚e3

0–1 was adequate in Semashev–Ozolinsh, Riga 1985.

19 ...   ♕h5

Certainly not 19 ... f4 20 ♗xf4 ♗xf4 21 ♕xh3 ♗xh3 22 ♖xe6 ♗xe6 (or 22 ... ♗xd2 23 ♖xc6 and White wins) 23 gf with an extra pawn for White in the ending.

20   f4

The only way to prevent ... f4, but Shamkovich and Schiller make the interesting suggestion of 20 ab!? f4 21 ♗xf4 ♖xf4 22 ♖xe6 ♗xe6 23 ba with advantage to White. Black should prefer 21 ... ♗xf4 22 ♖xe6 ♗xe6 23 gf ab, regaining the pawn on f4 with good play for the other pawn.

20   ...   ba

This move is best. Although Black voluntarily destroys his own queenside pawn structure, he gains time because White threatened to take on b5, then d5, then play ♕xb5, when the queen comes to d5 with tempo. Now, on the other hand, White cannot bring his queen to attack d5 with gain of tempo. A second point is that White's rook is deflected from the first rank leaving the other rook poorly defended. The alternatives are:

(1) **20 ... ♔h8?!** (illogical since if Black wants to unpin his knight like this he should adopt the Pawn Push line of Chapter 6) 21 ♗xd5 cd 22 ab a5 (22 ... ab 23 ♕xb5! ♖h6 24 ♘f1 ♗f3 25 b3! ♕h3 26 ♖a2 leaves Black unable to augment his attack) 23 b6! g5 24 ♕f2 ♖e4 25 ♘xe4 fe 26 b7! ♕f7 27 ♖xa5 ♕xb7 28 ♖ea1 gf 29 ♖a7 ♕b8 30 ♗xf4 1–0, Gallego–Fernandez Garcia, Spanish Ch. 1985.

(2) **20 ... g5?!** 21 ab ab 22 fg (22 ♖a6? was played in Reucki–Ostapenko, USSR 1970, and since this is just line B41 below with Black having an extra pawn on b5 it is not surprising that Black had fair chances; readers should compare is just line B41 below with Black but the Ostapenko game went 22 ... gf 23 ♖xc6 fg 24 ♕g2 f4 25 ♗xd5 f3 26 ♗xe6+ ♔h8 27 h3 f2+ 28 ♔f1 ♗xe6 29 h4 ♕xh4 30 ♗g5 fe♕+ 31 ♔xe1 ♕xg5 32 ♖xd6 ♖f2 0–1; note that the extra pawn comes in handy in the line after 26 ♗xf3) ♖xe3 23 ♖xe3 f4 24 ♕f3 and Ostapenko assessed this position as clearly better for White. However 24 ... ♗xf3 25 ♕xf3 ♕xf3 (25 ... ♕xg5 26 ♘e4) 26 ♘xf3 fg is not so clear, e.g. 27 ♘e5 gh+ 28 ♔xh2 ♗xe5+ (28 ... ♖f2+ 29 ♔g1! ♖xb2 30 ♗xd5+ cd 31 ♖a8+ ♔g7 32 ♖a7+ ♔g8 33 ♘g4 is good for White) 29 de ♖f2+ 30 ♔g3 ♖xb2 31 ♗xd5+ cd and only careful analysis would show whether White can win this ending. However it is true that few

players would aim for such a position from the opening!

(3) **20 ...** ☖**fe8** (once popular, this has now fallen into disrepute) 21 ab*(6)* and now:

(3a) **21 ...** ☖**xe3** 22 ☖xe3 ☖xe3 23 bc! (in view of the strength of this move, analysis of the unclear 23 ba ♗b8 24 a7 ♗xa7 25 ☖xa7 h6! is redundant) ☖e2 24 ♗xd5+ ♚f8 (24 ... ♚h8 25 h3! wins after 25 ... ♗xh3 26 ♗f3 ♗xf1 27 ♗xh5 ☖xd2 28 ♚xf1 ☖xb2 29 ☖xa6 or 25 ... ☖xd2 26 ♛xa6 ♛e8 27 hg ☖xb2 28 gf h5 29 f6 gf 30 c7 ♗xc7 31 ♛xf6+ ♚h7 32 ♛f5+ ♚g7 33 ♗e4) 25 h3! ♗xh3 (25 ... ☖xd2 26 ♛xa6 and now 26 ... ☖e2 27 ♛c8+ ☖e8 28 ♛d7 or 26 ... ♛e8 27 hg ☖xb2 28 gf h5 29 f6 h4 30 fg+ ♚xg7 31 ♛a7+ ♚h6 32 ♛d7 ♛e3+ 33 ♚h1 ☖h2+ 34 ♚xh2 hg+ 35 ♚h1 winning in both cases) 26 ♗f3 ♗xf1 27 ♗xh5 ☖xd2 28 ♚xf1 ☖xb2 (28 ... ♚e7 29 ☖xa6 ♗c7 30 ☖a7

♚d6 31 ♗f3 was also lost in Mollekens–Dodson, corr. 1983) 29 ☖xa6 g6 30 ♗e2 ♗b8 31 ☖a5! h5 32 ☖d5 h4 33 ☖d8+ ♚e7 34 ☖d7+ ♚e8 35 hg ♗xf4 36 ☖g7 1–0, Gurevich–Grzeskowiak, corr. 1968/9.

(3b) **21 ... ab** 22 ♗xd5 (22 ♗f2 ☖e2!? 23 ☖xe2 ☖xe2 24 ☖a8+ is not dangerous for Black, e.g. 24 ... ♗f8 25 c4 bc 26 ♘xc4 ♗h3 and now 27 ♛ moves allows 27 ... ♛f3, while 27 ♘b6 ♗xf1 28 ♘xd5 is met by 28 ... ♚f7!; alternatively 24 ... ♚f7 25 ♛g2 ☖xd2 26 ♗xd5+ ♚f6 is possible) cd 23 ♛xb5 and now:

(3b1) **23 ...** ♛**f7** (not 23 ... ☖xe3? 24 ☖xe3 ☖xe3 25 ♛xd5+) 24 ♗f2! (24 ♛d3 g5 25 fg f4 26 fg ♗xf4 27 ♘f1 ♗xg5 and White's exposed king gave Black genuine counterchances in Griso–van Vyve, corr. 1966; 24 ♛xd5 ☖xe3 25 ♛xf7+ ♚xf7 26 ☖xe3 ☖xe3 27 ♘c4 ☖e6 is unclear) and Black does not have enough for the two pawns.

(3b2) **23 ...** ♗**xf4** and in Pichler–Wachter, corr. 1985, White contented himself with a draw by 24 gf ♗f3 25 ♘xf3 ♛xf3 26 ♗f2 ☖g6+ ½–½, but 24 ♛xd5! is the critical move. Personally I cannot see a good reply for Black.

Now (after 20 ... ba) we have the first major branch of this section:

A **21 ♗xd5**
B **21 ⬜xa4**

The first line is an attempt to exploit Black's move-order (18 ... f5 instead of 18 ... ba), but this alternative is no reason for Black to give up 18 ... f5, since with best play the result appears to be a draw.

A

21 ♗xd5 cd
22 ♕g2

Certainly not 22 ⬜xa4? walking into 22 ... ♕e8!

22 ... ⬜fe8

This is safest, but Black has a second playable line: 22 ... ⬜e4 23 ⬜xa4 (23 ♘xe4 fe with ... g5 to come leaves White with nothing better than 24 ⬜xa4) g5 (23 ... ♗h3 24 ♕e2 ♗g4 25 ♕xa6 ♗xf4 26 gf ♗h3 27 ♘xe4 fe 28 ♕e2 ♕g6+ 29 ♔h1 ♗g4 is refuted by 30 ⬜a6! when 30 ... ⬜f6 31 ⬜xf6 gf 32 ♕xg4 ♕xg4 33 ⬜g1, 30 ... ♗xe2 31 ⬜xg6

♗f3+ 32 ⬜g2 and 30 ... ♕h5 31 ♕f2 g5 32 ♕g3 win for White) 24 ⬜xa6 gf *(8)* with three choices for White:

(1) **25 ⬜xd6** fe (Blatny recommends 25 ... ⬜xe3, but 26 ♕xd5+ appears good for White as 26 ... ♔h8 fails to 27 ⬜xe3 and 28 ♕e5+) 26 ♘xe4 fe 27 ⬜xe3 ♗h3 transposes into line 2, which should be a draw.

(2) **25 ♘xe4** fe 26 ⬜xd6 (26 ♗xf4 ♗xf4 27 gf ♔h8 28 ⬜ea1 ⬜g8 29 ⬜a8 ♗c8 was unclear in Jiu Shihan–Levitina, Tbilisi 1982) fe 27 ⬜xe3 ♗h3 (not 27 ... ♕f5? 28 h4! and White's king is safe at h2, Romanchuk–Belokopiat, corr. 1978) 28 g4! ♕h4 29 ♕xh3 ♕f2+ 30 ♔h1 ⬜a8 31 ⬜d8+ ⬜xd8 32 g5 (or 32 ♕g3 ♕xb2 33 ⬜e1 ½–½, Matsukevic–Nasilbulin, corr. 1983) ⬜a8 33 ♕e6+ ♔g7 34 ♕f6+ (White could have given perpetual check) ♕xf6 35 gf+ ♔xf6 and after 36 ⬜e2? ♔g5

37 ♖f2 e3 Black even succeeded in winning, Lang–van der Zwan, corr. 1983/4. After the correct 36 ♔g2 ♔f5 Black's protected passed pawn should enable him to hold the draw despite the minus pawn.

(3) **25 gf** is optimistically assessed as clearly better for White by *ECO*, but 25 ... ♖f6 26 ♘xe4 fe 27 ♗f2 ♖g6 28 ♖xd6! ♖xd6 29 ♗g3 ♗f3 30 ♕f1 ♖g6 31 ♔f2 is not at all clear, Black's strong pressure compensating for the two pawns.

23	♕xd5	♔h8
24	♗f2(9)	

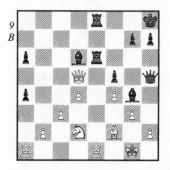

9
B

24 ...   ♗e2

Once again this is the main line, but an acceptable alternative exists: 24 ... ♖xe1+ (but not 24 ... ♗e2 25 ♖xe2 ♖xe2 26 ♕xd6 ♕e8 27 ♘c4 and White wins) 25 ♖xe1 ♖xe1+ 26 ♗xe1 ♕e8 27 ♗f2 h6! (not 27 ... ♕b8? 28 ♘c4 ♗c7 29 ♘e5 ♗xe5 30 ♕xe5

♕xe5 31 fe ♗e2 32 e6 ♔g8 33 d5 ♗c4 34 e7 ♔f7 35 d6 ♔e8 36 ♗d4 g6 37 ♔f2 ♔d7 38 ♔e3 ♗f7 39 ♗c5 ♔c6 40 ♔f4 ♗e8 41 ♗a3 h6 42 ♔e5 ♔d7 43 ♔f6 1–0, V. Agzamov–G. Agzamov, Erevan 1981) 28 ♕xd6 (not 28 ♔g2 ♕e2 29 ♘c4 ♗xf4 30 gf ♗h3+! mating) ♕e2 (surprisingly enough White cannot avoid a draw despite his large material advantage) 29 ♘f1 ♗h3 (or 29 ... ♕d1 30 ♕xa6 ♗e2 31 ♕c8+ ♔h7 32 ♕xf5+ ♔h8 33 ♕h3 ♗g4 34 ♕g2 ♗f3 ½–½, Matsukevic–Filipchenko, corr. 1983) 30 ♕b8+ ♔h7 31 ♘e3 ♕d3 (threat ... ♕b1+ mating) 32 ♘g2 ♕e4 33 ♘e1 ♕e2 34 ♘g2 with a draw, Matsukevic–Chevshenko, corr. 1983.

25   ♔g2

There are a number of alternatives, which deserve attention because the choice of ♔g2 as the main line is purely subjective:

(1) **25 ♖xa4** and now:

(1a) **25 ...   ♗xf4** (probably best) 26 gf ♗c4 and now 27 ♖xc4 ♖xe1+ 28 ♗xe1 ♖xe1+ 29 ♘f1 ♖xf1+ 30 ♔xf1 ♕d1+ or 27 ♕xc4 ♕g4+ 28 ♔h1 ♖xe1+ 29 ♗xe1 ♖xe1+ 30 ♘f1 ♕f3+ 31 ♔g1 ♕e3+ with a draw in both cases.

(1b) **25 ...   ♗c4** (there seems little reason to play this as White can force Black to take a draw in any case) 26 ♕xc4 (26 ♖xc4 ♖xe1+ 27 ♗xe1 ♖xe1+ 28 ♘f1 ½–½, Popovic–Pinter, Hastings 1980/1) ♖xe1+ 27 ♗xe1 ♖xe1+ 28 ♘f1 ♕e8 29 ♔f2 ♖b1 30 ♖a2 ♕e1+ 31 ♔g2 ♕e4+ 32 ♔h3 and in view of the threats of ♕c8+ and ♘d2 I doubt if Black has enough for the two pawns.

(2) **25 ♕g2** is an untested idea; Black may try **25 ... g5** 26 fg ♕xg5 27 ♘f3, **25 ... h6** 26 ♖xa4 g5 27 fg (27 c4 gf 28 ♖xa6?! ♗xc4 is fine for Black) hg 28 d5 ♖6e7 29 h4 g4 30 c4 or 25 ... a3 26 ba (26 b4 a5) ♗c7, which should all be good for White in varying degrees. The best line is probably **25 ... ♖g6!?** 26 ♖xa4 ♗xf4 with an unclear position.

(3) **25 ♘c4** (probably the weakest move as now White has no clear route to equality) ♗c7! (25 ... ♗xf4 26 ♖xe2 ♖xe2 27 gf ♖xf2 28 ♔xf2 ♕xh2+ 29 ♔f1 a3 is usually given the somewhat mysterious verdict of unclear; Black has still to prove his sacrifice correct) 26 ♘e5 ♗xe5 27 ♖xe2 (27 de ♗f3 28 ♕c4 ♕xh2+ wins, a constant danger once the knight has given up control of f3) ♕xe2 28 de ♕xb2 29 ♖xa4 ♕xc3 30 ♖c4 ♕a1+ 31 ♔g2 h6 (there is no argument about Black's advantage; the only question is whether or not it is enough to win) 32 ♕d3?! (32 ♖c6 ♖xc6 33

♕xc6 ♖g8 34 e6?! ♕f6 is very good for Black, but 32 ♖c7 would have kept Black's advantage to a minimum after 32 ... ♕a3 33 ♕b7 or 32 ... ♕b1 33 h4 intending ♗c5 followed by ♕d7) ♕a2! 33 ♖c7 (33 ♖c2 ♕b1 34 ♕xf5 ♖c6 35 ♕f7 ♕xc2 36 ♕xe8+ ♔h7 and 37 ... ♕e4+ wins) ♖b6! 34 ♖c2 ♖b2 35 ♖xb2 ♕xb2 36 ♕xa6 ♕c2 37 ♕b7 ♖d8 38 h3 ♖d2 39 ♕f3 ♖d3 40 ♕a8+ ♔h7 41 g4 ♕e2 42 gf ♕h5 43 ♕e4 ♕xh3+ 44 ♔g1 ♕f3 0–1, Tseshkovsky–Agapov, Kiev 1984.

25 ... h6!

Better than 25 ... ♖h6?! 26 ♘f3! ♕e4 27 ♘h4 ♖f6 28 ♖xa4 ♗d3 29 ♖aa1 h6 30 ♖ed1 ♕e2 31 ♖xd3! ♕xd3 32 ♘xf5 ♗xf4 33 ♕d7 ♖g6 34 ♘e7 and wins, Yim–Kaliwoda, corr. 1981/2.

26 ♘f3

26 ♖xa4 turned out badly after 26 ... ♗xf4 27 gf ♕g4+ 28 ♗g3 (28 ♔h1 ♗c4 29 ♕xc4 ♖xe1+ 30 ♗xe1 ♖xe1+ 31 ♘f1 ♕f3+ 32 ♔g1 ♕e3+ 33 ♔h1 ♕e4+ 34 ♔g1 ♖e2 is also very good for Black) ♖e3 29 ♔f2 ♗d3! 30 ♖xe3 ♖xe3 31 ♕f3 ♖xf3+ 32 ♘xf3 ♗e4 33 ♘e1 ♕d1 and Black won in Lang–Ramon, corr. 1985.

26 ...   ♗xf4(10)
and now:

(1) **27 gf** ♕g4+ 28 ♗g3 ♗xf3+ 29 ♕xf3 ♖e2+ 30 ♖xe2

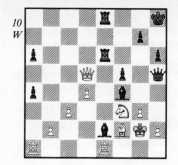

10
W

♖xe2+ 31 ♕f2 h5 32 d5 h4 33 d6
♖xf2+ 34 ♔xf2 hg+ 35 hg ♕g6
36 ♖d1 and by far the most likely
result is perpetual check after, for
example, 36 ... ♔h5.

(2) **27 ♘g1** ♗d2 28 ♖xe2 ♖xe2
29 ♘xe2 ♕xe2 30 ♕xf5 ♗e3 31
♕f7 ♗xf2 32 ♕xf2 ♕b5 33 ♕f7
♕xb2+ ½-½, Matsukevic–Fili-
pov, corr. 1983.

B

21   ♖xa4*(11)*

The most natural move; White
keeps his white-squared bishop
for the moment and prepares to
demolish Black's queenside by
♖xa6 and ♖xc6. Now Black has
four major lines:

11
B

B1   21 ...   ♔h8
B2   21 ...   ♖fe8
B3   21 ...   ♖b8
B4   21 ...   g5

Line B4 is the old main line,
now more or less refuted. Lines
B1 and B2 are both interesting
and have received few practical
tests. The analysis given below
indicates an advantage for White
in B1, but B2 is not so clear and
these lines are fertile ground for
research. The current main variation is line B3; the move ... ♖b8
induces White to take on d5,
when Black has achieved his objective of avoiding ♔h8. Unfortunately for Black it is this line,
which has always appeared
Black's best option after 21
♖xa4, that has recently suffered a
severe setback. Although these
variations may continue to
achieve good practical results,
particularly at club level, the
theoretical situation looks bad for
Black.

B1

21   ...   ♔h8
22   ♘c4

Or 22 ♗xd5 cd 23 ♖xa6 (this is
also critical) ♖fe8 (23 ... ♕e8 24
♕f2 ♕b5 25 ♖a2 ♖fe8 gives
Black reasonable play, but White
may improve by 24 ♗f2! with the
idea 24 ... ♗e2? 25 ♖xd6 and
wins) transposing to the note to
Black's 22nd in line B2 below.

22 ...   ♗xf4!?

Theory only gives 22 ... ♘xe3 23 ♘xe3 with a clear advantage for White. Unfortunately the capture on f4, although ingenious, is not adequate.

23   ♗xf4

Not 23 gf ⌶g6 with advantage for Black.

23 ...   ♘xf4

24 ⌶xe6 (not 24 gf ♗h3) ♘xe6 25 ♘e5! (Black has regained his pawn, but now suffers from his bad pawn structure) f4 26 ♗xe6 ♗xe6 27 ⌶xa6 ♔g8 28 ♘xc6! (28 ♕f3? ♗f5 29 ⌶a1 ♗d5 is good for Black) ♗h3 29 ⌶a5! ♕h6 (29 ... ♕g4 30 ♘e5) 30 ♕f3 and Black's attack has run out of steam.

B2

21 ...   ⌶fe8(12)

22 ⌶xa6(?)

On the basis of the main line this move is a mistake, and after it White will be very lucky to draw. The alternative is 22 ♕f2 (not 22 ♘c4? ♗xf4) g5 (the lines 22 ...

⌶8e7 23 ⌶xa6 ♕e8 24 ♘c4 and 22 ... ♔f8 23 ♗xd5 cd 24 c4 dc 25 ⌶xa6 are good for White) and now:

(1) **23 ⌶xa6** gf 24 gf ♔h8 (24 ... ⌶g6 25 ♔h1 ♔h8 26 ♗xd5 cd 27 ⌶g1 ♗xf4 was played in Cvachoucek–Kruglov, corr. 1973 and now 28 ⌶xg6! ♗xe3 29 ⌶e1 is good for White) 25 ♗xd5 (25 ⌶xc6 ♗xf4! is good for Black) cd 26 ♘f1 ⌶g8 27 ♘g3 ♗f3 28 ⌶a8 ⌶eg 29 ⌶xg8+ ⌶xg8 30 ⌶f1 ♗e4 followed by ... ♕h3 and ... h5–h4, giving Black a dangerous initiative for the two sacrificed pawns.

(2) **23 fg!?** After this the critical continuation is 23 ... f4 24 gf ♗h3!, when the game Junge–Wegner, Bundesliga 1989 continued 25 ♔h1 ♕g4 26 ♘f3 ⌶xe3 27 ⌶xe3 0–1. A good line for White on move 25 is hard to find, e.g. 25 ♘f1 ♗xf1 26 ♔xf1 ♕h3+, or 25 ♗d1 ⌶xe3 26 ♗xh5 ⌶e1+ 27 ♘f1 ⌶8e7 intending ... ♗xf4. Perhaps White should try 25 ♔h1 ♕g4 26 ⌶g1, although this appears to be a draw at best.

22 ...   ⌶xe3

Or 22 ... ♔h8 (this is important as line B1 may reach it by transposition) 23 ♗xd5 cd 24 ♕f2 (24 ♕b5 g5 seems to be slightly better for White after 25 ♕xd5 gf 26 ⌶xd6 ⌶xe3 27 ⌶xe3 fe 28 ⌶d8 ed 29 ♕e5+ ♔g8 30 ⌶xe8+ ♕xe8 31 ♕xe8+ ♔g7 32

♕a4 d1=♕+ 33 ♕xd1 ♗xd1, but 24 ... ♖h6! is a good reply since 25 h4 is met by 25 ... ♗xf4 26 gf ♖xa6 27 ♕xa6 ♕xh4, while 25 ♘f1 ♗f3 26 ♗f2 ♖g8! gives Black dangerous attacking chances) g5 25 fg and now Suetin continues 25 ... f4 26 gf h6 27 c4 hg 28 ♖xd6 ♖xd6 29 fg ♗h3 30 cd ♕g4+ 31 ♕g3 with advantage to White, but he makes no mention of the obvious 25 ... ♗xg3, which looks unclear.

23 ♖xe3 ♖xe3
24 ♖xc6 ♕e8

Black has two somewhat similar lines, and there is disagreement on which is the best. After 24 ... ♖e2!? 25 h4 (why not 25 h3, meeting 25 ... ♗xh3 by 26 ♗xd5+ and 27 ♗f3?) ♕e8 (25 ... ♖xd2 26 ♖xd6 ♕e8 may be possible) 26 ♗xd5+ ♔f8 27 ♘e4 fe 28 ♖xd6 ♕b8 (not 28 ... ♕a4? 29 f5 ♗f3 30 f6 gf 31 ♖xf6+ ♔e7 32 ♖f7+ ♔e8 33 b3 ♕a3 34 ♖xf3 winning, Miskovsky–Goth, corr. 1985) 29 ♖a6 ♕xb2 and Black wins according to van der Tak. However this is doubtful, since White has the defence 30 ♖a8+ ♔e7 31 ♖a7+ ♔d6 (or else perpetual check as the king cannot reach the b-file) 32 ♗xe4! ♗h3 33 ♖a6+ and Black cannot avoid the checks. This line, together with 25 h3!?, should be enough to turn Black players away from 24 ... ♖e2.

25 ♗xd5+ ♔f8

26 ♘e4 fe! (not 26 ... ♖xe4? 27 ♗xe4 fe 28 ♖xd6 e3 29 ♕b1 ♕a8 30 d5 e2 31 ♔g2 ♔e7 32 ♖c6 ♔d7 33 h3 winning for White, Dragunov–Konstantinopolsky, corr. 1965) 27 ♖xd6 ♖d3 and again Black wins according to van der Tak. This time I suspect he is right, for example 28 ♖a6 ♕b5 or 28 ♗b3 e3! In any case White is in serious trouble.

The real test of 21 ... ♖fe8 is 22 ♕f2, but there is not enough practical experience to give a reliable verdict. As the other Black 21st moves look dubious, this could be Black's best chance against 21 ♖xa4.

B3

21 ... ♖b8

The threat is 22 ... ♖xb3, and White's best reply is the simple capture on d5. Although Black has avoided wasting time with ... ♔h8 the rook on b8 is not especially well placed and often returns to the e-file. Moreover White's queen sometimes gets to d5, and then Black once again has problems with his king position.

22 ♗xd5

Not 22 ♕xa6 ♖xb3 23 ♘xb3 ♖xe3 winning, nor 22 ♕f2 ♖xb3 23 ♘xb3 ♗d1 with a good game for Black, while 22 ♖xa6 ♖xb3 23 ♘xb3 ♘xe3 24 ♖a8+ ♔f7 25 ♕f2! ♗h3 26 ♕e2 ♕xe2 27 ♖xe2 ♘c4 is probably slightly better for

Black. However there is one interesting idea which is not very well known, namely **22 ♗f2!?** After **22 ... ♖xe1 23 ♕xe1 ♖e8 24 ♕f1 ♖e2 25 ♖xa6 ♗h3 26 ♕d1 ♗g4 27 ♕f1 ♗h3** White played **28 ♖xc6!** in Rohde–Belyavsky, Alicante 1978, collecting bishop, knight, three pawns and the advantage for the queen. Harding suggests **22 ... ♗e2** (22 ... ♖h6 23 h4) 23 ♕g2 (or 23 ♗xd5 cd 24 ♕g2 ♕f7 25 ♘f3 ♕e8 26 ♖aa1 ♕b5 27 ♘e5 ♗xe5 28 de ♗d3 29 b4 ♗e4 30 ♕f1 ♗d3 ½–½, Usati–Gabran, corr. 1975/7) ♖xb3 24 ♘xb3 ♗f3 (he also suggests 24 ... ♘xf4 and 24 ... ♗xf4 but these are less convincing) and it seems to me that this is fine for Black, e.g. 25 ♕f1 (25 ♖xe6 ♗xg2 26 ♔xg2 ♕g4! 27 ♖e1 ♘xf4+ 28 ♔g1 ♘h3+ 29 ♔g2 f4 is very good for Black) and now Black can take a draw by 25 ... ♗e2 26 ♕g2 (26 ♖xe2 ♖xe2 threatening 27 ... ♘e3 is good for Black) ♗f3 or play for a win by 25 ... ♖h6 or 25 ... ♘xf4!?, the latter being

proposed by Shamkovich and Schiller.

| 22 | ... | cd*(13)* |

There is a further branch here, with B32 being the critical line.

| **B31** | 23 | ♕g2 |
| **B32** | 23 | ♖xa6 |

The remaining possibility is 23 b3 ♗be8 24 ♕f2 g5 25 fg f4 26 gf ♗h3 27 ♖xa6 (27 ♘f1? ♗xf1 28 ♔xf1 ♗xf4 was good for Black, Ioseliani–Blatny, Baden-Baden 1988), when Black has at least two ways of forcing a draw, but probably cannot do better:

(1) **27 ... ♗xf4** 28 ♖xe6 ♕g4+ 29 ♕g3 ♗xg3 30 ♖xe8+ ♔f7 31 ♖e7+! ♔f8 (31 ... ♔xe7 32 ♗f2+ is not better for Black, but 31 ... ♔g6 32 ♖e6+ ♕xe6 33 hg ♕c6 is a risky winning try) 32 ♖e8+ ♔f7 with perpetual check.

(2) **27 ... ♕g4+** 28 ♕g3 ♖xe3 29 ♖xe3 ♕d1+ 30 ♕e1 and now Black should give immediate perpetual check by 30 ... ♕g4+ since 30 ... ♕xe1+ 31 ♖xe1 ♖xe1+ 32 ♔f2 leads to an ending which is probably also a draw, but any winning chances lie with White.

B31

	23	♕g2	♕e8
	24	♕xd5	♔h8
	25	♔f2	

Or 25 ♘c4 (25 ♘f1? ♗f3 26 ♕xf5 ♖f6 27 ♕a5 ♖b5 28 ♕xa6

13
W

♗b7 29 ♕a7 ♕c6 wins for Black)
♗xf4! 26 gf ♖g6 and now:

(1) **27 ♔h1?** ♕d7! 28 ♕g2 ♗h3
0–1, Johansson–Mortensen,
Glucksburg 1977.

(2) **27 ♔f2?!** ♕xa4 28 ♗d2 is
suggested by Maric, but 28 ...
♗h3 29 ♘e5 ♖g2+ 30 ♔f3 h6
appears very promising for Black.

(3) **27 ♘d6!** with a further
branch:

(3a) **27 ... ♗h3+** (a risky winning try) 28 ♔f2 ♖xb2+ 29 ♖e2
♖g2+ 30 ♕xg2 ♖xe2+ 31
♔xe2 ♕h5+ 32 ♕f3 ♗g4 33
♕xg4 fg (not 33 ... ♕xg4+? 34
♔d2 ♕g2+ 35 ♔d3 g6 36 ♖b4
winning for White, Markland–
Weiner, corr. 1983) 34 ♔d3 (34
♖xa6 g3+ 35 ♔e1 ♕f3 wins)
♕xh2 35 ♖xa6 ♕h1 36 ♖b6 h6
37 ♘f7+ (not 37 f5? ♕d1+ 38
♗d2 g3 39 f6 ♕f1+ 40 ♔e4
♕xf6 41 ♗e3 g2 42 d5? ♕e7+
0–1, Canfell–Blatny, Altensteig
1988, but 37 d5 ♕xd5+ 38 ♗d4
activating the bishop is unclear
according to Blatny) ♔h7 38 ♘e5
♕d1+ 39 ♔e4 (39 ♗d2? g3 40
♖g6 ♕f1+ 41 ♔e4 g2 42 ♗e3
♕h1 43 ♔d3 h5 is good for
Black) ♕h1+ 40 ♔d3 ♕d1+
with perpetual check.

(3b) **27 ... ♗f3+** (the safe option) 28 ♔f1 ♗xd5 29 ♘xe8
♖xb2 30 ♖e2 (and not 30 ♖b4?
♗g2+ 31 ♔g1 ♗e4+ 0–1,
Heaven–Hessenbruch, Groningen
1978/9) ♖b1+ 31 ♖e1 ♖b2

drawing by repetition, Tshuva-
sov–Eglitis, corr. 1975.

25 ... g5

After 25 ... ♖xb2 26 ♖a2
♖xa2 27 ♕xa2 g5 the game Chiburdanidze–Tseshkovsky, Tashkent 1980, continued 28 ♘c4 gf
29 ♘xd6 fe+ 30 ♖xe3 ♕h5 31
♕xe6 ♕xh2+ 32 ♔f1 ♕h1+ ½–
½, but Matsukevic proposed 28 d5
as an improvement. However 28
... ♖xe3 29 ♖xe3 ♗c5 30 ♘f1 gf
31 gf ♗h3 appears good enough
to hold the balance, e.g. 32 ♕xa6
(32 ♕c4 ♕e7 or 32 ♔g3? ♕g6+)
♗xf1 33 ♕f6+ ♔g8 and its
about time White gave perpetual
check. This represents a reserve
line for Black if the main variation should turn out badly.

26 ♖xa6

26 h3? is bad because of 26 ...
gf 27 gf ♗e7!.

26 ... ♖xb2

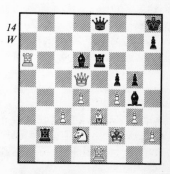

27 ♖a2

Certainly not 27 ♖xd6? ♖xe3
and Black wins, but 27 ♖a8 is
reasonable and could transpose to

the main line after 27 ... ♗b8 28 ♖a2 ♖xa2 29 ♕xa2 gf 30 gf ♗xf4. Finally, Popolitov–Trushakov, corr. 1980/1 went 27 ♕a8 ♖b8 28 ♕c6 ♕h5 29 h3 ♕xh3 (29 ... gf 30 ♗xf4 ♖xe1 31 ♔xe1 ♖e8+ 32 ♘e4! ♖xe4+ 33 ♔d2 ♗xf4+ 34 gf ♖e8 35 ♕f6+ ♔g8 36 ♖a7 is good for White) 30 ♕g2 gf 31 ♕xh3 ♗xh3 32 gf with a slightly better ending for White. However 30 ... ♕h5 looks better, when Black has considerable pressure for the pawn.

27	...	gf
28	gf	♖xa2
29	♕xa2	♗xf4!

and now:

(1) 30 ♕xe6 ♕xe6 31 ♗xf4 ♕a2 32 ♖e5 ♕c2 33 d5 ♔g8 34 d6 ♕xc3 35 ♖d5 ♕c6 36 ♖d4 ♕c5 37 ♘b3 ♕c2+ 38 ♘d2 ♕d1 ½–½, Burkhart–Scherfke, corr.1976.

(2) 30 ♘f1 ♖e4 31 ♕d2 ♗d6 (or 31 ... ♗c7 32 d5 f4 33 ♗c5 ♖xe1 34 ♕xe1 ♕d8 35 ♕e7 ♕xe7 36 ♗xe7 and Black held the draw by 36 ... ♗b6+ 37 ♔e1 ♔g7 38 ♗d6 ♗a5 39 ♗e5+ ♔g6 40 ♘d2 ♔f5 41 ♗d4 ♗d8 42 c4 ♗a5 43 c5 ♗f3 44 d6 ♗c6 45 ♔d1 ♗xd2 46 ♔xd2 ♔e6 ½–½ in Polsterer–van der Weijer, corr. 1986/8) 32 ♗g5 f4 33 ♗f6+ ♔g8 34 h4 ♕c6 35 ♘h2 ♖e3 36 ♖xe3 fe+ 37 ♕xe3 ♗xh2 38 ♕g5+ ♔f7 39 ♕g7+ ½–½, Kosenkov–Gabran, corr. 1975.

B32

23	♖xa6	♖be8(15)

There are two other possibilities, the second of which deserves investigation since the main line appears bad for Black:

(1) **23 ... ♖xb2** and now:

(1a) **24 ♕g2!** ♖b5 (24 ... ♕e8 25 ♕xd5 ♔h8 26 ♘c4 wins while 24 ... ♕f7 25 ♕xd5 ♖xd2 26 ♖xd6 ♖xd6 27 ♕xf7+ ♔xf7 28 ♗xd2 ♗f3 29 ♖e5 ♖d5 30 ♔f2 ♖xe5 31 de leads to a won ending for White) 25 c4 dc 27 ♕c6 (not 26 ♘xc4? ♗f3 27 ♕f2 ♗b4! with a dangerous attack, e.g. 28 ♖xe6 ♗xe1 29 ♕c2 ♗xg3 and Black won in Broeken–van der Weijer, Netherlands 1989) ♕e8 27 ♘xc4 ♕xc6 28 ♖xc6 ♖d5 29 ♖a1 was very good for White in Wikstrom–Smith, corr. 1969.

(1b) **24 ♖a8+** (this is dubious) and now:

(1b1) **24 ... ♖e8** 25 ♖xe8+ ♕xe8 26 ♕a6 ♗f8 27 c4 ♗b4 28 cd ♕f8 29 ♕e6+ ♔h8 30 ♘c4 wins.

(1b2) **24 ... ♔f7** 25 ♖a7+ ♔g8 (the alternatives 25 ... ♗e7 26 c4, 25 ... ♖e7 26 ♖xe7+ ♗xe7 27 ♕g2 and 25 ... ♔g6 26 c4 are all good for White) 26 ♕a6 ♖xe3 (26 ... ♖h6 27 h4 ♖b8 28 ♕c6 wins) 27 ♖xe3 ♖xd2 28 ♖a8+ ♔f7 29 ♖f8+! wins.

(1b3) **24 ... ♗f8!** 25 c4 ♖xe3 26 ♖xe3 ♖xd2 27 h4 ♖d1 28 ♖e1

(28 ♕xd1 ♗xd1 29 ♖ee8 ♕xe8!
30 ♖xe8 dc wins for Black) ♗e2
29 ♕f2 ♗xc4 and Black should
win.

(2) 23 ... ♕e8 24 ♗f2! ♕d7 (24
... ♗e2 25 ♖xd6 ♗xf1 26 ♖dxe6
wins for White) 25 ♖xe6 ♕xe6 26
c4 (Chandler later criticized this
move, since White does not appear able to win the resulting ending) dc 27 ♕xc4 ♕xc4 28 ♘xc4
♗e2 29 ♖c6 ♗xc4 30 ♖xc4
♖xb2 31 ♖c3 ♔f7 32 ♖d3 ♖c2
33 ♔g2 h6 34 ♖b3 g5 35 fg hg 36
h4 f4 37 gf ♗xf4 38 ♔f3 gh 39
♗xh4 and Black held the draw in
Chandler–P. Littlewood, London
(Lloyds Bank) 1987.

Now there is a final branch,
with 24 ♕b5! apparently refuting
Black's system:

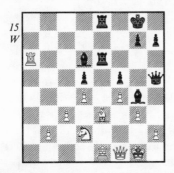

15
W

B321   24 ♕g2
B322   24 ♕f2
B323   24 ♕b5!

B321

24   ♕g2   ♖xe3

25   ♖xe3   ♖xe3
26   ♕xd5+
26 ♖xd6 ♖e1+ 27 ♘f1 ♗f3
and now 28 g4 is the only move,
for otherwise 28 ... ♖e2 wins, but
even then 28 ... fg is good for
Black.

26   ...   ♕f7
Better than 26 ... ♔h8 27
♕xd6 ♖e1+ 28 ♘f1 h6 29
♕f8+ ♔h7 30 ♖a8 winning for
White.

27   ♕xd6
Or 27 ♕xf7+ ♔xf7 and now
28 ♖xd6 ♖e1+ 29 ♘f1 ♗h3 30
♔f2 ♖xf1+ 31 ♔e3 and 28 ♘c4
♖e1+ 29 ♔f2 ♖e2+ 30 ♔f1
♗b8 lead to endings which are at
least equal for Black since the
three pawns are not yet advanced
while Black's pieces are very active.

27   ...   ♖e1+
28   ♘f1
After 28 ♔f2 ♖e2+ 29 ♔f1
Black may force a draw by 29 ...
♕e8 30 ♕d5+ ♔h8 31 ♖a8
♗h3+ 32 ♔g1 ♖e1+. Ftacnik
suggests 29 ... ♕b7, but after 30
d5 the most likely result is again a
draw, by 30 ... ♖xd2 31 ♖b6
♖d1+ 32 ♔f2 ♕a7 33 ♕e6+
♕f7 34 ♕c8+ etc.

28   ...   h6!
Ftacnik's drawing line 28 ...
♕b7 29 ♖c6 ♕a8 30 ♕d5+ ♔h8
31 ♕c5 ♖xf1+ 32 ♔xf1 ♕a1+
may be improved by 31 ♕c4!

♜xf1+ 32 ♚xf1 ♛a1+ 33 ♚f2
♛xb2+ 34 ♚g1 ♛c1+ 35 ♛f1
♛e3+ 36 ♛f2 ♛c1+ 37 ♚g2
and Black runs out of checks.

After 28 ... h6! Blatny considers that Black has enough compensation for the three pawns.

B322

 24 ♛f2 g5*(16)*

Blatny suggests 24 ... ♛f7 with an 'unclear' assessment, but this idea does not convince me.

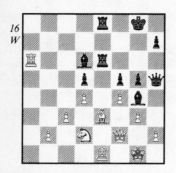

16
W

 25 ♜xd6

A crucial moment. The exchange sacrifice leads to equality, so various improvements have been put forward:

(1) **25 fg** ♝xg3 26 ♛xg3 (26 ♜xe6 ♝xf2+ 27 ♝xf2 ♜xe6 28 ♜xe6 f4 is also good for Black) ♜xa6 is probably good for Black.

(2) **25 c4** gf 26 gf ♜g6 27 ♚h1 dc 28 d5. This must be fine for Black, who is only one pawn down yet still has very strong pressure.

(3) **25 b3!?** gf 26 gf ♛h3! (better than 26 ... ♜g6 27 ♚h1 ♚h8 28 ♜g1, when 28 ... ♝xf4 fails to 29 ♜xg6 ♝xe3 30 ♜e1!) and a draw was agreed here in Ernst–Blatny, Poznan 1987 (this is similar to the note to White's 22nd move in line B2). Indeed, Black threatens 27 ... ♜xe3 28 ♜xe3 ♜xe3 29 ♜xd6 ♜e2, while after 27 ♞f1 ♜g6 28 ♞g3 h5 he has dangerous threats.

 25 ... ♜xd6
 26 fg ♜de6
and now:

(1) **27 h4?** (now Black is better) f4! 28 gf ♝h3! 29 ♞f1 ♝xf1 30 ♚xf1 ♛g4 31 ♝d2 ♜xe1+ 32 ♝xe1 ♛h3+ 33 ♚g1 ♛e6 34 ♚f1 ♛e4 35 ♛d2 ♛f3+ 36 ♝f2 ♜e4 37 g6 h5 38 c4 ♜xf4 39 ♛e1 ♛h3+ 0–1, Prandstetter–Blatny, CSSR Ch. 1986.

(2) **27 ♛f4!** ♝h3 28 ♚f2 ♜e4 29 ♞xe4 (not 29 ♛d6? f4 30 ♛xd5+ ♝e6! 31 ♛xe4 ♛xh2+ 32 ♛g2 fg+ winning, while after 29 ♛f3 ♝g4 30 ♞xe4! fe 31 ♛h1 ♜b8! 32 ♝c1 ♝h3 Black has a continuing attack) fe 30 ♚g1 ♜f8 31 g4 ♝xg4 (or 31 ... ♜xf4 leading to a draw by perpetual check) 32 ♛e5 ♛f7 33 ♛g3 with an unclear and roughly balanced position according to Blatny.

B323

 24 ♛b5! ♛f7*(17)*

The point of ♛b5 as opposed to ♛g2 is that White may meet 24

... ≜xe3 25 ≜xe3 ≜xe3 by 26 ≜xd6 and Black cannot cut off the queen's attack on d5 by ... ≜e1+ and ... ≜f3. This line wins for White after 26 ... ≜e1+ 27 ♘f1 h6 28 ♕xd5+ ♔h7 29 ≜d8, so the capture on e3 is impossible.

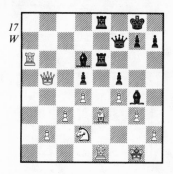

17
W

25 h3! ≜h5

Equivalent to resignation, but even 25 ... ≜xh3 26 ♘f3 h6 (26 ... ≜xe3 27 ≜xe3 ≜xe3 loses to 28 ≜xd6 h6 29 ♔f2 followed by ♕xd5) 27 ♘e5 ≜xe5 28 ≜xe6 ≜xe6 29 de is very bad for Black, who has no compensation for the minus pawn.

26 ♕xd5 ≜xf4

Or 26 ... ≜xe3 27 ♕xf7+ ♔xf7 28 ≜xe3 ≜xe3 29 ≜xd6 ≜e1+ 30 ♘f1 ≜e2 (the preliminary h3 has cut out ... ≜h3 here; if 30 ... ≜e2 then 31 ♔f2) 31 g4! fg 32 ♘g3 winning for White.

27 ≜xe6 ≜xe6

28 ♘f1 ≜xg3 29 ♘xg3 f4 30 ♕xh5 ≜g6 31 ♔h2 1–0, Short–Pinter, Rotterdam 1988.

B4

21 ... g5
22 ≜xa6

22 ≜a5 is inferior and after 22 ... gf (or 22 ... ♔h8 23 ≜xd5 cd 24 ≜xd5 ≜h6! 25 ♕f2 gf 26 ≜xf4 ≜xf4 27 gf ≜g8 28 ♔h1 ≜h3 and now 29 ♘f3 ≜hg6! 30 ♘g5 h6 31 ♘f7+ ♔h7 32 ≜d7 ≜g1+ wins so White must play 29 ♘f1 ≜g2+ 30 ♕xg2 ≜xg2 31 ♔xg2 ♕h3+ 32 ♔f2 ♕h4+ with an edge for Black) 23 ≜xd5 (23 ≜xf4 ≜xf4 24 ≜xe6 ≜xd2 25 ≜xc6 ≜e3+ wins) fg 24 ♕g2 (24 hg cd! 25 ≜xd5 f4! 26 ≜xe6+ ≜xe6 27 ≜xf4 ≜d5 is dangerous for White) cd 25 ≜xd5 f4 Black had a winning attack in Curtis–Hazai, Canberra 1986; the finish was 26 ≜xf4 ≜xf4 27 hg ≜xd2 28 ≜xe6 ♔h8! 29 ≜e5 ♕h6 30 ♕e4 ≜f3 31 ♕h4 ≜e3+ 0–1.

22 ... gf(18)

Certainly not 22 ... ♔h8? 23 ≜xc6 ♘xe3 24 ♕f2 ♘d1 25 ≜xd1 ≜xe1+ 26 ♕xe1 ≜e8 27 ♕f1 ≜xd1 28 ≜xd6 winning, nor 22 ... ♕e8? 23 ≜xc6! ≜xe3 24 ≜xd5+ ♔h8 25 ≜xe3 ♕xe3+ 26 ♕f2 and wins, Schuler–Hallier, corr. 1966.

We now have a major division:
B41 23 ≜xc6
B42 23 ≜xf4!

The first line was considered critical for many years, but it now appears that the refutation lies in 23 ♗xf4!.

B41

    23   ♖xc6

Astonishingly for such a sharp position Black has three playable moves, and it is quite unclear which is the best:

B411 23 ... fe
B412 23 ... fg
B413 23 ... ♖h6

Only 23 ... ♖xe3? is definitely bad, e.g. 24 ♗xd5+ ♔h8 25 ♖xd6 fg 26 h3! ♗xh3 27 ♖xe3 ♗xf1 28 ♘xf1 f4 29 ♖e7! g2 (or 29 ... f3 30 ♖dd7 and White strikes first) 30 ♘h2 ♕d1+ 31 ♔xg2 ♕c2+ 32 ♔g1 and White wins, Matsukevic–Kutsherov, corr. 1983.

B411

    23   ...   fe
    24   ♗xd5   ♔h8!

Not 24 ... ed 25 ♖xe6 ♔h8 26

♗b3 and White wins after 26 ... ♗b8 27 ♕c4 ♗xg3 28 hg ♗f3 29 ♖c8, 26 ... ♖b8 27 ♖exd6 ♖xb3 28 ♖d8+ or 26 ... ♗xg3 27 hg ♗f3 28 ♖h6 ♕g4 29 ♖cg6 ♕e4 30 ♖e6 ♕g4 31 ♕h3.

    25   ♗xe6   ed
    26   ♖a1! *(19)*

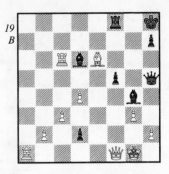

Not 26 ♖xd6? ♗h3 and Black wins. After 26 ♖a1! we have:

(1) Van der Tak gives two lines leading to a draw: **26 ... ♗e2** 27 ♕f2 ♗b5 28 ♖xd6 d1(♕)+ 29 ♖xd1 ♕xd1+ 30 ♔g2 ♗d3 31 ♕f4 ♗e4+ and **26 ... ♗xg3** 27 hg ♗f3 followed by ... ♗e4 and ... ♕h1+ with perpetual check in both cases. Both lines seem convincing, e.g. in the first variation 31 ♗d5 ♖e8 32 ♗f3 ♗e2 33 ♗c6 ♗f1+ 34 ♕xf1 ♖e2+ is fine for Black.

(2) **26 ... ♗e7** (26 ... ♗h3? 27 ♕d3 and 26 ... ♗b8?! 27 ♗b3 ♖e8 28 ♗b6! f4 29 ♗d1 ♖e1 30 ♖xb8+ ♔g7 31 ♖a7+ ♔f6 32

♖b6+ ♔g5 33 ♖a5+ win for White) 27 ♕f4! (not 27 ♗b3? f4!) ♗g5 28 ♕e5+ ♗f6 29 ♕c5 ♖e8 30 ♖c8 d1(♕)+ 31 ♖xd1 ♗xd1 32 ♕c6 ♖xc8 33 ♕xc8+ ♔g7 34 ♕d7+ ♔f8 35 ♕c8+ ♔g7 36 ♕g8+ ♔h6 37 ♕f8+ ♗g7 38 ♕xf5 ♕g5 39 ♕xg5+ ♔xg5 40 ♔f2 ♔f6 41 ♗g8 h5 42 ♔e3 ♗h6+ 43 ♔d3 and the four pawns eventually overwhelmed the piece, Helsloot–van der Zwan, corr. 1982/3.

B412

23	...	fg
24	♕g2	

Or 24 hg f4 (not 24 ... ♗xg3? 25 ♕g2) 25 ♖xd6 (White should avoid 25 ♗xd5? fe 26 ♗xe6+ ♗xe6 27 ♕e2 ed 28 ♕xe6+ ♔h8 29 ♖xd6 d1(♕)! or 25 ♗xf4? ♗xf4 26 gf ♖xf4, Carleton–Harding, corr. 1976, and Black wins in both cases) fg 26 ♕g2 ♖xd6 27 ♕h1! (not 27 ♘e4 ♗f3 28 ♕xg3+ ♖g6) ♔g7 28 ♕xh5 ♗xh5 29 ♘e4 ♖dd8 30 ♗xd5 ♖xd5 31 ♘xg3 ♗f3 32 c4 ♖d6 33 d5 ♖g6 34 ♔h2 ♖g4 35 ♘h5+ ♔g6 36 ♘f4+ ♔f5 37 ♘e6 ♖g2+ 38 ♔h3 ♖fg8 39 ♘d4+ ♔e4 40 d6 ♖2g3+ with a likely draw, Shakin–Rapoport, corr. 1976/77.

24	...	f4!

Not 24 ... ♔h8 25 ♗xd5 ♖g6 26 ♖xd6 ♖xd6 27 hg and White wins.

25	♗xd5	f3

26 ♗xf3! (but not 26 ♗xe6+? ♔h8! 27 ♕xg3 ♗xg3 and Black won in Meissner–Leisebein, corr. 1985) ♗xf3 27 ♘xf3 ♖xf3 28 ♖xd6 ♖xd6 29 hg ♖xg3 (29 ... ♖g6 30 ♗f2) 30 ♕xg3 ♖g6 with a near-certain draw.

B413

23	...	♖h6

This appears less reliable than the other 23rd moves.

24	♗xd5+	♔h8
25	♕g2	

25 ♕g2 (25 ♘f3 fe 26 ♖xe3 f4 is good for Black) fg 26 ♕g2 gh+ (Harding also suggests 26 ... f4 or 26 ... ♗h3) 27 ♔h1 f4 is often given as unclear but it looks very dangerous for White to me.

25	...	fe(20)

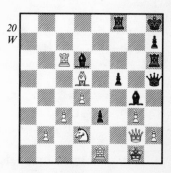

26	♘c4

Or 26 ♖xe3 (26 ♘f1 ♗h3 27 ♕f3 ♗g4 forces repetition since 28 ♕xe3 f4 is good for Black) f4 (better than 26 ... ♗h3 27 ♕e2 f4) 27 gf ♗xf4 (not 27 ... ♖xf4? 28 ♖c8+ ♗f8 29 ♖f3! and Black's attack falls apart) 28 ♖g3 (not 28 ♘f1 ♖xc6 29 ♗xc6 ♗xe3+ 30 ♘xe3 ♗h3 31 ♕d2 ♕h6! threatening both 32 ... ♕xc6 and 32 ... ♕xe3+, when the forced 32 ♗g2 loses a piece by 32 ... ♗xg2 33 ♔xg2 ♕g5+ 34 ♔h1 ♖f3) ♖xc6 (not 28 ... ♗xg3 29 ♖xh6 ♕xh6 30 ♕xg3 and with ♕e5+ coming the knight and three pawns are worth more than a rook) 29 ♗xc6 (29 ♖xg4? ♗xh2+) ♗xg3 when we have:

(1) **30 ♕xg3 ♖g8!** 31 ♔f2 (31 ♔h1 ♗d7 32 ♗f3 ♖xg3 33 ♗xh5 ♗c6+ wins) ♕h6! (this appears safer than 31 ... ♕f5+ 32 ♗f3 ♖f8, although 33 ♕e5+ is also a likely draw) 32 ♕e5+ ♖g7 and with d2 and c6 under attack White cannot do more than draw.

(2) **30 hg ♕f5** (30 ... ♕h6 may now be met by 31 ♕e4! since the knight on d2 cannot be captured) 31 ♗e4 (31 ♕e4? ♕f2+ 32 ♔h1 ♕xg3) ♕b5 32 ♘f1 (32 b4 ♕a4) ♗e2 33 ♘d2 ♗d3 (Black can of course take the draw by 33 ... ♗g4) 34 ♗xd3 (Shamkovich and Schiller suggest 34 c4 ♗xc4 35 ♔h1 ♕d7 36 ♕xh7+ ♕xh7 37 ♗xh7 ♔xh7 38 ♘xc4, but 35 ... ♖f7 appears better) ♕xd3 35 ♘e4? ♖f3! 36 ♔h2 ♕xe4 0-1, Jackson–van der Weijer, corr.

1986/7. Despite this success I am sure that the correct result should be a draw after, for example, 35 ♘f1.

26	...	**f4**
27	**♖xd6**	

27 gf? ♗h3 28 ♕f3 ♖g8+ and 27 ♘xd6 f3 win for Black.

27	...	**♖xd6**
28	**♘xd6**	**f3**
29	**♗xf3**	**♖xf3**

After 29 ... ♗xf3?! 30 ♕c2 White should defend.

39	**♖f1**

White has a promising alternative in 30 b4!? (but not 30 h4 ♗e6 31 ♖f1 ♗d5!, which is dangerous for White) e2 (this may not be the best, but good moves are not easy to find; White threatens ♕a2, while 30 ... ♖f2 31 ♕a8+ ♔g7 32 ♘e8+ looks unpleasant) 31 ♖xe2 ♗h3 32 g4! ♕d5 33 ♖e8+ ♔g7 34 ♘f5+ ♔f7 35 ♖e7+ ♔f8 36 ♖d7! ♗xg2 (36 ... ♕a8 37 ♖d8+, 36 ... ♕e4 37 ♖f7+ and 36 ... ♕c6 37 ♖d8+ ♔f7 38 ♕a2+ ♔f6 39 ♖f8+ ♔g5 40 ♕d2+ ♖f4 41 ♕xf4+ ♔xf4 42 ♘e7+ all win for White) 37 ♖xd5 ♗h3 38 ♖d8+ ♔f7 39 ♖d7+ ♔e8 40 ♖e7+ 1–0, Bryck–van der Weijer, corr. 1986/7.

30	...	**e2!**

Not 30 ... ♔g7? 31 ♖xf3 ♗xf3 32 g4! ♗xg4 33 ♕g3 e2 34 ♔f2 ♔f8 35 ♕f4+ ♔e7 36 ♕e5+

1–0, Basic–Radulovic, corr. 1983.

31 ♖e1 ♛d5

Not 31 ... ♗h3? 32 ♛xe2 ♖f1+ 33 ♛xf1! with ♖ + ♘ + 4 ♙ v ♛.

32 ♖xe2

32 ♘e8? ♖f1+! 33 ♖xf1 ♛xg2+ 34 ♔xg2 ♗h3+ would be unfortunate for White.

32 ... ♛xd6

33 ♖f2 ♖xf2 34 ♛xf2 and with four pawns for a bishop White has some winning chances, but with queens on the board it will be hard for him to advance the pawns without allowing perpetual check.

B42

23 ♗xf4! *(21)*

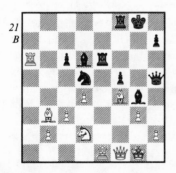

21
B

There are no visible improvements for Black in the subsequent analysis, so this must be considered the refutation of 21 ... g5!

23 ... ♗xf4

24 ♖xe6

Better than 24 ♖xc6 ♗e3+ 25 ♖xe3 ♖xe3 26 ♗xd5+ ♔h8 (threat ... f4) 27 ♛f4 ♖e1+ 28 ♘f1 ♗h3 29 ♗c4 ♛d1 30 d5 (30 ♖h6 ♗xf1 31 ♗xf1 ♖fe8 32 ♖f6 ♖xf1+ 33 ♛xf1 ♖e1 34 ♖xf5 should also be a draw) ♗xf1 31 ♗xf1 ♛xd5 Tal–Geller, USSR Ch. 1975.

24 ... ♗xd2

25 ♗xd5! cd

26 ♛g2 f4

26 ... ♗f3 27 ♛xd2 ♗e4 28 ♖h6 ♛f3 29 ♛g5+ wins for White, as does 26 ... ♗g5 27 ♛xd5.

27 ♛xd2 fg

27 ... ♗xe6 28 ♖xe6 fg 29 hg ♛g4 30 ♖e3 ♖a8 31 ♛e2 is just as bad.

28 ♖f6!

Not 28 hg? ♖f1+! 29 ♔xf1 ♛h1+ 30 ♔f2 ♛h2+ with at least a draw for Black, while after 28 ♖e1 ♗f3! (not 28 ... ♖f2 29 ♛h6 gh+ 30 ♔xf2 nor 28 ... gh+ 29 ♛xh2 ♛g5 30 ♛g2 and White wins) 29 h3 ♗e4 intending ... ♛f3 Black is not dead yet.

28 ... ♖e8

28 ... ♖xf6 29 ♖xf6 gh+ 30 ♛xh2 ♛g5 31 ♛b8+ mates.

29 hg ♖e2

30 ♛h6 ♖e1+ 31 ♖f1 ♖xf1+ 32 ♔xf1 ♛f5+ 33 ♛f4 ♛d3+ 34 ♔g1 ♛xa6 35 ♛xg4+ ♔f7 36 ♛h5+ ♔f8 37 ♔f2 1–0, Hauptmann–Sieberg, corr. 1986.

3 Main Line: 17 ... ♖e6 18 a4 Others

1 e4 e5 2 ♘f3 ♘c6 3 ♗b5 a6 4 ♗a4 ♘f6 5 0-0 ♗e7 6 ♖e1 b5 7 ♗b3 0-0 8 c3 d5 9 ed ♘xd5 10 ♘xe5 ♘xe5 11 ♖xe5 c6 12 d4 ♗d6 13 ♖e1 ♛h4 14 g3 ♛h3 15 ♗e3 ♗g4 16 ♛d3 ♖ae8 17 ♘d2 ♖e6 18 a4 *(22)*

There are two reasonable alternatives to 18 ... f5. The first of these is 18 ... ba, which often transposes into Chapter 2 after 19 ♖xa4 f5 20 ♛f1 ♛h5 21 f4. One reason why Black players sometimes prefer this move order is that it cuts out the line 18 ... f5 19 ♛f1 ♛h5 20 f4 ba 21 ♗xd5 cd 22 ♛g2. However there are arguments on both sides, because 18 ... ba gives White the option of 19 ♖xa4 f5 20 ♛f1 ♛h5 21 c4, which does not exist after 18 ... f5. Everything then depends on the assessment of the position after 21 c4; if this is satisfactory for Black then 18 ... ba gives White less choice, while otherwise 18 ... f5 is to be preferred. As 21

c4 is largely untested, while the line with 21 ♗xd5 cd 22 ♛g2 is probably just a draw, my personal opinion is that 18 ... f5 is more accurate.

The second alternative is 18 ... ♛h5, the Spassky Variation. Retreating the queen voluntarily appears odd, but by covering d5 Black avoids the possible disintegration of his queenside pawn structure by ♗xd5 and therefore need not take on a4. Thus although Black has fewer immediate attacking chances in the Spassky Variation, White's

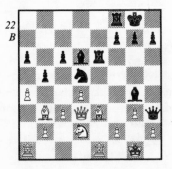

22
B

queenside counterplay is also held up. Currently the Spassky Variation has a good reputation.

A 18 ... ba

B 18 ... ♕h5

A

18 ...   ba

19 ♖xa4

19 ♗xa4 is inferior because of 19... ♗f4! 20 ♗xf4 ♘xf4 21 ♕f1 ♘e2+ and now:

(1) 22 ♖xe2 ♖xe2 23 ♘c4 (23 ♕xh3 ♗xh3 24 ♘c4 ♖fe8 25 ♘e3 ♖xb2 26 ♗xc6 ♖eb8 27 ♗e4 g6 is slightly better for Black) ♕h5 (the only real question is whether White can equalize; perhaps 23 ... ♖e6 was better, for example 24 ♘e5 ♕xf1+ 25 ♖xf1 ♗h3 26 ♖a1 c5 27 ♗d7 ♖xe5 28 ♗xh3 cd 29 cd ♖b5 and Black keeps an edge) 24 ♗d1 ♖e6 25 ♗xg4 ♕xg4 26 ♘e3 ♕g6 27 ♖xa6 ♖fe8 28 ♖a1 h5 29 ♕b1 ♖e4 30 ♕d1 h4 31 ♕f3 h3 32 g4 ♕h6 33 ♖a5 g6 34 ♔f1 ♖f4 35 ♕g3 ♖fe4 ½–½, Tozic–Hazai, Vrnjacka Banja 1984.

(2) 22 ♔h1 ♕h6 23 ♖ad1 and now 23 ... ♖fe8 was promising in Tolush–Mukhin, Leningrad 1964, but why not 23 ... ♕xd2 24 ♖xd2 ♗f3+ 25 ♕g2 ♘xg3+ 26 hg ♖xe1+ 27 ♔h2 ♗xg2 28 ♔xg2 with an extra exchange?

19 ...   f5

Black has nothing better, e.g. 19... ♖fe8 20 ♕f1 ♕h5 21 ♖xa6

f5 (21 ... ♘f4 22 ♗xe6 ♘e2+ 23 ♖xe2 ♗xe2 24 ♗xf7+ ♔xf7 25 ♖a7+ and 26 ♕g2 gives White three extra pawns, while 21 ... ♗h3 22 ♕c4 ♘xe3 23 ♖xe3 ♖xe3 24 fe ♖xe3 25 ♖a8+ ♗f8 26 ♔f2 ♖e6 27 ♘f3, Vitomsky–Gubanov, corr. 1963, is good for White since 27 ... ♖f6 28 ♗d1 ♗g4 is met by 29 ♕c5; finally 21 ... g5 22 ♖xc6 ♖h6 23 h4 ♘f4 24 ♗xf4 ♖xe1 25 ♕xe1 gf 26 ♕e8+ ♔g7 27 f3 wins) 22 ♖xc6 f4 23 ♖xd6 ♖xd6 24 ♗xf4 ♖xe1 25 ♕xe1 ♖e6 26 ♗e5 and White wins.

20 ♕f1 *(23)*

Certainly not 20 f4? ♗xf4! and now:

(1) 21 gf ♖g6 22 ♗xd5+ ♔h8! 23 ♔h1 ♖h6 24 ♖e2 cd 25 ♖g2 ♖g6 26 ♔g1 ♕xg2+ 27 ♔xg2 ♗e2+ wins for Black.

(2) 21 ♗xd5 cd 22 gf ♖fe8 23 ♖aa1 (23 ♕f1 ♖xe3 24 ♕xh3 ♖xe1+ 25 ♕f1 ♖8e2 26 ♖a1 ♖xf1+ 27 ♘xf1 ♗h3 with a fantastic ending for Black) ♖xe3 24 ♖xe3 ♖xe3 25 ♕xa6 h6 26 ♕f1 ♕h4 and Black's attack is worth far more than a pawn.

(3) 21 ♗f2 ♖xe1+ 22 ♗xe1 ♖e8 (0–1, Novopashin–Spassky, USSR Ch. 1963) 23 ♕f1 ♗e3+ 24 ♗f2 ♗xf2+ 25 ♕xf2 ♖e2 0–1, Perkins–Botterill, England 1964.

20 ...   ♕h5

23
B

Once again play is more or less forced. After 20 . . . f4 21 ♕xh3 ♗xh3 22 ♖xa6! fe 23 ♖xe3 (or 23 fe ♗e7 24 ♖xc6 ♖xc6 25 ♗xd5+ ♖e6 26 e4 ♔h8 27 ♗xe6 ♗xe6 28 ♔g2 with four good pawns for a piece, Plunge–Bohringer, corr. 1965/6) ♖xe3 (23 . . . ♘xe3 24 fe ♔f7 25 ♖xc6 ♔e7 26 ♗xe6 ♗xe6 27 ♖a6 ♗b8 28 ♔g2 was also very good for White in Szabo–Barczay, Hungary Ch. 1964) 24 fe ♗e7 25 e4! ♗g5 26 ed ♗xd2 (26 . . . ♗e3+ 27 ♔h1 ♖f2 28 d6+ causes a back-rank disaster) 27 dc+ ♔h8 28 ♖a1 g6 (28 . . . g5 is no better, e.g. 29 ♗d5 ♗e3+ 30 ♔h1 ♖f2 31 c7 ♔g7 32 ♖e1 ♗d2 33 ♗e6 ♗g2+ 34 ♔g1 winning, Schwartz–Dahlhaus, corr. 1973/5) 29 ♗d5 ♗e3+ 30 ♔h1 ♖f2 31 c7 ♖xb2 32 ♖e1 ♗xd4, Parma–Spassky, Yugoslavia–USSR 1965, White could have won easily by 33 g4! ♗xg4 34 cd ♖c2 35 ♖e7.

21 c4

This is the only significant alter-

native to 21 f4, which would transpose to Chapter 2, because 21 ♖xa6? f4 22 ♖xc6 (22 gf ♖g6 or 22 ♗xf4 ♗h3) fe 23 ♖xe3 ♘xe3 24 ♗xe6+ ♗xe6 25 ♕e1 ♗d5 26 ♖xd6 ♘g4 27 h4 ♘xf2 gives Black a decisive attack.

21 . . . f4

After 21 . . . ♘xe3 22 fe c5 *ECO* gives 23 ♖aa1 intending ♗a4–c6 as good for White, but in my view Black has enough compensation for the pawn, e.g. 23 . . . ♔h8 24 ♗a4 cd 25 ed ♗e2 followed by . . . f4 with a strong attack. Since the main line appears risky for Black this is probably his best choice.

22 cd ♖xe3

Not 22 . . . fe 23 de ♖xf2 24 e7+ ♔h8 25 e8(♕)+ ♕xe8 26 ♖xe3 ♖xf1+ 27 ♘xf1 and here the two rooks are worth more than the queen.

23 fe fg

24 dc+ ♔h8 25 hg ♖xf1+ 26 ♖xf1 ♕g5 (26 . . . ♕e8 27 ♘c4 ♗xg3 28 ♘e5! is good for White, while 26 . . . ♕h3 27 ♘e4 g6 28 ♖xa6 ♗f5 29 ♖a8+ ♔g7 30 ♖a7+ ♔h8 31 ♖xf5 ♕xf5 32 ♘xd6 1–0 was Bueno–Esteban, corr. 1984) 27 ♖f4 ♗xf4 28 ef ♕e7 29 ♘f1 ♕e2 30 ♖b4 and in this critical and unclear position Black should play 30 . . . h5 rather than 30 . . . g6 as in Suetin–Geller, USSR Ch. 1964, when 31 ♖b8+ ♔g7 32 ♖b7+ would probably have been good for White.

B

18   ...   ♛h5
19   ab

There is no reason for White to delay this capture. 19 ♛f1 transposes to line B of Chapter 5.

19   ...   ab*(24)*

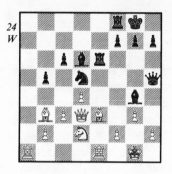

24
W

B1   20 ♘f1
B2   20 ♛f1

Other moves are less dangerous:
(1) 20 ♗xd5 and now:

(1a) 20 ... cd (I don't understand this move, even though it has been played more than once, since the whole point of 18 ... ♛h5 is to recapture with the queen) 21 ♖a5! (simple and strong) g5 22 ♛xb5 ♖h6 23 h4 gh 24 ♛xd5 hg 25 ♛xh5 ♖xh5 25 ♖xh5 gf+ 27 ♔xf2 ♗xh5 (Black has no compensation for the pawn) 28 ♘e4 ♗e7 29 ♗f4 f5 30 ♘c5 ♖e8 31 ♖e5 ♗xc5 32 ♖xe8+ ♗xe8 33 dc ♗f7 34 ♔e3 ♔f8 35 b4 ♔e7 36 ♔d4 ♔d8 37 c6 1–0, Schuler–Hentzgen, corr. 1981.

(1b) 20 ... ♛xd5 21 b3 (21 c4 bc 22 ♛xc4 ♛h5 23 ♖a6 ♖fe8 24 ♖xc6 ♖h6 25 h4 ♖g6 26 d5 ♗d7 27 ♔g2 ♛f5 was good for Black in Veksler–Solovyev, USSR 1969; note that 22 ♘xc4 is met by 22 ... ♗h3) ♛h5 22 c4 bc 23 bc ♗f5 24 ♛e2 ♛xe2 25 ♖xe2 ♗d3 26 ♖ee1 ♗b4 with equality (Harding).

(2) 20 c4?! ♘xe3! (20 ... bc 21 ♘xc4 ♗b4 22 ♖ec1 ♗e2 23 ♗d1 ♗xd3 24 ♗xh5 ♗xc4 25 ♖xc4 ♘xe3 26 fe ♗d2 ½–½, Parma–Geller, Yugoslavia–USSR match 1966, is totally equal, but 20 ... ♘xe3 is even better) 21 ♖xe3 (21 fe ♗xg3 22 hg ♖h6) ♗e2 22 ♛c2 ♖h6 23 h4 ♗f4! 24 ♖e4 (24 ♖c3 b4 traps the rook) g5 with a dangerous attack for Black.

(3) 20 ♗d1? ♘xe3 (in Hellers–I. Sokolov, Haninge 1989, Black overlooked this forced win and played 20 ... ♗xd1 21 ♖axd1 f5, also winning quickly) 21 fe ♗xg3 22 hg ♖h6 wins.

B1

20   ♘f1   ♖fe8

There is nothing better, e.g. 20 ... f5? 21 ♗f4! ♖xe1 22 ♖xe1 ♗xf4 23 gf ♗f3 (the only way to activate the bishop, but it fails tactically) 24 ♘g3 ♛g4 25 ♖e3 ♗e4 26 f3! and after 26 ... ♗xd3 27 ♗xd5+ cd 28 fg Black is a clear pawn down in the ending.

21   ♗d1   ♗xd1

22 ♕xd1

22 ♖axd1 ♕f3 leaves White somewhat tangled up, e.g. 23 ♕e2 ♕e4 and after 24 ♘d2 ♕c2 or 24 ♕d2 ♕f5 White is not making progress.

22 ... ♕f5(25)

It is not easy to see Black's compensation for the pawn since unlike other lines of the Marshall he has no immediate prospect of a direct attack on White's king. However White has serious problems freeing himself and putting his extra pawn to work. There is pressure on e3 and given time Black may develop counterplay by pushing his h-pawn. I believe Black should have enough compensation to hold the draw, but there is no doubt that only White has winning chances.

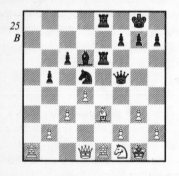

25
B

23 ♗d2

White exchanges one pair of rooks at the cost of having his bishop buried at e1. 23 ♖a6 was

the alternative, with the idea 23 ... ♗b8 24 ♗d2 and c6 becomes weak, but 23 ... h5! 24 ♖xc6 h4 is more dangerous, with unclear complications.

23 ... ♖xe1

24 ♗xe1 h5

The h-pawn arrives just in time to prevent White freezing himself, e.g. 25 ♔g2 h4 and 26 ♕f3 is impossible, or 25 ♗d2 h4 26 ♘e3 ♘xe3 27 ♗xe3 hg 28 hg ♗xg3.

25 h4 c5

Once again Black must interfere with the plan of ♗d2 and ♘e3, this time by preparing to give White an isolated d-pawn should he try ♗d2, which would give Black further possibilities for counterplay. *ECO* stops here and gives the strange assessment of a slight plus for Black, when in fact Black must still play accurately to equalize. We now follow the game Chandler–Nunn, Hastings 1987/8.

26 b3 cd?

A very risky idea which should have been punished by White. 26 ... g6 was correct, defending the queen and the weak h-pawn. Then 27 c4 bc 28 bc ♘f6 29 d5 (29 ♘e3 ♕e4 threatens ... ♗xg3) ♘g4 followed by ... ♘e5 gives Black sufficient counterplay.

27 ♕xd4 ♖e4

28 ♕d3 ♗c5 29 ♖a8+? (White plays to exploit the pinned rook,

but this idea is surprisingly refuted; 29 c4! was best, when 29 ... bc 30 bc ♘f6 31 ♔g2 intending ♘d2 or f3 leaves Black in a very awkward position) ♔h7 30 ♖e8 (it appears that exchanges are now forced, but ...) ♘xc3! (... and suddenly it is White who must defend accurately to achieve a draw) 31 ♔g2! (not 31 b4? ♘e2+ 32 ♔g2 ♘f4+! 33 gf ♕g6+ 34 ♘g3 ♖xe8 and the bishop on e1 hangs; 31 ♖xe4 ♘xe4 32 ♕e2 should also draw, but the move played is the simplest) ♗g6! 32 ♖xe4 (White could have set a trap by 32 ♖g8 and if 32 ... ♕d5? 33 ♖xg7+! ♔xg7 34 ♗xc3+ ♗d4 35 f3 and Black will be a pawn down after 35 ... ♖e2+ since 35 ... ♖g4 36 ♘e3 is a disaster; however the trap would have rebounded after 32 ... b4! and the rook is not doing anything on g8) ♕xe4+ 33 ♕xe4+ ♘xe4 34 f3 ♘d6 35 ♗f2 ♘b7 36 ♘d2 ♔f5 ½–½.

B2

20 ♕f1 ♖fe8

The alternative is 20 ... ♗h3 21 ♗d1 (Sax–Nunn, Reykjavik 1988, continued 21 ♕e2 ♗g4 22 ♕f1 ♗h3 23 ♕e2 ♗g4 ½–½) ♕f5 22 ♕e2 and now:

(1) **22 ... ♗f4!?** (White was threatening to free himself by ♘f3 so quick action is needed) 23 ♕f3 (23 ♘f1 ♗xf1 is equal) ♖fe8

(Black cannot regain his pawn by taking on e3 immediately, for example 23 ... ♗xe3 24 fe ♕xf3 25 ♗xf3 and c6 is hanging) and now:

(1a) **24 ♘f1 ♗xf1 25 ♖xf1** ♘xe3 36 fe ♗xe3+ 27 ♔g2 and although White still has a slight advantage Black should draw without real difficulty.

(1b) **24 gf!** and although this looks very risky for White I cannot see how Black can justify his piece sacrifice, for example 24 ... ♖g6+ (24 ... ♘xf4 25 ♘f1 defends) 25 ♔h1 ♗g4 (25 ... ♗g2+ wins the queen, but at too high a cost, while 25 ... ♘xf4 26 ♖g1 leads to nothing; finally 25 ... h5 fails to 26 ♗c2!) 26 ♕e4! and White exploits the weak back rank to nullify Black's attack.

(2) **22 ... ♘f4!?** 23 ♕f3 ♕g6 24 ♗e2 ♘xe2+ 25 ♕xe2 f5 26 ♕d3 f4 27 ♕xg6 ♖xg6 and Black won a piece in Nocci–Kuhnel, corr. 1984. If correct, this is an important improvement for Black, but only further practical examples will reveal the truth. One possibility is 24 ♗b3!?, meeting 24 ... ♗g4 by 25 ♕xc6 and 24 ... ♗g2 by 25 ♕d1.

(3) **22 ... c5!?** (a logical move exploiting the tangle of White pieces) 23 ♘f1 cd4 24 cd4 ♘b4 (preventing ♗c2 and threatening 25 ... ♘d3 26 ♗c2 ♕d5) 25 ♖a3 ♘c6 26 ♖d3 ♗b4 27 d5 ♖d6 28

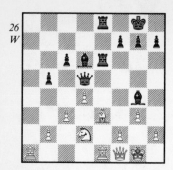

26
W

♗d2 ♖xd5 29 ♗xb4 ♘xb4 30 ♖f3 ♕d7 31 ♗b3 ♗g4 32 ♗xd5 ♕xd5 33 ♘e3 ♕xf3 ½–½, Sax–I. Sokolov, Haninge 1989.

21 ♗xd5 ♕xd5 *(26)*

and now:

(1) **22 ♕g2** is given by theory, but this must be a weak move. After 22 ... ♕h5 Black's queen has been driven to a good square and since White can never take on c6 his own queen is not very well placed.

(2) **22 h3!?** this has received only one practical test, when in Watson–Pein, London 1989 the continuation 22 ... ♗f5 23 ♕g2 h5 24 ♕xd5 cd 25 ♔g2 ♗d3 gave Black two good bishops and active pieces to balance the extra pawn. Moreover there is a threat of ... f5–f4. My view is that Black probably has enough compensation to draw, possibly by eliminating queenside pawns with ... b4.

(3) **22 f3** was successful in Chandler–Sarfati, Wellington 1988, after 22 ... ♗h5 23 ♕f2 f5 24 b3 f4 25 ♗xf4 ♗xf4 26 gf b4 27

♖xe6 ♕xe6 28 cb ♕g6+ 29 ♔h1 ♕d3 30 ♖e1 ♖xe1+ 31 ♕xe1 ♗xf3+ 32 ♔g1 ♕xd4+ 33 ♔f1 ♕d3+ 34 ♔f2 ♗h5 35 ♕e6+ ♔f8 36 ♕e3 and White eventually converted his extra pawn into a win. The immediate 22 ... ♗f5 is met by 23 ♗f2, but 22 ... ♗h5 23 ♕f2 ♗g6 looks promising, e.g. 24 b3 ♗d3 and White has problems freeing himself.

(4) **22 c4** ♕f5!? (22 ... bc is also possible) 23 cb ♗b4! 24 f3 (24 bc loses to 24 ... ♗h3 followed by taking on d2 and ... ♕f3, but 24 ♕c4! would have forced a draw after 24 ... ♗xd2 25 ♗xd2 ♖xe1+ 26 ♖xe1 ♖xe1+ 27 ♗xe1 cb) ♗h3 25 g4 ♕d5 (now Black is better) 26 ♕xh3 ♖xe3 27 ♖xe3 ♖xe3 28 ♕g2 (surprisingly the check on a8 doesn't help White much and only causes a loss of tempo after a later ... cb) cb 29 ♕f2 ♗xd2 30 ♕xd2 ♖xf3 31 ♖e1 h6 (31 ... g6! was much stronger) 32 ♖e3 ♖f6 33 ♕d3 g6 34 ♖e5 ♕a2 35 ♕d2? (timetrouble; 35 ♕xb5 is a likely draw) ♕c4 36 ♖e2 ♔g7 37 h3 ♖f3 38 h4 ♖d3 39 ♕f4 0–1, Large–Nunn, London 1988.

The Spassky Variation is one of Black's soundest lines in the Marshall. Although White can usually keep his extra pawn Black's positional compensation often makes it very hard for White to make use of it.

4 Main Line: 17 ... ♖e6 18 ♙xd5

1 e4 e5 2 ♘f3 ♘c6 3 ♗b5 a6 4
♗a4 ♘f6 5 0-0 ♗e7 6 ♖e1 b5 7
♗b3 0-0 8 c3 d5 9 ed ♘xd5 10
♘xe5 ♘xe5 11 ♖xe5 c6 12 d4
♗d6 13 ♖e1 ♕h4 14 g3 ♕h3 15
♗e3 ♗g4 16 ♕d3 ♖ae8 17 ♘d2
♖e6 18 ♗xd5 cd(27)

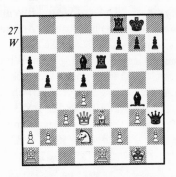

27
W

It is probably not necessary to
repeat the comment that White
should not make this exchange
voluntarily. Black is relieved of
any immediate problems on the
a2–g8 diagonal and he gains the
square e4. Despite this, many
White players have taken on d5,
so it is worth considering the line
in more detail. White may
exchange on d5 before move 18,
but this gives Black the extra option of adopting the Pawn Push
without having to play ... ♔h8
(see Chapter 6, note to White's
18th move).

19 ♕f1
Or 19 a4 and now:
(1) **19 ... b4** 20 ♕f1 ♕h5 21 c4
dc 22 ♕xc4 g5 23 d5 ♖h6 24 h4
♖c8 25 ♕d3 gh 26 ♗xh6 hg 27 fg
♕xh6 28 ♖ac1 was good for
White in Tal–Krogius, USSR Ch.
1961.
(2) **19 ... ba** and now:
(2a) **20 c4** (after 20 ♕f1 Black
can transpose to the main line by
20 ... ♕h5, or try 20 ... ♖b8!?)
♗b4 (20 ... dc 21 ♘xc4 ♗f3 22
♕f1 ♕h5 23 ♘d2 ♗c6 24 f3 was
slightly better for Black in Villa-
longa–Roche, corr. 1983, but 21
♕xc4 is better) 21 cd ♗xd2 22
♗xd2 ♖b6 and in view of the
opposite-coloured bishops a draw
is a very likely result. Note that 23
♖xa4 ♖xb2 (threat ... ♖xd2) 24

♗f4 fails to 24 ... ♖xf2 25 ♔xf2 ♕xh2+ 26 ♔e3 ♖e8+ 27 ♗e5 ♕xg3+ 28 ♔d2 ♕f2+ 29 ♖e2 ♗xe2 30 ♕xe2 ♕xe2+ 31 ♔xe2 f6 and Black has excellent winning chances.

(2b) **20 ♖xa4?** (now Black is better) f5 21 f4 (White has no time for 21 ♕f1 because of 21 ... f4 22 ♕xh3 ♗xh3 23 gf ♖xf4 24 ♘f1 ♖g4+ 25 ♘g3 h5 with a very strong attack) ♖fe8 (21 ... ♗xf4 22 gf ♖fe8 is also good, transposing to Chapter 3, line A, note to White's 20th move, variation 2) 22 ♖xa6 g5 23 ♖xd6 (23 fg f4) ♖xd6 24 ♕b5 ♖de6 25 ♕xd5 ♔h8 26 ♘f3 gf 27 ♘g5 ♖xe3! 28 ♖xe3 fe 29 ♘e6 ♕h6 30 ♕e5+ ♔g8 31 d5 f4 32 gf ♗xe6 33 de ♕xe6 0–1, Fordham-Hall-Breach, corr. 1970/1.

(3) **19 ... f5 20 ab?** (20 ♕f1 ♕h5 transposes into the main line, while 20 f4? ♖fe8 is bad since 21 ab again allows 21 ... ♗xf4!) ♖fe8 21 f4 ♗xf4! 22 gf ♖h6 23 ♘f1 ♗f3 24 ♕d2 ♖g6+ 25 ♘g3 ♖xg3+ 26 hg ♕h1+ and White is mated.

19 ...   ♕h5
20   a4(28)
Or:
(1) **20 f4** ♖fe8 21 ♕f2 and now Black has good chances after the simple 21 ... ♕f5, intending to start a minority attack by ... b4, but 21 ... f5 22 a4 is also possible, transposing to line B below.

(2) **20 ♕g2** ♖fe8 21 a4 ba (21 ... b4!? is a promising idea, e.g. 22 ♖ac1 ♗e2! 23 c4 dc 24 ♘xc4 ♗f3 25 ♕f1 ♗d5 26 ♘d2 f5 or 22 c4 dc 23 d5 ♖g6 24 ♗f4 ♖f8 25 ♗xd6 ♖xd6 26 ♘xc4 ♗f3 27 ♕f1 ♖xd5 and Black is slightly better in both cases) 22 ♖xa4 and now *ECO* recommends 22 ... ♗f4 as good for Black, but 23 ♖a5! ♗xe3 24 ♖xe3 ♖xe3 25 fe ♖xe3 26 ♕xd5 is unclear. Perhaps 22 ... ♗h3 is best, when 23 ♕f3 ♗g4 24 ♕h1 is the only way to avoid the repetition, but then 24 ... ♗c7!? is unclear.

(3) **20 f3** ♗h3 (better than 20 ... ♖f6 21 ♕e2 ♗xf3 22 ♘xf3 ♕xf3 23 ♕xf3 ♖xf3 and White may be slightly better, Anand-Mannion, London 1986) 21 ♕f2 g5 threatening 22 ... f5, and Black has good attacking chances.

After 20 a4 there are two lines for Black:

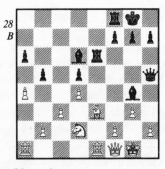

28
B

A   20 ... ba
B   20 ... f5

Line A is recommended; the analysis below shows that only Black can hope for an advantage in this variation. Line B is probably equal, but there has been much less practical experience.

A

20 ...   ba

21 ♖xa4

21 ♕g2 may be met either by 21 ... ♖fe8 as above (although Black has lost the ... b4 option) or by 21 ... ♖b8 22 ♖xa4 ♗h3 23 ♕f3 ♗g4 24 ♕h1 ♖xb2 25 ♖xa6 h6 which appears quite promising for Black.

21 ...   f5

21 ... ♖fe8 is less natural; 22 ♕g2 transposes to line 2 above, but 22 ♖xa6 is better, with an unclear position.

22   ♖xa6(29)

Or:

(1) **22 f4?** ♕e8! 23 ♗f2 (23 ♖xa6 ♖xe3 24 ♖xe3 ♕xe3+ 25 ♕f2 ♕e6 was also winning for Black, Ippel–Buys, corr. 1979) ♖xe1 24 ♕xe1 ♕xa4 25 ♕e6+ ♖f7 26 ♕xd6 ♕d1+ 27 ♘f1 h6 28 ♕d8+ (28 ♕xa6 ♗h3 followed by ... ♖e7–e2 wins) ♔h7 29 ♕xd5 ♗h3 0–1, Kindermann–Lukacs, Budapest 1987.

(2) **22 f3** ♗h3 (22 ... ♕e8 wins after 23 ♖xa6 ♖xe3 24 ♖xe3 ♕xe3+ 25 ♕f2 ♕e7 26 fg fg 27 ♕g2 ♕e3+, but 23 ♗f2! ♖xe1 24 ♕xe1 ♕xa4 25 ♕e6+ ♖f7 26 ♕xd6 is unclear) 23 ♕f2 (23 ♕d3

f4 24 ♗f2 fg 25 hg ♗xg3 wins) ♖fe8, threatening ... f4, with an edge for Black.

After 22 ♖xa6 Black may play:

(1) **22 ...** ♗h3 23 ♕e2 (23 ♕d3 f4 24 ♖xd6 ♖xd6 25 ♗xf4 ♖xf4 wins for Black, while 23 ♕b5 f4 24 ♖xd6 fe 25 ♖xe6 ef+ 26 ♔h1 f1(Q)+ 27 ♖xf1 ♖xf1+ leads to mate; note that 24 ... ♖xd6 25 ♗xf4 ♖xf4 is not possible in the second line because of 26 ♕b8+) ♕xe2 24 ♖xe2 f4 25 ♖xd6 (25 ♗xf4 ♖xe2 wins) and now Black may choose between forcing a draw by 25 ... ♖xd6 26 ♗xf4 ♖xf4 27 gf ♖g6+ or reaching a ♗ v 3 ♙ ending by 25 ... fe 26 ♖xe6 ed. This ending appears good for Black as White has only one passed pawn.

(2) **22 ...** f4 23 ♗xf4 ♖xe1 24 ♕xe1 ♗xf4 25 gf ♗e2! (25 ... ♖e8 is not so good since 26 ♕a1 ♗h3 27 f3! leaves Black with no obvious attacking continuation, Velders–van der Weijer, Dieren

1986) with advantage for Black,
e.g. 26 ♖b6 ♕g4+ 27 ♔h1 ♖e8
28 ♕b1 ♕xf4 (28 ... ♗d1! appears even better) 29 ♖b7 ♕xd2
0–1, Isaksen–Iversland, corr.
1983.

B

20 ... f5
21 f4

ECO gives 21 ab f4 22 ♗xf4
♗h3 23 ♕d3 ♗f5 24 ♕f3 ♗g4
with a draw by repetition.

21 ... ♖fe8

Or 21 ... g5 (21 ... ba transposes to Chapter 2, line A, which
is roughly equal) 22 fg (22 ab is
also playable) ♖fe8 23 ♕f2 h6 24
gh f4 25 gf ♖xh6 26 ♘f1 (the
position looks dangerous for
White, but in this game Black
could not break through) ♗f3 27
ab (greed pays in this case) ♖g6+
28 ♘g3 ab 29 ♗d2 ♖e4 30 ♖a6
♕g4 31 ♖b6 ♖ee6 32 ♖xe6
♖xe6 33 h3 ♕xh3 34 ♕xf3 ♖g6
35 ♔f2 ♕h2+ 36 ♕g2 ♕h6 1–0
Grootjans–de Boer, corr.

22 ♗f2

There are two alternatives:
(1) **22 ♕f2** g5 (22 ... b4!?) 23 fg
f4 24 ♗xf4? ♖e2 25 ♖xe2 ♖xe2
26 ♕xe2 ♗xe2 27 ♗xd6 ba was
good for Black in Pilnik–Geller,
Santiago 1965, but 24 gf h6 25 gh
transposes to Grootjans–de Boer
above, which was won by White.
(2) **22 ab** ♖xe3 23 ♖xe3 ♖xe3
24 ba ♗b8 25 ♕b5 (25 a7 ♗xa7
26 ♖xa7 ♕e8 27 ♖a1 ♖e2 with
advantage to Black) ♕e8 26

♕xe8+ (26 ♕xd5+ ♔h8 27 ♘f1
♖e7 28 b4 ♗a7 gives White four
pawns for the piece, but Black's
active pieces and attacking
chances are more important)
♖xe8 and Black has the better
ending because 27 a7 ♗xa7 28
♖xa7 ♖e1+ regains the piece.

22 ... ♖e2

Or 22 ... ba (22 ... ♗h3 23
♕d3 ♖xe1+ 24 ♖xe1 ♖xe1+
25 ♗xe1 ♕d1 26 ♕e3 ♔f7 27 ab
ab 28 ♘f3 is slightly better for
White, Gurevich–Sadomsky,
corr. 1965) 23 ♕g2 (23 ♖xe6
♖xe6 24 ♕xa6 ♕e8 25 ♕xa4
♕xa4 26 ♖xa4 ♖e2 27 ♘f1
♖xb2 should probably be a draw,
Driksna–Juhandi, corr. 1965)
♕f7 24 ♘f3 ♖xe1+ 25 ♖xe1
♗xf3 26 ♕xf3 ♖xe1+ 27 ♗xe1
♕e6 ½–½ Oliveau–van der Weijer,
corr. 1986.

23 ♕g2 h6

23 ... ♕f7 24 ab ab 25 ♘f3
♖xb2 26 ♘g5 ♖xe1+ 27 ♖xe1
♕b7 28 ♖e8+ ♗f8 29 h3 is good
for White according to Tal.

24 ab ♖xd2

25 ba ♗b8 26 ♖xe8+ ♕xe8 27
h3 ♗h5 28 a7 ♗xa7 29 ♖xa7
♕e2 30 g4 fg 31 hg ♖d1+ 32
♔h2 ♗xg4 33 ♗h4 ♕xg2+ 34
♔xg2 ♖d2+ 35 ♔g3 ♗f5 ½–½,
Kogan–Mitchell, corr. 1967/8.

Summing up, the lines in this
chapter offer White no chances
for the advantage and in many
cases he has to play accurately to
hold the balance.

5 Main Line: 17 ... ♖e6 18 Others

1 e4 e5 2 ♘f3 ♘c6 3 ♗b5 a6 4
♗a4 ♘f6 5 0-0 ♗e7 6 ♖e1 b5 7
♗b3 0-0 8 c3 d5 9 ed ♘xd5 10
♘xe5 ♘xe5 11 ♖xe5 c6 12 d4
♗d6 13 ♖e1 ♕h4 14 g3 ♕h3 15
♗e3 ♗g4 16 ♕d3 ♖ae8 17 ♘d2
♖e6 *(30)*

Apart from 18 a4 and 18 ♗xd5, there are three other moves worthy of consideration.

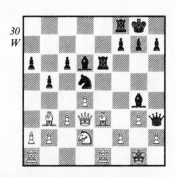

A 18 ♗d1
B 18 ♕f1
C 18 c4

Black should not be troubled by any of these moves. Lines A and C are at least equal for Black,
while line B gives Black a kind of Spassky Variation in which he has an important extra option.

A

18 ♗d1

This innovation was introduced by Ljubojevic in two games at Amsterdam (OHRA) 1988.

18 ... ♗xd1

The obvious tries lead to nothing, e.g. **18 ... ♘f4 19 ♕f1** or **18 ... ♗f4 19 ♗xg4 ♕xg4 20 ♗xf4 ♘xf4 21 ♕f3 ♘e2+ 22 ♔g2**, so P. Nikolic played **18 ... ♗f5**, but now White forced the exchange of queens by 19 ♕f1 ♖fe8 20 ♕xh3 ♗xh3. Nikolic had expected the e-file pin to regain the pawn, but he had not taken into account the bishop's return 21 ♗b3! Now Black has little for his sacrifice and Ljubojevic finished efficiently by 21 ... ♖6e7 22 ♘f1 ♔f8 23 ♗d2 ♖e2 24 ♖ad1 ♗g4 25 ♔g2 ♖xe1 26 ♖xe1 h5 27 ♖xe8+ ♔xe8 28 ♗c2 a5 29 b3 ♗e6 30 ♘e3 g6 31 ♗d3 ♗c7 32 c4 bc 33 bc ♘f6 34

♗c3 ♗e7 35 h3 ♗d8 36 f4 ♗c8
37 f5 g5 38 g4 hg 39 hg ♗a6 40
♗c2 ♗b6 41 ♔f3 ♗b7 42 c5 ♗c7
43 ♘c4 1–0, Ljubojevic–P. Nikolic, Amsterdam (OHRA) 1988.

19 ♖axd1   f5

This is the correct answer.
Although the exchange of bishops
reduces Black's attacking force,
he gains time because there is no
pin along the b3–g8 diagonal.
Moreover White cannot easily
dispose of the powerful knight at
d5.

20 ♘f3

A good move and the only
effective answer to the threat of
. . . f4. **20 ♗g5** ♖g6 is bad, as is **20
f4** ♖fe8 21 ♘f1 ♗xf4, while **20
♕f1** ♕h5 21 ♕e2 (21 ♘b3 f4 22
♗c1 fg wins for Black) ♕g6 (21
. . . ♕e8!?) 22 ♔h1 f4 23 gf ♘xf4
24 ♕f1 ♘d3 25 ♕g2 ♕h5 26 ♘f1
♖xe3 27 ♘xe3 ♖xf2 28 ♖xd3
♖xg2 29 ♔xg2 ♕g6+ 0–1 was
Boucchechter–Spassky, Tel-Aviv
1964.

20 . . .   ♖g6! *(31)*

Not 20 . . . ♘xe3 (20 . . . f4 21
♘g5 is also bad) 21 ♖xe3 ♖xe3
22 ♕xe3 f4 23 ♘g5! ♕xh2+ (or
23 . . . ♕h5 24 ♕e6+ ♔h8 25
♖e1 and Black has nothing for
the pawn) 24 ♔xh2 fe 25 f4 and
the advanced e-pawn will be lost
in a few moves (e.g. by ♔g2–f3
and ♘e4, or perhaps ♖e1 and
♘f3–e5).

31
W

After 20 . . . ♖g6! we follow the
game Ljubojevic–Nunn, Amsterdam (OHRA) 1988: 21 ♕f1 (the
only move since 21 ♘g5 ♕h5 22
f4 fails to 22 . . . h6, while after 21
♗g5 f4 22 ♗h4 fg 23 fg ♗xg3! 24
♗xg3 ♖xg3+ 25 hg ♕xg3+ 26
♔h1 ♖xf3 Black has a decisive
attack) ♕h5 22 ♘e5 ♗xe5 23 de
f4 24 ♗c1 (24 ♗c5 is wrong
because of 24 . . . fg 25 hg ♘f4!
with the threat of 26 . . . ♖h6, but
24 ♗d2 may be slightly more accurate because when the e-file
becomes open an extra defence of
e1 is useful) ♖h6 25 ♕g2 f3 26
♕h1 (26 g4 appears strong, but
the reply 26 . . . ♖g6! is awkward,
for example 27 ♖d4 ♘f4! 28 gh
♘h3+ wins, while after 27 h3
♕h4 28 ♕h2 h5 the attack on g4
cannot be met by 29 g5 due to 29
. . . ♘f4) ♖e6 27 h4 ♖xe5 (27 . . .
♖f5 28 ♕h3 ♖fxe5 29 ♖xe5
♕xe5 30 ♕g4 ♕e2 31 ♖f1 is
slightly better for Black) 28 ♕h3
♖xe1+?! (28 . . . ♘f6! would

have delayed the emergence of White's queen and prepared to post the knight at g4, but 29 ♖xe5 ♕xe5 30 ♕f1 would have left Black with only a very small plus) 29 ♖xe1 ♖e8 30 ♖e6! h6 (an essential precaution since 30 ... ♕f7 allows 31 ♖xc6 h6 32 ♖c8) 31 ♗e3 ♘xe3 32 ♖xe3 ½-½.

B

18 ♕f1

This will often transpose to lines considered in Chapters 2 and 3.

18 ... ♕h5

19 a4

Or:

(1) **19 ♗d1 ♗xd1 20 ♖axd1 f5** transposes into the note to White's 20th move in line A.

(2) **19 c4 ♘xe3 20 ♖xe3** (20 fe ♗b4) **♖h6 21 ♕g2 c5!** 22 d5 ♗e5 23 ♖ae1 ♗xb2 24 h4 ♖b6 25 ♖e8 ♕g6 was good for Black in Suetin–Borisenko, USSR Ch. 1950.

(3) **19 ♕g2 ♖fe8 20 ♘f1 f5** (20 ... ♗f3 21 ♗d1!) 21 ♗d2 ♗f3 22 ♗d1 ♖e2! 23 ♖xe2 (23 ♗xe2? ♖xe2 24 g4 fg 25 ♘g3 ♕g6! wins for Black) ♗xg2 24 ♖xe8+ ♕xe8 25 ♔xg2 ♕e4+ 26 ♔g1 f4 27 a4 g5 28 ab ab 29 ♗b3 h5 30 ♖c1, Kuzmin–Belyavsky, Lvov 1978, and now 30 ... h4! would have given Black real winning chances.

After 19 a4 the position is iden-

tical to line 1 of the Spassky Variation (see Chapter 3, line B) except that White has not yet exchanged pawns on b5. This has significance in one important line where White normally has a tactical resource based on a back rank mate. This arises after 19 ... ♗h3 (19 ... ba 20 ♖xa4 f5 transposes to Chapter 3, line A) 20 ♗d1 ♕f5 21 ♕e2 ♗f4! 22 ♕f3 ♖fe8 and now there is nothing better than 23 ♘f1 (23 gf ♖g6+ 24 ♔h1 ♗g4 25 ♕e4 doesn't work here!) ♗xf1 24 ♖xf1 ♘xe3 25 fe ♗xe3+ 26 ♔g2 with just a minute advantage for White. There is never time for White to interpose ab in this line.

If Black does not take up this position White will play ab and transpose to Chapter 3.

C

18 c4

This move had a brief flurry of popularity, but the current assessment is that it leaves White struggling for equality (and probably not getting it!).

18 ... ♗f4! *(32)*

Clearly best; 18 ... bc 19 ♘xc4 ♗f4 20 ♕f1 ♕h6 21 ♗c1! ♗h3 22 ♖xe6 fe 23 ♕d1 ♗xc1 24 ♖xc1 ♕f6 25 f3 ♕xf3 26 ♕xf3 ♖xf3 27 ♘e5 ♖f8 28 ♘xc6 gave White a solid extra pawn in R. Byrne–Geller, Las Palmas 1976.

After 18 ... ♗f4 there are two main lines for White:

32
W

C1   19 cd
C2   19 ♕f1

Certainly not 19 gf? ♖h6 20 ♕e4 ♕xh2+ 21 ♔f1 ♖e6 and Black wins, nor 19 ♗xf4?! ♘xf4 20 ♕f1 ♘e2+ when 21 ♔h1? loses to 21 ... ♕h6 22 ♖ad1 ♕xd2 23 ♖xd2 ♗f3+ 24 ♔g2 ♘xg3+ 25 hg ♖xe1+ 26 ♔h2 ♗xg2, so 21 ♖xe2 is relatively best, but still good for Black.

C1

19	cd	♖h6
20	♕e4	♕xh2+
21	♔f1	f5

This has been played most often, but strangely enough the move which was played in the very first game with this variation is probably stronger: 21 ... ♗xe3 22 ♖xe3 ♖f6 (22 ... ♕h1+!? 23 ♕xh1 ♖xh1+ 24 ♔g2 ♖xa1 25

dc a5! and ... a4 is unclear;) 23 f3 (23 ♘f3? ♖xf3 24 ♖xf3 ♕h1+ 25 ♔e2 ♗xf3+ 26 ♕xf3 ♖e8+ wins the queen, while 23 f4 cd is also very good for Black) ♗f5 24 ♕e5 ♕xd2 (not 24 ... ♕h1+?? 25 ♔e2 ♕xa1 26 dc and White won in Timman–Johansson, Reykjavik 1976) 25 ♔g1 cd 26 ♗xd5 ♕xb2 and Black is a pawn up. In fact the badly placed rook on f6 gives White drawing chances after, for example, 27 ♖d1 ♗e6 28 ♖e2 ♕c3 29 ♗e4, but even so the position is unpleasant for White.

22   dc+

Clearing d5 for the queen is better than 22 d6+ ♔h8 23 ♕xc6 ♖xd6 (not 23 ... ♗xe3? 24 ♖xe3 ♖xd6 25 ♖e8! and White wins) 24 ♕b7 ♗xe3 25 ♖xe3 f4 26 ♖e7 (26 gf ♕xf4) fg 27 ♖f7 ♖f6 28 ♖xf6 gf 29 fg ♖e8! 30 ♘e4 ♕e2+ 31 ♔g1 ♗f3 0–1, Geszosz–Fabry, CSSR 1977.

22	...	♔h8
23	♕d5	♗xe3

23 ... ♖d6, which worked in the last note, fails when the queen is on d5 because 24 ♗xf4 ♖xd5 25 ♗xd5 gives White too many pieces for the queen.

24	♖xe3	f4

Not 24 ... ♖d6? 25 ♘f3! ♕h3+ 26 ♔g1 ♖xd5 27 ♗xd5 and although White has only ♖,

♞ and ♟ v ♛, the out of play Black queen and the passed c-pawn give White the advantage.

25 gf   ♛xf4*(33)*

33
W

26 ♞f3!

This is the move that keeps White on the board. Black wins after 26 ♜e2? ♜h2 27 f3 ♝h3+ 28 ♚e1 ♜h1+ 29 ♚f2 ♜h2+ 30 ♚e1 ♜h1+ 31 ♚f2 ♜xa1 32 ♛e4 ♛g5 33 ♞b1 ♜xb1 34 ♛xb1 ♛g2+ 35 ♚e3 ♜xf3+ 36 ♚d2 ♛g5+ 37 ♚d1 ♜f1+ 0–1, Brito–P. Littlewood, Hastings 1980/1.

26 ...   ♜h1+
27 ♚e2   ♜xa1
28 ♝c2   ♜c1
29 ♚d2!

Better than 29 ♝e4 ♛h2 30 ♜c3 ♜a1 31 ♝f5 ♛g2 32 ♝xg4 ♜f1 33 c7 ♜xf2+ 34 ♚e3 ♜e2+ 35 ♚d3 ♛f1! 36 ♜c2 ♜xf3+ 37 ♛xf3 ♛d1+ and Black wins, Suvalov–Poleshuk, corr. 1978.

29 ...   ♜f1

Not 29 ... ♝xf3? 30 ♛xf3 ♛xf3 31 ♜xf3 ♜xc2+ 32 ♚xc2 ♜xf3 33 c7 ♜f8 34 d5 and the connected passed pawns roll on.

30 ♛e4

The best move, since after 30 ♛e2 Black need not be content with a draw when he has the alternative 30 ... ♜xf2+ 31 ♚xf2 ♛h2+ 32 ♚e1 ♛xc2 with advantage.

30 ...   ♛h6

30 ... ♜xf2+?! 31 ♚e1 ♛xe3 32 ♛xe3 ♜xf3 33 ♛e7! is better for White.

After 30 ... ♛h6 the position is totally unclear, Sideif Zade–Poleshuk, corr. 1978, continued 31 ♚e2 ♜c1 32 c7 ♛h2 33 d5 ♛h5 34 ♚d2 ♜f1 35 ♚e2 ♜c1 36 ♚d2 ♜f1 (36 ... ♜xc2+?! 37 ♛xc2 ♛xd5+ 38 ♜d3 ♛xa2 39 ♛c3 threatening ♜d8 gives White the advantage) 37 ♞d4? (White should take the repetition by 37 ♚e2) ♜1xf2+ 38 ♚c3 ♜2f7 39 d6 ♜f6 40 ♛c6 ♝d7! 41 ♛b6 (41 ♛xd7 ♛c5+ wins) ♛d5 42 ♚b4 ♜xd6 0–1.

The main line offers chances to both sides, but the simple alternative given in the note to Black's 21st should be enough to put White off this line.

C2

19 ♛f1   ♞xe3

After 19 ... ♖xe3 20 ♖xe3 ♗xe3 21 ♕xh3 ♗xh3 22 fe ♘xe3 23 ♖e1 White has a very slight endgame advantage; there is no reason for Black to play this when the main variation is good for him.

20 ♕xh3 ♗xh3
21 cb(*34*)

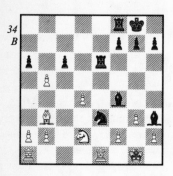

34
B

21 ... ♘c2

There is a second promising option for Black, namely 21 ... ♘d5 22 ♖xe6 fe 23 gf ab (even 23 ... cb 24 ♖e1 gives Black an edge) 24 ♖e1 ♖xf4 25 ♖e4 ♖f6 26 ♘f1 (26 ♗xd5? ♖g6+ wins, as does 26 ♖h4? ♖g6+ 27 ♔h1 ♗g2+ 28 ♔g1 ♗e4+ 29 ♔f1 ♗d3+), Hornung–Rogers, Canberra 1987, and now 26 ... ♘f4 would have maintained Black's advantages of a better pawn structure and safer king.

22 ♗xe6 fe!

The lines 22 ... ♗xe6 23 gf

♘xa1 24 ♖xa1 ab 25 ♖c1 and 22 ... ♘xa1 23 ♗xh3 ♗xd2 24 ♖xa1 cb 25 ♖d1 leave White a pawn up, while 22 ... ♗xd2 23 ♗xh3 ♘xe1 24 bc ♘f3+ 25 ♔h1 leaves Black's pieces badly coordinated in the fight against White's pawns.

23 gf ♘xa1

Better than 23 ... ♖xf4 24 ♖e3! with equality.

24 ♖xa1 ♖xf4
25 f3

Not 25 b6? ♖g4+ 26 ♔h1 ♗g2+ 27 ♔g1 ♗e4+ (if White had played 25 bc Black could take on c6 here) 28 ♔f1 ♗d3+ 29 ♔e1 ♖g1+ 30 ♘f1 ♖xf1+ 31 ♔d2 ♖xf2+ (if White had played 25 ba Black could take the rook here) 32 ♔xd3 ♖xb2 with two extra pawns for Black in the rook and pawn ending. 25 ♘f1 cb 26 ♖d1 ♖g4+ 27 ♘g3 h5 is even better for Black than the ending arising in the main line; Houtman–van der Kooij, corr. 1985 continued 28 f3 ♖g6 29 ♔f2 h4 30 ♘e4 ♖g2+ 31 ♔e3 ♖xb2 32 ♖d2 ♖xd2 33 ♔xd2 a5 34 ♔e3 b4 35 ♘c5 ♗f5 36 ♘b7 a4 37 ♔d2 ♗b1 38 ♘c5 a3 0–1.

25 ... cb

Material equality is re-established, but Black has the advantage. His bishop is superior to White's knight and he has fewer pawn islands. In practice White has failed to score from this position.

26 ♘e4   ♗f5!

26 ... ♖xf3 27 ♘g5 ♖d3 28 ♖c1 ♔f8 29 ♘xh7 ♔e7 30 ♖c3 gives White an easy time.

27 ♖e1

27 ♖c1 h6 28 ♖c6 ♖xf3 is tricky for White as 29 ♘c5?? ♗h3 is impossible.

27 ...   ♖xf3

28 ♘g5 (28 ♘c5 ♔f7 29 ♘xa6 ♖d3 30 ♘c7 b4 keeps an edge for Black) ♖d3 29 ♘xe6 ♔f7 (better

than 29 ... ♗xe6 30 ♖xe6 ♖xd4 31 ♖xa6 ♖d1+ 32 ♔f2 ♖d2+ 33 ♔g3 ♖xb2, Scheglmann–Attig, corr. 1984, and now 34 a4 draws) 30 ♘c5 ♖xd4 31 ♘xa6 ♖g4+! 32 ♔f2 ♖a4 33 ♘c5 ♖xa2 34 ♖e2 ♔f6 35 ♔f3 g5 36 ♘e4+ ♗xe4+ 37 ♔xe4 ♖a4+ 38 ♔f3 ♖b4 39 ♔g3 ♔f5 40 ♔f3 ♖b3+ 41 ♔g2 g4 42 ♔f2 h5 43 ♔g2 h4 44 ♔f2 h3 45 ♖c2 ♔e4 46 ♖d2 g3+ 0–1, Feldmus–Vitomskis, corr. 1983.

6   The Pawn Push: 17 ... f5

1 e4 e5 2 ♘f3 ♘c6 3 ♗b5 a6 4 ♗a4 ♘f6 5 0-0 ♗e7 6 ♖e1 b5 7 ♗b3 0-0 8 c3 d5 9 ed ♘xd5 10 ♘xe5 ♘xe5 11 ♖xe5 c6 12 d4 ♗d6 13 ♖e1 ♕h4 14 g3 ♕h3 15 ♗e3 ♗g4 16 ♕d3 ♖ae8 17 ♘d2 f5(35)

The Pawn Push replaces 17 ... ♖e6 of Chapters 2–5 with the direct attacking move ... f5. White has to block the advance of the f-pawn by playing f4 himself, when in order to make progress Black usually has to arrange ... g5. At the moment his d5 knight is pinned, so he normally plays ... ♔h8, when the pressure on e3 induces White to take on d5. Then it is a question of whether White's counterplay with a4 will take effect before Black's kingside threats become too serious. The critical line is variation A below, on which theory has yet to come to a final verdict.

There is one other 17th move which deserves a mention, namely **17 ... ♔h8**. The most likely result

is a transposition to the main line, but one independent example ran 18 c4 ♘xe3 19 ♖xe3 f5 20 ♕f1 ♕h5 21 cb f4 22 ♖xe8 ♖xe8 23 ♖e1 ♗e2 24 ♕g2 ♗b4 25 g4 ♕g6 26 f3 ♕d3 27 ♗c4 ♕xd4+ 28 ♕f2 ♕xd2 29 ♖xe2 ♖xe2 30 ♕xe2 ½–½, Geus–Schellingerhout, corr. 1983.

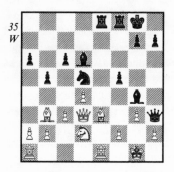

35
W

18   f4(36)

Just as in chapter 4, we need to consider the move 18 ♗xd5+, because this position can also arise if White takes on d5 earlier. Apparently an early ♗xd5 makes little sense because it gives Black the chance to save a tempo by avoiding the move ... ♚h8. In fact it is not so easy to make use of this factor, because ... ♚h8 is a useful move, so missing it out is no great advantage. However it may be that by delaying ... ♚h8 for a couple of moves Black can induce White to enter a line which is not considered best. This idea (21 ... ♚h8!? in line 3 below) represents the critical test for an early ♗xd5, but the whole question is rather academic since White loses nothing by delaying ♗xd5.

After 18 ♗xd5+ cd 19 ♕f1 (19 f4 g5 will transpose since White must play ♕f1 now) ♕h5 20 f4 g5 (20 ... ♚h8 transposes to the main line) White may play:

(1) **21 fg** ♖xe3 22 ♖xe3 f4 23 ♖f3 (more or less forced, since the defence 23 gf ♗xf4 24 ♖g3, as played in the main line, cannot be used here because the f8 rook is defended) ♕xg5!? (23 ... ♗xf3 24 ♕xf3 ♕xf3 25 ♘xf3 fg 26 ♚g2 gh is very drawish) with unclear complications, e.g. 24 gf ♖xf4!.

(2) **21 a4** is well met by 21 ... ba!, since 22 ♖xa4 gf 23 ♗xf4 ♗xf4 24 ♖xe8 ♕xe8 hits the stray rook on a4.

(3) **21 ♕g2** (this makes most sense, because the position of Black's king makes the threat of ♕xd5 stronger, but now that

White is committed to ♕g2 Black can play ... ♚h8) ♖e4 (21 ... gf transposes to the next note, but Black can play 21 ... ♚h8!? transposing into line 1 in the note to White's 21st) 22 fg (or 22 ♘xe4 fe and the result is probably a draw after 23 fg ♗h3 24 ♕d2 ♖f3 25 ♖f1 ♗xf1 26 ♖xf1 ♗xg3 27 ♖xf3 ♕xf3 28 hg ♕xg3+ 29 ♚f1 ♕h3+ 30 ♚e1 ♕h1+ with perpetual check) and now Black has a number of options, but none is fully satisfactory:

(3a) **22 ... ♗h3** 23 ♕f3 ♗g4 24 ♕g2 (24 ♕f2 ♚h8 25 ♗f4 ♗xf4 26 gf appears good for White to me) ♗h3 ½-½, Yanofsky–Tylor, Paignton 1952.

(3b) **22 ... f4** 23 ♘xe4 de 24 gf ♗xf4 25 ♗xf4 ♖xf4 26 ♕g3 ♖f3 27 ♕e5 ♗f5 28 ♖xe4 ♗xe4 29 ♕xe4 ♖f7 30 h4 is good for White.

(3c) **22 ... ♚h8** 23 h4! (23 a4 transposes to line 2a in the note to White's 21st, which is satisfactory for Black) ♖ee8!? (this appears strange, but the immediate 23 ... f4 fails to 24 ♘xe4 de 25 ♗xf4 ♗xf4 26 gf ♖xf4 27 ♖xe4! ♗f3 28 ♖xf4 ♗xg2 29 ♚xg2 and there is no perpetual check; Harding's suggestion of 23 ... h6!? is untested) 24 ♕f2 (Black's next move is ... f4 in any case) f4 25 ♗xf4 ♗e2 26 ♗xd6 (or else Black takes on f4 and plays ... ♕g4+)

♖xf2 27 ♔xf2 ♔g8 28 ♗e5 ♗g4 ½-½, Lang–Egorov, corr. 1959. I believe White is better in the final position.

36
B

18 ...   ♔h8

This preparatory move is almost always played, but the alternative 18 ... g5 19 ♕f1 ♕h5 is also possible. White may continue:

(1) **20 ♕g2** (this is normally given as the refutation of 18 ... g5, but its evaluation depends on line 1b below) and now:

(1a) **20 ... gf** (20 ... ♖e4? 21 ♘xe4 ♗f3 22 ♘xd6 should win) 21 ♗xd5+ cd (21 ... ♔h8 22 ♗xf4 ♗xf4 23 ♗xc6 ♗e3+ 24 ♔h1 is good for White after 24 ... ♖e6 25 ♗f3! or 24 ... ♗h3 25 ♕e2! ♗g4 26 ♗xe8 ♖xe8 27 ♕xe3 ♖xe3 28 ♖xe3 ♕f7 29 ♔g2 f4 30 ♖e5 fg 31 ♔xg3 ♕g6 32 ♖ae1, Kern–Dahlhaus, corr. 1973/7) 22 ♕xd5+ ♔g7 (22 ... ♔h8 23 ♕xd6 fe 24 ♖xe3) 23 ♗xf4 ♗xf4 24 gf ♔h8 (or 24 ...

♗e2 25 ♕g2+ ♔h8 26 ♕f2 with a clear plus for White, Unzicker–Pfleger, W. Germany 1963) 25 ♖e5 ♖g8 26 ♔h1 ♗h3 27 ♖xe8 ♕xe8 28 ♕e5+ ♕xe5 29 de ♗g2 30 ♖d1 with advantage for White according to Euwe. Black's active pieces give him some compensation for the two pawns but probably not enough.

(1b) **20 ... ♔h8!?** and now White has nothing better than to take on d5, transposing into line 1 in the next note, which is unclear.

(2) **20 a4!?** The question now is whether Black has anything better than moving his king, transposing to the main after an exchange on d5. The answer is probably not.

(3) **20 fg** ♖xe3 21 ♖xe3 f4 22 ♖f3 (if White ever takes on d5 we transpose to line 1 in the last note, with which this should be compared) ♗xf3 (22 ... ♕xg5!?) 23 ♕xf3 ♕xf3 24 ♘xf3 fg 25 ♔g2 gh is again drawish.

This analysis suggests that 18 ... g5 is no better than 18 ... ♔h8.

19 ♗xd5   cd
20 ♕f1   ♕h5(37)
21 a4(38)

21 ♕g2 is an interesting alternative, and now:

(1) **21 ... g5** 22 ♕xd5 ♖d8 (not 22 ... gf? 23 ♕xd6! fe 24 ♖xe3 winning for White) 23 ♕c6 (this position is very important because it may arise by transposition from

either of the last two notes) gf 24 ♗xf4 ♗xf4 25 gf ♗e2 26 ♔h1 ♖de8!? (not 26 ... ♖d6? 27 ♕g2 winning for White) 27 ♖gl (27 ♕g2 ♖e3! also gives Black compensation for the pawns) ♕h4 28 ♕g2 (White decides he has nothing better than a draw; 28 ♕d6 ♗g4 29 ♖ae1 ♕f2 30 ♖xe8 ♗f3+ is also drawn) ♖g8 29 ♕c6 ♖gf8 30 ♕g2 ♖g8 31 ♕c6 ½-½, A. Sokolov–Nunn, Rotterdam 1989.

(2) **21 ... ♖e4** and now:

(2a) **22 a4** g5 (this position can arise from earlier notes, so we need to analyse it even though 22 ♘xe4 appears strong) 23 fg ♗h3 24 ♕f3 (24 ♕f2 and 24 ♕e2 are also met by 24 ... ♖g4) ♖g4 25 ab f4 26 ♗xf4 ♗xf4 27 ba ♕xg5 28 a7 ♖a8 29 ♖e8+ ♖xe8 30 a8(♕) ♖xa8 31 ♖xa8+ ♔g7 31 ♖a7+ is a draw. Harding suggests that Black can play on by 28 ... ♕g8!?, when the critical reply seems to be 29 ♔h1.

(2b) **22 ♘xe4** fe 23 h4! h6 24 ♖f1 g5 25 ♕h2! gf 26 ♗xf4 ♖xf4

27 ♖xf4 ♗xf4 28 gf e3 29 ♕g3 e2 30 ♔f2 ♕f5 31 h5 won for White in Klover–Kant, Ostrava 1981.

The Klover–Kant game suggests that 21 ♕g2 is an underrated idea. Black's best chance appears to be line 1; if this is satisfactory for Black then 18 ... g5 is just as good as 18 ... ♔h8, while if not then the whole Pawn Push is in trouble.

Finally **21 ♕f2** is rare. The best line appears to be 21 ... h6 22 a4 g5 23 ab ab transposing to Nunn–Cooper in line B below, which is fine for Black. The alternative 21 ... ♖e6 (21 ... g5 22 fg ♖xe3 23 ♖xe3 f4 24 ♖e5 is good for White) 22 a4 was good for White after 22 ... ♖fe8 23 ab ab 24 ♘b3 g5 25 fg f4 26 ♗xf4, Barcons–Ramos, corr. 1983 or 22 ... ♕e8 23 ♘f1 ♖f7 24 ♗d2 ♖e4 25 ♘e3 ♕c6 26 ab ♕xb5 27 ♘xg4 fg 28 ♖xe4 de 29 b4 g5 30 ♖a5 ♕c4 31 ♖xg5 e3 32 ♗xe3 1-0, Stilling–Kelstrup, corr. 1980.

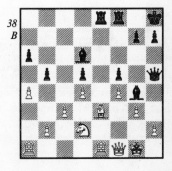

After 21 a4 there is a major division:

A **21 . . . ba**
B **21 . . . g5**

Although the first alternative severely weakens Black's queenside pawns, the necessary reply ♖xa4 deflects White's rook from the first rank and gives Black tactical chances; indeed, White's best response is simply to return the rook to a1. The resulting positions are quite unclear. Line B has for a long time been regarded as the main continuation, but the latest games indicate that best play for both sides leads to a bad ending for Black. I expect that future investigations will concentrate on 21 . . . ba.

A

21 . . . **ba**
22 ♖xa4

This is the best move. Alternatives lead to at most a draw:

(1) **22 ♛xa6** ♖e6 23 ♛b5 (23 ♛xa4 ♗e2 24 ♛d7 ♖h6 25 h4 ♛g4 26 ♔f2 ♗d3 27 c4 ♖g6 28 ♘f1 ♗xf1 29 ♖xf1 ♛xg3+ was very good for Black in Byway–Gillam, England 1985, while the untested suggestion 23 ♛f1!? looks unappealing) ♖h6 24 ♘f1 ♗f3 25 ♛d3 ♛g4 26 ♛d2 g5 27 ♖xa4 ♖g6 28 ♖a6 gf 29 ♖xd6 fg 30 hg ♖xd6 and White scraped a draw after 31 ♗f4 ♖g6 32 ♘h2

♛h5 33 ♘xf3 ♛xf3 34 ♛g2 ♛xg2+ 35 ♔xg2 ♖b6 36 ♖e7 ♖xb2+ 37 ♔f3 ♔g8 38 ♗e5 ♖f7 ½–½, den Broeder–van Oosterom, corr. 1981.

(2) **22 ♛g2** ♖e4 (22 . . . g5? 23 ♛xd5 gf 24 ♛xd6 fe 25 ♖xe3 wins) 23 ♘xe4 (not 23 ♖xa4 g5 24 ♘xe4 fe 25 ♖xa6 gf 26 ♖xd6 fe 27 ♖xe3 ♗h3 28 g4 ♛xg4 winning for Black, Kosten–Hebden, Ramsgate 1982 and Timman–Nunn, radio game 1983) fe 24 ♛f1 ♗f3 (24 . . . g5? 25 ♛xa6 ♗b8 26 fg ♗xg3 27 hg ♗f3 28 ♛h6! wins) 25 ♛xa6 ♛h3 (again Black must take care since 25 . . . ♗b8?! 26 ♛e6! is good for White) 26 ♖e2 (26 ♛f1?! ♛g4 followed by . . . h5–h4 is dangerous) ♗xe2 27 ♛xe2 g5 28 ♖xa4 gf 29 ♗xf4 ♗xf4 30 gf e3! 31 ♔h1 ♖xf4 32 ♖a8+ ♔g7 33 ♛g2+ ♛xg2+ 34 ♔xg2 ♖f2+ (the 1987 telex game Essen–London was agreed drawn here) 35 ♔g3 ♖xb2 36 ♖e8 e2 37 ♔f3 ♖c2 38 ♖xe2 ♖xc3+ 39 ♔f4 ♔f6 40 ♖a2 ♖h3 41 ♖a6+ ½–½, Hindle–P. Littlewood, England 1987.

22 . . . **g5**
23 ♖aa1!*(39)*

This paradoxical move is best. Firstly White removes the a4 rook from its tactically exposed position, and by defending e1 he ensures that he need not take with the pawn if Black exchanges on f4. The alternative 23 fg? (23 ♖xa6? gf is also fine for Black after 24 ♖xd6 fe 25 ♘b3 f4 26 gf ♗h3, 24 gf ♗h3 25 ♕f3 ♖g8+ or 24 ♗xf4 ♖xe1 25 ♕xe1 ♗xf4 26 gf ♗e2) is complicated but ultimately good for Black, e.g. 23 ... ♖xe3 (23 ... f4 amounts to the same thing since 24 ♗xf4 ♗xf4 25 gf ♗h3! 26 ♕f2 ♕g4+ 27 ♔h1 ♗g2+ wins for Black while 24 gf ♖xe3 25 ♖xe3 ♗xf4 transposes to the main line) 24 ♖xe3 f4 25 gf (25 ♖f3 fails to 25 ... ♗xf3 26 ♕xf3 ♕e8! followed by ... fg) ♗xf4 26 ♖g3 ♕e8! (this move is one of the points of ... ba) 27 ♖xg4 ♗e3+ (better than 27 ... ♗xd2 28 ♕xa6, when both 28 ... ♕h5 29 ♕e2! ♗e3+ 30 ♔h1 ♖f2 31 ♖a8+ ♔g7 32 ♖a7+ ♔f8 33 ♖a8+ and 28 ... ♕e1+ 29 ♔g2 ♖f2+ 30 ♔h3 ♖f3+ 31 ♖g3 ♖xg3+ 32 hg ♕h1+ 33 ♔g4 ♕e4+ 34 ♔h5 ♕h1+ lead to perpetual check) 28 ♔g2 (28 ♔h1 ♖xf1+ 29 ♘xf1 ♕xa4 30 ♘xe3 ♕a1+ and the a-pawn gives Black fair winning prospects) ♖xf1 29 ♘xf1 ♗c1! (29 ... ♕xa4 30 ♘xe3 ♕b3 31 ♔h3 ♕xb2 32 ♘xd5 a5 33 ♘f6 ♕xc3+ 34 ♔h4 a4 35 d5 a3 36 d6 ♕d2 was also good for Black in Schumann–Leisebein, corr. 1985, but 31 ♔f3! ♕xb2 32 ♘xd5 ♕xh2 33 ♖e4 followed by ♖e5 would have been unclear accord-

ing to van der Heijden) 30 ♖a5 (30 ♖b4 ♕e2+ 31 ♔g3 ♕xf1 32 ♖b8+ ♔g7 33 ♖b7+ ♔g8 34 ♖b8+ ♔f7 35 ♖b6 ♕d3+ 36 ♔h4 ♗d2 gives Black a dangerous attack against the king, e.g. 37 ♖f6+? ♔g7 38 ♔h5 ♗e1 39 h4 ♕g6+ wins) ♕e2+ 31 ♔g3 ♕xf1 32 ♖xd5, Ulmanis–van der Heijden, corr. 1986 and now 32 ... ♗e3! 33 ♖e4 ♕f2+ 34 ♔g4 ♕g2+ 35 ♔f5 ♕xg5+ 36 ♔e6 ♕g6+ 37 ♔e5 ♗g1 38 ♖d8+ ♔g7 39 ♖d7+ ♔f8 40 ♖f4+ ♔e8 41 ♖ff7 ♗xh2+ followed by ... ♕xf7+ would have won according to van der Heijden.

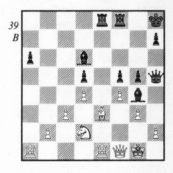

23 ...   ♖e6

Better than **23 ... a5** 24 fg f4 25 ♗xf4 and a draw was agreed in Schlosser–Nunn, Krefeld 1986, even though 25 ... ♗e2 26 ♕f2 ♗xf4 27 gf ♕g4+ 28 ♕g3 ♖xf4 29 ♕xg4 ♖xg4+ 30 ♔h1 is clearly good for White. **23 ... h6** is an untested alternative, with a possible transposition to line 2 below after 24 ♕f2 ♖e6.

24 ♕f2

24 ♖xa6? gf 25 ♖xd6 (25 ♗xf4? ♖xe1 26 ♕xe4 ♗xf4 27 gf ♗e2 0–1, Janosevic–Blatny, Bad Worishofen 1989) would be very good for White if Black were forced to play 25 ... ♖xd6 26 ♗xf4, but 25 ... fe 26 ♖xe6 ed 27 ♖1e2 f4! is good for Black. However **24 fg!?** must be critical, since 24 ... f4 leads to the same bad ending as in Schlosser–Nunn above; therefore Black should play 24 ... ♖fe8 and if 25 ♕f2 h6 transposes to line 1 below.

After 24 ♕f2 Black may try:

(1) **24 ... ♖fe8!?** 25 fg h6 is one idea, meeting 26 gh?! by 26 ... f4, when both 27 ♗xf4 ♖e2 and 27 gf ♖g6 are dangerous.

(2) **24 ... h6** 25 c4 ♖g8 26 cd ♖xe3 27 ♖xe3 gf 28 gf ♗f3+ 29 ♔f1 ♗g2+ 30 ♔g1 ♗f3+ 31 ♔f1 ♗g2+ 32 ♔e1 ♕xh2 33 ♖xa6 ♗xf4 34 ♘f1 ♗xe3 35 ♕xe3 (35 ♘xh2 ♗xf2+ 36 ♔xf2 ♗xd5 37 ♖xh6+ ♔g7 will be a draw) ♕h4+ 36 ♔d2 ♔h7 37 ♖a7+ ♔g6 38 ♕e6+ ♔h5 39 ♕xf5+ ♖g5 40 ♕f7+ ♖g6 41 ♖a4 ♗xf1 42 ♕xf1 ♕h2+ 43 ♕e2+ ♕xe2+ 44 ♔xe2 ♖g2+ 45 ♔f3 ♖xb2 46 ♔f4 ♔g6 47 ♖a6+ ♔f7 and the ending of ♖ and doubled pawn v ♖ is a draw, McClelland–Gillam, corr. 1986.

(3) **24 ... ♖g6!** (preventing fg) 25 c4 ♗h3 26 cd ♕g4 (by now ... gf is a very serious threat) 27 ♖f1 ♗xf1 28 ♖xf1 gf 29 ♗xf4 ♗xf4 30 ♕xf4 ♕xf4 31 ♖xf4 ♖d6 and Black won the ending in Mol–van Oosterom, corr. 1981.

B

21 ... g5
22 ab ab(40)

Better than 22 ... a5 23 fg ♖e4 (23 ... ♖xe3 24 ♖xe3 f4 25 ♖f3 ♗xf3 26 ♕xf3 ♕xf3 27 ♘xf3 fg 28 ♔g2 gh 29 ♘xh2 ♗xh2 30 ♔xh2 ♖f2+ 31 ♔g3 ♖xb2 32 ♖xa5 should win for White) 24 ♗f4! ♗xf4 25 gf h6! 26 h3! (26 gh ♖g8 and 26 ♖xa5 ♗h3 are unclear, as is 26 ♔h1 after 26 ... ♖e2 or 26 ... ♖fe8; finally 26 b6 hg 27 ♘xe4 fe 28 b7 ♗f3 29 h3 gf 30 ♔h2 ♖b8 was even good for Black in Tarnoy–Papai, corr. 1983) ♗xh3 (26 ... ♗e2 27 ♕g2) 27 ♕f3 ♕h4 (27 ... ♗g4 28 ♕g3! hg 29 ♘xe4 fe 30 f5! ♗xf5 31 ♕h2 ♗h3 32 ♖e3 g4 33 ♕e5+ should win for White) 28 ♘xe4 fe 29 ♕f2 ♕g4+ 30 ♔h2 ♖xf4 31 ♕g3 ♕f5 32 gh! ♗f2+ 33 ♔h1 ♗g4 34 ♕e5+! ♕xe5 35 de ♖xb2 36 ♖ab1! (not 36 ♖eb1? ♗f3+ 37 ♔g1 ♖g2+ 38 ♔f1? e3! and Black wins) ♗f3+ 37 ♔g1 ♖g2+ 38 ♔f1 ♖h2 39 b6 and White won in Varadi–Papai, corr. 1984.

The position after 22 ... ab is

critical for the assessment of the Pawn Push variation. There are three different theoretical recommendations which supposedly give White the advantage, but two of them are doubtful. We take the third as the main line.

23 fg

The other moves are:

(1) **23 ♖a6** gf 24 ♗xf4 and now the simplest line is **24 ... ♗h3!** winning the queen since 25 ♕f2 ♖xe1+ 26 ♕xe1 ♗xf4 27 gf ♕g4+ 28 ♕g3 ♕d1+ is catastrophic. White's compensation for the queen is probably not even enough to equalize. Moreover Black has a second satisfactory line in **24 ... ♖xe1** 25 ♕xe1 ♗xf4 26 fg ♗e2 27 ♘f1 ♕f3! with a very dangerous attack for the pawn; after 28 ♕f2 (28 ♘g3 ♕e3+ 29 ♕f2 ♕c1+ 30 ♔g2 ♗d3 is the same) ♕d3! 29 ♘g3 (29 ♖e6 ♗xf1 30 ♕xf1 ♖g8+ 31 ♔f2 ♕d2+) ♕d1+ 30 ♔g2 ♗d3 the bishop transfer to e4 causes

serious problems, since if White takes it he will be defenceless along the g-file.

(2) **23 ♕f2** h6 and now:

(2a) **24 b3** was played in Nunn–L. Cooper, Swansea 1987, but after 24 ... ♖g8 25 c4 ♗h3 26 fg hg 27 ♖a6 Black could have played 27 ... ♗b4! and White cannot meet the threat of ... f4.

(2b) **24 ♘f1** and now 24 ... ♗f3? 25 fg f4 26 gf hg 27 ♘g3! ♕g4 28 h3 ♕xh3 29 ♕xf3 gf 30 ♗xf4 ♖xe1+ 31 ♖xe1 ♖xf4 32 ♕h5+ ♕xh5 33 ♘xh5 was effective in Leander–Enegren, corr. 1981/2. However 24 ... ♖e4! is a big improvement and poses awkward problems for White.

(2c) **24 ♖a5** (this looks dreadful) gf 25 ♗xf4 ♖xe1+ 26 ♕xe1 ♗xf4 27 gf ♖e8 28 ♕f2 ♗h3 29 ♘f3 ♖g8+ 30 ♔h1 ♗g2+ 31 ♕xg2 ♖xg2 32 ♔xg2 ♕g4+ 33 ♔f2 ♕xf4 34 ♖xb5 ♗e4 35 ♖b7 f4 and Black won in Madler–Sarink, corr. 1980.

| 23 | ... | ♖xe3 |

23 ... ♖e4 has been suggested but not played.

24	♖xe3	f4
25	gf	♗xf4
26	♖g3	♕xg5
27	♔h1 *(41)*	

27 ♘f3!? is also untried; the best reply is 27 ... ♕g7.

| 27 | ... | ♗d6! |

27 ... ♖g8 28 ♘f3 ♕f5 was

41
B

played in Boleslavsky–Tal, USSR 1962, and now 29 ♘e5! ♗xg3 30 hg ♗f3+ 31 ♘xf3 ♖xg3 32 ♘h4! ♕xf1+ (32 ... ♖h3+ 33 ♔g1 is similar) 33 ♖xf1 ♖h3+ 34 ♔g2 ♖xh4 35 ♖f5 gives White a winning rook and pawn ending.

28   ♕g2

Better than 28 ♕e1 ♗xg3 29 hg (29 ♕xg3 transposes) ♕h5+ 30 ♔g1 ♗e2! (but not 30 ... ♖e8 31 ♕f2 with advantage to White), which virtually paralyses White. Black can increase the pressure by 31 ... ♕e8 (this is the answer to 31 ♖a6, for example) and 32 ... ♕e3+, followed by the advance of the h-pawn, and it seems to me that White has no hope of any advantage.

28   ...   ♗xg3
29   ♕xg3   h5

29 ... ♕xd2 30 ♕xg4 ♖g8 31 ♕f3 ♕g5 32 ♖f1 gives White very good winning chances.

30   ♖f1

Much better than 30 ♖a7 h4,

which gives Black a dangerous attack after 31 ♕g2 (31 ♕c7 ♖f1+ 32 ♔g2 ♗e2+ 33 ♔h3 ♕g4 mate, or 31 ♕e1 ♗h3 32 ♕e2 ♖g8 with strong threats) ♖g8 with the threats of 32 ... ♕xd2 and 32 ... ♗f3, or a superior ending after 31 ♕e5+ ♕xe5 32 de ♗h3 33 ♖a1 ♖f2 34 ♘b3 ♖xb2.

30   ...   ♖xf1+

30 ... ♖g8 31 h3 ♕xd2 32 ♕e5+ ♖g7 33 hg hg 34 ♕h5+ ♔g8 35 ♕xd5+ ♔h7 36 ♕f5+ followed by ♖f2 is very good for White.

31   ♘xf1   ♕c1
32   ♔g1   ♕xb2 *(42)*

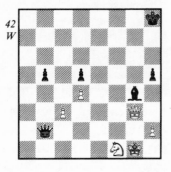

42
W

In my opinion all the moves since 21 ... g5 have been best play for both sides, so the assessment of this ending is important for the entire Pawn Push. *ECO* naively assesses it as equal, but in fact White has a clear advantage. The only question is whether or not Black can draw.

33 h3!   ♗d1!

This is the only move, e.g. 33 ... ♗e6/f5 34 ♕e5+, 33 ... ♗d7 34 ♕e5+ followed by ♕e7+ or ♕xd5+, 33 ... ♗c8 34 ♕e5+ followed by ♕c7+ or ♕e8+, or 33 ... ♗e2 34 ♕e5+ ♔h7 35 ♘g3 ♕c1+ (35 ... ♗d1 36 ♘f5) 36 ♔f2 ♗d1 37 ♘f5 ♕d2+ 38 ♔f1 ♔g5 39 ♕xd5 with a pawn more and the better position. The final possibility is 33 ... b4, but 34 hg bc 35 ♕e5+ ♔h7 (35 ... ♔g8 36 gh c2 37 h6) 36 ♕xh5+ etc., followed by a timely ♘e3 should win for White.

34 ♘e3

Timman suggested 34 ♕e1, so as to gain a tempo over Timman–Nunn below after 34 ... ♕e2 35 ♕xe2 ♗xe2 36 ♘g3 ♗d1 37 ♘f5. Whether this is sufficient to change the evaluation of the position is not clear, but in any case Black may play 34 ... ♕c2, meeting 35 ♘e3 by 35 ... ♕e4. Note that 34 ♕e5+ ♔h7 35 ♘e3 is inferior, since Black may reply 35 ... ♕c1!

34 ...   ♕b1!

Once again the only move, since 34 ... ♕c1? loses to 35 ♕e1. Now 35 ♕e1 may be met by 35 ... ♕e4.

After 34 ... ♕b1! there are two moves:

(1) **35 ♕e5+** (exchanging queens gives White some advantage, but it appears that Black can just hold the draw) ♔h7 36 ♕f5+ ♕xf5 37 ♘xf5 (at first sight this ending looks awful for Black, with all three pawns fixed on white squares, but Black controls just enough space to prevent White from penetrating) ♔g6! 38 ♘e3 (after 38 ♘e7+ ♔g5 39 ♘xd5 ♗b3 both 40 ♘e3 ♔f4 41 ♔f2 ♔e4 42 ♔e2 h4 followed by ... b4, and 40 ♘c7 ♗c4 41 d5 ♔f6 42 d6 ♗e6 43 ♘xb5 ♗xh3 44 c4 ♗d7 45 ♘c7 ♔e5 46 c5 ♔d4 lead to a draw), Timman–Nunn, Brussels 1988, and now I played 38 ... ♗b3 when the game ended in a draw on move 89. However it is simpler for Black to play 38 ... ♗f3 39 ♔f2 ♗e4, setting up the optimum defensive position right away, e.g. 40 ♔g3 ♔g5 41 h4+ ♔g6! 42 ♔f4 ♔f6. This is a corresponding squares position which is a draw provided Black defends precisely. White can also reach a position with ♔b4 v ♔b6, but the corresponding squares are similar and again Black can draw.

(2) **35 ♔g2!** (Haba's move gives White good winning chances) and now:

(2a) **35 ... b4** 36 ♕e5+ ♔h7 37 ♘f5, Haba–Dobrovolsky, Czechoslovakia Ch. 1988, and **35 ... ♕e4+** 36 ♔f2 ♗b3 37 ♕e5+

♕xe5 38 de ♔g7 39 ♔g3 should win for White.

(2b) **35 ... ♕b2+** 36 ♕f2 ♕c1 (36 ... ♕xf2+ 37 ♔xf2 ♗b3 38 ♘g2! ♔g7 39 ♘f4 ♔h6 40 h4 completely ties Black up, when White can penetrate with his king on the queenside) 37 ♕f6+ ♔h7 38 ♕e7+ ♔g6 39 ♘xd5 is very good for White. Note that the tactical idea 39 ... ♗f3+ 40 ♔xf3 ♕f1+ (40 ... ♕h1+ 41 ♔f4) fails to 41 ♔g3! (41 ♔e4? ♕f5+ 42 ♔e3 ♕xh3+ draws) ♕g1+ 42 ♔f4 ♕h2+ 43 ♔e4 and wins.

(2c) **35 ... ♗c2** 36 ♕e5+ ♔h7 37 ♕xh5+ ♔g7 38 ♕e5+ ♔h7 39 ♕c7+ ♔g6 40 ♕c6+ ♔h7 41 ♘g4 ♕e1 (41 ... ♗e4+ 42 ♔g3) 42 ♕h6+ ♔g8 43 ♕e3 and again White has good winning prospects.

7 Other Black 16th Moves

1 e4 e5 2 Nf3 Nc6 3 Bb5 a6 4 Ba4 Nf6 5 0-0 Be7 6 Re1 b5 7 Bb3 0-0 8 c3 d5 9 ed Nxd5 10 Nxe5 Nxe5 11 Rxe5 c6 12 d4 Bd6 13 Re1 Qh4 14 g3 Qh3 15 Be3 Bg4 16 Qd3(43)

In this chapter we deal with two less common Black 16th moves, 16 ... f5 and 16 ... Nxe3. The normal result of 16 ... f5 is a transposition into the Pawn Push, but here we examine an independent line in which Black tries to save time by missing out ... Rae8 in the hope of playing the rook to f8 without losing a tempo. 16 ... Nxe3 is based on a different principle. Black abandons his hopes of a direct attack and plays for positional compensation based on the two bishops. This line is considered dubious and is never played today.

Apart from 16 ... Kh8, when a transposition to chapter 6 is virtually inevitable, other 16th moves are bad, e.g. 16 ... g5?! (16 ... Nf4? 17 Bxf4 Bxf4 18 Qe4! is very good for White) 17 Bxg5 f5 and now White has a choice of promising lines:

(1) **18 Bh4 f4 19 Qf1**, given by Barden, looks very good for White.

(2) **18 Qf1 Qh5 19 f4 Rae8 20 Nd2 Kg7 21 Bxd5 cd 22 Qg2** (22 Qf2 is also good) **Rxe1+ 23 Rxe1** (Black has no real compensation for the two pawns) **Re8 24 Qf2 Qg6 25 Re3 a5 26 Qe1 Rxe3 27 Qxe3** and White won in Yim–Nussle, corr. 1983.

(3) **18 Nd2 f4 19 Ne4 fg 20 fg Rf3** (20 ... Bf3 21 Qd2 Bc7 22 Bh6 Rf5 23 Ng5 Qxh6 24 Nxf3 Qg7 25 Qg2 is no better, Rathmann–Hindre, corr. 1966) **21 Qd2 Raf8 22 Bh4** with a clear plus for White.

A 16 ... f5
B 16 ... Nxe3
A

    16 ... f5
    17 f4

After 17 Qf1 Black can continue 17 ... Qh5 with a likely

transposition to the main line, but in Kindermann–I. Sokolov, Biel 1988 Black tried 17 ... ♛xf1+!? 18 ♚xf1 f4 19 gf ♗xf4 20 ♚g1 (20 ♗xf4 ♖xf4 21 ♘d2 ♖af8 22 ♘e4 ♗f5 23 ♘g5 h6 24 ♘e6 ♗h3+ is good for Black) ♗c7 and White's broken kingside gave Black good compensation for the pawn. The continuation was 21 ♘d2 ♖f6 22 ♘e4 ♖g6 23 ♘g3 ♖f8 24 ♗c2 ♗f5 25 ♗xf5 ♖xf5 26 ♗d2 h5 27 ♖e4 ♗f4! with a slight advantage for Black.

17 ...   g5

After 17 ... ♚h8 18 ♗xd5 cd 19 ♘d2 Black should play either 19 ... ♖ae8 transposing to Chapter 6 or 19 ... g5 transposing to the main line below, avoiding 19 ... ♖g8? 20 ♛f1 ♛h5 21 a4 which was good for White in Euwe–Donner, Dutch Ch. 1950. Once Black has played 17 ... g5 he can no longer return to the main line of Chapter 6, so this is a committal decision.

18   ♛f1   ♛h5
19   ♘d2

Not 19 fg (19 ♗xd5+ cd 20 ♘d2 ♖ae8 transposes to Chapter 6, note to White's 18th move) f4 20 ♗xf4 (20 gf ♖ae8) ♖xf4 21 gf ♖f8 and Black obtains a much more favourable version of the main line.

19 ...   ♚h8

19 ... ♖ae8 leads to Chapter 6, note to Black's 18th move.

20   ♗xd5   cd
21   fg

The other idea is 21 a4, which aims to reach a favourable version of the main line by first of all opening up the queen's path to a6. After 21 a4 ba (21 ... ♖ae8 leads to a position from Chapter 6 considered favourable for White) White may play:

(1) **22 ♖xa4** ♖ae8 leads to Chapter 6. If the main line of this section is satisfactory for Black, then White will have to fall back on this transposition, in which case 17 ... g5 is only an alternative move-order.

(2) **22 c4** ♖ab8 23 ♖ab1 ♗h3 24 ♛f2 ♛g4 25 cd gf 26 ♗xf4 ♗xf4 27 ♛xf4 ♛xf4 28 gf ♖b4 29 ♚f2 ♖xd4 30 ♘f3 ♖xd5 with a fully satisfactory ending for Black, Short–Ehlvest, Skelleftea 1989.

(3) **22 fxg5** f4 23 ♗xf4 ♖xf4 (since there seems to be no improvement for Black after this he should try 23 ... ♗xf4 24 gf ♖ab8, when it is not clear if

White can prove any advantage)
24 gf ♖f8 25 ♖e5 ♗xe5 26 de h6
27 ♕xa6 (the interpolation of a4
and ... ba gives White a much
better version of the main line) hg
28 ♕d6 ♖xf4 29 ♖f1 ♗f5 30
♕xd5 ♗h3 31 ♖xf4 gf 32 ♕f3,
Sax–Ehlvest, Skelleftea 1989, and
White converted his material advantage into a win.

21 ... f4
22 ♗xf4 ♖xf4

This combination allows Black
to make use of the fact that he has
not played ... ♖ae8. The alternative 22 ... ♗xf4 (22 ... ♖f5 23
♕g2 ♗xf4 24 gf ♖xf4 25 ♕xd5
♖af8 26 ♖f1 is also very good for
White) 23 gf ♗h3 24 ♕e2 (24 ♕f2
♕g4+ 25 ♕g3 ♖xf4 26 ♖e3
♖g8 27 ♔h1 ♕xg3 28 ♖xg3 ♖f2
is less clear and Black eventually
won in Helsloot–de Klerk, corr.
1983) ♕xe2 25 ♖xe2 ♖xf4 26
♘f1 ♖g4+ 27 ♘g3 ♖xg5 28
♖ae1 ♖ag8 29 ♖e5 won for
White in Neishtadt–Antos, corr.
1959.

23 gf ♖f8
24 ♖e5 ♗xe5
25 de h6 *(44)*
26 ♖e1

The alternatives are:

(1) **26 a4** hg 27 ab ♗e2 28 ♕f2
♖xf4 29 ♕e3 ♗xb5 30 e6 d4! is
unclear according to Lindroos.

(2) **26 ♕d3** hg 27 ♕xd5 gf 28
♕d6 ♖g8 29 ♕f6+ ♖g7 30 h4
♗d1+ 31 ♔h1 ♕g4 32 ♕d8+

44
W

♖g8 33 ♕f6+ ♔h7 34 ♕f7+
♖g7 0–1, Rosellio–Lindroos,
corr.

(3) **26 gh!?** ♖g8 27 ♔f2
♕xh2+ 28 ♔e3 and after 28 ...
♗h3 29 ♘f3 ♖g3 30 ♕e2 White
went on to win in Hansel–Leh-
mann, corr. 1980. However, 28 ...
♕g3+! wins for Black after 29
♘f3 ♖f8 or 29 ♔d4 ♖f8.

26 ... hg
27 f5 ♖xf5

Not the time-wasting 27 ...
♗h3?! 28 ♕e2 ♗g4 29 ♕d3 ♗h3
30 f6! of Lundblad–Lindroos,
corr. 1974.

28 ♕d3 ♖f2!

Better than 28 ... ♗h3 29 e6
(not 29 ♕xd5 ♕h4 30 ♕e4 ♖f4)
♖f4 30 ♕e2! and now:

(1) **30 ... ♖g4+** 31 ♔h1
♗g2+ (31 ... ♕e8 32 e7 d4 33
♕f3 also wins) 32 ♕xg2 ♖xg2 33
♔xg2 ♕e8 34 e7 and White wins.

(2) **30 ... ♗g4** 31 ♕e3 ♗f5 32
e7 ♗e4 33 ♘xe4 ♖xe4 (33 ... de
34 ♖f1) 34 ♕d4+! ♖xd4 (34 ...
♔h7 35 ♖xe4) 35 e8(♕)+ winning.

(3) **30 ... ♕h4 31 ♔h1** (but not
31 ♕e5+? ♔h7 32 ♖e2 ♕g4+
33 ♔h1 ♖f1+!) ♖f2 32 ♕e5+
♔h7 33 e7 ♗d7 34 ♘f3 and
White wins, Koti–Riszt, corr.
1982/3.

29 ♘f1!

Better than 29 h3 (not 29
♔xf2?? ♕xh2+ 30 ♔e3 ♕f4
mate), when 29 ... ♕h4 30 ♖f1
♗f5 31 ♕e3 ♖xf1+ 32 ♘xf1
♗xh3 33 e6 ♕g4+ ½–½, A. Sokolov–Ehlvest, Rotterdam 1989,
was a safe draw, but Black could
try 29 ... ♖f4!?, when 30 hg?
♕xg4+ 31 ♔h1 ♖f2 wins, while
30 e6 ♗xh3 threatens 31 ...
♕g4+.

29 ...   ♖xb2(45)

45
W

and Leander's analysis continued
with the two lines:

(1) **30 e6 ♗f3 31 ♕d4+ ♔g8
32 ♘d2 ♕h3 33 ♕f2** and now it
seems to me that the simplest continuation is 33 ... ♕g4+ 34 ♔f1
♗g2+ 35 ♕xg2 ♕xg2+ 36
♔xg2 ♖xd2+ and 37 ... ♔f8

when only Black has winning
chances.

(2) **30 ♘d2 ♗h3 31 ♕d4 ♖xd2
32 ♕xd2 ♕g4+ 33 ♔f2 ♕g2+
34 ♔e3 ♕e4+** with perpetual
check.

However this analysis was
dented in Klatt–Leisebein, corr.
1986, when White added a third
line:

(3) **30 ♕xd5 ♗f3 31 ♕d8+
♔h7 32 ♕d7+ ♔h8 33 ♘d2 g4
34 ♕d8+ ♔h7 35 ♖e3!** with advantage for White. However, this
is not completely convincing
because Black can play 31 ...
♔g7!, so as to meet 32 ♕d7+ by
32 ... ♕f7 33 ♕xf7+ ♔xf7 with
a drawn ending. Black can always
make sure that he meets ♕d7+
by ... ♕f7 and since White can
only play ♘d2 when g4 and d2
are covered, I cannot see anything
better for him than perpetual
check.

If this holds up, then White
should play 21 a4, followed by
either 22 ♖xa4 or 22 fg.

B

16 ...   ♘xe3

17 ♖xe3

Not 17 ♕xe3? (17 fe? ♗xg3 18
hg ♗f3) ♖ae8 18 ♕xe8 ♗f3 19
♗xf7+ ♔h8 and Black wins.

17 ...   c5

Black tries to open up the position for his two bishops. 17 ...
♔h8 is good for White after 18

♘d2 f5 19 ♕f1 ♕h5 (or 19 ...
♕h6 20 f4 g5 21 ♖e6 ♖f6 22 fg
♕xg5 23 ♘f3 with a clear plus for
White) 20 ♗d1 f4 21 ♗xg4 ♕xg4
22 ♖e4 (Gutman's suggestion 22
♕e2 ♕h3 23 ♖e6 is also strong)
♕g6 23 ♕h3 fg 24 fg and it is
hard to see what Black has for the
pawn, Tomson–Euole, corr. 1966.

18   ♕f1 (46)
18 ♗d5 ♖ad8 19 ♘d2 ♗c7 20
♗g2 ♕h6 is inferior and in Barczay–Adorjan, Budapest 1970,
Black's active pieces enabled him
to hold the balance.

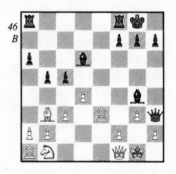

18   ...   ♕xf1 +
Avoiding the exchange also
fails to equalize, e.g: 18 ... ♕h6
(18 ... ♕h5 19 ♘d2 ♖ad8 20
♗d1) 19 ♘d2 ♖ad8 20 ♘f3
♗xf3 (20 ... c4 21 ♗c2 f5 22 ♘e5
♗xe5 23 ♖xe5 f4 24 ♗e4 gave
White a clear extra pawn,
Kuijpers–Bouwmeester, Rotter-

dam 1965) 21 ♖xf3 cd 22 cd ♕d2
23 ♖d3 (Donner considered 23
♖d1 ♕xb2 24 ♖fd3 to be even
better) ♕g5 (23 ... ♕xb2? 24
♖b1) 24 ♖c1, Fischer–Donner,
Santa Monica 1966, and the only
question is whether White can
convert his extra pawn into a win.
Donner drew the game after a
blunder by Fischer, but there is no
doubt that Black's position is very
unpleasant.

19   ♔xf1   ♖ad8
20   ♔g2!
The most accurate. 20 ♘d2 cd
21 cd ♗b4 and 20 a4 cd 21 cd
♗b4 22 ab ab 23 d5 ♗c5 are
satisfactory for Black.
After 20 ♔g2! Black is worse.
Poleshuk–Rapaport, corr. 1974–6
continued 20 ... c4 21 ♗c2 f5 22
♘d2 ♗h5 23 ♗d1 ♗f7 24 ♗f3
with a clear plus for White, so
Harding suggests 20 ... cd 21 cd
♗c7 22 ♖d3 ♗f5 23 ♖d1 ♖fe8
(23 ... ♗b6 24 d5 ♖fe8 25 ♘c3
b4 26 ♘a4 ♗a7 27 ♖c1 is also
good for White). Although this
may offer Black better drawing
chances than Poleshuk–Rapoport, the continuation 24 ♘c3 b4
25 ♘a4 ♖e2?! 26 ♖ac1 followed
by ♗c4 is still very good for
White.
The conclusion is that 16 ...
♘xe3 is bad for Black.

8 . Other Black 15th Moves

1 e4 e5 2 ♘f3 ♘c6 3 ♗b5 a6 4
♗a4 ♘f6 5 0-0 ♗e7 6 ♖e1 b5 7
♗b3 0-0 8 c3 d5 9 ed ♘xd5 10
♘xe5 ♘xe5 11 ♖ ♕xe5 c6 12 d4
♗d6 13 ♖e1 ♕h4 14 g3 ♕h3 15
♗e3 *(47)*

Black has tried a number of
moves apart from 15 ... ♗g4, but
with little success. These alternatives are hardly ever played today.

47
B

A   15 ... ♗f5
B   15 ... ♖e8

Or:

(1) **15 ... ♖a7** is possible, nor-
mally·transposing to line B.

(2) **16 ... ♘f6** 16 ♕f3 (16 ♘d2

♗g4 17 ♕b1 ♖ae8 18 ♕d3 is
probably also good; Black has
'gained' the tempo ... ♘f6, but in
fact the knight is worse placed on
f6 than on d5) ♗b7 17 ♘d2 ♔h8
18 ♗d1 ♖ae8 19 ♕g2 ♕f5 20
♗f3 ♖e6 21 a4 and Black has
inadequate compensation for the
pawn,   Zhukhovitsky–Pitksaar,
USSR 1953.

(3) **15 ... ♗e6** 16 ♘d2 (in view
of the next note 16 ♕f3 is more
accurate) ♖ae8 (16 ... ♗g4! is
better since 17 f3 ♗xg3 18 hg
♕xg3+ 19 ♔f1? ♗h3+ 20 ♔e2
♘xe3 21 ♔xe3 ♖ae8+ wins for
Black after 22 ♘e4 ♖xe4+ 23
♔xe4 ♖e8+ or 22 ♔d3 ♖xe1 23
♕xe1 ♗f5+, so White should
play 17 ♕b1 ♖ae8 and he probably has nothing better than 18
♕d3 transposing to normal lines)
17 ♕f3 f5 18 ♕g2 ♕h5 19 ♗d1
♕f7 20 ♘f3 f4 21 ♗d2 ♕d7 22
♘g5 ♗f5 23 ♗f3 ♗c7 24 g4 ♗g6
25 ♘e4 with a clear plus for
White, Gligoric–Nyman, Stockholm 1954.

(4) **15 ... h5** 16 ♕f3 h4 17
♗xd5 cd 18 ♘d2 ♗e6 (after 18
... hg 19 fg ♗g4 there seems no
reason why White should not take
the pawn on d5) 19 ♗f4 ♗g4 and
now 20 ♕g2 ♕xg2+ 21 ♚xg2
h3+ 22 ♚g1 ♗xf4 23 gf ♖fd8 24
f3 gave White a promising ending
in Fischer–Wade, Havana 1965.
However Black's solid position
makes it hard to turn the advantage into a win and Black drew in
the end, so 20 ♕xd5 deserves attention. After 20 ... ♗xf4 21 gf
♕d3 (21 ... ♖ae8 22 ♕g2 ♕d3
23 f3 is also very bad for Black) 22
♘e4 Black has little to show for
the two pawns.

A

15 ...   ♗f5

Since Black usually ends up
playing ... ♗g4 later, this move
often leads to the loss of a tempo.

16 ♕f3

16 ♗xd5 cd 17 ♕f3 is refuted
by 17 ... ♗e4, winning.

16 ...   ♖ae8

17 ♘d2

17 ♗xd5 cd 18 ♘d2 ♗e4 19
♘xe4 de 20 ♕g2 ♕h5 intending
... f5–f4 gave Black good counterplay in Ekblom–Asaritis, corr.
1966.

17 ...   ♗g4

17 ... ♖e6 18 ♗xd5 cd 19
♕xd5 h5 was played in Hallier–
Schmitzer, corr. 1966, and now 20
♕g2 ♕g4 21 f3 ♕g6 22 ♗f2

leaves Black with insufficient
compensation for the pawns.

18 ♕g2   ♕h5

19 a4(48)

Comparing this position with
the Spassky Variation (Chapter
3), one finds that firstly White's
queen is on g2 instead of f1 and
secondly White has an extra
tempo. The first difference has
little effect, since the queen is not
any better placed on g2 than on
f1, but the spare tempo clearly
tips the balance in White's favour.
Perhaps the most surprising thing
is that White's advantage is not
more clear-cut.

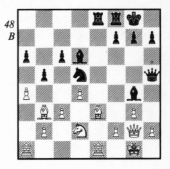

19 ...   ♖e6

Black could try 19 ... ♗h3 20
♗d1 ♕f5 21 ♕f3 ♕e6, intending
... f5–f4, which at least makes use
of the fact that his rook is not yet
blocking e6.

20 ab   ab

21 ♖a6

Harding correctly points out that Gutman's 21 ♗xd5 is not very convincing, e.g. 21 ... cd 22 ♖a5 (this is one case in which White would prefer to have his queen on f1) ♗e2 23 b3 (threat c4) ♗c7 24 ♖a2 ♗d3 and Black has good play for the pawn.

21 ... ♘f4?!

This appears unsound. After 21 ... ♗h3 (21 ... ♗f4? 22 ♗xd5) 22 ♕f3 (22 ♗d1? ♕xd1 23 ♖xd1 ♗xg2 24 ♔xg2 ♖xe3) ♗g4 23 ♕h1 ♗c7 24 ♗xd5 cd 25 ♖ea1 ♕f5 26 ♖a8 ♗b8 27 ♕g2 h5 28 ♖8a5 ♗e2 29 ♖e1 ♗d3 30 ♕f3 Black's position fell apart in Mukhin–Faibisovich, USSR 1970. Black could have improved by 25 ... h6, waiting for White to come up with a plan, but White still has some advantage.

22 gf

and after 22 ... ♗h3 (22 ... ♖g6 23 ♘f1 ♗f3 24 ♘g3 ♗xg2 25 ♘xh5 ♗d5+ 26 ♘g3 ♗xb3 27 ♖xc6 leaves Black two pawns down) 23 ♗d1 ♕h6 24 ♕f3 ♗xf4 25 ♘f1 Black's attack is not worth a piece, for example Harding's suggestion of 25 ... ♖g6+ 26 ♘g3 ♖e8 is refuted by 27 ♗d2! ♖ge6 28 ♖xe6 ♕xe6 29 ♗e3!

B

15 ... ♖e8*(49)*

Black ams to double rooks on e8 and e7. The positive points are

that the knight on d5 will not be pinned against a rook on e6, and that by leaving the bishop on c8 for the moment Black reserves the option of playing it to h3 in one move. The problem is that the whole plan is rather slow and since Black forfeits ... f5–f4 his attacking chances are less than in other lines.

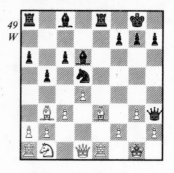

16 ♗xd5

Or 16 ♕f3 (not 16 a4? ♘xe3 and ... ♗xg3, nor 16 ♘d2? ♗g4, while after 16 ♕d3 Black may play 16 ... ♖a7 as below or 16 ... ♘f4!? 17 ♕f1 ♗h5, which is unclear according to Gutman) ♗g4 (or 16 ... ♖a7 17 ♘d2 ♖ae7 and now not 18 ♘f1? ♘f4! 19 ♕h1 ♕g4 20 ♗xf4 ♖xe1 21 ♖xe1 ♖xe1 22 ♗xd6 ♕e2 23 ♕g2 ♗f5 24 f4 ♕e3+ 25 ♕f2 ♗h3 0–1, Astafiev–Petrov, corr. 1968, but 18 ♗xd5 transposing to the main line) 17 ♕g2 ♕h5 18 ♘d2 ♗h3 19 ♗d1 ♕f5 20 ♕f3

♕d3, given as unclear by Geller. Black has a tempo more than in line A, note to Black's 19th move, but on the other hand the wrong rook is on e8.

16 ...   cd

17 ♕f3

The counterattack on d5 is important, so 17 ♕d3 ♖a7 18 ♘d2 ♖ae7 19 a4 f5 20 f4 g5 gives Black unnecessary attacking chances.

17 ...   ♖a7

18 ♘d2   ♖ae7

and now:

(1) 19 ♘f1 (not 19 ♕g2 ♕h5 and if nothing else Black will be two tempi up over line A when he plays ... ♗h3 in one move! Tseshkovsky–Kuzmin, USSR 1975, continued 20 a4 b4 21 c4? dc 22 ♘xc4 ♗b7 with advantage to Black) h5 20 ♗d2 h4 21 ♖xe7 ♖xe7 22 ♘e3 is Gutman's untested *ECO* suggestion. However 19 ... ♖e4! is a big improvement, threatening 20 ... ♗g4 21 ♕g2 ♕h5, and I cannot see any better reply than 20 ♘d2.

(2) 19 a4 ba (19 ... b4 20 c4 dc 21 ♘xc4 ♗b8 22 ♗d2 ♖xe1+ 23 ♖xe1 ♖xe1+ 24 ♗xe1 ♕e6 and now 25 ♘e3 ♗a7 26 ♕d5 ♕b6 led to a draw in Unzicker–Rossolimo, Staunton Mem. 1952, so White should have played 25 ♕e3! with winning chances) 20 ♖xa4 and the two practical examples were both good for White:

(2a) **20 ... ♔h8** 21 ♖ea1 f5 22 ♖a5 g5 23 ♖xd5 g4 24 ♕g2 ♕xg2+ 25 ♔xg2 ♗b7 26 ♖aa5 ♗c7 27 ♔f1 f4 28 gf ♗xd5 29 ♖xd5 ♖f7 30 ♖e5! ♗xe5 31 fe with a clear plus for White, Geller–Jansa, Amsterdam 1974.

(2b) **20 ... h5** 21 ♖a5 ♗b7 22 ♖aa1 h4 23 ♕h5 ♗c8 24 ♘f3 hg (after 24 ... ♗xg3 25 hg ♖xe3 26 ♖xe3 ♖xe3 Boleslavsky gives the murky 27 ♕xf7+, but why not 27 ♘g5 ♖xg3+ 28 fg ♕xg3+ 29 ♔h1?) 25 ♕xh3 ♗xh3 26 hg ♗xg3 27 fg ♖xe3 28 ♖xe3 ♖xe3 29 ♔f2 ♖e6 30 ♖a5 with a promising ending for White, Tseshkovsky–Ivanov, USSR 1976.

Thus 15 ... ♖e8, although superficially attractive, seems to be inadequate against accurate play.

9 Other White 15th Moves

1 e4 e5 2 ♘f3 ♘c6 3 ♗b5 a6 4
♗a4 ♘f6 5 0-0 ♗e7 6 ♖e1 b5 7
♗b3 0-0 8 c3 d5 9 ed ♘xd5 10
♘xe5 ♘xe5 11 ♖xe5 c6 12 d4
♗d6 13 ♖e1 ♕h4 14 g3 ♕h3*(50)*

In this chapter we cover alternatives to 15 ♗e3. Two of these,
15 ♗xd5 and 15 ♖e4, are quite
important. Although a number of
other moves have been tried, they
have little to recommend them.

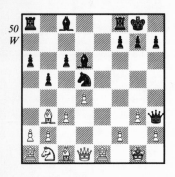

A   15 ♗xd5
B   15 ♖e4

Or: (1) **15 ♕d3** (the result of
this is that White has to play ♕f1

very early, which gives Black
extra options) and now:

(1a) **15 ... ♘f6** (simple and
effective) 16 ♕f1 (16 ♘d2 ♗b7 17
♕f3 ♖ae8 18 ♖e3 ♘g4 19 ♖xe8
♕xh2+ 20 ♔f1 ♕h3+ was a
draw in Vasilchuk–Smirnov,
Moscow 1963) ♕f5 17 ♗e3 (17 c4
may be met by 17 ... bc 18 ♗xc4
c5 or by 17 ... c5!) ♗b7 18 ♘d2
and now both 18 ... c5 19 f3 c4 20
♗d1 h5, Bonch-Osmolovsky–
Liublinsky, USSR 1952, and 18
... ♖ae8 19 c4?! ♗b4 20 c5 ♗c8
21 ♖ad1 ♘g4 are fine for Black.

(1b) **15 ... ♗f5** (after 15 ...
♗g4 White should transpose
back to normal lines with 16 ♗e3)
16 ♕f1 ♕h5 17 ♗e3 (not 17
♗d1? ♕g6 18 ♘d2 ♘f4!, Biv-
shev–Sidorov, USSR 1950) with
another branch:

(1b1) **17 ... ♖ae8** 18 ♘d2 ♖e6
and now White can transpose to
normal lines by 19 a4 ♗h3 (see
the discussion at the end of line B
in Chapter 5). However he has
two other options, namely **19**

♗d1 ♗g4 20 ♗xg4 ♕xg4 21 f3 ♕h5 22 ♗f2 ♖g6, which gives Black fair play for the pawn, or 19 c4!?, when Suetin–Borisenko, Kiev 1954, continued 19 ... ♘xe3 20 ♖xe3 ♖h6 21 ♕g2 c5 22 d5 ♗e5 23 ♖ae1 ♗xb2 24 h4, and White is better according to Harding, although this seems unclear to me. In any case Black's other options are better, so this assessment is irrelevant.

(1b2) 17 ... ♗h3 18 ♗d1 ♕f5 19 ♕e2 ♖ae8 20 ♘d2 (not 20 ♕h5? ♘xe3 21 fe ♖xe3) and we have the same position as in Chapter 5, line B, except that the moves a4 and ... ♖e6 have been omitted. On the basis of the following analysis this change favours Black. The continuation runs 20 ... c5!? (20 ... ♖e7 21 ♕h5 ♕d7 22 ♗f3 ♗f5 23 ♗xd5 cd 24 f3 ♖fe8 25 ♗f2 ♖e2 26 ♘b3 g6 27 ♕g5 ♖xb2 28 ♘c5 ♕d8 29 ♕xd8 ♖xd8 30 ♘xa6 h5 ½-½, Zagorovsky–Klass, corr. 1959/60, was also adequate) 21 ♘f3 (not 21 ♕f3 cd 22 ♕xf5 ♗xf5 23 cd ♗b4!, but 21 a3 cd 22 cd ♗f4 23 ♕f3 ♗xe3 24 fe ♕xf3 25 ♗xf3 ♘xe3 ½-½, Boleslavsky–Bronstein, match 1950, may be White's best) ♗f4! (not 21 ... ♘f4 22 ♕c2 ♘d3 23 ♘h4! with advantage to White, Boleslavsky–Saigin, Sverdlovsk 1951) 22 ♘h4 (22 ♕d2 ♘xe3 23 fe ♗h6 24 ♘e5

f6 25 ♗c2 ♕g5 26 ♘f3 ♕xe3+ is a wishful variation from Bronstein) ♕f6 (22 ... ♕g5 is also possible) 23 ♕f3 cd 24 cd ♘xe3 25 ♕xf4 (25 fe? ♗xe3+ 26 ♖xe3 ♖xe3) ♕xf4 26 gf ♘f5! with the better endgame for Black.

(2) 15 a4 ♗g4 16 ♕d3 ♖ae8 17 ♗e3 ♘f4! 18 ♕f1 ♕h5 19 ♗d1 (19 ♗xf4? ♗h3) ♘h3+ 20 ♔g2 ♘xf2 21 ♕xf2 ♗xd1 22 ab ab 23 ♘d2 ♗g4 with advantage to Black, S. Garcia–Plachetka, Polanica Zdroj 1975.

(3) 15 ♕f3 ♗g4 16 ♕g2 (this line is very doubtful, since White just sets himself up for ... ♗f3) ♕h5 17 ♗e3 (17 ♗xd5 cd 18 f4 may be relatively best, but this is no recommendation for 15 ♕f3) ♗f3 18 ♕f1 f5 19 ♘d2 f4 20 ♘xf3 fe 21 ♗d1 (not 21 fe? ♖xf3 22 ♕e2 ♗xg3! and White collapses, Berner–Pfleger, Hitzacker 1961) ♖ae8! (21 ... ♖xf3 22 ♗xf3 ♕xf3 23 fe is unclear) and Black has a very dangerous attack, e.g. 22 ♘e5 (22 fe ♘xe3 23 ♕e2 ♘xd1 24 ♕xd1 ♕xf3 wins) ♕h6 23 f4 ♗xe5 24 de g5 with a clear advantage for Black.

(4) 15 ♗c2 ♗g4 16 ♕d3 ♖ae8 17 ♗e3 f5 18 ♕f1 ♕h5 19 c4 f4 20 cd fg 21 hg ♗f3 0–1, Kuppe–Rautenberg, Weidenau 1947.

A

15	♗xd5	cd
16	♕f3	

This is the usual follow-up to the capture on d5. After other moves the most likely result is a transposition to Chapter 4 or the note to White's 18th in Chapter 6, e.g: 16 ♗e3 ♗g4 (16 ... ♖e8 is Chapter 8, line B) 17 ♕d3 f5 (for 17 ... ♖ae8 18 ♘d2 see Chapters 4 and 6) 18 ♕f1 (18 f4 will transpose to Chapter 6 after 18 ... ♖ae8 or Chapter 7 after 18 ... g5 19 ♕f1 ♕h5) f4 (the only independent line as 18 ... ♕h5 19 f4 leads to earlier chapters) 19 ♕xh3 ♗xh3 and Black has reasonable play for the pawn after 20 ♗d2 ♖ae8 or 20 ♗xf4 ♗xf4 21 gf ♖xf4 22 ♖e3 ♖g4+ 23 ♖g3 ♖e8.

16 ...   ♗f5! *(51)*

Marshall's move and undoubtedly the best, since after 16 ... ♗g4 17 ♕xd5 ♖ae8 18 ♖xe8 ♖xe8 19 ♗e3 White makes off with his extra pawns.

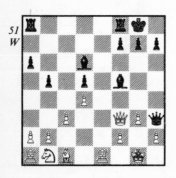

51
W

17   ♕xd5

The only dangerous move. Alternatives:

(1) **17 ♕g2** and now:

(1a) **17 ... ♕h5** 18 ♕xd5 (18 f3 ♗h3 19 ♕f2 f5 is fine for Black) ♖ad8 19 ♕c6 (19 ♕g2 ♗h3 is dangerous for White as 20 ♕h1 ♗g4 21 ♘d2 ♖ae8 gives Black an enormous attack) ♗e6 20 ♕e4 and now theory gives 20 ... ♗d5 21 ♕e2 ♗f3 22 ♕f1 f5 23 ♘d2 ♗d5 24 f3 ♖de8 25 ♖e2 ♖xe2 26 ♕xe2 ♖e8 27 ♕f2 ♖e6 with sufficient compensation for the two pawns. However Black has a number of promising alternatives, for example 20 ... ♖de8 (threat ... ♗d7) 21 ♕e2 ♕d5 22 ♗e3 (22 ♕f1 ♗h3) ♗h3 23 f3 f5 with very strong threats.

(1b) **17 ... ♕g4** (this is less convincing) 18 f3 ♕g6 19 ♗e3 ♖ac8 (19 ... ♖ae8 20 ♘d2 ♗d3 21 ♘b3 ♖e7 ½-½ was Grigic–Ledic, Vinkovci 1982; although this may not have been a serious game 19 ... ♖ae8 is probably better than 19 ... ♖ac8) 20 a3! (20 ♘d2 b4 is worse; with White's kingside weakened the minority attack is dangerous because White cannot afford to remove defenders from the other side of the board; Buslayev–Demuria, USSR 1957, continued 21 ♖ac1 bc 22 ♖xc3 ♖xc3 23 bc ♗c8 24 ♗f4 h6 25 ♗xd6 ♕xd6 26 ♖e5 ♗d3 27 ♘b3 ♖xc3 and with the fall of the c-pawn Black gained the advantage) a5 21 ♘d2 b4 22 ab ab 23 ♖a6 (thanks to 20 a3 White's active rook gives him the advantage) bc 24 bc ♖fe8 25 f4 ♖e6 26 ♕xd5 h5 27 ♖a8 ♖xa8 28 ♕xa8+ ♔h7 29 ♘f3 ♗e7 30 ♘e5 ♕f6 31 ♕f3 g6 32 d5 1–0, van der Drift–Helslott, corr. 1983.

(2) 17 ♘d2 ♖ae8 18 ♖e3 ♖e6 19 ♕xd5 ♗d3 20 ♖xe6 fe 21 ♕xd6 (21 ♕g2 ♕h5 22 f3 e5 is unclear) ♖xf2 22 ♔xf2 ♕xh2+ 23 ♔f3 ♕e2+ 24 ♔f4 h6 25 ♕d8+ ♔h7 26 ♕e7 ♔h8 with a draw by repetition.

17 ...   ♖ae8
18 ♗d2*(52)*

Not 18 ♖e3? ♕h5 19 f3 (19 ♕xd6 ♗h3 wins) ♕g6 20 ♖xe8 ♖xe8 21 ♘d2 ♗xg3 22 ♘e4 ♗xh2+ 0–1, Foltys–Thelen, Prague 1943.

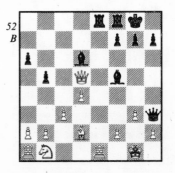

52
B

18 ...   ♗f4!
I believe this is best, although

other moves have been more popular in practice:

(1) 18 ... ♗d3 19 ♘a3 ♗xa3 20 ba ♗c4 21 ♕f3 ♕d7 22 ♖xe8 ♖xe8 23 ♖e1 h6 24 ♖xe8+ ♕xe8 25 h3 ♗xa2 26 ♔h2 ♕e6 27 ♕e3 ♕c6 gave White an edge in Chandler–Nikolic, Leningrad 1987, but White never came close to turning it into a win.

(2) 18 ... ♖e6 (Marshall's original recommendation) 19 ♖xe6?! (dubious; 19 ♘a3 is the critical move, but this has never been tested in practice) fe 20 ♕g2 ♕h5 with sufficient compensation for the two pawns. Dabrowski–van der Weijer, corr. 1986/8, continued 21 h4? (a clear error, but a decent line for White is hard to find) ♕d1+ 22 ♕f1 ♕f3 23 ♕g2 ♕d1+ 24 ♕f1 ♕g4 25 ♗e1 ♗e4 26 ♘d2 ♗xg3 27 ♘xe4 ♗xf2+ 28 ♔h1 (28 ♔h2 ♕xh4+ 29 ♕h3 ♕xe4) ♕xe4+ 29 ♕g2 ♕xh4+ 30 ♕h2 ♗xe1 0–1.

(3) 18 ... ♕g4 19 ♘a3! (not 19 ♕xd6 ♖xe1+ 20 ♗xe1 ♕d1 21 ♕e7 ♗e6 22 ♘a3 ♕xa1 23 ♔f1 ♗h3+ 24 ♔e2 ♕xb2+ 0–1, Szekely–Adorjan, Hungarian Ch. 1968/9) ♗xa3 20 f3 and Black has an inferior version of Chandler–Nikolic above.

19 ♖xe8
Other lines cause Black no trouble:
(1) 19 ♕g2 ♖xe1+ 20 ♗xe1

♗c1! 21 ♕xh3 (21 a4 ♖e8 22
♗d2 ba 23 ♖xa4 ♗xd2 24 ♘xd2
♖e1+ 25 ♘f1 ♕xg2+ 26 ♔xg2
♗e4+ 27 f3 ♗d3 is also winning)
♗xh3 22 ♘d2 ♗xb2 23 ♖b1
♗xc3 24 ♘b3 ♖c8 25 f3 ♗f5 0–1,
Sakhalkar–Barczay, corr. 1959/
60.

(2) **19 gf** ♖xe1+ 20 ♗xe1
♕g4+ 21 ♔h1 ♗e6! 22 ♕e4
♕d1! is good for Black

(3) **19 ♕c6** ♖xe1+ 20 ♗xe1
♕h5 21 f3 ♗c1 (or 21 ... ♕g5 22
♘a3 ♗c1) is also not recommended.

19 ... ♖xe8
20 ♕c6

20 ♕g2 ♕h5 21 gf loses to 21
... ♗h3.

20 ... ♗d7

20 ... ♔f8 has been suggested
but not played; White has a draw
by 21 ♕c5+, but can he do
better?

21 ♕g2 ♕h5
22 f3 *(53)*

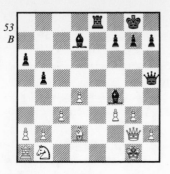

This position is assessed as
clearly better for White in *ECO*,
but according to my analysis
Black has good chances.

22 ... ♗c6!
23 gf

Or 23 ♗xf4 (23 ♔f2 ♗xf3! 24
♕xf3 ♕xh2+ 25 ♔f1 ♗xd2 and
23 g4 ♕h4 are very bad) ♗xf3
and Black wins after 24 g4 ♖e1+
25 ♔f2 ♖e2+ 26 ♔xf3 ♕d5+
27 ♔xe2 ♕xg2+ and 28 ...

♕xb2 or 24 ♕f1 ♖e2 25 h3
♖g2+ 26 ♕xg2 ♗xg2 27 ♔xg2
♕e2+.

23 ... ♖e6!

24 ♔f2 (24 f5 ♕xf5 doesn't
help) ♖g6 25 ♕h1 ♕h4+ with a
tremendous attack, e.g. 26 ♔f1
♖g3, 26 ♔e3 ♖e6+ 27 ♔d3 ♕f2
or 26 ♔e2 ♕h3 (perhaps even 26
... ♖g3!?).

B 15 ♖e4

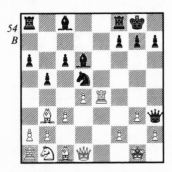

This move aims to interfere
with Black's attack by preventing
both ... ♗f5 and ... ♗g4. It

might seem that White threatens to start a kingside attack himself by ♖h4 and ♗c2, but this is normally not dangerous. However the possibility of ♖h4 is so inconvenient that Black almost always replies 15 ... g5, intending to regain the time lost by playing ... ♗f5 next move. White typically offers the exchange at e4 in return for a pawn and kingside attacking chances. This idea has been played quite frequently over the past few years and it represents one of White's best deviations from the main line.

15 ... g5

Or: (1) **15 ... ♗b7** is a suggestion by Korchnoi, lining up on the rook and the exposed g2 square. *ECO* continues 16 ♗xd5 cd 17 ♖e1 ♖ae8 18 ♗e3 ♗c8, but now White is worse off than in the normal main lines of the Marshall, since although both sides have lost two tempi Black has jumped his queen's rook over his bishop. Perhaps 16 ♗c2!? is the real test.

(2) **15 ... ♗d7** (15 ... ♘f6 16 ♖h4 ♕f5 17 ♗f4 is bad for Black) 16 c4 (16 ♗c2 h6 17 ♘d2 ♖ae8 18 ♕f1 ♘f6 19 ♕xh3 ♗xh3 20 ♖xe8 ♖xe8 21 ♘f3 is just slightly better for White, Tal–Stein, USSR 1967) bc 17 ♗xc4 ♖ae8 18 ♘d2 ♘f6 19 ♖h4 ♕f5 20 ♘f3 with advantage for White,

Sakharov–Peterson, USSR 1969.

(3) **15 ... ♕d7** 16 ♘d2 ♘f6 17 ♖h4 ♗b7 18 ♘f3 c5 (18 ... ♖ae8? 19 ♗g5 ♘e4 20 ♗c2 f5 21 ♗b3+ ♖f7 22 ♗f4 1–0, Tal–Krogius, USSR Ch. 1971) and now 19 ♗f4 or 19 ♗g5 gives White some advantage.

Now there are two main lines, of which the second is better:

B1 16 ♕f1
B2 16 ♕f3!

16 ♘d2? (16 ♗xg5?? ♕f5) f5 17 ♖e2 (17 ♖e3 f4! 18 gf ♕h6 is very dangerous for White) f4 18 ♕f1 ♕h5 gives Black a very strong attack.

B1

16 ♕f1 ♕h5 (55)

Or: (1) **16 ... ♕xf1+** 17 ♔xf1 f5 18 ♖e1 f4 19 ♔g2 ♖a7 is often recommended but is not completely clear, for example after 20 ♘d2 ♗f5 21 ♘f1 (not 21 ♘e4? f3+ 22 ♔f1 ♖e7 23 ♗c2 ♖fe8 with advantage for Black, Camilleri–Philippe, Skopje Ol. 1972) Black clearly has a strong initiative, but in the absence of queens it is not clear whether it is worth a pawn. My own feeling is that Black is not worse, but because the main line is promising for Black there has been no incentive for Black to explore this possibility.

(2) **16 ... ♕h6** 17 f3 ♔h8 18

♘d2 ♗h3 19 ♕e1 ♘f4 20 ♘f1 (not 20 gf gf 21 ♔h1 ♖g8 22 ♖e2 ♕g7 23 ♕f2 ♗e7 followed by 24 ... ♗h4 and Black wins) ♕g7 21 ♕f2 (threat 22 gf gf+ 23 ♔h1 ♖g8 24 ♗xf4) ♘d3 22 ♕d2 ♘xc1 23 ♖xc1 f5 24 ♖e6 ♖ad8, Krum Georgiev–Tseshkovsky, Moscow 1985, and now 25 ♕f2!, preventing ... c5, would have been good for White.

17   f3

Other moves are no better:

(1) **17 ♗d2?!** ♗f5 (17 ... f5 18 ♖e1 f4 is also good) 18 ♖e1 ♗h3 19 ♕e2 ♗g4 20 ♕f1 ♖ae8 21 ♘a3 ♗h3! (21 ... ♗e2 22 ♗d1) 22 ♕d3 ♘f4! 23 ♗xf4 (23 gf gf 24 ♔h1 f3 wins for Black) gf 24 ♘c2 ♗g4 25 ♖xe8 ♖xe8 26 ♖e1 ♗e2 27 ♕d2 ♕f3 (27 ... f3 also wins) 28 d5 c5 29 ♘a3 fg 30 ♕g5+ (30 hg ♔h8 and 31 ... ♗xg3) ♔h8 31 hg ♖g8 32 ♕h4 ♗xg3 0–1, Smolensky–Heffner, corr. 1985.

(2) **17 ♕e2** ♕g6 18 ♖e8 ♗f5

(18 ... ♗h3 19 ♖xa8 ♖xa8 20 ♗e3 f5 21 ♕f3 ♖e8 22 ♘a3 f4 was also good for Black in Dornieden–Hecht, Berlin 1961) 19 ♖xa8 ♖xa8 20 ♘d2?! (20 ♗xd5 cd 21 a4 was better, but even then the only question is how big Black's advantage is) ♗d3 21 ♕e1 ♘f4!? 22 gf gf+ 23 ♔h1 ♔h8 24 ♕g1 ♕f6 25 f3 ♖e8 26 a4? (26 ♗d1 was the last chance) ♕h4 and Black won in Ernst–Hebden, Gausdal 1987.

17 ...   ♗f5

Better than 17 ... ♗h3 18 ♕f2 and now **18 ... f5** 19 ♖e6 f4 20 ♖xd6! fg 21 hg ♖xf3 22 ♖xd5! wins, so Cardoso–Quinones, Skopje Ol. 1972, continued **18 ... ♘f6** 19 ♖e1 ♖fe8 20 ♗e3 ♖e7 21 ♘d2 ♖ae8 22 ♗c2 h6 23 ♘e4 ♖e6 24 ♗d2 with a small plus for White.

After 17 ... ♗f5 Black will continue with ... ♖ae8, with sufficient compensation for the pawn. In Rodriguez–Krilov, corr. 1959/60, White defended badly and lost quickly: 18 ♗xd5 cd 19 ♖e1 ♖ae8 20 ♗e3 ♗h3 21 ♕f2 f5 22 ♘a3? f4! 0–1, in view of 23 gf gf 24 ♗d2 ♔h8 25 ♔h1 ♖xe1+ 26 ♖xe1 ♖g8 27 ♖g1 ♖xg1+ 28 ♔xg1 ♕g6+ 29 ♔h1 ♕d3! and wins by ... ♗e7–h4.

B2

16   ♕f3   ♗f5*(56)*

Not 16 ... f5? 17 ♖e5! ♗xe5 18

de ♗e6 19 ♘xg5 with two solid pawns for the exchange.

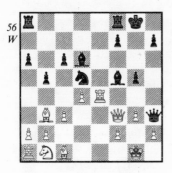

56
W

17   ♗c2

There is a major alternative in 17 ♗xd5 (17 ♘d2?! ♖ae8 18 ♗c2 ♘f6 19 ♖e5 ♗xc2 and 17 ♖e1? ♖ae8 18 ♗d2 ♖xe1+ 19 ♗xe1 ♘f4 are very good for Black) cd 18 ♖e3 ♗e4 19 ♖xe4 de 20 ♕f6 ♕g4 (if the main line turns out well for White, then perhaps Black should try 20 ... ♗f4 21 ♗xf4 gf 22 ♕xf4 f5 23 ♘d2 ♔g7 24 ♘f1 ♕h6 ½-½, Stean–Radulovic, Schilde 1970) 21 ♕xg5+ ♕xg5 22 ♗xg5 (this ending has always been thought satisfactory for Black, but recent postal games have put this assessment in doubt) f5 (22 ... ♔g7 23 ♘d2 ♖ae8 24 a4 h6 25 ♗e3 f5 26 ab ab 27 ♖a5 ♖b8 28 ♖a6 ♖f6 29 b3 ♔g6 30 c4 with advantage to White, Trautmann–Dittmar, corr. 1981, is similar to van der Weijer–Jackson below) 23 ♘d2 ♖ae8 (in view of White's next move this looks

wrong; the immediate 23 ... ♔g7 is better) 24 a4! (not 24 ♖e1 ♔f7 25 ♔f1 ♔g6, Blackstock–Radoicic, Hastings II 1970/1, and Black may even be slightly better) and now both 24 ... ♖a8 25 f3 ef 26 ♔f2 ♔g7 27 ♘xf3 f4 28 g4 h6 29 ♗h4 ♖ac8 30 ab ab 31 ♖a6 ♗c7 32 ♗e7 ♖f7 33 ♗c5 ♖f6 34 ♖a7 ♔f7 35 ♖b7 ♔e6 36 ♖xb5, Trautmann–Nicklich, corr. 1981, and 24 ... ♔g7 25 ab ab 26 ♖a6 ♖e6 27 b3 ♖g6 28 ♗h4 ♖e8 29 ♖b6 ♖b8 30 ♖xb8 ♗xb8 31 ♔f1 ♗a7 32 ♗e7 ♖c6 33 ♗b4 ♔f6 34 ♔e2, van der Weijer–Jackson, corr. 1986/8, were good for White.

This line deserves closer attention from over-the-board players, since Black is hardly able to avoid it.

17   ...   ♗xe4

Black's best move is far from clear. Here are the other possibilities:

(1) **17 ... ♗f4!?** (Harding analysed this as Black's best, but strangely enough it has only appeared very rarely in practice) 18 ♘d2 (18 ♘a3 g4 19 ♕e2 ♗xe4 20 ♗xe4 ♗xc1 21 ♖xc1 ♖ae8 gives Black a clear plus, and 18 ♗xf4 gf 19 ♘d2 fg 20 fg ♗xe4 21 ♘xe4 f5 22 ♘g5 ♕g4 23 ♕xg4 fg 24 ♘xh7 ♖fe8 25 ♖f1 ♖a7 26 ♘g5 ♔g7 is slightly better for Black) ♘f6! and now:

(1a) **19 gf** ♕xf3 20 ♘xf3 ♗xe4 21 ♗xe4 ♘xe4 22 fg f6 23 gf ♖xf6 24 ♔g2 ♖a7 intending ... ♖g7+, and Black wins.

(1b) **19 ♖xf4** gf 20 ♗xf5 ♕xf5 21 ♘b3 ♘d5 22 ♗xf4 ♘xf4 23 gf ♖ae8 24 ♔h1 ♖e4 25 ♖g1+ ♔h8 26 ♖g4 ♖g8 with advantage to Black.

(1c) **19 ♖e3** ♗xc2 20 gf ♕xf3 21 ♘xf3 ♘d5 and 19 ♖e7 ♗xc2 20 gf ♕xf3 21 ♘xf3 ♘d5! 22 ♖d7 gf 23 ♘e5 ♗f5! are fine for Black.

(1d) **19 ♖e5** ♗g4 20 ♕xc6 ♗xe5 21 de ♘d7 22 ♘f3 ♖ac8 23 ♕e4 ♕h5 24 ♗d1 ♖fe8 and Black's strong initiative is worth more than White's theoretical material advantage.

(1e) **19 ♖e1!** ♗xc2 (19 ... ♖ae8 20 ♖f1 ♘g4! 21 ♕g2 ♕xg2+ 22 ♔xg2 ♗xc2 23 gf gf 24 ♘f3 ♖e6 25 ♗xf4 ♖g6 gives Black good compensation for the pawn, but 20 ♘e4! ♘xe4 21 ♗xf4 ♗g4 22 ♕g2 gives White the advantage) 20 gf g4, Wang Zili–Ye Jiangchuan, China Ch. 1988, is assessed as equal by *Informator*, but I suspect that White is slightly better.

(2) **17 ... ♖ae8?!** 18 ♗xg5 ♗xe4 19 ♗xe4 ♖e6 20 ♘d2 f5 (or 20 ... ♖fe8 21 ♖f1 intending ♗f5) 21 ♗xd5 cd 22 ♕xd5 f4 23 ♖e1 ♖e8 24 ♗f6! (threat ♕g5+) ♔f8 25 ♗e5 ♗xe5 26 de ♖h6 27 ♘f3 ♖e7 28 ♕d8+ ♖e8 29 ♕d4

fg 30 fg ♖h5 31 ♖e4 ♖f5 32 ♖h4 1–0, Shamkovich–Iskov, Reykjavik 1982.

(3) **17 ... ♘f4?!** 18 ♗xf4! gf (18 ... ♗xe4 19 ♗xe4 gf 20 ♗xc6 and 18 ... ♗xf4 19 ♘a3 ♗xe4 20 ♗xe4 are also dismal for Black) 19 ♘d2 ♖ad8 20 ♖ae1 fg 21 fg ♗xe4 22 ♘xe4 f5 23 ♘g5 ♕g4 24 ♕xg4 fg 25 ♗b3+ ♔h8 26 ♘f7+ and the extra pawn gives White excellent winning chances (Harding).

18 ♗xe4 ♕e6! *(57)*

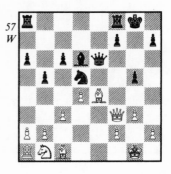

57
W

19 ♗xg5

19 ♗f5 ♕e1+ 20 ♔g2 ♕xc1 21 ♘a3 ♕xa1 22 ♕h5 ♖fe8 23 ♕h6 ♖a7! 24 ♗xh7+ drawing is an oft-repeated line (*ECO* and Harding), but Black emerges a rook up after 21 ... ♕xb2! (21 ... ♕d2 22 ♖d1 is slightly less clear-cut) 22 ♗xh7+ (22 ♕h5 ♘e3+) ♔g7!

19 ... f5

20 ♗d3 h6!

More accurate than 20 ... f4 (20 ... ♕e1+ 21 ♔g2 f4 22 ♕e4! is also a little better for White) 21 ♕e4 ♕h3 (the lines 21 ... ♕f7 22 ♘d2 ♖ae8 23 ♕f3 and 21 ... ♕xe4 22 ♗xe4 ♖ae8 23 ♘d2 ♖e6 24 ♔g2 ♔g7 25 g4 h6 26 ♗h4 ♖fe8 27 ♔f3, Staniszewski–Blatny, Naleczow 1985, both give an edge to White) 22 ♗h4 ♖a7 23 ♘d2 ♖g7 24 ♗f1! ♕d7 (24 ... ♕xh4?! 25 ♕e6+ and ♕xd6 is again slightly better for White) 25 ♖e1 ♗e7 26 ♗xe7 ♖xe7 27 ♕b1 fg 28 hg ♖fe8?! (28 ... ♖ef7 offered fair chances of equality) 29 ♖xe7 ♖xe7 30 ♘f3 and again White can claim some advantage, Krum Georgiev–Lukacs, Baile Herculane 1982.

After 20 ... h6! both **21 ♗d2** ♖a7, with the idea of ... ♖g7 and ... f4, and **21 ♗h4** ♖a7 22 ♘d2 ♖g7 (threat ♘f4–g6) 23 ♔f1 f4 give Black a completely satisfactory position.

There are many unanswered questions in this section, for example is 17 ♗xd5 good for White, and what is the correct verdict on Harding's 17 ♗c2 ♗f4? If other variations fail to give White the advantage, I expect 15 ♖e4 to become more popular, since many of the endgames arising from this move are safe for White, while offering some winning chances.

10 The 13 ♖e2 Line

1 e4 e5 2 ♘f3 ♘c6 3 ♗b5 a6 4
♗a4 ♘f6 5 0–0 ♗e7 6 ♖e1 b5 7
♗b3 0–0 8 c3 d5 9 ed ♘xd5 10
♘xe5 ♘xe5 11 ♖xe5 c6 12 d4
♗d6 13 ♖e2 *(58)*

Just a few years ago 13 ♖e2
rated barely a note in opening
books; now it has become one of
White's main lines against the
Marshall. Theory is still being ac-
tively developed and while many
lines remain in a state of flux,
enough is known to give tentative
opinions on the main variations.
As so often with new ideas, 13
♖e2 scored well to begin with,
but then Black started to fight
back. At the present time it is
impossible to say whether 13 ♖e2
is better or worse than 13 ♖e1.
Both moves have merits, and both
have drawbacks. The idea behind
♖e2 is to keep the path d1–f1
open so that White can expel
Black's queen from h3 by playing
♕f1 directly, rather than going
via d3. The problem is that the
rook is tactically exposed on e2.

58
B

There are four main lines to
consider:

A 13 ... ♗g4
B 13 ... ♗c7
C 13 ... ♕h4 14 g3 ♕h5
D 13 ... ♕h4 14 g3 ♕h3

Line A more or less forces
White to take on d5 in a couple of
moves, when the question is
whether the two bishops and lead
in development compensate for
White's extra pawn. In practice
Black has done quite well, but the
theoretical position is less clear.
Line B is a recent and unexplored
idea. It is too early to say how

good it is. 13 ... ♕h4 is the main
line, but Black has a choice after
the forced reply 14 g3. The initial
preference was for 14 ... ♕h5,
since moving to h3 seemed to be
falling in with White's plan to
play ♕f1. Recent games seem to
show that 14 ... ♕h5 just fails to
equalize, and therefore the current trend is to play 14 ... ♕h3.
At the moment this line can only
be assessed as unclear.

A

13	...	♗g4
14	f3	♗h5

Or 14 ... ♗f5 and now:

(1) **15 g3!?** (an interesting idea,
trying to exploit the choice of ...
♗f5 instead of ... ♗h5) ♕c7 16
♔f2 h5 17 ♘d2 ♘f6?! 18 ♘f1
♗h3 19 ♗g5 ♘d5 20 ♕d3 ♕d7
21 ♖ae1 ♗xf1 22 ♖xf1 ♕h3 23
♔g1 h4 24 ♗xd5 hg 25 hg cd 26
♖h2 ♕xg3+ 27 ♖g2 and White
won in Mokry–Panczyk, Breiten-
brunn 1984.

(2) **15 ♗xd5** (just as after 14 ...
♗h5, 15 ♘d2 ♘f4 is fine for
Black) cd 16 ♘d2 ♗d3? (a poor
move which wastes time; Nikolic
suggests 16 ... b4 while I prefer 16
... ♕c7 as in the main line; Black
should be slightly better off here
because his bishop is more effective on f5 than h5, but note that
line 2 below cannot be played
with the bishop on f5) 17 ♖f2
♕c7 18 g3 ♖ae8 19 ♘f1 ♗g6 20

♘e3 ♕d7 (Black is in a mess
because ♕b3 will win his d-pawn)
21 ♘xd5 ♗xg3 22 ♘f6+ gf 23 hg
with an extra pawn and a positional advantage for White, Kir.
Georgiev–P. Nikolic, Wijk aan
Zee 1988.

15 ♗xd5

After 15 ♘d2 ♘f4 16 ♖f2 ♘d3
the result should be a draw as 17
♖f1? ♕h4 is bad.

15	...	cd
16	♘d2(59)	

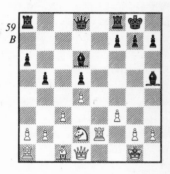

and now:

(1) **16 ...** ♕h4 17 ♘f1 ♖ae8 18
♗e3 is slightly better for White.

(2) **16 ... f5** (note that this line,
which may be Black's best, is impossible after 14 ... ♗f5) 17 ♘f1
f4 (attempting to seal in White's
minor pieces) 18 a4 ♗e8 19 b3
♖c8 20 ab (20 ♗b2 is better, but
Black seems to have enough for
the pawn) ♗xb5 21 ♖c2 ♕b6 22
♗b2 ♖fe8 23 ♖f2 ♗e7!, Perenyi–

Blatny, Hajduszoszlo 1987, and the coming ... ♗h4 gives Black good compensation.

(3) **16 ... b4** 17 cb ♕b8 18 ♘f1 ♕xb4 19 ♗d2 ♕xd4+ 20 ♗e3 ♕c4 21 b3 ♕b5 with a slight advantage for White, Kosten–Hebden, Gausdal 1987.

(4) **16 ... ♕c7** 17 ♘f1 ♖fe8 18 ♗e3 (18 ♗g5 is critical, intending ♗h4–g3) ♕c4 19 a4 ♗g6 20 ♖d2 ♖ac8 21 ab ab 22 ♖c1 (22 ♕e2 ♕xe2 23 ♖xe2 ♗d3 24 ♖ee1 ♗xf1 is a likely draw, although White is slightly better, so Black should prefer 22 ... ♕b3) ♖e6, van der Sterren–Pein, Brussels 1984, and by now Black has good play for the pawn.

Playing for positional compensation by 13 ... ♗g4 is a solid option for Black, although it is not clear whether he gets full value for the pawn.

B

      13 ...   ♗c7
      14 ♘d2

Or 14 ♗c2 (14 ♗xd5 ♕xd5 15 ♘d2 is an untested idea) ♕d6 (both 14 ... ♕h4 15 g3 ♕h5 16 ♘d2 ♗h3 and 14 ... ♗g4 15 f3 ♗h5 16 ♘d2 are unclear) 15 g3 ♗g4 16 f3 ♗h5 (16... ♗xf3?? 17 ♕d3) 17 ♘d2 f5 18 a4 ♖ab8 19 ab ab 20 ♕e1 ♕d7 21 ♕f2 ♗d6 22 ♘f1 ♗f7 23 ♗d2 b4 24 c4 b3 25 ♗d3 ♘b4 26 ♗xb4 ♖xb4 27 ♘d2 ♖d8 28 f4 ♗h5 29 ♖e3 ♗f8

30 ♗e2 ♕xd4 31 ♗xh5 ½–½, Watson–Motwani, British Ch. 1988.

      14 ...   ♘f4
      15 ♖e3 *(60)*

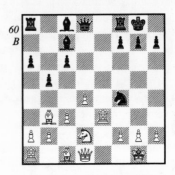

60
B

      15 ...   c5

The alternative is 15 ... ♕g5 16 ♕f1 (16 ♖g3 ♕e7 17 ♖e3 ♕g5 is a draw, but 16 g3!? may be possible) ♕h5! (16 ... ♘h3+?! 17 ♔h1 ♕f4 18 ♘f3 ♗g4 19 ♖e7! ♕d6 20 ♖xf7 ♖xf7 21 ♗xf7+ ♔xf7 22 ♘e5+ ♔g8 23 ♘xg4 h5 24 ♘e5 wins for White) 17 h3 ♗g4 with obscure complications. Since the main line appears good for White, this is the critical variation.

      16 ♘e4!

Not 16 ♘f3 ♗b7 17 dc ♕f6 and Black's attack is worth more than two pawns. Oll–Tseshkovsky, Sverdlovsk 1987, continued 18 ♕d7 ♖ac8 19 ♕e7 (after 19 ♕g4 h6 the slow plan of ... ♖cd8 and ... ♗c8 is surprisingly hard to meet) ♕c6 20 ♗c2

(20 ♗d2 h6! 21 ♕h4 g5 wins) f5
21 ♗b3+ ♚h8 22 ♖e6 (22 ♗f7
♖fd8 23 ♗d2 ♘xg2 24 ♚xg2 f4
wins) ♘xe6 23 ♕xe6 ♕xe6 24
♗xe6 ♖ce8 25 ♗d7 ♖d8 0–1.

After 16 ♘e4! White has the
advantage, e.g. 16 ... cd (or 16 ...
♗b7 17 dc ♕h4 18 g3 ♘h3+ 19
♚f1 and Black cannot follow up
his attack) 17 ♕xd4 ♕h4 18 ♘g3!
(18 g3 ♕g4 is unclear) ♗e6 (18
... ♗b7? 19 ♕xg7+ wins),
Klovans–Sulman, USSR 1988,
and now 19 ♗xe6 fe (19 ... ♖ad8
20 ♗d7 wins) 20 ♖e1 ♖ad8 21
♕e4, given by Klovans, consoli-
dates the extra pawn.

C

	13	...	♕h4
	14	g3	♕h5
	15	♘d2*(61)*	

Better than the old line 15 ♖e4
♕g6 16 ♗c2 and now:

(1) **16 ...** **♗f5** 17 ♖e2 ♖ae8
(Pinkus–Altman, US Ch. 1944) 18
♗e3! (not 18 ♗xf5 ♕xf5 19 ♗e3
♕g6! followed by ... f5–f4, with a
strong attack) ♗xc2 19 ♕xc2
♕xc2 20 ♖xc2 ♘xe3 21 fe ♖xe3
with equality.

(2) **16 ... f5** 17 ♖e2 ♕h5! (both
sides have lost two tempi, but in
addition White has spent a move
on the useless ♗c2) 18 ♘d2 f4 19
♗e4 (19 ♘e4 fg 20 hg ♗g4) fg 20
hg ♖xf2! 21 ♗xd5+ cd 22 ♖e8+
♕xe8 23 ♚xf2 ♕g6 24 ♕f3 ♗b7
25 ♚g2 ♖f8 26 ♕e3 ♗f4 27 ♕f2

♗xd2 28 ♕xd2 ♕e4+ 0–1,
Elmes–Romanenko, corr. 1960/1.

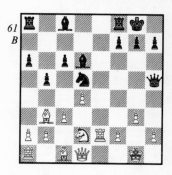

61
B

	15	...	♗h3

Or 15 ... ♗g4 (15 ... ♗f5 16
♖e1! ♕g6 17 ♘f3 ♗g4 18 ♘h4
♕h5 19 f3 ♗h3 and now 20 ♘g2
♖ae8 21 ♖e4 g5 22 ♗d2 ♖e6 23
♕e2 ♖h6 24 ♘e3 was complex
but good for White in Sax–Pinter,
Hungary Ch. 1981, and according
to Matanovic 20 ♕d3 ♖ae8 21
♗d2 ♖e6 22 ♘g2 was a safer
route to the advantage) 16 f3
♗xf3 17 ♘xf3 ♕xf3 and now:

(1) **18 ♕f1** ♕h5 (or 18 ... ♕g4
19 ♗d2 ♖fe8, Balashov–Tseshkovsky, USSR Ch. 1980/1, with
the same type of position) 19 ♗d2
f5 20 ♖e6 ♖ad8 21 ♗xd5 cd 22
♗f4 ♗xf4 23 ♕xf4 a5 24 ♖ae1
with just an edge for White, Sznapik–Duric, Ljubljana 1981.

(2) **18 ♖f2** (better, because it
virtually forces the exchange of
queens, when White has a small
long-term advantage based on his

two bishops and queenside pawn majority) ♕e4 (18 ... ♕xd1+ leads to a similar ending) 19 ♕f3! (19 ♗c2 ♕e6 20 ♕d3 g6 followed by ... f5 sets up a barier to White's bishop) ♖ae8 20 ♗d2 ♘f6 21 ♖e1 ♕xf3 22 ♖xf3 ♖xe1+ 23 ♗xe1 ♖e8 24 ♔f1 ♖e7 25 h3 h5 26 c4 ♗c7 27 a4 ♘e4 28 cb cb 29 ab ab 30 ♗d5 ♘d6 31 ♗b4 with a slight advantage for White, Sax–Nikolic, Plovdiv 1983.

Few players enjoy defending an ending with a permanent slight disadvantage, where there is no hope of winning or even of real counterplay, so 15 ... ♗g4 has disappeared even though objectively Black may be able to draw.

16 f3(62)

Other moves are inferior:

(1) **16 ♖e4 ♕g6** (16 ... ♕xd1+ 17 ♗xd1 f5 18 ♖e2 ♖f6 looks inadequate, although after 19 ♘f3 ♗g4 20 ♖e1 f4 21 ♘e5 ♗xd1 22 ♖xd1 ♖e8 23 ♘xc6 fg 24 hg ♖e2 25 ♖f1 ♗xg3 26 fg ♖xc6 Black's active pieces enabled him to draw in Korchnoi–van Oosterom, Netherlands 1982/3) 17 ♕e1? (17 ♖e1 intending ♘f3 is the critical test) f5 18 ♖e2 f4 19 ♘e4 ♕h5 20 f3 fg 21 ♘xd6 ♖f3 22 ♘e4 gh+ 23 ♔xh2 ♗f1+ 0–1, Mokry–Franzen, CSSR Ch. 1984.

(2) **16 ♖e1?!** (this is very dubious) ♖ae8! 17 f3 f5 (Geller suggests 17 ... ♕g6 18 ♘f1 ♗xf1 19 ♔xf1 ♗xg3 20 hg ♕xg3, which is probably a draw) 18 c4 ♘e3 19 c5+ ♔h8 20 ♖xe3 ♖xe3 21 cd f4! 22 ♘e4 (22 ♔f2 ♗g4 23 gf ♖fe8 wins for Black) ♖xf3 23 ♗xf4! (the best chance; 23 d7 fg 24 d8(♕) gh+ 25 ♔h1 ♗g2+ 26 ♔xg2 h1(♕)+ 27 ♕xh1 ♕g4+ mates next move) ♖8xf4 24 d7 (24 ♘d2 ♕e8 25 ♘xf3 ♕e3+ 26 ♔h1 ♕f2 27 ♘h4 ♖xh4 wins for Black) ♗xd7 25 ♘d2 ♗h3! 26 ♘xf3 ♖xf3 27 ♕d2 ♖f8! 28 ♕e3 ♕f5 29 ♕e2 c5 30 ♗c2 (or 30 dc ♕xc5+ 31 ♔h1 ♗d7 winning), Psakhis–Geller, Sochi 1982, and now Geller gives 30 ... ♕f6 31 dc ♕d4+ 32 ♔h1 ♗g4 as a win for Black.

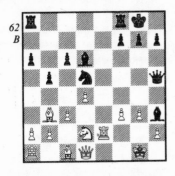

62
B

16 ... ♗c7

The idea is to take the sting out of a possible ♘e4, but White can play it anyway. Other moves:

(1) **16 ... ♖ae8** 17 ♖xe8 ♖xe8

18 ♘e4 ♕g6!? (18 ... ♗c7 19 ♗d2 ♕g6 20 ♗c2 ♗f5 21 ♕f1 h5 22 ♕g2 ♖e6 23 a4! ♘f6 24 ab cb 25 ♖e1 was clearly better for White, S. Garcia–Pinter, Lucerne 1982) 19 ♗xd5 (19 ♗c2 is a better test of Geller's idea) cd 20 ♘xd6 ♕xd6 gave Black reasonable play for the pawn in Mithrakanth–Geller, Delhi 1987.

(2) **16 ... f5** 17 c4! (simple and strong; 17 a4 has also been recommended, but I can find no practical examples) bc 18 ♘xc4 ♗c7 19 ♘e5 and White is better, A. Rodriguez–Malaniuk, Erevan 1984.

(3) **16 ... ♖ad8** 17 ♘e4 (the same move as below, but Aseev suggests the more ambitious plan of 17 ♕e1!? intending ♕f2, ♘e4 and ♗d2, developing while holding on to the pawn) ♕xf3 18 ♘g5 ♕h5 19 ♘xh3 ♕xh3 20 ♕f1 ♕g4 21 ♗d2 with the usual very slight advantage for White, Aseev–Taborov, USSR 1986.

17 ♘e4*(63)*

This simple move gives White an edge, but there is a second possible line in 17 a4 (Kuporosov suggests 17 ♕e1 f5 18 ♕f2) b4 18 c4 ♘f6 and now:

(1) **19 ♖e1** (19 ♕e1 ♖ae8! is also dangerous, e.g. 20 ♘e4? ♕xf3! or 20 ♕f2 ♖xe2 21 ♕xe2 ♖e8 22 ♕f2 ♕f5, and White's position is full of holes) ♖ad8 20 ♘e4 ♘xe4 21 ♖xe4 ♗f5 22 ♖e1

♕h3! (22 ... ♗b6 23 ♗e3 ♗xd4 24 ♗xd4 c5 is unclear after 25 ♖e5!? ♖xd4 26 ♕e2 or 25 ♗xc5 ♖xd1 26 ♗xd1 ♖d8 27 ♗xb4) 23 ♖e2 ♖fe8 24 ♗g5! f6 26 ♗e3, Kuporosov–Malaniuk, USSR 1985, and now 25 ... ♗xg3 26 hg ♖xe3 27 ♖xe3 ♕xg3+ 28 ♔f1 ♕h3+ is a draw.

(2) **19 ♘e4** and now:

(2a) **19 ... ♘xe4** 20 ♖xe4 ♗f5 (20 ... ♕g6 21 ♗f4! f5 22 ♖e6 wins for White) 21 ♖e7! ♗d6 22 ♖e3 with advantage to White.

(2b) **19 ... ♕xf3** (best) 20 ♘g5 ♕h5 21 ♘xh3 ♕xh3 22 ♗g5 ♘g4 (22 ... ♕f5 23 ♗h4 is very good for White after 23 ... g5 24 ♖f2 ♕g6 25 ♗c2 ♕h6 26 ♕d3 or 23 ... ♖ad8 24 ♗c2 ♕h5 25 ♗xf6 gf 26 ♖e4) 23 ♕f1 ♕h5 with reasonable counterplay, e.g. 24 ♗f4 ♗xf4 25 ♕xf4 ♖ae8 26 ♖ae1 c5! is fine for Black or 24 ♗e7 ♖fe8 25 ♕g2 ♘e5!?.

(2c) **19 ... ♕g6** 20 ♘f2! ♗f5 (20 ... ♗xg3 21 ♘xh3 wins) 21 ♗c2 ♖fe8 (21 ... ♗xg3 22 hg ♕xg3+ 23 ♔f1 ♗h3+ 24 ♘xh3 ♕xh3+ 25 ♔g1 wins, but 21 ... ♖ad8 22 ♗xf5 ♕xf5 23 ♖d2, intending ♖d3 and ♔g2, while still good for White, would have been a better chance) 22 ♗xf5 ♕xf5 23 ♖xe8+ ♖xe8 24 ♔g2 and White is a pawn up for nothing, Short–Nunn, Brussels 1986.

Whether 17 ♘e4 or 17 a4 is better depends on the assessment of line 2b above.

63
B

17 ...   ♖ae8?!

Continuing to play for the attack, but in my view this is a mistake. After 17 ... ♕xf3 (17 ... f5 18 ♘f2) 18 ♘g5 ♕h5 (18 ... ♕g4 19 ♕e1! is good for White) 19 ♘xh3 ♕xh3 20 ♗d2 White has his usual edge, but Black should be able to defend. Ehlvest–Nikolic, Zagreb 1987 continued 20 ... ♖ae8 21 ♕f1 ♕d7 22 ♖ae1 ♖xe2 23 ♕xe2 a5? (Ehlvest suggests 23 ... ♗d8!, intending ... ♗f6 and ... g6) 24 ♕e4 ♗d8 25 ♗c2 g6 26 ♗h6 ♘f6 27 ♕f3 ♖e8 28 ♖xe8+ ♕xe8 29 ♕e3 ♕xe3 (White's king is slightly more exposed, so Black should have kept the queens on) 30 ♗xe3 and now White has a clear advantage.

18 ♕d3

Not 18 ♘f2?? ♕xf3 winning.

18 ...   f5

A better chance than 18 ... ♖e6 (Belyavsky suggests 18 ... ♗c8 intending ... f5–f4) 19 ♗d2 (19 ♘f2 ♖g6 20 ♘xh3 ♕xh3 21 ♖g2 h5 is less clear) ♖g6 (19 ... ♖fe8 20 ♖ae1 ♕f5 21 ♗d1 followed by ♘f2 disentangles) 20 g4! ♗xg4?! (20 ... f5? 21 ♘g3 ♕h4 22 ♘xf5 wins, while 20 ... ♕h4 21 ♗e1 ♕d8 22 ♗xd5 ♕xd5 23 ♗g3! ♗xg3 24 ♘xg3 gives Black little, if anything, for the pawn) 21 fg ♖xg4+ 22 ♘g3 f5 23 ♖g2 ♕h3 24 ♖f1! ♖f6 25 ♖f3 h5 26 ♕e2 ♖fg6 27 ♗c2 1–0, Belyavsky–Malaniuk, USSR Ch. 1987.

19 ♘g5

Not 19 ♘f2 ♖xe2 20 ♕xe2 ♖e8 21 ♕d1 ♕xf3 and Black wins.

19 ...   f4

Geller gives 19 ... ♖xe2 20 ♕xe2 ♖e8 21 ♕f2 f4 as unclear, but I cannot see compensation for two pawns after 22 ♗xf4 ♗xf4 23 gf.

20 ♘xh3 fg

Geller optimistically assesses 20 ... ♕xh3 21 g4 h5 as unclear, but after 21 ♗xf4! ♗xf4 22 gf Black has very little for the pawn, e.g. 22 ... ♖xe2 23 ♖xe2 ♖xf4 24 ♖f1 ♖f6 25 ♕e8+ ♖f8 26 ♕e4.

After 20 ... fg the attack is unsound, e.g. 21 ♖xe8! (21 ♔g2? gh 22 ♗c2 ♕g6+ wins for Black)

♖xe8 (or 21 ... gh+ 22 ♔h1
♖xe8 23 ♗f4 and White wins) 22
♔g2 gh 23 ♗d2 ♔h8, Ehlvest–
Geller, Vrsac 1987, and now 24
♗xd5 cd 25 ♘g5 would have
repulsed the attack. The game
actually concluded 24 ♘g5? ♗f4!
(turning the tables) 25 ♘e4 ♖e6
26 ♔h1 ♗xd2?? (losing, just when
Black could have won by 26 ...
♘e3! 27 ♗d1 ♖g6 28 ♗xe3 ♕h3
29 ♕e2 ♗xe3) 27 ♗xd5 cd 28
♘xd2 ♕g5 29 f4 ♕h4 30 ♕f5
♖e8 31 ♖f1 h6 1–0.

If Black adopts this line he
should regain his pawn after
White's ♘e4, when he is slightly
worse, but should be able to hold
on. The current unpopularity of
this line is probably due to the
fact that this strategy is inconsistent with the original choice of the
Marshall Attack.

D

| 13 | ... | ♕h4 |
| 14 | g3 | ♕h3 |

This is currently thought to be
the best reply to 13 ♖e2.

| 15 | ♘d2 |

Or 15 ♕f1 (15 ♖e4 transposes
to Chapter 9) ♕h5 16 f3 (16 ♘d2?
♘f4 is unpleasant) ♗h3 (Sax and
Hazai assess the interesting line 16
... ♗f5!? 17 ♕f2 ♕g6 18 ♗xd5
cd 19 ♘d2 ♗d3 20 ♖e3 f5! 21 f4!
♗e4 22 ♖e1 ♖ae8 23 ♘xe4 fe 24
♗e3 h5 as unclear) 17 ♕f2 f5 (17
... ♖ae8 18 ♖e4!) and now:

(1) **18 ♘d2** ♖ae8 19 ♖xe8
♖xe8 20 c4 (in view of the reply
the solid 20 ♘f1 is preferable)
♘f4!? (20 ... bc 21 ♘xc4 is good
for White) 21 c5+!? (if 21 gf then
not 21 ... ♗xf4? 22 ♘f1 ♗xc1 23
cb+ ♔f8 24 ♖xc1 ♕g5+ 25
♕g3 ♕xc1 26 ♕xh3 and White
wins, but 21 ... ♕g6+! 22 ♕g3
♖e1+ 23 ♔f2 ♕e8 24 ♘e4
♖f1+ 25 ♔e2 fe 26 cb+ ♔f8 27
♕xh3 ef+ 28 ♔d2 ♕e2+ 29
♔c3 with an unclear position;
White can play 26 c5+ in this
line, which leads to a draw as in
the next bracket) ♔f8 22 cd?
(White could have forced a draw
by 22 gf! ♕g6+ 23 ♕g3 ♖e1+
24 ♔f2 ♕e8 25 ♘e4 ♖f1+ 26
♔e2 fe 27 ♕xh3! ef+ 28 ♔d3
♕e2+ 29 ♔c3 ♕e1+ 30 ♗d2
b4+ 31 ♔c4 ♕e2+ 32 ♔xb4
♕xd2+ 33 ♔a3 ♗xc5+ 34 dc
♕a5+ 35 ♗a4 ♕xc5+ 36 b4
♕c3+ 37 ♗b3 ♖xa1 38 ♕c8+
♔e7 39 ♕c7+) ♖e2 23 d7 ♔e7
24 ♗c2 ♖xf2 26 ♔xf2 ♘e6 26
♘b3 ♗g4 and wins, Kapengut–
Malaniuk, USSR 1985.

(2) **18 c4** and now the oft-
quoted game Gracs–Pogats,
Budapest 1951 continued 18 ...
♘b4 19 ♘d2 ♔h8 20 ♘f1 ♖ae8
21 ♖xe8 ♖xe8 22 ♗e3 ♘d3 23
♕e2 f4 24 g4 (24 gf ♗xf4! 25
♕xd3 ♕xf3) ♕g6 25 c5 ♗xf1! 26
♕xf1 fe 27 ♗d1 ♗c7 28 ♗e2 ♘f4
29 ♖c1 ♕f6 0–1. Unfortunately I

cannot see why **19 c5+** ♔h8 20 cd
doesn't simply win a piece, e.g. 20
... ♘d3 21 ♕e3 f4 22 ♕xd3 fg 23
♘d2. Therefore Black should try
18...f4!?, when 19 g4 (19 cd fg 20
hg ♖xf3) ♗xg4 20 fg (20 cd
♗xf3) ♕xg4+ 21 ♔g2 ♕h5 is
unclear. Even so, 15 ♕f1 is an
interesting idea which makes
good sense and deserves further
tests.

15 ... ♗f5(64)

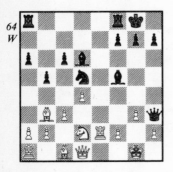

Now White has a wide choice:

D1 16 ♘e4?!
D2 16 ♕f1
D3 16 ♗xd5
D4 16 ♗c2
D5 16 a4

The final choice is 16 f3, but the
single example 16 ... ♗d3 17
♗xd5 (17 ♖f2 gives Black at least
a draw by 17 ... ♗xg3 18 hg ♘e3
19 ♕e1 ♕xg3+ 20 ♔h1 ♕h4+)
♗xe2 18 ♗xf7+ ♖xf7 19 ♕xe2
♖af8 20 b3 h5 21 ♗b2 h4 22 ♕g2

♕e6 23 gh ♗f4 0–1, Smirin–
Naumkin, Vilnius 1988, was not a
good advertisement.

Of the above lines, D1 is bad
for White, while D2 has hardly
been investigated. D3 is playable
but not very promising, while D4
has been tried a number of times
and appears satisfactory for
Black. Finally D5, although relatively untested, may be the best of
the five choices.

D1

16 ♘e4?!

This move is a tactical mistake;
Black wins the exchange for
inadequate compensation.

16 ... ♗g4

and now:

(1) **17 ♕f1** ♕xf1+ 18 ♔xf1
♖ae8 (18 ... ♗xe2+?! 19 ♔xe2
♖ae8 20 ♔d3 gives White fair
compensation) 19 ♘xd6 (19 ♖e1
♗h3+ 20 ♔g1 f5 wins for Black)
♗xe2+ 20 ♔g2 ♖e6 and Black
has good chances to convert his
material plus into a win.

(2) **17 ♘xd6** ♕h5! (this is the
tactical justification for 15 ...
♗f5) 18 ♔f1 (18 f3 ♗xf3 19 ♔f2
♖ad8 20 c4 ♖xd6 21 cd cd 22
♗f4 ♖e6 23 ♗e5 f6 wins for
Black, Sznapik–Panczyk, Polish
Ch. 1987) ♕xh2 19 ♔e1 ♕h1+
20 ♔d2 ♕h6+ 21 ♔c2 ♕xd6 22
♕d3 ♗xe2 23 ♕xe2 c5 and Black
wins, Zuckerman–Pavlovic, New
York 1987.

(3) **17 ♘g5** (relatively the best)
♗xe2 18 ♕xe2 ♕d7 19 ♕d3 f5
(19 ... ♘f6 20 ♗c2 g6 21 ♕f3 is
unclear) 20 ♗d2! (not 20
♗xd5+? cd 21 ♗f4 ♗xf4 22 gf,
Geller–Lukacs, Coimbatore 1987,
and now 22 ... ♕d6! 23 ♕g3 ♖f6
24 ♔h1 ♖e8 is very good for
Black) ♖ae8 (20 ... h6 21 ♘f3 f4
22 ♗c2! and 20 ... ♔h8 21 a4 h6
22 ♘f3 f4 23 ab ab 24 ♖xa8
♖xa8 25 ♗c2 are unclear according to Lukacs) 21 a4 ♔h8 and
Black has only a slight advantage.

D2

16   ♕f1

A reasonable alternative, even
though the move ... ♗f5 gains
point because White must spend a
tempo dealing with the threat of
... ♗d3.

16   ...   ♕h5
17   ♗d1

Better than 17 ♗xd5 (17 ♘e4?
fails to 17 ... ♗h3 and 18 ...
♕f3) cd 18 ♕e1 ♗g4 19 ♖e3 f5
20 f4 (20 f3 ♗h3 21 f4 g5 is no
better) g5 21 ♘f1 ♖ae8 (21 ... gf
22 ♖e6 ♖ae8 23 ♗xf4 is unclear)
22 ♖e5 ♗h3 23 ♗e3 ♗xe5 24 de
♕f3 25 ♕f2 ♕xf2+ 26 ♔xf2
♗xf1 27 ♔xf1 gf 28 gf ♔f7 with
some advantage for Black, Tisch-
bierek–Blatny, Leipzig 1988.

17   ...   ♕g6

17 ... ♗d3 and 17 ... ♗h3 are
both well met by 18 ♖e4.

18   ♕g2   ♖ae8(65)

65
W

with the possibilities:

(1) **19 ♘f1** ♗e4 20 f3 ♗d3 21
♖xe8 ♖xe8 22 ♗d2 ♗xf1 23
♕xf1 ♗xg3 24 hg ♕xg3+ 25
♕g2 ♖e1+ 26 ♗xe1 ♕xe1+
with a draw by perpetual check
(Sax and Hazai).

(2) **19 ♘f3** ♖xe2 20 ♗xe2 ♖e8
and now Blatny gives the following lines:

(2a) Not **21 ♘h4?** ♖xe2! 22
♘xg6 ♖e1+, nor 21 ♕f1 ♗g4 22
h3 ♗xf3 23 ♗xf3 ♗xg3 24 fg
♕xg3+ and Black wins in both
cases.

(2b) **21 ♗d1** ♗g4 22 ♕f1 (22 h3
♕d3 and 22 ♗d2 ♕h5 intending
... ♖e6–f6 are satisfactory for
Black) ♕h5 23 ♕d3 ♗f5 24 ♕d2
(after 24 ♕f1 ♗h3 both 25 ♕d3
♕xf3! and 25 ♘g5 ♗xf1 26 ♗xh5
♖e1 27 ♘f3 ♖d1 28 h4 g6 win for
Black) ♗f4! 25 gf ♕g4+ 26 ♔f1
♘xf4 and White is mated.

(2c) **21 ♗f1** ♗g4 22 h3 ♗xf3 23
♕xf3 ♖e1 24 ♔g2 ♗f4! 25 ♗d3

f5 26 ♗xf4 ♖xa1 27 ♗e5 ♘e7
with advantage to Black.

(2d) **21 ♗e3!** ♕e6! (21 ... ♘xe3
22 fe ♖xe3 23 ♕f2 intending ♘h4
could be unpleasant) 22 ♘h4
♘xe3 23 fe ♕xe3+ 24 ♕f2
♕xf2+ 25 ♔xf2 ♗e4 with a
roughly level position.

D3

16 ♗xd5 cd

Although White faces no immediate danger in this line, the
active bishops and White's weakened kingside virtually guarantee
Black enough positional compensation. In comparison with line A
above Black has forced the weakening move g3 and his pieces are
better placed.

17 f3 *(66)*

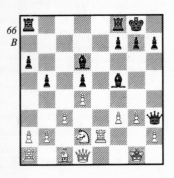

17 ... ♖ae8

Simple development is natural,
but other moves are possible:

(1) **17 ... ♗d3?!** (loses time) 18
♖f2 (18 ♖e3 ♗xg3 is a draw)
♖ae8 19 ♘f1 ♗g6 20 ♘e3 ♖e6

21 ♕f1 ♕h5 22 ♗d2 (22 ♘g2!
intending ♗f4 is even better)
♖fe8 23 ♖e1 with some advantage for White, Kuporosov–
Deiko, Minsk 1983;

(2) **17 ... ♕h5!?** 18 ♖f2 ♖ae8
19 ♘f1 ♖e6 20 a4 (if White ever
plays g4, Black replies ... ♕g6)
♖fe8 21 ♗f4 (a panicky move)
♗xf4 22 gf ba 23 ♘g3 ♕h3 24
♕xa4 ♗d3 25 ♕d1 ♗b5 26 ♖g2
h5 27 f5 ♖e3 28 ♕d2 h4 29 ♘h5
♖e2 30 ♕g5 ♖e1+ 31 ♖xe1
♖xe1+ 32 ♔f2 ♖f1+ 33 ♔e3
♕xf3+ 0–1, Nijboer–Peelen,
Amstelveen 1984. Rather feeble
play by White, but a good illustra-
tion of how Black's pressure can
gradually increase.

18 ♘f1 h5!

and now:

(1) **19 ♗e3?!** h4 (19 ... ♖e6 20
♕d2 h4 21 g4 ♗h7 22 ♖f2 f5 is
good for Black, while 20 ♗f2
♖g6 21 ♕d2 h4 22 ♖ae1 ♗d7
followed by ... f5 is unclear) 20
♗f2 ♗d7! 21 gh?! (21 ♖xe8 ♖xe8
22 ♕d3 ♖e6 23 ♖e1 hg 24 ♗xg3
♗xg3 25 ♖xe6 ♗xh2+ 26 ♘xh2
♕g3+ 27 ♔h1 ♗xe6 is slightly
better for Black) ♖xe2 22 ♕xe2
♖e8 23 ♕d3 ♖e6 gave Black
more than enough for the pawns
in Grunfeld–Pinter, Zagreb 1987.
Black won after 24 ♗g3 ♖g6 25
♔f2 b4 26 a4 ba 27 b3 ♗e7 28 c4
dc 29 bc ♖b6 30 ♖a2 ♕f5 31
♕xf5 ♗xf5 32 c5 ♖b2+ 33

♖xb2 ab 34 ♘d2 a5 35 c6 ♗b4
0–1.

(2) **19 ♘e3** (19 ♗g5? h4! 20
♗xh4 f6 wins for Black) h4! (19
... ♗g6?! is bad after 20 ♘g2!
followed by ♗f4) 20 g4 (20 ♘xf5
♕xf5 21 ♖xe8 ♖xe8 22 ♔g2 hg
23 hg ♕g6 is unclear) ♗g6 21
♖f2 f5! 22 gf (22 ♕f1 fg 23 ♕xh3
gh 24 ♗d2 ♗g3! 25 hg hg 26 ♖f1
♗d3! is also murky) ♗xf5 23
♘xf5 ♖xf5 24 ♗d2 (after 24 ♕f1
♖xf3! 25 ♕xh3 ♖xh3 Black has a
slight endgame advantage) ♖xf3
25 ♕xf3 ♗xh2+ 26 ♔h1 ♗g3+
is a draw

D4

16 ♗c2(67)

White exchanges the dangerous
bishop, but this clears the way for
Black's f-pawn.

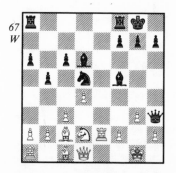

67
W

16 ... ♗xc2

Or 16 ... ♖ae8 17 ♗xf5 ♕xf5
18 ♖xe8 (18 ♕e1?! ♘f6 19 ♘f1
h5 20 ♘e3 ♕f3 with good compensation for Black, Sabena–

Svensson, corr. 1960) ♖xe8 19
♘f1 (Ciric suggests 19 ♘f3) ♘f6
(even though Black's attack appears very slow, White is way
behind in development) 20 ♗e3
h5 21 ♕e2 h4 22 f3 (22 ♖e1 may
be better, but what is White's
plan?) hg 23 hg g6 24 ♖e1 ♔g7 25
g4?! (25 ♕g2 is unclear) ♕d7 26
♕d2 ♖h8 27 ♗f4 ♘d5 28 ♗xd6
♕xd6 29 ♖e4 ♕f6 30 ♕f2 ♘f4
31 ♕g3 g5 32 ♖e3 ♕g6 33 ♕e1
♕h7 34 ♕g3 ♕c2 35 ♖e4 ♖h3
0–1, Sklarczyk–Muller, corr.
1985. In this game Black's compensation appeared nebulous, yet
White went under without doing
anything seriously wrong.

18 ♕xc2 f5

White's queen and rook are
badly placed to deal with the
threat of ... f4–f3, so quick action
is needed.

18 c4

18 f4 ♕g4 19 ♘f1 ♗xf4 20 ♖f2
♗d6 (after the simple 20 ... ♗xc1
21 ♖xc1 f4 Black has a completely satisfactory position) 21 c4
bc 22 ♕xc4 f4 23 ♕xc6 ♕e6 24
♗xf4 led to a very unclear position in Sokolov–Khalifman,
Sochi 1982.

18 ... ♕g4

The sacrifice 18 ... ♘f4 19 gf
♕g4+ 20 ♔f1 ♖ae8 is refuted by
21 ♕d3, but Ciric suggests 18 ...
♘f6, intending ... f4 followed by
... ♘g4.

19 ♖e6?! *(68)*

After this move Black is at least equal. The main alternative is 19 ♖e1 (19 ♘f1 ♘b4? 20 ♕d2 bc 21 ♘e3! is good for White, but 19 ... bc 20 ♕xc4 f4 21 ♕xc6 fg is fine for Black) f4 20 f3 ♕h3 21 cd fg 22 ♘f1 gh+ 23 ♔h1 ♖f6 with a horribly unclear position. Mokry–Panczyk, Polancia Zdroj 1984, continued 24 f4 ♖h6 25 ♕f2 ♖f8 26 ♖e6 ♖xe6 27 de ♕xe6 28 ♗d2 ♗xf4 29 ♗xf4 ♕e4+ 30 ♔g2 ♕xf4 31 ♘xh2 ♕xd4 and with three pawns for the piece Black is not worse. The game actually ended in a draw.

68
B

19 ...   ♘f4

This probably leads to a draw by perpetual check. Therefore 19 ... f4! is slightly better, since it forces White to play accurately to make the half-point. After 19 ... f4! 20 ♕e4 (not 20 cd fg 21 hg ♗xg3 22 f3 ♕xd4+ 23 ♔h1 ♕h4+ mating, nor 20 ♖xd6 fg

21 hg ♖xf2 22 ♔xf2 ♖f8+ and Black wins) ♘e3! (threat ... ♕d1+) and now:

(1) **21 fe** ♕d1+ 22 ♔g2 (22 ♘f1 fg) fg! (Black need not be satisfied with a draw by 22 ... ♕e2+) 23 hg (23 ♖xd6 ♖f2+ 24 ♔h3 ♖xh2+ 25 ♔xg3 ♕g1+ leads to mate) ♕e2+ 24 ♔h3 ♖f2 and White faces a very dangerous attack.

(2) **21 ♘f1** ♘xf1 22 ♔xf1 ♕h3+ 23 ♔g1 (23 ♔e1 ♕xh2 24 ♖xd6 fg 25 fg ♖f2 wins) fg 24 hg ♗xg3 and Black wins.

(3) **21 ♘f3!** (the only way to defend) fg (21 ... ♘xc4? 22 b3) 22 ♕xg4 (not 22 hg ♕xe4 23 ♖xe4 ♘c2 nor 22 ♗xe3 gf+ 23 ♔xf2 ♖xf3+ 24 ♕xf3 ♕xe6 with a winning position for Black in both cases) gf+ 23 ♔xf2 ♘xg4+ 24 ♔g2 ♖f6 and Black has a very slight advantage but of course the result should be a draw.

20 ♖xd6?

This move loses. The right line was 20 f3 ♘h3+ 21 ♔g2 ♘f4+ 22 ♔g1 ½–½, Hübner–Timman, Tilburg 1987, but the crucial question is whether White can play for a win by 22 ♔h1 ♕h3 23 gf ♗xf4 (23 ... ♖ae8? 24 ♖e5! wins) 24 ♖e2 ♖ae8 25 ♕d1 (25 ♕d3 ♗xh2) and now:

(1) **25 ...** ♖e7 (25 ... ♖e6 26 d5! is no better, while 25 ... ♖e3 26 ♖f2! is good for White after 26

... Rfe8 27 Ne4! or 26 ... Bg3 27 Qf1) and now:

(1a) **26 Qf1!** Qxf1+ 27 Nxf1 Rxe2 28 Bxf4 Rxb2 (28 ... bc 29 Rc1 is somewhat better for White) and White may have an edge, but a draw is much the most likely result.

(1b) **26 Rg2** Qh4! (not 26 ... Rfe8 because of the tactical point 27 Ne4! Bxc1 28 Nf6+ and wins) with a promising position for Black.

(1c) **26 Rf2** Rfe8 27 Nf1 Bg3! (27 ... Re1? 28 Bxf4 wins) 28 Nxg3 Re1+ 29 Rf1 Qxf1+! (29 ... R8e2 30 Qxe2 Rxe2 31 Nxe2 Qxf1+ 32 Ng1 bc 33 b3 is unclear) 30 Nxf1 Rxd1 and Black wins.

(2) **25 ... Qh5!** (this attempts to reach the same type of position as in 1b above, but without allowing White to liquidate to an ending as in 1a) 26 Rf2! (the threat was 26 ... Rxe2 27 Qxe2 Re8 28 Qf2 Re1+, and 26 Rg2 Qh4! is similar to 1b) Qh4 (26 ... Bg3 27 Qg1) 27 Qf1 (27 Qg1 Be3) Rf6 with a very dangerous attack since 28 Nb3 is met by 28 ... Bg3.

We now follow Ljubojevic–Nunn, Szirak 1987.

20 ... Rae8 (69)
21 cb

Or 21 Nf3 (21 Nf1 Nh3+ 22 Kg2 Re2 wins after 23 Qd3 Rxf2+ 24 Kh1 Rxf1+ 25 Qxf1

69
W

Qe4+ 26 Kg2 Qe1+ or 23 Ne3 Rxc2 24 Nxg4 fg 25 Be3 Nxf2 26 Kg1 Nh3+ 27 Kh1 Re8) Re2 22 Qb3 Nh3+ 23 Kh1 Rxf2 24 cb+ Kh8 25 Bf4 (25 Bh6 Rxf3 26 Qf7 Rf1+ mates) Rxf3 26 Qf7 Rg8 27 Re1 Rxf4 and White's only possible defence 28 Qxg8+ fails because Black's king can hide from the rook checks on h5. The move 21 cb looks suicidal, but although Black can easily force a draw by 21 ... Nh3+ 22 Kg2 Nf4+ or 21 ... Qh3 22 Qc4+ Kh8 23 gf Qg4+, it is not so easy to win, e.g. 21 ... Re1+ 22 Nf1 Qh3 23 Qc4+ Kh8 24 Bxf4 and the attack rebounds.

21 ... Re2!
22 Qc4+

22 Qxc6 Re1+ 23 Nf1 Rxf1+ 24 Kxf1 Qd1 mate and 22 Qb3+ Kh8 23 Nf3 Qxf3 lose more quickly.

22 ... Kh8
23 Qxe2

The only way to stop 23 ...
♘h3+ 24 ♔f1 (or 24 ♔g2
♖xf2+ 25 ♔h1 ♕d1+) ♖fe8
followed by mate since 23 d5 costs
the queen after 23 ... ♖e1+ followed by a knight check.

23	...	♘xe2+
24	♔g2	

24 ♔f1 ♖e8 followed by ...
♕h3+ wins easily.

24	...	f4!
25	bc	

25 f3 and 25 h3 are both met by
the queen sacrifice 25 ... fg! 26 fg
(26 ♖d8 ♘f4+) ♖f2+ leading to
mate next move.

25	...	fg
26	hg	♘f4+ 0–1

D5

16 a4*(70)*

Sax's important innovation;
Black is not threatening anything,
so White activates the a1 rook
while waiting to see Black's intention. Experience is very limited,
but this appears to be White's best
move.

Black may reply:

(1) **16 ...** ♘f4 17 gf ♖ae8 fails
to 18 ♖e5!, while 16 ... b4 17
♘e4 ♗g4 18 ♘xd6 ♕h5 is met by
19 ♗c4.

70
B

(2) **16 ... ♖ae8** 17 ♖xe8 (17
ab? ♘f4!) ♖xe8 18 ♘f1! h5 (since
g3 is well defended White may
answer 18 ... ♗g4 or 18 ... ♗e4
by 19 f3, and 18 ... b4 19 c4 ♘f6
20 f3 is also good for White) 19
♗xd5 cd 20 ab ab 21 ♘e3 with
advantage to White, Sax–Nunn,
Brussels 1988.

(3) **16 ... ♗d3!** 17 ♖e1 ♖ae8
18 ♘f3 ♖xe1+ 19 ♕xe1 h6 is
suggested by Sax and Hazai. After
20 ab ab 21 ♖a7 ♘f6 a curious
position arises in which neither
player has any obviously con-
structive moves. Black is tied
down to the defence of f7, while
White must cover f1 and prepare
to meet ... ♗e4 or ... ♘g4.
Therefore the position must be
judged unclear, although if White
can break the deadlock his extra
pawn might be important.

11 Kevitz Variation: 12 ♗xd5 and 14 ♖e3

1 e4 e5 2 ♘f3 ♘c6 3 ♗b5 a6 4
♗a4 ♘f6 5 0-0 ♗e7 6 ♖e1 b5 7
♗b3 0-0 8 c3 d5 9 ed ♘xd5 10
♘xe5 ♘xe5 11 ♖xe5 c6 12 ♗xd5
cd

The idea of the early exchange
of d5 is to enable the rook to
retreat to e3 instead of e1, supporting the endangered kingside.
However the rook may become
exposed to an ... f5–f4 attack,
and as always with an early
exchange on d5, there is the
danger of Black's two bishops
providing good positional compensation. This line has recently
shown signs of a revival and I
expect a number of further games.

13 d4

Not 13 ♕f3 ♗d6 14 ♖e3 (14
♖xd5 ♗b7 15 ♖xd6 ♕e7 wins
for Black) ♕g5 15 g3 ♗g4 16
♕g2 ♖ae8 17 d4 ♕h5 18 ♕f1
♗h3 19 ♕e1 ♕f3! 0–1,
Botechko–Semashev, Chernovtsi
1985.

13 ... ♗d6

14 ♖e3 *(71)*

14 ♖e1 ♕h4 15 h3?! (15 g3
transposes to Chapter 9, line A)
♗xh3 16 gh ♕xh3 17 f4 (17 ♖e3?
♗h2+ 18 ♔h1 ♖fe8 is crushing)
is at least a draw, and 17 ... ♖ae8
is a reasonable winning attempt.

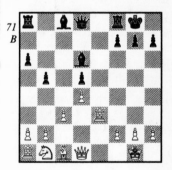

71
B

After 14 ♖e3 there are two
possible lines:

A 14 ... f5
B 14 ... ♕h4

The continuation 14 ... ♗f5 15
♘d2 ♕h4 16 ♘f1 ♖ae8 17 ♕e1
♖e6 18 ♖xe6 fe 19 ♗e3 ♖c8 20

a3 ♕g4 21 ♕d2 ♕e4 22 ♖c1 ♕d3 23 ♕e1 ♖e8 24 ♘d2 a5 25 ♘f3 gave Black insufficient compensation for the pawn in I. Ivanov–Hebden, New York 1983.

Line A attempts to exploit the position of the rook on e3, but the advance of the f-pawn doesn't by itself generate a strong attack. Moreover it allows the manoeuvre ♘d2–f3–e5. Both theoretical analyses and practical results have favoured White, so it is not surprising that recent games have shown a preference for 14 ... ♕h4, which appears good for equality.

A

14 ... f5

15 ♘d2

Or 15 ♕f3 (15 ♖h3? f4 16 ♖xh7 ♕e7! 17 ♖h5 ♗g4 wins for Black, while after 15 ♖e1 f4 White should play 16 ♘d2 transposing to the main line, rather than 16 f3? ♕g5 17 ♔h1 ♗d7 18 ♘d2 ♕h4 19 ♘f1 g5 with a strong attack, Yanofsky–Ed. Lasker, New York 1949) ♖a7 16 ♘d2 (taking the second pawn is asking for trouble, but otherwise the queen blocks the knight's best square) ♖af7 (*ECO* gives 16 ... g5 as good for Black) 17 ♘b3 f4 18 ♖e1 ♖f5 with a promising attack, Teichgraber–Wirsam, corr. 1966.

15 ... f4

16 ♖e1 *(72)*

72
B

16 ... ♕g5

Not necessarily best. Other moves:

(1) **16 ... ♖f5** 17 ♘f3 ♖a7 18 a4 ba 19 ♕xa4 ♗d7 20 ♕d1 ♗b5 21 b3 ♖c7 22 ♗b2 ♕f6 23 ♖c1 g5 24 ♘e5! ♗xe5 25 de ♖xe5 26 ♖xe5 ♕xe5 27 c4 ♕xb2 28 ♕xd5+ ♖f7 29 ♕xg5+ ♔h8 30 ♕d8+ ♔g7 31 ♖d1! and White won in Zagorovsky–Dalko, corr. 1965.

(2) **16 ... ♕f6** (suggested by Barden) 17 ♕b3! ♗e6 18 ♘f3 with some advantage for White.

(3) **16 ... ♔h8** 17 ♕h5 ♗f5 18 ♘f3 ♗e4 19 ♗d2 ♖f5 20 ♕g4 ♕f6 21 a4 ba 22 ♖xa4 g6 23 c4 ♖h5 24 ♘e5 ♖h4 25 ♕g5 with a clear plus for White, Zurakhov–Mnatsakanian, USSR 1963.

(4) **16 ... g5** 17 ♕h5 ♕f6 18 h4 (not the move I would have played! 18 ♘f3 should be good for White) h6 19 ♘f3 ♖a7 20

♗d2 (taking the second pawn turns out to be impossible as 20 hg hg 21 ♕xg5+ ♕xg5 22 ♘xg5 ♖g7 23 ♘f3 ♗h3 is too dangerous) ♖g7 21 ♖e8 and White might still be slightly better, Z. Nilsson–Nyman, Stockholm 1954.

(5) **16 ... ♖a7** 17 ♘f3ˀ(17 h3? looks bad and after 17 ... g5 18 ♕b3 ♔h8 19 ♘f3 g4 20 hg ♗xg4 21 ♘e5 ♖g7 Black was better in Orlov–Gibaidulin, Liepaya 1976) ♗g4 (17 ... g5 18 ♘e5 ♖g7 19 a4 is good for White) 18 a4 ba (18 ... b4 19 ♗d2 is no improvement) 19 ♖xa4 g5 and now *ECO* gives 20 b3 ♖e8 21 ♕d3 as slightly better for White. I prefer 20 ♕d3 ♗f5 21 ♕f1, when a6 and g5 are attacked, and after 21 ... a5 22 ♕b5 ♗b8 23 ♘e5 White has a clear advantage.

(6) **16 ... f3** (tempting, but unsound) 17 ♘xf3 ♗g4 18 ♖e3 ♖a7 (the alternatives 18 ... ♗f4? 19 ♖d3 ♗f5 20 ♗xf4 ♗xd3 21 ♗g5 and 18 ... ♕c8 19 ♕d3 ♗f4 20 ♖e5 ♗xe5 21 ♘xe5 ♗f5 22 ♕d1 are also good for White) 19 h3! ♗h5 20 g4 ♗g6 21 ♘e5 ♗xe5 (or 21 ... ♕h4 22 ♕e1 ♗xe5 23 de and after 23 ... ♖f4 24 ♖g3, 23 ... ♗e4 24 f4 or 23 ... ♖af7 24 f4 ♕e7 25 ♖g3 White keeps his extra pawns) 22 de d4 (22 ... ♕h4 23 ♕e1 transposes to the last bracket) 23 cd ♖d7 24 ♕b3+

♔h8 25 e6 ♖xd4 26 e7 ♖d1+ 27 ♔g2 ♕a8+ 28 f3 1–0, Tal–Hermlin, Tallinn 1964.

17 ♘f3   ♕h5(73)

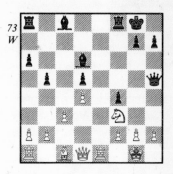

73
W

and now:

(1) **18 a4?!** ba (18 ... ♗g4? 19 ab ab 20 ♖xa8 ♖xa8 21 ♕e2 is good for White) 19 ♖xa4 (19 ♕xa4? ♗h3 is very bad) ♗g4 20 ♕d3 ♗f5 21 ♕f1 ♗e4 22 ♖xa6 ♖ad8 23 ♘e5 (23 ♘d2? f3 24 g3 ♗f5 25 ♖e3 ♗h3 26 ♕d3 ♗xg3! wins for Black) with a slight advantage to Black according to *ECO*.

(2) **18 ♕b3?!** and now:

(2a) **18 ... ♗g4** 19 ♘e5 ♗e6 20 f3 (20 ♘f3 ♗g4 is a draw) ♖f6 21 ♗d2 ♖af8 22 ♖e2 ♖h6 23 h3! (23 g4 fg 24 ♗xh6 ♗xe5 25 de ♕xf3! 26 ♕c2 ♗h3 27 hg ♕xg3+ 28 ♖g2 ♗xg2 29 ♕xg2 ♕xg2+ 30 ♔xg2 gh with a draw, Schmidt–Prameshuber, Clare Benedict Team Tnt. 1964) ♕g5 (after 23 ... ♗xh3 24 gh, the line

24 ... ♕xh3 25 ♕xd5+ ♚h8 26 ♖g2 ♕h1+ 27 ♚f2 ♕xa1 28 ♘f7+ wins for White, so Vasiukov–Barczay, Skopje 1970 continued 24 ... ♗xe5 25 ♕xd5+ ♚h8 26 ♕xe5 ♖g6+ 27 ♖g2 ♕xf3 28 ♖xg6 hg 29 ♕g5 ♕xh3 30 ♗xf4 1–0) 24 ♘g4 ♖g6 25 ♖ae1 ♕f5 (25 ... ♗f7! would have been unclear) 26 a4 h5 27 ♘f2 ♕g5 28 g4 hg 29 ♘xg4 ♕h4 30 ♖g2 ♖f5 31 ab ♕xh3 32 ♖xe6 ♖xe6 33 ba ♕xf3 34 a7 ♖g6 35 a8(Q)+ ♗f8 36 ♕a1 ♕h3 37 ♕f1 f3 38 ♘f6+ ♖fxf6 39 ♕xd5+ ♚h8 40 ♖xg6 ♖xg6+ 41 ♚f2 ♖g2+ 42 ♚e3 ♕h6+ 43 ♚xf3 ♕h3+ 44 ♚e4 ♖g4+ 45 ♗f4 ♕xf1 46 ♕h5+ ♚g8 47 ♕xg4 ♕b1+ 48 ♚d5 ♕xb2 and White won the ending in Weiner–Kaliwoda, corr. 1983. This game was very complicated, but my feeling is that White was better from move 26 onwards.

(2b) **18 ... ♚h8!** 19 ♘e5 (19 ♗d2 ♗g4 20 ♘e5 f3 21 ♕xd5 ♖ad8 22 gf ♗h3 is good for Black according to Boleslavsky) ♗e6 20 f3 ♖f6 21 ♖e2 ♖af8 and in comparison with line 2a Black has gained the move ... ♚h8. Since the check on d5 was crucial to White's defence this makes a big difference and *ECO* now assesses the position as clearly better for Black.

(3) **18 ♘e5!** (natural and good)

f3 19 gf (19 ♘xf3? ♗g4 is bad as Black has gained two tempi over 16 ... f3 above, while 19 ♖e3?! ♗xe5 is unclear after 20 de ♖f7 or 20 ♖xe5 ♕g4 21 ♖g5 ♕e4) ♗f5 (this is Harding's suggestion; 19 ... ♗xe5 20 ♖xe5, 19 ... ♖f5 20 f4 ♖xe5 21 de and 19 ... ♗h3 20 f4 ♕h4 21 ♕f3 ♖ae8 22 ♕g3! are all very good for White) 20 ♗f4! and Black does not have enough for the two pawns.

About the best Black can hope for after 16 ... ♕g5 is an opposite-coloured bishop position a pawn down. The other 16th moves are relatively unknown territory, but I am not impressed by any of them. It follows that 14 ... f5 is a poor choice.

B

14   ...   ♕h4*(74)*

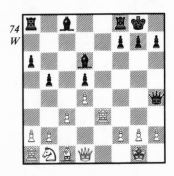

74
W

15   h3*(75)*

The usual choice, but 15 g3 is also playable and now:

(1) **15 ... ♗g4** with the branch:

(1a) **16 ♕f1** ♕h5 17 ♘d2 f5 18 f4 ♖ae8 19 ♘b3 ♗h3 20 ♕e1 ♗xf4! is definitely bad for White.

(1b) **16 gh** ♗xd1 17 ♘d2 f5 18 ♘f1 f4 19 ♖e1 ♗h5 gives Black adequate compensation for the pawn.

(1c) **16 f3** ♗xg3 17 ♕e2 (17 hg ♕xg3+ 18 ♔f1 ♗h3+ 19 ♔e2 ♕g2+ 20 ♔e1 ♖ae8 21 ♕e2 ♕h1+ 22 ♔d2 ♗f1 23 ♕f2 ♖xe3 24 ♕xe3 h5! and White faces serious problems stopping the h-pawn) ♗f4 18 fg f5! 19 gf (19 ♖h3 ♕xh3 20 ♗xf4 fg 21 ♗e5 ♖f3 22 ♘d2 ♖e3 23 ♕f1 ♖f8 and the ending is at least equal for Black) ♖xf5 20 ♖e8+ ♖xe8 21 ♕xe8+ ♖f8 22 ♕e6+ ♔h8 and Black should be able to give perpetual check.

(1d) **16 ♕e1** ♕h5 17 ♘d2 f5 18 f3 ♗h3 19 f4 g5 20 ♕f2 ♖ae8 21 ♘f3 gf 22 ♖xe8 ♖xe8 23 ♗xf4 ♗xf4 24 gf ♔h8 25 ♔h1 ♖e4 26 ♘g1 ♗g4 and Black has strong pressure for the pawn, Janssen–Van der Weijer, Netherlands 1987.

(1e) **16 ♕d3** ♕h5 17 ♘d2 f5 18 f3 (Harding gives 18 f4 g5 19 ♖e6 ♖ad8 20 ♘f1 ♔f7 21 ♕e3 gf 22 gf ♖g8 with advantage for Black) ♗h3 19 f4 ♕g4 20 ♖f3 ♖ae8 21 ♔f2 ♗xf4! and Black is better.

(2) **15 ... ♕h3** 16 ♘d2 ♗g4 (16 ... ♗f5 17 a4 ♖ae8 18 ♘f1 h5 19 ab ab 20 ♖a6 ♗b8 21 ♕e2 ♖e6 22 ♕xb5 h4 23 ♖a8 ♔h7 24 ♖xe6 fe 25 ♖xb8 ♗e4 26 ♘e3 ♗xf2 27 ♔xf2 ♕xh2+ 28 ♔e1 ♕xg3+ 29 ♔d2 h3 30 ♖f8 h2 31 ♕e8 1–0, Richardson–Zapletal, corr. 1976) 17 f3 (17 ♕f1!? is also possible, when 17 ... ♕h5 leaves Black a tempo down over 1a above) f5 (17 ... ♗xg3 18 ♘f1) 18 fg f4 19 ♖f3 fg 20 hg ♗xg3 21 ♘f1 was good for White in Vasiukov–Geller, USSR 1965.

Line 2 bears comparison with variation D3 in Chapter 10. It seems that the rook is slightly better placed on e3 than e2, so whereas the earlier line was roughly level, here 15 ... ♕h3 gives White an edge. However with the rook on e3 Black has the tactical idea 15 ... ♗g4, which equalizes.

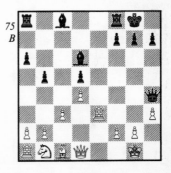

75
B

After 15 h3 Black has three possibilities:

B1   15 ... g5

B2   15 ... ♕f4!
B3   15 ... f5

15 ... ♗f4? 16 g3 ♕g5 17 ♖e5 wins, while 15 ... ♗e6 16 ♘d2 ♖ae8 17 ♘f3 ♕h5 18 ♗d2 and 15 ... ♗f5 15 ♘d2 ♖ae8 17 ♕f3 ♗f4 18 ♖xe8 ♖xe8 19 ♘f1 ♖e1 20 ♕xd5 g6 21 ♗xf4! are very good for White.

Line B1 and B3 are relatively risky, although line B1 is not clearly bad. Line B2 is certainly the safest, and appears to offer Black excellent equalizing chances.

B1

    15   ...   g5
    16   ♕f3

16 ♘d2? g4 17 ♘f1 ♔h8 18 hg ♗xg4 19 ♕e1 ♖g8 20 ♗d2 ♗f4 gave Black a clear plus in van den Berg–Beredewout, Netherlands Ch. 1965.

    16   ...   ♗e6
    17   ♕f6(76)

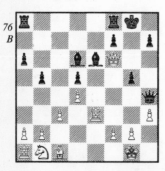

    17   ...   ♕h5
This is probably not the best move. The alternatives are:

(1) 17 ... ♖ae8 and now:

(1a) 18 ♘d2 ♕f4! 19 ♕xf4 ♗xf4 20 ♖e1 (20 ♖f3 ♗d7 21 ♔f1 b4 22 c4 ♖e7 is good for Black) ♗xh3 21 ♖xe8 (for 21 ♘f3 see line 2 below) ♖xe8 22 ♘f3 ♗xc1 23 ♖xc1, Browne–Gilden, USA Ch. 1974, and now both 23 ... ♗f5 and 23 ... ♗g4 24 ♘xg5 f6 25 ♘h3 ♗xh3 26 gh ♖e2 suffice to equalize.

(1b) 18 ♘a3! ♕h5 19 ♗d2 (19 ♖e1 ♗e7 20; ♕e5 ♗xh3 21 gh ♗xa3 22 ♕xe8 ♖xe8 23 ♖xe8+ ♗f8 is equal according to *ECO*) ♗f4 (or 19 ... h6 20 ♘c2 ♗f4 21 ♖d3 ♕e2 22 ♗xf4 gf 23 ♘e1 ♕xb2 24 ♖ad1 ♔h7 25 ♕xf4 ♕xa2 26 ♖e3 ♖c8 27 ♘d3 ♕c2 28 ♖a1 ♕xc3 29 ♖xa6 with a clear plus for White, Hübner–Pinter, Euro. Club Ch. 1989) 20 ♖d3 ♗xd2 21 ♖xd2 and now the combination 21 ... ♗xh3? 22 gh ♕xh3 backfires after 23 ♕xg5+ ♔h8 24 ♕f6+ ♔g8 25 ♖d3! ♕xd3 26 ♔h2 and wins.

(2) 17 ... ♖fe8! 18 ♘d2 (after 18 ♘a3 the tactical line in 1b above doesn't work since after 26 ♔h2 Black plays 26 ... ♖e6 27 ♖g1+ ♔f8 28 ♕h8+ ♔e7 29 ♕xa8 ♖h6+ 30 ♔g2 ♕h3 mate) ♕f4 19 ♕xf4 ♗xf4 20 ♖e1 ♗xh3 21 ♘f3 (for 21 ♖xe8+ see line 1a above) ♖xe1+ 22 ♘xe1 ♗xc1 23 ♖xc1 ♗f5 24 ♘c2 ♗xc2 25 ♖xc2 ♖e8 26 ♔f1 h5 27 ♖c1 f6 ½–½, Zagorovsky–Nyman, corr. 1968.

18 ♘d2

Better than 18 ♖e1 h6 19 ♗e3 (19 f4 ♕h4 20 ♖f1 ♗xh3 21 ♕xd6 ♗xg2 draws) ♔h7! 20 ♘d2 ♖g8 21 ♘f1 (21 ♕f3 g4 22 hg ♕h2+ 23 ♔f1 ♗xg4 24 ♕xf7+ ♖g7 wins for Black) ♖g6 22 ♕f3 g4 23 hg ♖xg4 24 ♘g3 ♕g6 25 ♘e2 ♖g8 26 g3 ♕h5 27 ♔g2 ♕h3+! 0–1, Ermakov–Sikov, corr. 1966.

18 ... g4

18 ... ♗f4 19 ♖e1 ♗xh3 20 gh ♕xh3 21 ♘f1 ♕g4+ 22 ♘g3 ♗xg3 23 ♕xg5+ was slightly better for White in Vasiukov–Golovko, USSR 1964.

19 ♖xe6 fe

20 ♕xe6+ ♕f7 21 ♕xd6 ♕xf2+ 22 ♔h2 ♖ae8 23 ♕g3 is slightly better for White according to Tal. The position is still very complicated, but Tal appears to be correct e.g. 23 ... ♖e2 24 ♕xg4+ ♔h8 25 ♘f1! ♖g8 (25 ... ♕xf1 26 ♗h6) 26 ♗g5 ♖e4 27 ♕h5 ♕f5 28 ♘g3 wins, while 23 ... ♕xg3+ leads to Tal's 'slight advantage'.

B2

15 ... ♕f4

The safest option. White has not been able to prove the slightest advantage after this move.

16 ♖e5

Not 16 ♖g3 ♕f5 (16 ... ♕f6 17 ♖f3 ♕g6 18 ♕d3 ♖e8 19 ♗d2 ♖e4 20 ♘a3 ♗f5 21 ♕f1 ♖h4 was also good for Black in

Boudy–Rodriguez, Cienfuegos 1983) 17 ♖f3 ♕h5 18 ♕d3 ♗g4! with advantage to Black, according to Keres.

16 ... ♕f6

17 ♖e1

Not 17 ♖xd5 ♗b7 18 ♖g5 ♖fe8 with an enormous attack, while 17 ♖e3 is just a draw.

17 ... ♕g6

18 ♕f3

After 18 ♔h1 Black should play for positional compensation. *ECO* recommends 18 ... ♗e6 19 ♘d2 (19 ♗e3?! f5 gives Black a target) ♖ac8 switching to a minority attack plan, although after 20 a3! I am not sure how effective this is since playing ... a5 and ... b4 will let the a1 rook into the game. The flexible 18 ... ♗f5 is probably best, and I believe the position is level.

18 ... ♗e6(77)

18 ... ♗f5?! 19 ♗e3 ♗e4 (or else just ♘d2) 20 ♕g4 h5 21 ♕xg6 ♗xg6 22 ♘d2 was good for White in Tal–Spassky, match 1965.

77
W

19 ♗f4

19 ♗e3 (19 ♘d2 ♖ae8 threatening ... ♗g4 is bad) ♕c2 20 ♕e2 ♕g6 is no better.

19 ... ♗xf4

20 ♕xf4 ♗xh3 21 ♕g3 ♕c2!? (21 ... ♕xg3 22 fg ♗f5 23 ♘d2 ♖fe8 24 ♘b3 and now either 24 ... ♔f8 25 ♘c5 a5 26 ♖xe8+ ♖xe8 27 a4 ba 28 ♖xa4 ♖e2, Tal–Spassky, match 1965, or 24 ... f6 25 ♘c5 ♖xe1+ 26 ♖xe1 ♔f7 27 a4 ba as suggested by Lilienthal, and in both cases White is slightly better although Black should draw) 22 c4 ♗e6! 23 cd ♗xd5 24 ♘c3 ♖ad8 25 ♖e2 ♕g6 26 ♕xg6 hg 27 ♘xd5 ♖xd5 28 ♖d1 ♖fd8 29 ♖ed2 f6 ½–½, Holmov–Tal, Kislovodsk 1966.

B3

15 ... f5(78)

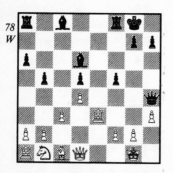

78
W

An ambitious but risky continuation. Black proceeds with his attack, but risks exposing his own king.

16 ♕f3

Or:

(1) **16 ♕b3** ♗b7 17 ♘d2 f4 18 ♘f3 and now:

(1a) **18 ... ♕f6** (suggested by Popov, but it blocks the direct attack by ... ♖f6–g6 as in 1b below) 19 ♖e1 ♖ae8?! (this achieves very little, but in any case I can see no natural defence to the threat of a4) 20 ♗d2 g5 21 a4 h5 22 ab g4 23 ba ♗a8 24 hg hg 25 ♖xe8! ♖xe8 26 ♘h2 g3 27 fg fg 28 ♘g4 ♕h4 29 ♕b6 ♖e4 30 ♕xd6 ♖xg4 31 ♕h6 1–0, Bryck–van der Weijer, corr. 1986/7.

(1b) **18 ... ♕h5!** (Keres assessed this position as unclear) 19 ♖e6 (19 ♖e1 ♖f6 20 a4 ♖g6 21 ♔h1 ♖f8 22 ♕d1 ♗c8 gives Black an enormous attack) ♖ad8 20 ♖e1 ♗c8?! (it is hard to see why the position of the rook at d8 improves White's position so 20 ... ♖f6 should be good, or possibly Harding's suggestion of 20 ... ♔h8 21 ♘e5 f3 22 ♘xf3 ♖xf3) 21 ♘e5, Poliak–Olifer, USSR 1960, and now 21 ... ♗xe5 22 de ♕g6 23 ♔h2 f3! gives Black good attacking changes according to Popov.

(2) **16 ♘d2** f4 17 ♘f3 ♕h5 18 ♖e1 ♗xh3 19 gh ♕xh3 20 ♘g5 ♕h4 21 ♘f3 ♕g4+ 22 ♔f1 ♖ae8 with a very strong attack for the piece.

16 ... ♗b7

17 ♘d2   g5
18 ♕e2!

Hübner's innovation casts doubt on Black's play. Other moves are good for Black, e.g. 18 ♘f1 (or 18 ♖e6 ♖ad8 19 ♕e2 f4 20 ♘f3 ♕h5 21 ♘h2 ♕f7 22 ♕e1 ♗c8 23 ♖e2 ♗f5 with a tremendous initiative for the pawn) ♖f6 19 ♕e2 ♔f7 20 f3 (20 ♗d2 f4 21 ♖d3 ♖e8 22 ♕g4 ♕xg4 23 hg ♗c8 24 ♘h2 h5 and the position of the rook on d3 gives Black the advantage, Bangiev–Vitomski, corr. 1972) f4 21 ♖d3 ♖e8 22 ♕f2 ♕h5 23 ♖d1 ♖fe6 24 ♕c2 ♖e2 25 ♖d2 ♖e1 26 ♖f2 ♗c8 27 b4 ♔f6 28 ♗b2 ♖xa1 29 ♗xa1 ♖e1 with more than enough for

the pawn, Houdek–Nejezezchleba, corr. 1980.

After 18 ♕e2! Black is in serious trouble, for example:

(1) **18 ... g4** 19 ♖e6 ♖ad8 20 ♘f1 gh 21 ♖h6 ♕g4 22 ♕e6+ ♔h8 23 ♖xh3 and Black cannot even play 23 ... ♖g8 because of 24 ♖xh7+.

(2) **18 ... f4** 19 ♘f3 ♕h5 (19 ... ♕h6 20 ♖e6 ♖f6 21 ♖xf6 ♕xf6 22 ♘xg5 is no better) 20 ♘xg5! ♕g6 (20 ... ♕xg5 21 ♖g3 fg 22 ♕e6+! wins) 21 ♖e6 ♕xg5 22 ♖xd6 ♖ae8 23 ♖e6 ♔f7 24 ♖e5 with a winning position for White, Hübner–Nunn, Skelleftea 1989.

12 Other White 12th Moves

**1 e4 e5 2 ♘f3 ♘c6 3 ♗b5 a6 4
♗a4 ♘f6 5 0-0 ♗e7 6 ♖e1 b5 7
♗b3 0-0 8 c3 d5 9 ed ♘xd5 10
♘xe5 ♘xe5 11 ♖xe5 c6**(79)

We have already considered 12
d4 and 12 ♗xd5, but there are a
number of other ideas for White.
These have become increasingly
popular over the past few years as
White players have explored ways
of avoiding the huge mass of
theory in the main lines. There are
three important moves for White.

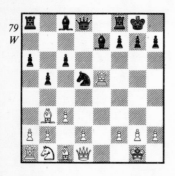

79
W

A   12 g3
B   12 ♖e1
C   12 d3

These three lines all aim to
reach the same position, namely
that arising after 12 d3 ♗d6 13
♖e1 ♕h4 14 g3 ♕h3, but each
move order has its own distinctive
features. Move order C occurs
most often in practice, but by
abandoning the usual ... ♕h4–h3
plan and instead developing by
... ♗f5 Black reaches a satisfactory position. Line A has the same
objective, but White reserves the
right to play d4 if Black adopts
the ... ♗f5 plan. The trouble is
that Black can develop his
bishops to f6 and b7, exploiting
the open long diagonal. Line B is
probably the most accurate way
of executing White's plan. Here
White waits for ... ♗d6 before
playing g3. In this case Black can
still experiment with ... ♗f5 or
... ♖e8, but if these prove un-
satisfactory then he must fall in
with White's plan. We therefore
consider the critical position
(after 12 ♖e1 ♗d6 13 d3 ♕h4 14
g3 ♕h3) under line B.

Finally 12 Qf1 has been played a few times. The idea is to save a tempo by avoiding Qd3–f1, but Black regains the lost move by playing ... Qh4–h5 instead of ... Qh4–h3–h5, and then gains a second tempo by playing his bishop to h3 in one go. The continuation is 12 ... Bd6 13 Re1 Qh4 (13 ... Bf5 14 d4 Qh4 15 g3 Qh5 transposes into the analysis of 15 Qd3 at the start of Chapter 9) 14 g3 Qh5 15 d4 Bh3! (15 ... Bg4 transposes to Chapter 8 after 16 Be3, or to Chapter 10, line D, note to White's 15th move, variation 1 after 16 Nd2 Rae8 17 f3 Bh3 18 Qf2 f5 19 Rxe8 Rxe8) 16 Bd1 (after 16 Qd3 Black need not take the draw by repetition as 16 ... Rae8 gives him a crushing attack) Qf5 17 Qe2 c5 (or 17 ... Qd7 18 Qf3 Rae8 19 Rxe8 Rxe8 20 Be3 f5 21 Bb3 f4 22 gf Re6 with advantage for Black, Murei–Smirnov, Moscow 1971) with a favourable version of line 1b2 in the note to White's 15th move in Chapter 9. Since that note was equal, this position must be good for Black.

A

12 g3 Bf6

Or 12 ... Nf6 (12 ... Bd6 13 Re1 transposes to line B) 13 d4 Bd6 (Spassky suggests 13 ... c5!?) 14 Re1 Bg4 and now:

(1) 15 f3 Bh3 (15 ... Bh5 16 Nd2 c5 17 Ne4 Nxe4 18 Rxe4 c4 19 Bc2 f5 20 Re1 f4 21 g4 Bxg4! 22 fg f3 threatening ... Qh4 is good for Black according to Mikenas) 16 Bg5 Qc7 17 Bxf6 gf 18 f4?! (18 Kf2 is an improvement) Bxf4! 19 Qh5 Bxg3 20 Re2 Rfe8 with complications favouring Black, Yudovich–Zalpetal, corr. 1972/5.

(2) 15 Qd3 c5 16 dc (16 Bc2! c4 17 Qf1 Qd7 18 f3 Bh3 19 Qf2 is slightly better for White) Bxc5 17 Qxd8 Raxd8 18 Bf4 (18 Bg5 Rfe8 19 Nd2 Re1+ 20 Rxe1 h6 21 Bxf6 Rxd2 is level) h6 19 Na3 g5 20 Be3 (20 Be5 Rd2) Bxe3 21 Rxe3 Rd2 with equality, Fischer–Spassky, Santa Monica 1966.

13 Re1 c5

This move is the most logical since it prepares to exploit the weakened long white diagonal. 13 ... Ra7?! (Wade suggests 13 ... Bf5) 14 d4 Re7 15 Rxe7 Qxe7 16 Na3! is good for White according to I. Zaitsev.

14 d4

After 14 d3 Black should play 14 ... b4! since 14 ... Bb7 15 Nd2 b4 16 Ne4 bc 17 Rb1 Bd4 18 Bg5 f6 19 Be3 Kh8 20 Rxd4 cd 21 Nc5 Qc8 22 Nxb7 Qxb7 23 Qf3 was slightly better for White in Poznyak–Rapoport, corr. 1973/4.

14 ... Bb7

Better than 14 ... cd 15 cd ♗b7 16 ♘c3 ♘xc3 17 bc ♛d7 (17 ... b4 18 ♗b2 bc 19 ♗xc3 ♛d7 20 ♖c1 ♖ac8 21 ♛d3 ♖c5 22 d5 was good for White in Matanovic–Ostojic, Yugoslavia Ch. 1969) and now Matanovic–Geller, Sousse 1967, continued 18 ♗e3 ♖fe8 ½–½, but 18 ♗b2 would have been slightly better for White according to most commentators.

15 dc(80)

15 ♗e3 ♖e8 16 ♘d2 ♘xe3 17 fe cd 18 cd ♗xd4 19 ed ♛xd4+ 20 ♔f1 ♛f6+ 21 ♔g1 ♛c6 is very good for Black, while **15 a4** has been suggested, but another non-developing move looks very risky.

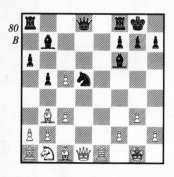

80
B

15 ...   ♖e8

15 ... ♛d7 is an interesting alternative, when Ernst–Dam, Lugano 1988 continued 16 ♘d2 ♘xc3 17 bc ♗xc3 18 ♖b1 ♖ad8 (Geller suggests 18 ... ♖fe8) 19

♖e2 ♛c6 20 f3 ♛xc5+ 21 ♔g2 ♗xf3+ 22 ♔xf3? (22 ♘xf3! ♖xd1 23 ♗xd1 ♛d5 24 ♗c2 ♛c4 25 ♖f2 ♖e8 would have been slightly better for White after 26 ♗b2 ♖e2 27 ♗xc3 ♖xf2+ 28 ♔xf2 ♛xc3 29 ♗b3 a5 30 ♖d1 or 26 ♗f4 h6 27 h4 ♖e2 28 ♖f1) ♖d3+ (the best move, since after 22 ... ♛c6+ 23 ♔f2 ♗d4+ 24 ♔e1 ♛h1+ 25 ♘f1 ♗c3+ with the idea 26 ♗d2?! ♗xd2+ 27 ♖xd2 ♖xd2 28 ♛xd2 ♛e4+ 29 ♔f2 ♛xb1, White can play 26 ♔f2! ♖xd1 27 ♗xd1 ♗d4+ 28 ♗e3 with a small plus) 23 ♔g2 ♛c6+ 24 ♔g1 ♗d4+ 25 ♖f2 ♗xf2+ 26 ♔xf2 ♛b6+ 27 ♔f1 (27 ♔g2 ♛c6+ 28 ♔h3 ♛h6+ and 27 ♔e2 ♖e8+ 28 ♔xd3 ♖e3+ 29 ♔c2 ♛g6+ 30 ♔b2 ♛f6+ are both draws) ♛f6+ 28 ♔e2? (an unjustified winning attempt) ♛f5 29 ♛h1 ♖e8+ 30 ♔d1 ♖xd2+! 31 ♔xd2 ♛f2+! 32 ♔c3 ♖c8+ 33 ♔d3 ♖d8+ 34 ♗d5 ♛f5+ 35 ♔e2 ♛xb1 36 ♗d2 ♖e8+ 37 ♔f2 ♛d3 0–1. In view of the note to move 22 in this line, it seems that Geller's move is best.

16 ♘d2   ♘xc3!
17 bc   ♗xc3
18 c6!

Or:

(1) **18 ♖b1** ♛d7 gives Black more than enough compensation for the piece, e.g. 19 ♖b2 (19

♖xe8+ ♖xe8 20 ♘f3 ♕c6 21 ♗e3 ♕xf3 22 ♕xf3 ♗xf3 is good for Black) ♖xe1+ 20 ♕xe1 ♖e8 21 ♕d1 ♕h3 22 f3 ♗d4+ 23 ♔h1 h5 24 ♖c2 (24 ♘f1? ♖e1 wins) h4 25 g4 (or 25 c6 ♗xc6 26 ♖xc6 hg winning) ♗c6 26 ♗b2 ♗e3 with a decisive attack for Black.

(2) **18 ♖xe8+ ♕xe8 19 ♖b1 ♖d8 20 ♖b2** (20 ♕c2 ♕c6 21 f3 ♗xd2 22 ♗xd2 ♕xf3 23 ♗f4 ♖e8 is also bad) ♗xb2 21 ♗xb2 ♕c6 22 f3 ♕xc5+ 23 ♔g2 ♕e3 24 ♗c1 ♕c3 25 ♕e1 g5 26 g4 (the immediate 26 ♕e7? loses to 26 ... ♖xd2+ 27 ♗xd2 ♕xf3+) ♔f8 intending ... a5–a4 or ... b4 and ... ♖c8, with advantage for Black.

18	**...**	**♗xc6**
19	**♖xe8+**	**♕xe8**
20	**♖b1**	**♖d8**(81)

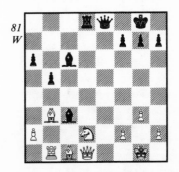

81
W

21 ♕c2!

Not 21 ♖b2 a5! 22 ♖c2 ♕e4 23 f3 ♕d4+ 24 ♔g2 a4 25 ♖xc3 ♕xc3 26 ♗c2 (26 ♕c2 b4 wins) ♗xf3+ 27 ♕xf3 ♕xc2 and Black wins, nor 21 ♕h5 g6 22 ♕g5 ♖e1+ 23 ♘f1 ♕e4 24 ♕xd8+ ♔g7 25 f3 ♕xf3 26 ♘e3 ♕h1+ 27 ♔f2 ♕e1 mate.

21	**...**	**♗xd2**

Not 21 ... ♕e1+? 22 ♘f1 ♗e4 23 ♗g5 and White turns the tables.

22	**♗xd2**	**♗e4**

23 ♗xf7+ (23 ♖e1 ♗xc2 24 ♖xe8+ ♖xe8 25 ♗xc2 ♖e2 wins) ♔xf7 24 ♕b3+ ♗d5! (24 ... ♕e6 25 ♖e1 is a draw) 25 ♕b4 ♕e4 (according to Braga 25 ... ♗xa2 would have given Black fair winning chances) 26 ♕xe4 ♗xe4 27 ♖b2 ♖d4! with an edge for Black as the a-pawn is weak, Braga–Geller, Amsterdam II 1986.

If this complicated analysis is all correct then 12 g3 is a bad move, and White must choose one of the other methods of aiming for his target position.

B

12	**♖e1**	

This move aims to play a g3 system as in line A, but only after Black has committed his bishop to d6, thus cutting out the line of Braga–Geller.

12	**...**	**♗d6**
13	**g3**(82)	

13 d3 transposes to line C.

13	**...**	**♕d7**

82
B

The most common move, but there are numerous alternatives:

(1) **13 ...** ♗f5 (relatively untested, but quite playable) 14 d4 ♕d7 15 ♗e3 ♖ae8 16 a4?! (16 ♘d2 ♗g4 17 ♕b1 h5 18 ♗xd5 cd 19 a4 h4 is unclear, Anikaev–Faibisovich, USSR 1970, or 16 ♗xd5 cd 17 ♘d2 ♗g4 18 ♕b3 with equality according to Kapengut, but rather than chase the queen to an active square I prefer 17 ... b4 18 cb ♗xb4 19 a3 ♗d6) ♗g4 17 ♕d3 ♘f4! 18 gf (18 ♕d2 ♗f3 19 ♗d1 ♘h3+ 20 ♔f1 ♘g5 wins for Black) ♗f3 19 f5 ♖e4! 20 ♗d1, Butnorius–Kapengut, USSR 1970, and now 20 ... ♖g4+ 21 ♔f1 ♗e4 22 ♕d2 ♕xf5 gives Black a winning attack.

(2) **13 ...** f5 14 f4 (14 c4 f4 15 ♘c3 fg 16 hg bc 17 ♗xc4 ♔h8 18 d4 ♘xc3 19 bc ♕c7 20 ♖e3 ♗d7 21 ♗d2 ♖f6 22 ♗e2 ♖af8 was unclear in Kapic–Draskovic, corr. 1984, but 14 d4 f4 15 ♘d2 followed by ♘e4 and ♕h5 looks

good to me, and I doubt if Black has enough for the pawn) g5 15 d4 gf 16 ♗xd5+ cd 16 ♗xf4 ♗xf4 (Black's attacking chances are poor when his bishop is stuck inside the pawn chain) 17 gf ♕h4 18 ♖f1 ♖a7 20 ♘d2 ♖g7+ 21 ♔h1 ♖g4 22 ♕f3 with a clear plus for White, Ahlers–Dahlhaus, corr. 1973/7.

(3) **13 ...** ♖a7 14 d3 ♗f5 (14 ... ♖e7!? is more consistent) 15 ♘d2 ♗xd3 16 ♘e4 ♗xe4 17 ♖xe4 ♖d7 (returning the pawn has given White an advantage based on his two bishops; 17 ... ♖e7 18 ♗xd5 cd 19 ♕xd5 ♖xe4 20 ♕xe4 ♖e8 21 ♗g5! ♖xe4 22 ♗xd8 ♖e2 23 ♗b6! leads to an advantageous ending for White) 18 ♕f3 ♗c5 19 ♗f4 a5 20 ♖ae1 ♘xf4 21 ♖xf4 a4 22 ♗c2 ♕b6 (22 ... ♖d2 23 ♗xh7+ ♔xh7 24 ♕h5+ ♔g8 25 ♕xc5 ♖xb2 26 ♕xc6 wins a pawn) 23 ♗xh7+! ♔xh7 24 ♖h4+ ♔g8 25 ♕f5 f6 26 ♕e6+ ♖df7 27 ♕h3 ♖e7 28 ♖h8+ ♔f7 29 ♕h5+ g6 30 ♕h7+ ♔e8 31 ♕xg6+ ♔d7 32 ♖d1+ ♔c7 33 ♖xf8 ♗xf2+ 34 ♔g2 ♕c5 35 ♖f7 1–0, Lobron–Duric, Sarajevo 1984.

(4) **13 ...** ♖e8 (this move seems to have been unfairly dismissed by *ECO*) 14 d4 ♗g4 (14 ... ♖a7 15 ♖xe8+ ♕xe8 16 ♗xd5 cd 17 ♗e3 f5 18 ♕f3 f4 19 gf ♕g6+ 20 ♕g2 ♕h5 21 ♘d2 was good for

White, Svenn–Plachetka, Rilton Cup 1978/9) 15 ♖xe8+ ♕xe8 16 ♕xg4 (after 16 ♕f1 ♖a7 17 ♗xd5 cd 18 ♗e3 f5 19 ♕g2 ♕e6, Sagarin–Ermakov, corr. 1966, Black's attacking prospects on the kingside give him good compensation for the pawn) ♕e1+ 17 ♗g2 ♕xc1 18 ♕e2 ♘f4+ 19 gf ♕xf4 20 ♕h5 reaching a critical position for the assessment of 13 ... ♖e8. *ECO* stops here with an evaluation of clearly better for White, while Harding continues with the game Kopakkala–Nuutilainen, corr. 1973, where Black gained the advantage after 20 ... ♕e4+ 21 ♕f3 ♕g6+ 22 ♔h1 ♕h6 23 h3 ♕c1+ 24 ♔g2 ♕xb2 25 ♗xf7+ ♔h8 26 ♕xc6 ♖d8 27 ♕b6 ♗e7 28 d5 ♕xa1. I cannot see any convincing improvements for White in this game, so Harding seems to be correct.

(5) **13 ... ♕g5** (13 ... ♘f6 transposes to line A, while 13 ... ♗e6 14 d4 ♕d7 is an untested suggestion) 14 d4 ♕g6 15 ♗xd5 cd 16 ♕f3 ♗f5 17 ♗f4 ♗g4 **18 ♕xd5** is good for White according to Pachman, but 18 ... ♗xf4 19 gf ♖ae8! 20 ♖xe8 (20 ♘d2 ♗d1+) ♖xe8 21 ♘d2 ♗h3+ 22 ♕g5 ♕c2 seems to be better for Black. However **18 ♕e3!** is genuinely good for White.

13 ... ♗f5 and 13 ... ♖e8 are the most promising alternatives to the usual 13 ... ♕d7, and are well worth a practical test.

14 d3

14 d4 ♕h3 transposes to Chapters 2–9.

14 ...   ♕h3

The alternatives are inferior:

(1) **14 ... ♕f5** 15 ♘d2 ♕g6 (15 ... ♕xd3?? 15 ♗c2) 16 ♘e4 ♗c7 17 ♕f3 ♗g4 18 ♕g2 ♖ad8 (18 ... f5? 19 ♘g5 f4 20 ♗xd5+ cd 21 ♕xd5+ ♔h8 22 ♖e7! wins, and 18 ... ♕h5 19 ♗e3 ♗f3 20 ♗d1 forces exchanges) 19 ♗g5 f6 20 ♗e3 f5 21 f4! ♔h8 22 ♘f2 ♖h5 23 ♗d4 ♖fe8 24 ♗e5 ♗xe5 25 fe ♕h6 26 d4 ♘e3 27 ♕h3 c5 28 ♘d3! winning, Byrne–Hebden, New York 1983.

(2) **14 ... ♗b7** 15 ♘d2 f5 16 f4 c5 17 ♘f3 ♖ae8 18 ♗d2 ♔h8 19 ♔f2 ♕c6 20 c4 ♘f6 21 h3 was unclear in Grunfeld–Sharp, Fort Worth 1984, but what would Black have played after 16 c4?

(3) **14 ... ♘f6** 15 ♘d2 ♕h3 16 ♘f1 ♗g4 17 f3 ♗d7 18 ♗g5 ♕f5 19 ♗e3 c5 20 ♘d2 ♗c6 21 ♘e4 ♗c7 22 ♕e2 ♖ad8 23 ♗c2 ♖fe8 24 ♕f2 with advantage to White, Richardson–van Oosterom, corr. 1985.

15 ♖e4*(83)*

This move is the point of White's play. In contrast to Chapter 9, Black cannot play 15 ... g5 when the pawn is on d3 because the rook is defended and

83
B

White can simply take on g5.

15 ...　　　♕f5

The following alternative lines should be compared with those in Chapter 9, line B, note to Black's 15th move:

(1) **15... ♗d7** 16 ♘d2 ♖ae8 17 ♖h4 ♕f5 18 ♘f1 ♕g6 19 ♗d2 ♗f5 20 ♗xd5 cd 21 ♘e3 ♗e6 22 a4 ♗e7 23 ♖f4 ♗g5 24 ♖f3 b4 25 c4 ♗xe3 26 ♖xe3 a5 27 c5 d4 28 ♖e4 was good for White in Murei–Geller, Amsterdam 1987.

(2) **15... ♘f6** 16 ♖h4 ♕f5 17 ♗f4! (after 17 ♗c2 ♖e8 18 ♘d2 g5 19 ♘e4! White has the advantage, but 17... ♕g6 18 d4 ♗f5 19 ♗xf5 ♕xf5 20 ♗f4 g5 21 ♗xd6 ♖fe8 22 g4 ♕d5 was less clear in Ueter–Rieke, Bundesliga 1983/4) g5 18 ♗xd6 gh 19 ♗xf8 ♔xf8 (*ECO* gives 19 ... hg 20 hg ♔xf8 21 ♘d2 ♕xd3 22 ♕f3 as slightly better for White, which is true, but White can also try 21 ♕e2 hanging on to the pawn) 20 ♕e2 ♗b7 21 ♘d2 c5 22 f3 (the solid

outpost at e4 makes it hard for Black to achieve anything) hg 23 hg ♕g5 24 ♕f2 ♖d8 25 ♗c2 ♘h5 26 ♘f1 ♕d5 27 ♖e1 ♕xf3?? (a terrible blunder, but otherwise White plays ♖e3 and is then ready to free himself by ♕h2–h4) 28 ♕xc5+ 1–0, Anand–L. Cooper, British Ch. 1988, since the d8 rook falls with check.

(3) **15 ... ♗b7** 16 ♖h4 ♕f5 17 ♗c2 ♕e6 18 c4 (not a move White wants to play, but after the obvious 18 d4 f5 the rook on h4 is stranded) ♘b4 19 c5 ♘xc2 20 ♕xc2 f5! 21 ♘d2 (21 cd? ♕e1+ 22 ♔g2 c5+ 23 f3 ♖ae8 wins for Black) ♗e7 22 ♖d4 ♕e5 23 ♘f3 ♕xc5 and Black is better, Tukmakov–Jansa, Student Olympiad 1967.

(4) **15 ... ♕d7** (this looks very odd; can Black really be claiming that White has nothing better than 16 ♖e1?) 16 ♕f1 (16 ♘d2 is better, as in the corresponding position from Chapter 9) ♗b7 17 ♗xd5? cd 18 ♖e1 d4 19 h3 ♕c6 20 ♔h2 ♖ae8 21 ♗d2 ♕f3 0–1, Larsson–Nyman, corr. 1966.

These lines deserve further investigation because having the pawn on d3 instead of d4 should favour Black. Perhaps 15 ... ♗b7 is the pick of the bunch.

16　♘d2

Or 16 ♗c2 ♕g6 17 ♕f1? (17 d4 ♗f5 18 ♖e2 ♖ae8 19 ♗xf5 ♕xf5

20 ♕e1 ♘f6 21 ♗e3 was played in Hennigan–Motwani, British Ch. 1988, and White is now a tempo down over Chapter 10, line D4, note to Black's 16th move, although he does have the advantage of having played ♗e3 before ♘d2; the position is roughly level) f5 18 ♖e1 f4 19 ♕g2 ♕h5 (Black has the advantage) 20 ♖e4 ♗h3 21 ♕h1 fg 22 hg ♗xg3 23 fg ♖f1+ 24 ♔h2 ♗g4+ 0–1, Sakharov–Hodzhayev, Lvov 1949.

    16 ...   ♕g6*(84)*

There is no point to 16 ... ♘f6 because after 17 ♖e1 the capture on d3 leads to a very bad endgame by 17 ... ♕xd3 18 ♘e4 ♕xd1 19 ♘xf6+ gf 20 ♖xd1.

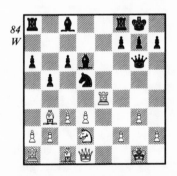

84
W

After 16 ... ♕g6 there is a major division:

B1   17 ♖e1
B2   17 ♘f1

These are the accepted continuations, but 17 a4!? is an interesting recent idea, and now:

(1) **17 ... ♗f5** 18 ab ab (18 ... ♗xe4? 19 de wins for White) 19 ♖xa8 ♖xa8 20 ♖e1 ♗xd3 (20 ... ♘f4?! 21 ♘e4 defends) 21 ♘f3 and according to Zapata the threats of ♘h4 and ♘d4 give White the advantage.

(2) **17 ... ♘f6!?** 18 ♖e1 ♗g4 19 f3 ♗h3 (19 ... ♗f5 20 ♘e4 ♗xe4 21 fe ♗xg3 22 ♖e2 ♗f4+ 23 ♖g2 ♕h6 24 ♗xf4 ♕xf4 25 ♕e2 gives White a clear plus) 20 ♘f1 ♖ae8 21 ♗e3 h5 22 d4 h4 23 ♗c2 ♗f5 24 ♗xf5 ♕xf5 25 ab ab 26 ♖a6 and Zapata claims White has a slight advantage, but here I am not so sure; 26 ... ♕d5 looks unclear.

(3) **17 ... f5?!** 18 ♖d4 f4 19 ♘e4 (not 19 ♖xd5?! cd 20 ♗xd5+ ♔h8 21 ♗xa8 fg 22 fg ♗xg3 23 ♗g2 ♗xh2+ 24 ♔xh2 ♕h6+ drawing) ♗g4 20 ♕f1 (20 f3? ♗xf3 21 ♕xf3 fg 22 ♕g2 gh+ 23 ♔h1 ♕xg2+ 24 ♔xg2 ♖f1 wins for Black) ♗e5 21 ♖xd5 cd 22 ♗xd5+ ♔h8 23 ♗xa8 fg 24 ♘xg3 and White ends up with numerous extra pawns, Zapata–Pavlovic, Belgrade Open 1988.

B1

    17 ♖e1   f5

This sacrificial move appears the most promising:

(1) **17 ... ♗b7** (17 ... ♕xd3?? 18 ♗c2) 18 ♘f3! ♖fe8 (18 ... c5

19 ♘h4 ♕f6 20 ♕g4 is good for White) 19 ♖xe8 + ♖xe8 20 ♘h4 ♕f6 21 ♗d2 b4 22 ♕f3 ♕xf3 23 ♘xf3 with advantage for White in Hjartarson–Hebden, London 1986.

(2) **17 ...** ♗c7 18 ♘f3! ♗g4 19 ♘h4 ♕h5 20 f3 ♗h3 21 ♕e2 (White is slightly better) ♖ad8 (21 ... ♗b6+ 22 d4 c5 23 ♕e5! is awkward) 22 d4 f5 23 f4 ♕xe2 (an admission of defeat; Black should have tried 23 ... ♗g4 24 ♕g2 g5 25 fg f4 with some attacking chances) 24 ♖xe2 ♖fe8 25 ♖xe8+ ♖xe8 26 ♔f2 with an extra pawn for White, Smagin–Malaniuk, USSR Ch. 1986.

18 c4

White is more or less forced to play sharply and accept Black's challenge. The greedy **18 ♕f3 ♔h8** 19 ♗xd5 cd 20 ♕xd5 ♖a7 gives Black a dangerous initiative, while **18 ♘e4?** fe 19 de fails to 19 ... ♗g4 20 ♕d4 ♕h5! 21 ed c5! with a decisive attack.

18	...	f4
19	♘e4	fg
20	fg	♗g4
21	♕c2	bc
22	dc	*(85)*

Or 22 ♕xc4!? ♗c7 (not 22 ... ♗e5? 23 ♘f2) 23 ♕c2? (after this Black gains the advantage; White should have played 23 ♗e3 ♔h8 24 ♗c5 ♘f4 25 ♗xf8 ♘h3+ 26 ♔g2 ♘f4+ 27 ♔g1 drawing,

although Black can speculate by 24 ... ♖f5!? or 24 ... ♖f3) ♔h8 24 ♗xd5 cd 25 ♘f2 (25 ♕xc7 de 26 de ♖ac8 and ... ♖c2 is very dangerous) ♖ac8 26 ♕a4 ♗d7 27 ♕h4 (27 ♕xd7? ♗xg3 wins) ♗d8 28 ♕b4 ♗c7 29 ♕h4 ♗d8? (29 ... ♖f5 is a good winning try) ½–½, Hellers–Wahls, World Junior Ch. 1988.

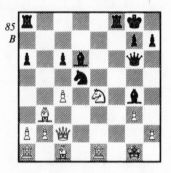

85
B

22	...	♖ae8

In this very sharp position there are two possible moves, and it is not clear which is better. The other line is 22 ... ♗b4 23 ♗d2 ♘f4! 24 ♗xf4 ♗xe1 25 ♖xe1 ♗f5 26 ♕g2, Smagin–Hebden, Moscow 1986, and now Black played 26 ... ♖fe8?! 27 ♗c2 ♖e6 28 g4! ♗xg4 29 ♘f1 ♗e2 (29 ... ♗h3 30 ♕xg6 ♖xg6+ 31 ♘g3 ♗xf1 32 ♗xg6 ♗xc4 33 ♗b1 was a much better chance, although White certainly has an advantage) 30 ♘g5! and White won. However

26 ... ♖ae8! was much better, when the line played by Smagin fails because the f4 bishop is attacked.

According to Hebden this move should lead to a draw, and if the analysis given below is correct, then this is Black's best line.

23 cd ♗f3

24 dc+

24 ♗f4 ♗xf4 25 ♕xc6 ♕h5 26 d6+ ♔h8 27 d7 ♕h3! (and not 27 ... ♖xe4? 28 ♕c8! winning) 28 ♕c2 ♕xd7 29 gf ♖xe4! and White cannot take the rook because of 30 ♖xe4 ♕g4+ 31 ♔f1 ♗xe4, so Black regains all his sacrificed material and keeps a crushing attack.

24 ... ♔h8 *(86)*

Until recently this position was regarded as favourable for Black, but there are two moves which cast serious doubts on this view.

25 ♗d5!?

Or:

(1) **25 ♗d2?** ♖xe4 26 ♖xe4 ♗xe4 27 ♕c3 ♕f5 and White lost on time in A. Ivanov–Agapov, USSR 1984, but in any case 28 ♗f4 ♗c5+ 29 ♔f1 ♗d3+ 30 ♔g2 ♕e4+ 31 ♔h3 ♖xf4 32 ♕xc5 ♖h4+ 33 gh ♕f3 is mate.

(2) **25 ♗f4!? ♗xf4 26 c7?!** (26 ♘f2! appears very strong, and I cannot see how Black can keep the attack going, e.g. 26 ... ♖xe1+ 27 ♖xe1 ♖e8 28 ♖xe8+ ♕xe8 29 ♕c3!) ♕b6+!? (if Black wants a draw then 26 ... ♗xe4 27 c8(♕) ♗xg3! 28 ♕xe4 ♗f2+ 29 ♔h1 ♕xe4+ 30 ♖xe4 ♖xc8 is a good choice; another possibility is 26 ... ♗xc7 27 ♕xc7 ♗xe4 and White's exposed king balances his extra pawn) 27 ♕f2 (27 ♘f2 ♗e3) ♗xc7! 28 ♘c5 ♗e5 (the two bishops and attacking chances are worth more than a pawn) 29 ♖f1 ♕d6 30 ♘e6 ♖f6 31 ♕xf3 ♖xf3 32 ♖xf3 h6 33 ♖d1 ♕b6+ 34 ♔g2 ♖xe6 35 ♗xe6 ♕xe6 36 b3 ♕c6 37 ♖d2 ♕e4 38 h3 h5 39 h4 ♗d4 0–1, Scholis–Skurovic Khasin, corr. 1987.

25 ... ♗xg3

Or 25 ... ♕f5 26 ♗e3 ♖xe4 27 ♗xe4 ♗xe4 28 ♕e2 ♗xc6 29 ♖ac1 ♕d5 (29 ... ♗b7 30 ♖f1 ♕e4 31 ♖xf8+ ♗xf8 32 ♔f2 ♕g2+ 33 ♔e1 ♗b4+ 34 ♔d1 ♕d5+ 35 ♗d2 wins for White) 30 ♖xc6 ♕xc6 31 ♗d4 and the extra pawn gives White fair winning chances.

26 hg &xe4

After 26 ... &xe4 (or 26 ... ♕h5 27 ♕h2 ♕xd5 28 &f4 &xe4 29 ♖ac1 g5 30 &e3 and White is clearly better) 27 &f4! ♖fxf4 (27 ... ♖xe1+ 28 ♖xe1 ♕xc2 29 &xf3 followed by ♖c1 wins, as does 27 ... ♕h5 28 ♕h2 ♕xd5 29 ♖xe4 &xe4 30 ♖c1 ♕d4+ 31 ♕f2 ♕xf2+ 32 &xf2 g5 33 &e3) 28 ♕f2 ♕h5 29 ♕h2 ♕xd5 30 gf White won in Andrievic–Pavlovic, Yugoslavia 1988.

27 ♖xe4 ♖xe4

28 &xe4 and now Andrievic's analysis continues 28 ... ♕xg3+ 29 ♕g2 (or 29 &g2 ♕e1+ drawing) ♕e1+ 30 &h2 ♖f2 (not 30 ... ♕h4+? 31 ♕h3 ♕xe4 32 &e3 and wins) 31 &f4 (31 c7 ♖xg2+ 32 &xg2 ♕h4+ draws) ♖xg2+ 32 &xg2 ♕h4+ 33 &g1 ♕xf4 34 ♖f1 ♕e3+ 35 ♖f2 ♕c1+ 36 ♖f1 with a draw. However I believe White can win by **31 &f3!** ♕e5+ (31 ... ♖xg2+ 32 &xg2 is hopeless) 32 &h3 ♕f5+ (32 ... ♕e6+ 33 &g4) 33 &g4! (33 &g3 ♖xg2+ 34 &xg2 ♕g6+ is less clear, as White has to give up his c6 pawn to avoid perpetual check) ♕d3+ 34 ♕g3 ♕f1+ 35 &h4 ♕h1+ 36 &h3 ♕e4+ 37 ♕g4 ♕e1 and now 38 ♕xg7+ or 38 &d2 wins.

In such a complex tactical line

it is hard to be sure of anything, as a small finesse can completely reverse the assessment of the whole line. However my impression is that 22 ... ♖ae8 is very doubtful, so Black must try 22 ... &b4 if he wants to keep his head above water.

B2

17 ♘f1*(87)*

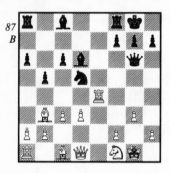

17 ... f5

A number of moves have been tried, with varying success:

(1) **17 ... &f5** and now:

(1a) **18 ♖d4!? &c5** 19 ♖xd5 cd 20 d4 &b6 21 &xd5 ♖ad8 22 ♕f3 &g4 23 ♕g2 ♖fe8 24 ♘e3 ♕d3 25 &b3 &h5 26 ♕f1 ♕e4 27 a4 ♕c6 28 &c2 &g6 29 &d1 b4 30 a5 &c7 31 d5 ♕c5 with an unclear position, Hansson–Hebden, London 1984, although White eventually won.

(1b) **18 &xd5 cd** 19 ♖d4 &c5 (19 ... &e6 20 ♘e3 &c5 21 ♘xd5 followed by ♘f4 wins for White)

20 ♖xd5 ♗g4 21 ♕d2 ♕c6 22 ♕g5 ♗h3 23 ♘e3 ♗xe3 24 ♗xe3 h6 25 ♕h5 g6 (or 25 ... ♖ad8 26 c4 and wins) 26 ♕e5 with ♕d6 to come, and White wins (analysis by Hübner).

(2) **17 ... ♘f6** 18 ♖e1 ♗g4 (18 ... ♗f5 19 d4 c5 20 ♘e3 is good for White) 19 f3 ♗f5 (19 ... ♗h3 20 ♗e3 ♗xf1 21 ♔xf1 doesn't help Black's attack) 20 d4 c5 (20 ... ♖ae8 21 ♗e3 ♘d5 22 ♗xd5 cd 23 ♕d2 ♗d3 24 ♖ad1 ♗c2 25 ♖c1 ♗d3 26 ♖cd1 ♗c2 27 ♖c1 ♗d3 28 ♗f4 ♗xf4 29 ♕xf4 ♗xf1 30 ♔xf1 ♕d3+ 31 ♔f2 h6 32 ♖cd1 gave White a clear extra pawn in Wedberg–Pinter, Haninge 1988, while 20 ... h5 21 ♗e3 h4 22 ♗f2 keeps the kingside intact) 21 dc ♗xc5+ 22 ♗e3 ♖ad8 23 ♕e2 with a small advantage for White according to Hübner.

(3) **17 ... h5** 18 a4 (18 ♘e3 ♘f6 is unclear, while 18 ♗c2 is met by ... f5 and ... f4) ♗g4 19 ♕e1 (19 f3 ♗f5) ♘f6 (not 19 ... ♗f3? 20 ab with a clear plus for White) 20 ♖e3 ♖ae8 21 ab ab 22 d4 h4 23 ♗d1 ♗f4 24 ♖xe8 ♖xe8 25 ♗e3 ♗h3 26 ♗f3 ♘d5 (26 ... hg 27 hg ♘d5 28 ♗g2 ♗xg2 29 ♔xg2 ♕e4+ 30 ♔g1 ♘xe3 31 fe ♗xe3+ 32 ♘xe3 ♕xe3+ 33 ♕xe3 ♖xe3 34 ♔f2 gives White an edge) 27 ♕d2 (27 ♗g2? ♗xg2 28 ♔xg2 ♕e4+ 29 ♔g1 h3 wins) ♗xe3 28 ♘xe3 ♘xe3 29 ♖e1 ♕f5

(29 ... ♖e6 30 ♖xe3 ♕b1+ 31 ♕d1 ♕xb2 is unclear) 30 ♗d1 ♕d5 31 fe ♖e6 32 e4 ♖xe4 33 ♖xe4 ♕xe4 34 ♕e2, Kuzmin–Sulman, USSR 1986, and now 34 ... ♕xe2 35 ♗xe2 hg 36 hg ♗d7 leads to a draw.

18 ♖d4

18 ♖e1? f4 19 c4 fg 20 fg ♗g4 wins for Black.

18 ... f4

After 18 ... ♔h8 (both 18 ... ♗e6 and 18 ... ♗b7 are met by 19 c4) 19 ♗xd5 cd 20 ♗f4 ♗c5 21 ♖xd5 ♕c6 22 ♖xc5 ♕xc5 23 d4 ♕e7 24 d5 ♕f6 (or 24 ... ♗b7 25 ♕d4 followed by ♘e3, b3 and c4 with a pawn roller) 25 h4 ♗b7 26 ♘e3 h6 (or 26 ... ♖ad8 27 ♕d3) 27 ♕h5 ♖ae8 28 ♖d1 White had a very pleasant position in Nijboer–van der Sterren, Wijk aan Zee II 1989, and won as follows: 28 ... ♖e4 29 d6 ♕e6 30 d7 ♖xe3 31 ♗xe3 ♕e4 32 ♔f1 ♖d8 33 ♖d8 33 ♖d4 ♕e6 34 ♕d1 ♗c6 35 ♖d6 ♕c4+ 36 ♔e1 ♕e4 37 ♕d4 ♕h1+ 38 ♔d2 ♗h7 39 ♔c2 a5 40 ♔b3 ♕f3 41 ♕f4 ♕xf4 42 gf ♗xd7 43 ♗b6 1–0.

19 ♖xd5 cd

20 ♗xd5+ ♗e6 21 ♗xa8 ♖xa8 22 ♕f3 (22 a4 ♗g4 23 ♕b3+ ♗e6 leaves White with nothing better than ♕d1) ♖f8 23 ♕e4 ♗f5 24 ♕d5+ ♔h8 25 a4, Timman–Hübner, Tilburg 1985, and now Hübner recommends

25 ... ♗xd3 26 ab ♗e4 27 ♕d4 fg 28 ♘xg3 (not 28 hg? ♕f5 29 ♗h6 ♗e5) ♗xg3 29 fg ab (29 ... ♕f5? 30 ♗h6) 30 ♗f4 h5 (30 ... h6? 31 ♗xh6) 31 ♕d6 with an ending which he assesses as a draw. Nevertheless Black is a pawn down, so he is on the worse side of the draw.

Perhaps 17 ... h5 is the most interesting move, but I have the impression that Black is struggling for equality. Since 17 ♖e1 also gives White better practical chances, the position after 15 ... ♕f5 must be judged slightly better for White. Black players who want more than an uphill fight for a draw should investigate earlier deviations, at move 13 or move 15.

C

| 12 | d3 | ♗d6 |
| 13 | ♖e1 | ♗f5! *(88)* |

Or 13 ... ♖a7 (13 ... ♕h4 14 g3 ♕h3 transposes to line B above) 14 ♘d2 (for 14 g3 see line

B, note to Black's 13th, variation 3) ♘f4 15 ♘e4 ♘xd3 16 ♗g5! ♗e7 (16 ... ♕d7? 17 ♖e3! wins) 17 ♗xe7 ♖xe7 18 ♖e3! (18 ♘f6+ is met by 18 ... ♔h8!) ♖d7 (18 ... ♘xb2? 19 ♘f6+ wins) 19 ♕h5!, threatening ♖f3, with a dangerous initiative for White, Popovic–Velimirovic, Bor 1985.

14 ♘d2

There are two alternatives:

(1) **14 ♗xd5** cd 15 ♘d2 (15 ♕f3 ♖e8 16 ♗d2 ♕d7 17 h3 ♗c7 18 ♘a3 ♕d6 19 g3 ♗xh3 was pleasant for Black in Zaitsev–Adorjan, Polanica Zdroj 1970) ♗xd3 and Black's two bishops compensate for the isolated pawn, for example 16 ♘f1 ♗g6 17 ♕d4 ♖c8 18 ♗e3 b4! 19 ♖ad1 bc 20 bc, Smyslov–Sokolsky, USSR Ch. 1949, and after 20 ... ♗b8 Black may even be slightly better.

(2) **14 ♕f3** ♖e8 (not 14 ... ♕d7 15 ♗xd5 cd 16 ♗f4 ♗xf4 17 ♕xf4 ♗xd3 18 ♘d2 ♖ae8 19 ♖e3 ♖xe3 20 ♕xe3, with a clear plus for White, Smagin–Geller, Moscow GMA Open 1989) 15 ♖xe8+ ♕xe8 16 ♗d2 (16 ♘d2 ♕e1+ 17 ♘f1 ♗g6 18 g3 ♖e8 19 ♗xd5 cd 20 ♕xd5 ♗c5! is very good for Black) ♕e5 (16 ... ♘f4!? may be playable) 17 g3 ♖e8 18 ♘a3 ♗xa3 19 ba ♗h3 20 d4 ♕e2 21 ♕xe2 ♖xe2 22 ♖e1 ♖xe1+ 23 ♗xe1 ♘b6 with a drawn ending.

14 ...   ♞f4

14 ... ♗xd3 15 ♞f3 ♗g6 16 ♗g5 ♕d7 17 ♞e5 ♗xe5 18 ♖xe5 ♖fe8 19 ♖xe8+ ♖xe8 20 ♕d2 h6 21 ♗f4 ♖d8 22 ♖d1 ♗f5 23 ♗g3 gives White an edge based on his two bishops and chances to break up Black's pawn structure by c4, Byrne–Angantysson, Reykjavik 1982.

15   ♞e4

15 d4 ♞xg2! is usually given, presumably based on the line 16 ♔xg2 ♕h4 17 ♞f1 ♕h3+ (17 ... ♗h3+ 18 ♔g1 ♗xf1 19 ♔xf1 ♕h3+ 20 ♔e2 is good for White) 18 ♔g1 ♗g4 followed by ... ♗f3.

Unfortunately 19 ♖e3! refutes the whole idea. Therefore Black should continue **15 ...** ♕g5 16 g3 (16 ♕f3? ♗g4 17 ♞e4 ♕h5) ♞h3+ 17 ♔g2 ♞f4+ 18 ♔h1 ♞d3 19 ♖e2 (19 ♞f3? ♕h5) ♖ae8 with good play for the pawn.

15 ...   ♞xd3

16 ♗g5 ♕d7 17 ♖e3 (17 ♞xd6 ♕xd6 18 ♗c2 ♕g6 19 ♗xd3 is a draw) ♗xe4 18 ♖xe4 ♖ae8 19 ♕g4 ♕xg4 20 ♖xg4 ♗e5 21 ♖b1 h5 22 ♖h4 ♞xb2! 23 ♗e3 (23 ♖xb2 ♗f4!) ♞d3 24 ♖d1 ♞b2 25 ♖b1 ♞d3 ½–½, Kir. Georgiev–Nunn, Dubai Ol. 1986.

13 Original Marshall: 11 ...♘f6

**1 e4 e5 2 ♘f3 ♘c6 3 ♗b5 a6 4
♗a4 ♘f6 5 0-0 ♗e7 6 ♖e1 b5 7
♗b3 0-0 8 c3 d5 9 ed ♘xd5 10
♘xe5 ♘xe5**
11 ♖xe5 ♘f6(89)
The original Marshall, rarely
played by GMs nowadays.

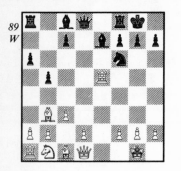

89
W

From the diagram:

A 12 ♖e1
B 12 d4!

(a) **12 h3 ♗d6** (12 ... c5!?) **13
♖e1!** transposes to A. Other retreats are bad: **13 ♖e2? ♘h5!** (13
... ♗b7!?) 14 d3 (14 d4? ♕h4 15
♕d3 ♗g4) 14 ... ♗b7 15 ♘a3

♕h4 16 d4 ♘f4! or **13 ♖e3?! ♗b7**
14 d4 ♘d5 15 ♖e1 ♕f6!

(b) Also unwise are **12 f3?** (12
♕e1? ♗d6 13 ♖e2 ♗xh2+ ∓ ∓
or 12 ♕f3? ♗g4 13 ♕c6 ♗d6 14
♖e1 ♖e8!) ♗d6 13 ♖e2 ♘g4 14
fg ♗xg4 15 ♕e1 ♗xe2 16 ♕xe2
♗xh2+ 17 ♔xh2 ♕h4+ 18 ♔g1
♖ae8 ∓ ∓ Gil–Medina, Barce-
lona 1942.

A

12 ♖e1 ♗d6
13 h3?!

Following Capablanca's original move order, which he used in
an attempt to get Marshall out of
his prepared analysis, but it is
better to transpose to B1 at once
by 13 d4!

13 ... ♘g4

(a) Shamkovich and Schiller
recommend **13 ... ♗f5!?** e.g. 14
d4 ♕d7 'intending ... ♗xh3
(possibly after ... ♖ae8)'.

(b) **13 ... ♗b7?!** 14 d4 ♕d7
(Tartakower) 15 ♗e3 ♕c6 16
f3 ± Golombek.

14 hg?!

Normally White transposes to B1 by 14 d4 or, as Capablanca in fact played, 14 ♕f3 ♕h4 15 d4! with the same result.

Others after 14 ♕f3 ♕h4 are bad: **15 d3?!** ♘xf2∓ or **15 ♖e4?** h5 (when 15 d4 is in B12) or **15 ♖e8?!** ♗b7! 16 ♖xf8+ ♖xf8 17 ♕xg4 ♖e8! 18 ♔f1 ♕e7 19 ♕d1 (19 ♗e6 ♗d5) 19 ... ♕e5 20 g3 ♕e4∓∓ Konstantinov.

14 ...   ♕h4
15 ♕f3

15 g3 ♗xg3 16 fg ♕xg3+ and ... ♗xg4∓∓.

15 ...   ♗h2+!

The refutation found by Shamkovich in the 1950s.

Not 15 ... ♕h2+ (nor 15 ... ♗xg4? 16 g3! ♕h5 17 ♕g2 ♖ae8 18 ♖e3!) 16 ♔f1 ♗xg4?! 17 ♕xg4 ♕h1+ 18 ♔e2 ♖ae8+ (Capablanca) 19 ♗e6!! ♖xe6+ 20 ♕xe6±± E.Palkin, 1954.

16 ♔f1   ♗xg4
17 ♕e4

If **17 ♖e4 ♗f4!** or **17 g3 ♕h5** or **17 ♕c6** ♗d6 18 g3 (18 f3 ♗g3 19 ♖e3 ♕h1+ 20 ♔e2 ♖ad8) ♗xg3 19 fg ♕xg3 20 ♗d5 ♖ad8 21 ♗g2 ♖d6 22 ♕e4 ♖f6+ 23 ♔g1 ♗f3∓∓ Shamkovich.

17 ...   ♗f4!
18 g3   ♕h2!∓∓

(a) **19 ♖e3 ♖ae8 20 ♕d5 ♗xg3!** or

(b) **19 ♗xf7+ ♔xf7! 20 ♕d5+** (20 ♕xf4+ ♔g8) ♔g6 21 ♖e6+

♗xe6 22 ♕xe6+ ♔h5 23 ♕d5+ ♗g5 24 ♕g2 ♖xf2+!∓∓ Shamkovich.

B

12 d4   ♗d6

12 ... ♘g4 13 ♖e1 ♕d6?! 14 g3 c5 15 ♗f4 ♕d7 16 h3 g5 17 ♕xg4±± Findlay–Crawley, British Ch. 1986.

After 12 ... ♗d6 White has:

B1 13 ♖e1
B2 13 ♖e2!

13 ♕f3?! ♗g4 14 ♕g3 ♗e6 15 ♗c2 (15 ♗h6 ♘h5) ♗xe5 16 de ♘h5 17 ♕f3 ♕h4 18 h3 f6 19 ♕c6 ♖ae8∓∓ Ahman–Barda, Gothenburg–Oslo radio match 1954.

B1

13 ♖e1   ♘g4

13 ... ♗b7 and **13 ... ♗f5** are both met by 14 ♗g5! while if **13 ... ♗xh2+ 14 ♔xh2 ♘g4+ 15 ♔g1 ♕h4 16 ♕f3±**.

14 h3!

14 g3?! has often been sloppily analysed in the past; the move is inferior, but does not lead to a forced mating attack for Black. The main possibilities are:

(a) **14 ... ♘xh2!?** is tempting but unconvincing:

(a1) **15 ♗d5** (15 ♔xh2? ♕h4+ 16 ♔g1 ♗xg3∓∓ or 15 ♖e4 ♗b7 16 d5 f5!∓) ♗xg3 (15 ... ♕f6! 16 ♗xa8 ♗g4 17 ♕d2 ♖xa8 Wade) 16 fg (16 ♗xa8 ♗g4

17 f3 ♕xa8 18 fg ♘f3+ ∓∓
ECO) ♕xd5 17 ♔xh2 ♗b7 18
♖g1 ♖ae8 19 c4! (19 ♗d2 ♖e6
20 ♘a3 ♖fe8 ∓∓ Pil–Pawlowski,
Poland 1972; 19 ♗f4 ♖e1! ∓∓
ECO) unclear (19 ... bc 20 ♘c3)
Wade.

(a2) **15 ♕h5!** ♘g4 16 ♗g5!
♘f6! 17 ♕h4 ♗f5 18 ♗xf6 ♕xf6
19 ♕xf6 gf 20 ♘d2 (S. Eriksson–
Roosvald, Stockholm 1967) ♖ae8
(Wade) when Black's two bishops
balance White's superior pawns.

(b) **14 ... ♕f6!?** 15 f4 (15 f3 or
15 ♖f1 ♘xh2!; 15 ♗e3 ♖e8 16
♕d2 ♘xh2!) ♕h6! with good
play for the pawn (Wade).

14 ...   ♕h4
(a) **14 ... ♘xf2!?** transposes to
B11 after **15 ♕f3! ♕h4.** Not **15
♔xf2?** ♕h4+ 16 ♔f1 ♗xh3 17
♗e3 ♗g4 18 ♕d3 ♖ae8 19 ♘d2
♗g3 ∓∓.

(b) **14 ... ♗h2+!?** 15 ♔f1
♘xf2!? is probably unsound but
worth another look: 16 ♕f3!
(White is in danger after 16 ♔xf2
♗b7—Pötzsch) 16 ... ♘h1 17
♗f4! (17 ♕xa8 ♕h4!) ♗b7 18 d5!
♗xf4 19 ♕xf4 g5 20 ♕f3
(material is level but the White
game is very solid and the need to
rescue the ♘ will force concessions) ♕d6 21 ♔g1 ♖ae8 22 ♘d2
♘g3 23 ♔f2 ♕f4 24 ♕xf4 gf 25
♔f3 (± endgame) ♔g7 26 c4 bc
27 ♗xc4 ♘f5 28 ♔xf4 ♘e7 29
♘f3 ♘xd5+ (now all the black

pawns are weaklings) 30 ♔g3
♘e3 31 ♗b3 ♖e7 32 ♔f2 ♖fe8
33 ♗a4 c6 34 ♘d4 ♔f8 35 ♗xc6
♗xc6 36 ♘xc6 ♖e4 37 ♖ac1
♖8e6 38 ♔g1 ♘c4 39 ♖xe4
♖xe4 40 ♖c2 ♘e5 41 ♘xe5
♖xe5 42 ♔f2 ♖a5 43 b3 ♔e7 44
♔e3 ♔d6 45 ♔d4 ♖f5 46 ♔e4
♖f1 47 ♔e3 f5 48 ♖c4 ♖e1+ 49
♔f3 a5 50 ♖a4 ♖e5 51 g3 ♖d5
52 ♔f4 ♔e6 53 ♖c4 ♖d2 54 ♖a4
♖d5 55 h4 h5 56 a3 1–0, Eslon–
Barczay, Kecskemet 1983.

15   ♕f3 *(90)*
(a) **15 hg?** ♕h2+ (15 ...
♗h2+!?) 16 ♔f1 ♕h1+! 17 ♔e2
♗xg4+ 18 ♔d3 ♕xg2 19 ♖g1
♗f5+ 20 ♔e2 ♖ae8+ 21 ♗e3
♖xe3+ ∓∓ Tal.

(b) **15 ♗e3?!** ♗h2+! 16 ♔f1
♗f4! 17 ♕d2 ♘xe3+ 18 fe ♗g3
19 ♖c1 (19 ♖e2? ♗g4; 19 ♖d1!?
Goransson) 19 ... ♗b7 20 ♘a3
♖ae8 Black plus (0–1, 41)
Tolush–Szabo,   Balatonfüred
1958.

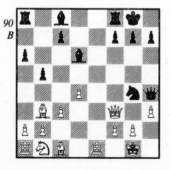

90
B

From the diagram:

B11   15 ... ♘xf2!?
B12   15 ... h5

15 ... ♗h2+ 16 ♔f1 ♗d6 (16
... ♗e6 17 ♗f4 ♗f5!? 18 ♗g3!±
Borodenko–Zhilin, RSFSR 1956)
17 ♗f4! ♗b7 18 d5 ♘f6 19 ♗e3!
♖ae8 20 ♘d2 ♗c8 21 ♗d4±
Palosevic and Vukcevich.

B11
15 ...   ♘xf2!?
This sacrifice is of great analytical as well as historical interest:

B111   16 ♖e2!
B112   16 ♗d2!?

Against other moves Black's attack grows very strong:

(a) 16 ♕xf2? ♗h2+! (Not 16
... ♗g3?? 17 ♕xf7+! ♖xf7 18
♖e8 mate) 17 ♔f1 ♗g3 18 ♕e2
(18 ♕xf7+?? ♖xf7+) ♗xh3! 19
gh (19 ♗g5 ♕xg5 20 gh ♖ae8!
0–1, Almeida–Biava, corr. 1985)
♖ae8!∓∓ Matanovic–Matulovic, Belgrade 1954.

(b) 16 ♗d5? ♘xh3+ 17 ♔f1
♗g4∓∓ Bajusz–S. Szilagyi, corr.
1968.

(c) 16 ♖e8? ♘xh3+ 17 gh
♗b7! 18 ♖xf8+ ♖xf8 19 d5 (19
♕xb7 ♕e1+ 20 ♔g2 ♖e8 or 19
♕e3 ♗f4! 20 ♕xf4 ♕e1+ ∓∓)
♕e1+ 20 ♕f1 ♗h2+ 21 ♔g2
♕g3+ 22 ♔h1 ♖e8 23 ♗d2? (23
♗f4 ♕xf4) ♖e2 24 ♗f4 (24 a4
♖f2) ♕d3!∓∓ Teodorescu–

Jurczynska,   Romania–Poland
1959.

B111
   16 ♖e2!
Capablanca's choice which
now seems vindicated. Although
ways have been suggested to
strengthen the Black attack,
nothing really challenges Capablanca's judgment that White's
position is defensible.

   16 ...   ♗g4
As played by Marshall.
Nothing better has been found
since in this position:

(a) 16 ... ♘g4?! is central to the
assessment of the variation:

(a1) *ECO* claims it equalizes,
following Tartakower's lines like
17 ♖e8 (17 ♗f4 ♗b7 18 ♕f1 ♘f6
19 ♗xd6 cd= or 17 ♕xa8?! ♕g3
with a dangerous attack) 17 ...
♘f6 19 ♗xd6 cd= or 17 ... ♘f6
18 ♖xf8+ ♔xf8 19 ♘d2 ♖b8 20
♘f1 ♗b7=.

(a2) But in fact it loses rapidly
to 17 g3!, the bonecrusher discovered by former US champion
John Grefe and published back in
1974! After 17 ... ♕xh3 (17 ...
♗xg3 18 ♕xf7+ ♖xf7 19 ♖e8
mate.) 18 ♕xa8 ♗xg3 19 ♕g2
White survives the attack with a
great material advantage: 19 ...
♗h2+ 20 ♔f1 ♕h5 21 ♘d2 1–0,
Winslow–Pustilnik, New York
Open 1986.

(b) Other tries are equally hopeless: **16 ... ♘xh3+?** 17 gh ♗xh3 18 ♖e4± ± or **16 ... ♗xh3?** 17 gh ♘xh3+ 18 ♔f1± ±.

17 hg!

'White could also play 17 ♕xf2 without losing, but it might give White an opportunity to draw' wrote Capablanca, presumably thinking of 17 ... ♗g3 18 hg! not 18 ♕f1 ♗xe2 19 ♕xe2 ♖ae8∓ Tartakower.

17 ...   ♗h2+

17 ... ♗g3!? (not 17 ... ♘xg4? 18 ♗f4) 18 ♖xf2 ♕h2+ 19 ♔f1 ♕h1+ transposes back to the text.

18 ♔f1   ♗g3

(a) Capablanca expected **18 ... ♘h1** after which he said (in *My Chess Career*) that White could defend in various ways, the best perhaps being 19 ♗e3 (e.g. 19 ... ♘g3+ 20 ♔e1 ♘xe2+ 21 ♔xe2 ♖ae8 22 ♘d2 ♕e7 23 ♖h1± ± (Golombek).

(b) He did not say what he intended against **18 ... ♘xg4**. After 19 ♕h3! (Panov's book on Capablanca gives 19 ♗f4 overlooking 19 ... ♗xf4 20 ♕xf4?? ♕h1 mate) 19 ... ♕f6+ 20 ♔e1 (20 ♕f3 ♕h4=) 20 ... h5 21 ♕xh5 ♗g3+ 22 ♔d2 Black has inadequate compensation for the piece.

'Throughout all these complications what saves White is the combined pressure of the ♕ and

♗ against Black's f-pawn, as well as the great defensive power of the ♕ at f3' wrote Capablanca.

19 ♖xf2

Capablanca's later suggestion 19 ♔e1 (hoping for 19 ... ♖ae8 20 ♕xf7+) is unclear after Golombek's 19 ... h6!

19 ...   ♕h1+
20 ♔e2   ♕xc1

Attempts to improve on Marshall's play have focused on this move. Instead Capablanca–Marshall, Manhattan Chess Club Masters 1918, went 20 ... ♗xf2 21 ♗d2! ♗h4 22 ♕h3 ♖ae8+ 23 ♔d3 ♕f1+ 24 ♔c2 ♗f2 25 ♕f3! ♕g1 (25 ... ♖e2 26 a4! ♕e1 27 ab) 26 ♗d5 c5 27 dc ♗xc5 28 b4 ♗d6 29 a4! a5 30 ab ab 31 ♖a6 bc 32 ♘xc3 ♗b4 33 b6 ♗xc3 34 ♗xc3 h6 35 b7 ♖e3 36 ♗xf7+! ♖xf7 37 b8(♕)+ ♔h7 38 ♖xh6+! 1–0.

21 ♕xg3!

After 21 ♗xf7+? ♔h8 22 ♖f1 ♕c2+ 23 ♘d2 ♖ae8+ 24 ♗xe8 ♖xe8+ 25 ♕e3 ♖xe3+ 26 ♔xe3 (Yates–O'Hanlon, British Ch. 1921) the Irish champion missed a great chance to win by 26 ... g5! (*BCM*) e.g. 27 ♖ad1 ♕xb2 28 ♘e4 ♗f4+ 29 ♔d3 ♕xg2 (or ♕xa2), or 27 ♖f8+ ♔g7 28 ♖af1 ♗f4+ 29 ♖8xf4+ gf+ 30 ♖xf4 ♕xb2.

21 ...   ♕xb2+
22 ♔d3!   ♕xa1

23 ♔c2   b4
24 g5!±

Black is at the end of his resources: 24 ... a5 25 g6 or 24 ... bc 25 ♕xc3 (Tartakower).

B112

16 ♗d2*(91)*

This move, first played by Ristic in 1947, is generally reckoned to be a safer refutation of Marshall's sacrifice, but there is still one chance for Black to muddy the waters:

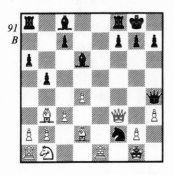

16 ...   ♗b7!

A necessary decoy sacrifice to regenerate the K-side attack during the temporary enforced absence of the white ♕ from its optimum square f3; this move also links rooks to answer the threat of ♕xf7+.

Others are certainly insufficient:

(a) **16 ... ♗d7?** 17 ♕xf2 ♗g3 (17 ... ♗h2+ 18 ♔f1 ♗g3 19 ♕f3±) 18 ♕f1 a5 19 ♘a3 ♖a6

20 ♖e3±± ♗xh3? 21 ♕xf7+! 1–0, Macles–Skembris, Paris 1983.

(b) **16 ... ♘g4?** (16 ... ♘xh3+? 17 gh ♗xh3 18 ♖e4±±) 17 ♖e8! (or 17 ♖e4 h5 18 ♗e1±) 17 ... ♘f6 18 ♖xf8+ ♗xf8 19 ♕xa8±± Diel–Oechslein, corr. 1963.

(c) **16 ... ♗xh3** (16 ... ♗g4? 17 ♕xf2 ♗h2+ 18 ♔f1 ♗g3 19 ♗g5±±) 17 gh ♘xh3+ 18 ♔f1 g5 (18 ... ♘g5 19 ♗xg5 ♕xg5 20 ♘a3± Gutman) 19 ♖e4 ♗f4 20 ♗xf4 ♘xf4 21 ♘d2 ♖ad8 22 ♖xf4! gf 23 ♘e4± Aronin–Demuria, Tbilisi 1957.

17 ♕xb7

Capturing the other piece definitely helps Black: 17 ♕xf2? ♗h2+! (17 ... ♗g3 18 ♕e2) 18 ♔f1 ♗g3 19 ♕g1 (19 ♕f5 g6 20 ♕g4 ♕f6+ or 19 ♕e2 ♖ae8 20 ♕xe8 ♕f6+ ∓∓) ♖ae8 20 ♖e3 ♖e6! 21 d5 (21 ♗xe6 fe+ 22 ♔e2 ♕h5+ 23 ♔d3 ♕g6+ 24 ♔e2 ♖f2+ 25 ♔d1 ♗xg2 26 ♖e1 ♕d3∓∓) ♖f6+ 22 ♖f3 ♖xf3+ 23 gf ♖e8 24 ♘a3 ♗c8 25 ♗e3 ♗f5 26 ♘c2 (26 ♖d1? ♕xh3+ 27 ♔e2 ♗f4 28 ♘c2 ♗xc2) ♗d3+ 27 ♔g2 ♗f4! (27 ... ♗f5 28 ♔f1 ♗d3+ =) 28 ♕f2? (28 ♗f2? ♖e2 with the idea 29 ♖e1 ♕g3+ 30 ♔f1 ♖xf2 mate; 28 ♗xf4!? ♖e2+ 29 ♔h1 ♕xh3+ 30 ♕h2 would struggle on) ♕g5+ 29 ♔h1 ♗xe3 30 ♘xe3 ♕xe3 31

Qxe3 Rxe3 32 Kg2 h5 (with a clearly superior endgame) 33 Kg3 g5 34 Bd1? Re1 0–1, Vukcevic–Minic, Yugoslav Ch. 197.

17 ... ♘d3

18 Re2

Others are bad, e.g. 18 Rf1? Qg3 19 Rxf7 Kh8∓∓ Lilienthal.

18 ... ♕g3!

Threatening mate in two. *ECO* only gives 18 ... Rae8? 19 Qf3 Rxe2 20 Qxe2 Qg3 (Lemoine–Prameshuber, Munich Ol. 1958) 21 Qf3! Qh2+ 22 Kf1 Qh1+ 23 Ke2 Nxb2 24 Be3±± Euwe.

19 ♔f1 ♘f4!

Not 19 ... Qh2 20 g4! (Vukovic, 1949) e.g. 20 ... Qxh3+ 21 Qg2 Qh4 22 Be3 (or 22 Qf3 Kh8 23 Bd5 f5 24 g5± Peiris–Dekar, Dubai Ol. 1986) Rae8 23 Nd2 Bf4 24 Nf3 Qh6 25 Bc2±± Rostov–Pensa, intercity telegraph match 1958.

20 ♖f2!

Others give Black chances:

(a) 20 Bxf4? Qxf4+! 21 Qf3 Qc1+ 22 Kf2 Bh2! when:

(a1) 23 Qe4 g6 24 Re1 Qxb2+ 25 Qc2 Qxa1 26 Rd1 (with the idea Nd2) b4 27 cb Be5! 28 Nc3 Bxd4+!= Titjen–Tistrup, corr. 1966.

(a) 23 Re1? Qxb2+∓∓ 24 Qe2 Qxa1 25 g3 c5 26 dc b4 27 cb Qd4+ 28 Kg2 Bxg3 29 Kxg3 Qxb4 30 Qe7 Ra7! 31 Re4

Qb8+ 32 Qe5 Rc7 33 Rg4 g6 34 Qg2 Re8 35 Qd6 Qb7+ 36 Kg3 Rd7 37 Qf6 Qc7+ 38 Rf4 Re4 39 Nc3? Rxf4 40 Qxf4 Rd3+ 0–1 Hansson–Westerinen, Esbjerg 1983.

(b) **20 ♕f3** (20 Re3!? Qh2 21 Qf3 Qh1+ 22 Kf2 Rae8 may be an impasse) Nxe2 21 Qxe2 (Westerinen's 21 Kxe2 Qg6! is also critical) Rae8 22 Qf3 Qh2 is unclear.

20 ... ♕h2

Most sources mention only 20 ... Qd3+ 21 Kg1 Ne2+ 22 Rxe2 Qxe2 23 Qf3 Qxf3 24 gf c5± (Wedberg, *Skakbladet*).

But after the text move (suggested by Pötzsch) Black also seems busted in view of **21 ♗xf4!** (21 g4? Qxh3+ = while others could even lose) Bxf4 22 g3! Qxh3+ (22 ... Qxg3 23 Qf3) 23 Qg2 Qxg3 24 Bxf7+ Kh8 25 Qxg3 Bxg3 26 Rf3±± (Nunn).

B12

15 ... h5!? *(92)*

This move, introduced by Shamkovich in 1956, leads (he now says) to a complicated position where White has rather better chances.

16 ♗e3!

(a) **16 ♗f4** Nxf2! 17 Bxd6 Nxh3+ 18 Kf1 Bg4! (18 ... cd? 19 Re4 Bg4 20 gh±±) 19 Bg3 Qg5 20 Re5! (20 Qe3? Qf4+ 21 Bf2 Rae8 22 Qd2 Rxe1+ 23

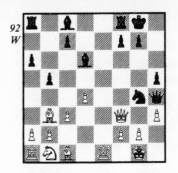

92
W

♚xe1   ♖e8+ ∓ ∓)   ♕c1+   21
♖e1 ♕g5= Shamkovich.

(b) **16 ♘d2** when:

(b1) **16 ... ♘xf2?!** (16 ... ♗b7?
17 ♘e4 ♖ae8 18 ♗g5!± ± Boleslavsky–Shamkovich, Harkov
1956) 17 ♕xf2! (17 ♖e2? ♗g4! 18
hg hg 19 ♕f5 g3! 20 ♖xf2 ♖ae8!
Poitner–Itin, corr. 1977) ♗g3 18
♕f1 ♗xe1 19 ♘f3!

(b2) **16 ... ♗h2+!** 17 ♚f1 (17
♚h1? ♘xf2+ 18 ♚xh2 ♘g4+)
♗d6 18 ♚g1= (18 hg? ♗xg4 19
g3 ♕h2 20 ♕c6 ♗xg3! ∓ ∓).

(c) **16 ♖e4 ♗b7** 17 ♖xg4 hg 18
♕xb7 ♖ae8 19 ♘d2 ♖e1+ 20
♘f1 gh ∓ ∓ Panov.

16 ...   ♘xe3

Relatively best. If 16 ... ♘h2!?
17 ♕xa8 ♗g4 (17 ... ♗xh3?! 18
♗xf7+!) 18 ♕e4! (18 ♕xf8+?
♚xf8 19 hg hg 20 ♘d2 f5! 21 g3
♗xg3 22 fg ♕xg3+ 23 ♚h1
♘f3 ∓ ∓ Suetin) ♘f3+ 19 gf
♕xh3 20 f4 ♗f3 21 ♕xf3 ♕xf3 22
♘d2 ♕g4+ 23 ♚f1 ♖e8! 24 ♗d5
h4? (24 ... ♕f5!? 25 ♗g2± Sue-

tin) 25 ♘f3 ♕h3+ 26 ♚g1! c6 27
♘g5 ♕g4+ 28 ♗g2± ± Suetin–
Witkowski, Byelorussia–Poland
1958.

17   ♖xe3   ♕f4
18   ♕xf4   ♗xf4
19 ♖e1! (19 ♖e7? ♗c1 Black
plus or 19 ♖e2 ♗f5=) 19 ... ♗f5
20 ♘a3± Shamkovich.

B2

13   ♖e2! *(93)*

White overprotects f2 to fore-
stall the typical tactical ideas of
the previous variations. 13 ♖e2 is
generally recommended as best to
give White a clear advantage
without having to defend a sacrificial attack on his king. Black must
seek different ways of building up
pressure; improvements may yet
be forthcoming because most of
the attention paid by analysts has
hitherto been given to the 13 ♖e1
lines.

93
W

From the diagram:

B21   13 ... ♗b7?!
B22   13 ... ♘h5

(a) **13 ... c5!?** might be considered (14 ♗e3 ♕c7).

(b) **13 ... ♘g4** 14 h3 ♕h4 15 ♘d2 (15 ♕d3 ♗b7 16 ♘d2± Korn–Winter, London 1949) ♗b7 (15 ... ♘h2 16 ♘e4± ±) 16 ♘f1 ♘f6 (16 ... ♖ae8 17 ♘e3 or 17 f3 Heemsoth) 17 a4 g5!?± Schmid–Pfeiffer, Travemunde 1951.

(c) **13 ... ♗g4** 14 f3 ♗f5 15 ♘d2 c5 16 ♘f1± Crombleholme–Radoicic, Southampton 1971.

B21

> **13 ... ♗b7?!**
> **14 ♘d2 ♕d7**
> **15 f3!**

With the idea of ♘e4. 15 ♘f1 may be good too: 15 ... ♕g4 16 ♘g3 ♕h4 17 ♕f1 ♗e4 (17 ... ♘e4!? Barden) 18 ♗c2 ♗xc2 (18 ... ♘g4 19 h3 ♘xf2 20 ♘f5!± ± *ECO*) 19 ♖xc2 c5 20 h3 ♖ad8 21 ♕d3± Kriukov–A. Zaitsev, corr. 1959.

> **15 ... ♖ae8**

Not 15 ... ♕f5?! 16 ♘f1± e.g. 16 ... ♕h5 17 ♗e3 ♘d5 (17 ... ♖ae8 18 ♕d2 ♘d5 19 ♗xd5 ♗xd5 20 b3± Konstantinopolsky–Russo, corr. 1953) 18 ♕d3 f5 19 a4 c6 20 ♗xd5 cd 21 ab ab 22 ♖xa8 ♖xa8 23 ♕xb5± ± Vasilchuk–Shishov, Moscow 1958.

> **16 ♘f1 c5!?**

16 ... ♘d5 17 ♗e3± (Hazai) looks relatively best; **16 ... ♘h5** 17 ♗e3 ♘f4 18 ♗xf4 ♗xf4 19 a4 b4 20 a5± Lein–Shakov, RSFSR 1959.

> **17 dc! ♗xc5+**
> **18 ♗e3 ♖xe3!?**

18 ... ♕e7 and **18 ... ♕c7** are both met by 19 ♗xc5 ♕xc5+ (19 ... ♕xe2 20 ♗xf8 ♔xf8 21 ♖b1±) 20 ♔h1 ♖xe2 21 ♕xe2 ♖e8 22 ♕d2± Hazai.

> **19 ♘xe3 ♕c6**

Pliester's suggestion after 19 ... ♕c7?! 20 ♔h1 ♘h5 21 ♘d5!± ± ♗xd5 22 ♗xd5 ♖d8 23 ♖d2 ♘g3+!? 24 hg ♕xg3 25 ♕e1 ♕g5 26 g3 ♖xd5 27 ♖xd5 ♕xd5 28 ♔g2 g6 29 ♖d1 ♕f5 30 ♖d8+ ♔g7 31 ♕e4 ♕f6 32 ♖d5 1–0, Hazai–Nikolac, Maribor 1985.

After 19 ... ♕c6 Nunn says:

(a) White has the safety-first line **20 ♔h1** ♘h5 21 ♗d5 ♘g3+ (21 ... ♕h6 22 ♘f5± ±) 22 hg ♕h6+ 23 ♔g1 ♗xe3+ 24 ♖xe3 ♕xe3+ 25 ♔f1 with a clear extra pawn.

(b) He may also try **20 ♕e1** to hang on to all the material and it is hard to prove anything for Black.

B22

> **13 ... ♘h5** *(94)*

94
W

From the diagram:

B221 14 ♕d3
B222 14 ♗e3!

(a) **14 ♖e4?** ♗f5 15 ♖e1 ♕h4 16 g3 (16 h3 ♗xh3 17 gh ♕xh3 18 ♗e3 ♖ae8 19 ♕d2 ♗h2+ 20 ♔h1 ♘f4 21 f3 ♗g3+ 22 ♔g1 ♗xe1 Fernandez) ♘xg3! 17 fg ♗xg3 18 ♖e2 (18 hg ♕xg3+ 19 ♔f1 [19 ♔h1 ♖ae8 20 ♗d2 ♖e4 etc] ♗h3+ 20 ♔e2 ♖ae8+ 21 ♔d2 ♕f4+ 22 ♔c2 ♗f5+ ∓∓) ♖ae8 (intending 19 ... ♗xh2+ 20 ♖xh2 ♖e1+) 19 ♗d2 (19 hg ♕xg3+ 20 ♔h1 ♗e4+ ∓∓ or 19 ♘d2 ♗g4 20 hg ♕xg3+ 21 ♖g2 ♕e3+ ∓∓ or 19 ♕f1 ♖xe2 20 ♕xe2 ♗xh2+ 21 ♕xh2 ♕e1+ 22 ♔g2 ♖e8∓∓) ♗h3 20 ♖xe8 ♗xh2+ 21 ♔h1 ♖xe8 22 ♕f3 ♗f4! 23 ♕xf4 ♖e1+ 24 ♗xe1 ♕xf4 25 ♘d2 ♕g5 0–1, Rosso–J. L. Fernandez, Buenos Aires 1987.

(b) **14 ♘d2** ♘f4 15 ♖e3 ♕g5!

and White should force a draw by 16 ♖g3! ♕e7 17 ♖e3! in view of 16 ♕f1?! (Hokhlovkin–Havsky, RSFSR Ch. 1956) 16 ... ♕h5! 17 ♘f3 (or 17 h3 ♗g4! 18 ♘e4 ♘e2+ 19 ♔h1 ♗f4) 17 ... ♗b7 18 h3 ♘xh3+ ∓∓ Shamkovich.

(c) **14 ♗d5?** (14 ♕f1 ♗f5!? or 14 ... ♗b7!?) ♗xh2+ 15 ♔xh2 ♕xd5 16 ♖e5 ♕d6∓ Saren–Westerinen, Helsinki 1965.

B221

14 ♕d3

Ravinsky's move, which is no longer thought the refutation of 11 ... ♘f6.

14 ... ♗g4

(a) **14 ... ♕h4?!** (14 ... ♗f4 15 ♕f3!) 15 g3 ♕h3 16 ♗d5! ♗f5 (16 ... ♗g4 17 ♖e3) 17 ♕e3!± Tal–Witkowski, Riga 1959.

(b) **14 ... ♕f6** (Sokolsky) 15 ♗d5 ♘f4! 16 ♗xf4 ♕xf4 17 g3 ♕c1+ 18 ♔g2 ♕h6!? 19 ♘d2 (19 ♗xa8?! ♗h3+) ♖b8 20 ♔g1± (but draw, 48) Gaprindashvili–Westerinen, Beverwijk 1966.

15 ♖e1

15 f3?! ♗d7 16 g4 ♘f4∓ (Statzenko–Sarsenbekov, corr. 1966).

15 ... ♖e8!

15 ... ♕f6? 16 ♗c2 g6 17 ♘d2 ♖ae8 18 ♘e4 ♕g7 19 ♗g5± Ravinsky–Neistadt, Moscow Ch. 1957.

16 ♖xe8+ ♕xe8
17 ♗e3

17 ♕e3?! ♕c6 18 f3 ♗f4 19 ♕e1 ♖e8 (threatening ... ♗c1 and ... ♗f3) Tal.

17	...	♘f4
18	♗xf4	♗xf4
19	♘d2	c5

(1) **20 ♗c2** f5 21 ♘f3 c4 22 ♕d1 ♕h5 23 h3 ♖d8= Gutman.

(b) **20 dc!?** and if 20 ... ♖d8 21 ♕e4± or 20 ... ♗e2 21 ♗xf7+!±± Pliester.

B222

14   ♗e3!

This is now the critical line of the 12 ♖e2 variation.

14   ...   ♗b7

Or 14 ... ♔h8 (Euwe) 15 ♘d2 f5 (15 ... ♗b7 below) 16 ♖e1! ♘f6 (16 ... ♕h4 17 ♘f3) 17 f3 f4 18 ♗f2± Hazai.

15   ♘d2   ♔h8

15 ... ♕h4!? 16 ♘f1 ♖ae8 17 f3 ♕f6 18 ♕d3 ♗f4 19 ♖ae1± Krupanszki–Freyer, corr. 1966.

16   ♖e1!

(a) **16 ♘f1?** f5 17 f3 f4 18 ♗f2 ♕g5 19 ♘d2 (19 ♖e1 ♘g3!? unclear—Hazai) ♘g3 20 hg!? fg 21 ♗e3 ♕h5 22 ♔f1 ♗f4 23 ♗g1 unclear (Shagalovich–Luik, Minsk 1957).

(b) **16 d5** ♘f6 (16 ... f5 17 ♘f3 f4 18 ♗d4± Shamkovich) 17 c4 bc 18 ♘xc4 ♗xd5 (18 ... ♘xd5?! 19 ♘d6 ♕xd6 20 ♖d2 intending ♖c1± *ECO*) 19 ♘d6 ♕xd6 (Shamkovich) 20 ♖d2 c6 21 ♖c1± Hazai.

16   ...   ♕h4

17   ♘f1

Safest. If 17 h3?! ♘f4 18 ♘f3 ♘xh3+! (18 ... ♕h5 19 ♗xf4 ♗xf3 20 ♕d2! ♕g6 21 g3 ♕h5 22 ♔h2± Kuijpers–Erny, Basle 1959) 19 gh ♕xh3 20 d5 ♖ae8 21 ♗c2 ♗c8 or 21 ... f5 with strong mating threats.

17   ...   f5

17 ... ♖ae8 18 f3 with the idea of ♗f2± Hazai.

18   f3   f4

19 ♗f2 ♘g3 20 ♕d3 ♕g5 21 ♗e6± Hazai.

Conclusion

Although, here and there, new ideas for Black may salvage some particular sub-variations, the likelihood of sufficient critical improvements being found to justify 11 ... ♘f6 is small.

14 Move 11 Alternatives

1 e4 e5 2 ♘f3 ♘c6 3 ♗b5 a6 4 ♗a4 ♘f6 5 0-0 ♗e7 6 ♖e1 b5 7 ♗b3 0-0 8 c3 d5 9 ed ♘xd5 10 ♘xe5 ♘xe5

11 ♖xe5

Apart from 11 ... c6 and 11 ... ♘f6 Black has tried three other moves, which reappear from time to time although they have never been considered much more than surprise weapons.

These are:

A 11 ... ♘b6
B 11 ... ♘f4
C 11 ... ♗b4

A

11 ... ♘b6 *(95)*

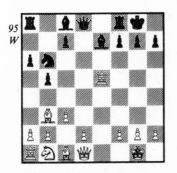

95
W

First seen in the 1960s, this is a positional treatment of the Marshall, designed to consolidate Black's grip on the queenside and so nullify White's material advantage. However, it has never been popular—probably because most people who play the Marshall do so with a strong desire to have a go at the white king! There has only been one recent high-level game in the variation:

12 d4

12 ♕h5 has also been seen but it gives no advantage after 12 ... ♘d7!? (12 ... ♗d6 13 ♖e3 ♗b7 14 ♖h3 h6 also seems good; if 15 ♕g6 ♘d5! or 15 d4 ♕f6) 13 ♖e1 ♘f6 14 ♕e2 ♗d6 which is a version of the 11 ... ♘f6 Marshall in which White has played the pointless ♕e2 instead of h3 or d4, e.g. 15 h3 (15 d4 ♖e8) c5! 16 d4 cd 17 cd ♗c7! with good chances for Black (Kerje–Sjöqvist, Swedish Ch. 1959).

12 ... ♗d6
13 ♗g5!

Also critical is 13 ♖h5!? (13

♖e1 ♕h4 14 g3 ♕h3 gives Black compensation) g6!? (13 ... h6 14 ♕f3) 14 ♗g5 ♕d7 15 ♖h4 ♗b7 16 ♘d2 ♕f5 17 ♗h6 ♖fe8 18 ♘f1 ± Tal.

13 ... ♕d7
14 ♖e1 ♗b7
15 ♘d2 ♖fe8

Formerly 15 ... ♖ae8 was played here, but this seems less in accord with the knight on b6, although in some variations it may not matter which rook goes first to e8. White has continued:

(a) **16 ♗h4** ♖xe1+ 17 ♕xe1 ♖e8 18 ♕d1 (Sokolsky's 18 ♕f1 might be met by 18 ... ♗f4 19 ♖d1 ♕g4 20 ♗g3 h5!?—unclear) 18 ... ♘d5 19 ♗g3 ♘f4 20 ♗xf4 ♗xf4 21 ♘f1 ± (Bertok–Stein, Stockholm 1962).

(b) **16 f3** ♕f5 17 ♗h4 c5 18 ♘f1 cd 19 cd ♘d5 20 ♗g3 ♘f4 = Nedeljkovic–Geller, Yugoslavia– USSR 1957.

(c) **16 ♕h5** ♕f5 17 ♘f1 ♘d5 (17... h6? 18 ♖xe8 ♖xe8 19 ♘e3 ♖xe3 20 fe± ±) 18 ♕h4 c5 with compensation for Black—Gutman.

(d) **16 ♗e3** ♘d5 17 ♘f1 ♖e6 18 a4 ♖g6 19 ♘g3 ♕c6 20 ab ab 21 ♕f3 ♖d8 22 ♗d2 ♗f8 23 ♖e5 ♖e6 24 ♖xd5 ♖xd5 25 ♖a7± Rozenshtein–Stapulis, USSR 1981.

16 f3!?

16 ♗h4± should probably transpose into note (a) above. The text move is designed to blunt the black bishop's long diagonal and give the white queen access to good squares after the rook exchange.

16 ... ♖xe1 +

Since this plays into White's hands, the critical move must be 16 ... ♕f5 as in note b above, hoping to demonstrate a drawback to the f3 move.

17 ♕xe1 a5
18 ♘e4 a4
19 ♗c2 ♗d5

Nunn–Nemet, Geneva 1987. Now 20 ♕h4! would have been very strong.

B

11 ... ♘f4

This is the Balogh Variation, named after the Hungarian postal chess master J. Balogh, although he was probably not the first to play it. Black signals a fairly crude intention to attack g2 with the ♘ in conjunction with the ♗b7. However, although it had some practical successes, the variation is rightly considered dubious.

12 d4!

This avoids the trap 12 ♕f3? ♗d6 13 ♕xf4 ♗xe5 14 ♕xe5 ♖e8∓∓.

12 ... ♘g6(96)
13 ♖h5!

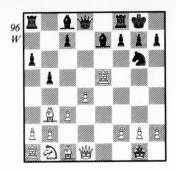

White cuts across Black's plans by fighting for the initiative on the kingside.

Black gets practical chances after 13 ♖e1 (13 ♖e2!? ♗d6 14 ♕f1! ♗b7 15 ♗e3 ♘h4 unclear) ♗b7 (13 ... ♗d6? 14 ♘d2 ♗b7 15 ♘f3 ♕f6 16 d5 h6 17 ♕d4± Vitomskis–Rapoport, Latvia 1968) 14 ♘d2 (14 ♗e3 ♗d6 15 ♘d2 ♔h8 and ... f5 Botterill) c5 (14 ... ♘h4? 15 g3!±) 15 ♘f3 c4 (15 ... ♗xf3? 16 ♕xf3 cd 17 cd ♕xd4 18 ♗xf7+ ♔h8 19 ♗e3 ♕xb2 20 ♕e4± Euwe) 16 ♗c2 f5 17 ♘e5 (17 b3?! ♗d6 18 ♘e5 ♕c7 19 f4 ♗xe5∓ —Gutman) ♕d5 18 f3 ♘xe5 when:

(a) **19 de** ♗c5+ 20 ♔h1 (Filipcic–Hribousek, corr. 1966–67) f4! 21 b3 (21 b4?! ♗e7 22 ♕e2 ♕e6 23 ♗e4 ♗xe4 24 ♕xe4 g5 25 a4 ♖ad8 26 ab ab 27 ♖a5 ♖d3 28 ♖xb5 ♖fd8∓ —Gutman) ♕xd1 22 ♖xd1 ♗c6 and Black has suf-

ficient compensation for his pawn—Tal.

(b) **19 ♖xe5** ♕d7! 20 ♗f4 ♗d6 21 ♗xf5 ♕d8 22 ♕e1 (22 ♗e6+ unclear—Tal) ♔h8! (Balogh) and Black is not worse in the complications.

13	...	♗b7
14	♕d3!	

14 ♕g4 is also strong, e.g. 14 ... ♖e8 (14 ... ♗c8 15 ♕e4±) 15 ♗e3 ♘f8 (15 ... c5!? 16 ♘d2! ♗f6 17 ♘f3± Gutman) 16 ♘d2 ♗f6 when:

(a) **17 a4** ♕d7 18 ♕xd7 (18 ♕g3!? Samarian) ♘xd7 19 ab ab 20 ♖d1 c6 21 ♘f3 and *ECO*'s± assessment was not so clear after 21 ... ♖e7 22 ♔f1 (Suta–Dalko, corr. 1969–70);

(b) **17 ♕g3!?** (intending ♗f4 or ♖c5) 17 ... g6 18 ♖c5 ♖e7 19 ♗f4± or 19 ♗g5± Shamkovich and Schiller.

14	...	♖e8

Black sets a trap: 15 ♖xh7? ♗g5!∓∓.

15	♗e3	c5
16	♕f5	c4
17	♗c2	♕c7
18	♘d2!	

18 ♖xh7 fails to 18 ... ♔xh7 (18 ... ♗a3!? Maric) 19 ♕xf7 ♕c6!

18	...	♖ad8
19	♕h3	h6
20	♗xg6!	

This appears to be the complete refutation of the Balogh variation. Black was following Kurtes–Balogh, Hungary 1966, which continued 20 ♗xh6? gh 21 ♗xg6 fg 22 ♖xh6 ♗f6 23 ♖xg6+ ♗g7 24 ♘f3 ♕f7 Black having a strong initiative.

20	...	fg
21	♕e6+	♔h7
22	♖xh6+	gh
23	♕f7+	♔h8
24	d5±±	

24 ... ♗d6 25 ♗d4+ ♖e5 (25 ... ♗e5 26 ♕xc7) 26 ♕xg6 ♗xd5 27 ♖e1 ♗f7 28 ♕xh6+ ♔g8 29 ♖e3 1–0, Kuhnert–Holzvoigt, corr. 1983.

C

| 11 | ... | ♗b7*(97)* |

This move was mentioned by Frank Marshall as one he had tried, but unfortunately he published no continuation and most examples stem from the period when it was rediscovered by Soviet players in the 1970s. Black's development is rapid and there is no clear-cut refutation as yet.

Nevertheless 11 ... ♗b7 has a serious drawback: Black can be forced to block the apparently powerful bishop's diagonal.

White has tried:

C1 12 ♕f3!
C2 12 d4

12 d3 ♕d7: see Chapter 15, line C1.

C1

| 12 | ♕f3! |

This move is very awkward to meet; any danger to White's queen is only apparent.

| 12 | ... | ♗d6 |
| 13 | ♗xd5! |

After 13 ♖xd5 ♖e8! all the complications favour Black: 14 ♕xf7+?! (or 14 ♔f1 ♕e7 15 ♕d1 ♕h4 16 ♖h5 ♕e4 Bajusz–Akos, corr. 1968) ♔xf7 15 ♖xd6+ ♔f8 16 ♖xd8 ♖xd8 17 ♔f1 ♗e4∓∓ Tal.

| 13 | ... | c6 |
| 14 | ♖e2 | |

White concentrates on establishing a sound position with his extra pawn, although victory is still a long way off.

14 ♖e1 usually transposes to the note at move 17, while 14 ♖h5!? cd 15 d4 (Kudryashov–Butnorius, Rostov 1976) looks more risky.

14	...	cd
15	d4	♕c7
16	g3	♖ae8

The minority attack might be accelerated with 16 ... b4!? (17 ♘d2 a5).

17 ♘d2!

Although 17 ♖xe8 ♖xe8 18 ♗e3 'seems to favour White' in the opinion of Shamkovich and Schiller, after 18 ... b4 victory has eluded White on all three occasions that we are aware of:

(a) **19 a3** a5 20 ab ab 21 cb ♕c2 22 ♘d2 ♗xb4 23 ♖a7 ♕c6 24 ♕d1 ♕b6 25 ♖a1 ♖a8 26 ♖xa8+ ♗xa8 27 ♘f3 ♗d6 28 ♕c2 ♗b7 29 ♕f5 (29 ♘g5 g6 30 ♔g2 ♕b5 31 ♘f3 ♗a6 draw in Tomizawa–Petterson, corr. 1979) h6 30 ♘e1± (½–½, 49) Tukmakov–Tseitlin, USSR Armed Forces Teams Ch. 1973).

(b) **19 cb** ♕c2 20 ♘d2 ♗xb4 21 ♕d1 ♖c8 22 ♘f3 f6 23 a3 ♗d6 24 ♖c1 ♕xd1+ 25 ♖xd1 a5 26 ♖c1 ♔f7 27 ♖xc8 ♗xc8 28 ♘d2 g5 29 f3 ♗a6 (Black's superior minor pieces balance the pawn minus) 30 ♘b1 ♔e6 31 ♔f2 h5 32 ♗d2 ♗d3 33 ♘c3 h4 34 f4 ♗e7 35 g4 ♗c4 36 ♘e2 a4 37 ♘g1 f5 38 gf+ ♔xf5 39 fg ♗xg5 40 ♗xg5 ♔xg5 41 ♔f3 ♗f1 42 ♔f2 ♗c4 43 ♘f3+ ♔g4 44 ♔e3 ♗b3 45 ♘g1 ½–½ (A. Sokolov–Ermolinsky, Vilnius 1984).

17 ... b4

Although the minority attack seems appropriate, White may have found the answer to it. The East German master Pötzsch has suggested 17 ... f5!? instead.

18	cb	♕c2
19	♖e3	♗xb4
20	♘f1	

A critical position for the variation:

(a) After **20 ... ♖xe3?!** 21 ♘xe3 ♕d3 22 ♕d1 ♕e4 23 f3± White consolidated his material advantage: 23 ... ♕e6 24 ♕b3 ♖c8 25 ♔f2 ♕b6 26 ♗d2 a5 27 ♗xb4! ab 28 ♖d1 ♕h6 29 h4 ♖e8 30 ♘g2 ♗a6?! (30 ... ♕d6 31 ♖e1!) 31 ♕xb4 ♖e2+ 32 ♔g1 g5 33 ♖e1 1–0, A. Sokolov–Haritonov, Vilnius 1984.

(b) **20 ... ♖e4!?** 21 a3! (21 ♖b3 a5∓ not now 22 a3?! ♗a6 23 ab ♗e2! 24 ♕c3 ♕d1∓∓ Haritonov) 21 ... ♗e1 (22 ... ♗d6 22 ♖c3 ♕e2 23 ♕xe2 ♖xe2 24 ♗d2 [threat ♖e3] 24 ... ♖fe8 25 ♖ac1 intending ♖3c2, ♗e2±) 22 ♖xe4 de 23 ♘e3!± Nunn.

C2

12 d4

This move gives Black a much

freer hand in his search for compensation.

12 ... ♕d7*(98)*

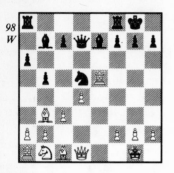

Also interesting is 12 ... ♗f6 (12 ... ♘f6!? M. Levy–Greenfeld, Thessaloniki Ol. 1984) 13 ♖e1 ♖e8 e.g. 14 ♘d2 (14 ♘a3 b4! 15 ♘c4 bc 16 ♘e5 ♕d6 = Mukhin–Romanishin, Vilnius 1971) b4 15 c4! ♘f4 16 d5 ♘d3 17 ♖xe8 + ♕xe8 18 ♗c2 ♘xb2?! 19 ♗xb2 ♗xb2 20 ♖b1 ♗c3 21 ♘e4 ♕e5 22 ♕d3 ♖e8 23 ♘xc3 bc 24 f4 ♕e2 25 ♕xh7 + ♔f8 26 h3 ♖e3 27 ♕h8 + ♔e7 28 ♕h4 + f6 29 ♖xb7 ♕xc2 30 ♖xc7 + ♔d6 31 ♖c6 + ♔e7 32 ♕g4 ♔f8 33 ♖c7 g5 34 fg ♖e1 + 35 ♔h2 ♕f2 36 ♖c8 + ♔e7 37 d6 + ♔xd6 38 ♖d8 + ♔c5 39 ♕c8 + ♔b4 40 ♕b7 + 1–0, de Firmian–Crawley, Lugano 1989.

From d7 the queen is ready to go to a variety of squares as required and in the meantime the rooks are linked. No reply has yet become established as best.

13 ♘d2!?

This leads to great complications. Others:

(a) **13 a4** ♗f6 14 ♖e1 b4 15 c4 ♘e7 16 d5 c6 17 d6 ♘f5 gave balanced chances in Ciocaltea–Tseitlin, Kragujevac 1974.

(b) Black has little to fear from **13 ♕h5** ♘f6 14 ♕f5 ♕xf5 15 ♖xf5 ♗e4! (Gardner–Harding, corr. 1975) or **13 ♕f3** (a move too late) ♖ad8 14 ♘d2 c5! 15 ♕f5 (15 dc ♗f6 16 ♖e1 ♘xc3 ∓ ∓ Tal and Gutman) ♕xf5 (15 ... ♗f6 16 ♕xd7 ♖xd7 17 ♖e1 cd 18 ♘e4! = Peiris–Sarfati, Dubai Ol. 1986) 16 ♖xf5 cd 17 cd ♗f6 18 ♘d2 ♘b4 while 13 g3? ♗f6 14 ♖e1 ♖ae8 15 ♘d2 ♘f4! ∓ ∓ is more Tal and Gutman analysis.

(c) However, **13 ♗xd5!?** ♗xd5 could prove the most troublesome to Black, in view of Dvoiris' suggested improvements on the following game: 14 ♗f4 (14 ♘d2!? ♗b7 15 f3) ♗b7 15 ♖e1 c5 16 dc (16 ♘d2 cd 17 ♘b3 ♕d5 18 f3 ±) ♕c6 17 ♕g4 ♗c5 18 ♘d2 ♖ae8 19 ♘b3? (19 ♘f3 ♖xe1 + 20 ♖xe1 ♖e8 21 ♗e5 f6 22 ♗d4 ±) ♖xe1 + 20 ♖xe1 ♖e8 21 ♖xe8 + ♕xe8 22 ♗d2 h5! with a strong initiative for the pawn(s) in Dvoiris–Ermolinsky, Vilnius 1984.

13 ... ♘f4

This attack on g2 is the culmination of Black's opening strategy but even so it may be insufficient. After other moves Black's compensation is nebulous, e.g. 13 ... c5?! (Not 13 ... ♗d6?? 14 ♖xd5 ♗xd5 15 ♗xd5 ♗xh2+ 16 ♔xh2 ♕xd5 17 ♘f1± ± de Firmian–Hebden, London 1986) 14 ♘f3 cd 15 cd ♗f6 16 ♖e1 ♖fe8 17 ♖xe8+ ♖xe8 18 ♗d2 ♕d6 19 h3 ♘f4 20 ♘e5!± ♗xe5 21 de ♕c6 (21 ... ♕xe5? 22 ♗xf4 ♕xf4 23 ♕d7± ±) 22 ♕g4 ♘d3 23 e6 f5 (23 ... fe? 24 ♗c3 ♖e7 25 ♗f6) 24 ♕g3 f4 25 ♕g5 h6 26 ♕g6 ♘e5 27 e7+ ♘c4 28 ♕xc6 ♗xc6 29 ♗b4 a5 30 ♗c5 a4 31 ♗xc4 bc 32 ♖d1 g5 33 ♖d6 ♗e4 34 f3 ♗b1 35 ♖xh6 ♔f7 36 a3 ♗g6 37 h4 ♔f6 38 h5 1–0, Klovan–Mark Tseitlin, USSR Armed Forces Teams Ch., Novosibirsk 1986.

14 ♘e4!

A major improvement on 14 ♘f3 ♘xg2! 15 ♖xe7 ♕xe7 16 ♔xg2 ♖ad8 17 d5 ♕e4 18 ♕d4 ♕g6+ 19 ♔f1 ♕h5∓ Tukmakov–Tseitlin, Odessa 1972.

14 ... ♗d6

Black tries to exploit White's uneasily-placed rook. Instead 14

... ♘xg2? would now be met by 15 ♔xg2 ♗f6 16 f3 ♗xe5 17 de ♕f5 18 ♗e3± (Dvoiris) while if 14 ... ♘g6 15 ♘c5 ♗xc5 16 ♖xc5 ♘h4 17 ♖g5 (S. Djuric).

15 ♘xd6 cd
16 ♖g5 ♘g6
17 ♗e3

17 d5!? (Djuric) would cope with the immediate threats but Black might be able to besiege the d-pawn.

17 ... ♖ae8
18 a4 ♗e4
19 ab ab

(a) 20 ♗c2? d5 21 ♗xe4 ♖xe4 22 ♕c2 f5 23 g3 ♕e6 24 ♖e1 ♘e7 25 ♕d1 g6 26 ♕d2 ♕f6 27 f3 ♖e6 28 g4 h6 29 gf ♘xf5 30 ♖xf5 ♕xf5 31 ♗xh6 ♖xe1+ 32 ♕xe1 ♖f7 33 f4 ♕g4+ 34 ♔h1 ♖a7 35 ♗g5 ♔f7 36 ♕f1 ♖a2 37 ♕b1 ♕e2! 0–1, Henao–Djuric, St John Open 1988.

(b) 20 d5 f5 21 ♖a7 (21 f3? ♗c2) ♕d8 22 ♗d4 is critical. In Djuric's line 22 ... ♖e7 23 ♖xe7 ♕xe7 24 ♖xg6 hg 25 f3 ♗xf3 Black may have just enough tactical chances to draw; he gives 26 gf (26 ♕xf3 ♕e1+ 27 ♕f1 ♕d2) ♕g5+ 27 ♔h1 ♕h4 28 ♕e2 ♖a8 unclear.

15 Marshall: Minor Lines

1 e4 e5 2 ♘f3 ♘c6 3 ♗b5 a6 4 ♗a4 ♘f6 5 0-0 ♗e7 6 ♖e1 b5

In this chapter we look at various rare or irregular lines which arise prior to move 11 and which do not fit neatly into other chapters. Some of these lines are trivial or just bad, but there are a few which any Marshall player needs to know, or which White can consider adopting to avoid main lines.

7 ♗b3 0–0

Two lines analogous to the Marshall are worth a mention:

The Trajkovic Variation 7 ... ♗b7!? still appears on the board occasionally and is not completely solved. White can meet it by:

(a) **8 c3** d5 9 ed ♘xd5 10 ♘xe5 ♘xe5 11 ♖xe5 ♘f4 with great complications, the main line being 12 d4 (12 ♖f5!? ♕d6 13 ♕g4 ♘xg2 14 ♖xf7! unclear—Nunn) ♘xg2 13 ♕e2 h6 14 ♕h5 g6 15 ♕h3 ♕d6! (15 ... ♕c8 16 ♕g3± Trajkovic) 16 ♘d2 (16 ♗g5 ♕xe5! 17 de ♗xg5 with compen-

sation) ♘h4 (16 ... ♘f4 17 ♕e3 ♘d5 18 ♗xd5 ♗xd5 19 ♘e4±) 17 ♘e4 ♕xe5! 18 de ♗xe4 19 ♗d1 g5 20 ♗e3 g4! (20 ... ♖d8 21 f3 ♗d5 22 ♗e2 ♖g8! 23 ♖d1 ♖g6 24 b3± Polovodin–Genin, USSR 1981) 21 ♕g4! (21 ♗xg4 ♖g8 or 21 ♕g3 0–0–0 22 ♕xg4+ ♗f5∓) ♗f5 22 ♕g7! 0–0–0 23 ♕xf7 ♖hg8+ 24 ♔f1 (24 ♔h1 ♖xd1+!) ♗h3+ 25 ♔e2 (Fershter–Faas, Tolush Mem. 1978) ♗g4+ 26 ♔f1 ♗h3+=.

(b) **8 d4** ♘xd4!? 9 ♘xd4 ed 10 e5 ♘d5 (10 ... ♘e4 11 ♕g4 c5 12 ♕xg7 ♖f8 13 ♕xh7 c4 14 ♖xe4 cb [Trajkovic] 15 ab! ♗xe4 16 ♕xe4± Kindermann) 11 ♕f3!? (11 ♕g4 ♔f8 12 ♗xd5 ♗xd5 13 ♕xd4 ♗c6 14 ♘c3 d6 15 ♗f4± Kindermann) 11 ... c6 12 ♕g4 ♕b6!? 13 ♕xg7 0–0–0 14 ♕h6!± (1–0, 31) Kindermann–Yilmaz, Dubai Ol. 1986.

In Oll–Kupreichik, Kuibyshev 1986, Black tried a deferred Marshall, 7 ... d6 8 c3 0–0 9 h3 d5?! White declined the challenge by

10 d4 (compare line B below), but after 10 ed! the move h3 is more likely to be a help than a hindrance to White, especially if he plays the Kevitz Variation.

8 c3 d5*(99)*

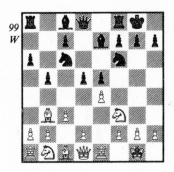

99
W

Now we discuss White divergences at move nine or ten from the Marshall accepted. Some of these unusual lines have been played quite a few times recently; this applies particularly to 10 a4. But the general impression is that Black has nothing to fear.

From the diagram:

A 9 d3
B 9 d4
C 9 exd5

9 a4 will lead to C3 below after 9 ... ♗b7 (or 9 ... b4, compare Chapter 18, B) 10 ed ♘xd5.

A

9 d3 de

This is a reliable answer to White's somewhat cowardly 9th move, although it tends to be drawish. 9 ... ♗g4?! is too risky after 10 h3 ♗h5 11 ♘bd2 (11 g4 ♗g6 12 ed ♘xd5 13 ♘xe5 ♘xe5 14 ♖xe5 ♘f6 15 ♗g5 h6 16 ♗h4 ♗d6 17 ♖e3 ♗f4! ∓) d4 12 g4! dc 13 bc ♗g6 14 ♘f1 ± Gutman.

10 de ♕xd1
11 ♗xd1

This avoids the simplifications of 11 ♖xd1!? ♖d8 (or 11 ... ♘xe4 12 ♖e1 =) 12 ♗c2 h6 13 ♘bd2 ♗e6 14 ♘f1 ♘d7 15 ♗e3 ♗c5 16 b4 ♗xe3 17 ♘xe3 ♘b6 = Boleslavsky–Lilienthal, USSR Ch. 1947.

11 ... ♗b7!?

This is the only move with recent master tests. 'Theory' is 11 ... ♘d7 12 ♗e3 ♘a5 13 ♘bd2 c5 ± Foguelman–Schweber, Villa Crespo 1959.

12 ♘bd2 ♘d7

12 ... ♖fd8 13 ♗b3 ♗c5 14 ♘f1 ♗b6 15 ♗g5 ♖d6 16 ♗xf6 ♖xf6 17 ♗d5 ♖e8 18 a4 ♗c8 19 ab ab 20 ♖a8 ♘e7 21 ♘e3 ± Hulak–Ivkov, Budva 1981.

13 ♘b3 a5
14 ♗e3 a4

15 ♘bd2 ♖fb8 16 a3 ♗c8 17 ♗c2 ♘c5 18 ♖ad1 f6 19 ♘f1 ♗e6 20 ♘h4 ♘a5 21 ♘f5 ♗f8 22 ♘5g3 c6 = (0–1, 59) Damljanovic–Franzen, Trnava 1982.

B

9 d4*(100)*

This sharp method of declining

the Marshall must be treated with respect, but it should give Black a good type of Open Spanish since he is not required to play... ♗e6.

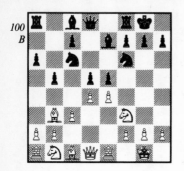

100
B

9 ... ed!

(a) **9 ... ♘xe4** is playable but an unlikely option for a Marshall player to select: 10 ♘xe5 (10 de is a direct transposition to the Open Spanish: see *ECO* C83) ♘xe5 11 de ♗b7 12 ♗e3 c5 13 ♘d2 ♘xd2 14 ♕xd2 ♕b6= Ciocaltea–Velimirovic, Smederevska Palanka 1979.

(b) Other moves favour White, e.g. **9... de?!** (9... ♗g4? 10 ed e4 11 dc ef—see Chapter 16, B1; or 10... ♘xd5? 11 h3 ♗h5 12 g4±) 10 ♘xe5 ♗b7 11 ♘d2! ♗d6 (11 ... ♘xe5 12 de ♘d7 13 ♘e4 ♘xe5 14 ♕h5 ♘d3 15 ♘g5± Neikirkh–Litkevich, DDR 1975) 12 f4 ef 13 ♘dxf3 ♘xe5 14 ♘xe5 (14 de ♗c5+ 15 ♘d4± Gutman) 14... c5 15 ♗g5 cd 16 cd! ♗e7 17

♕d3 ♗d5 18 ♗c2 g6 19 ♗b3± *MCO*.

10 e5

10 ed ♘xd5 is variation C2.

10 ... ♘e4

10 ... ♘e8 gives a position which can arise via 5 0-0 ♗e7 6 d4 ed 7 ♖e1 0–0 8 e5 ♘e8 9 c3 b5!? 10 ♗b3 d5. Recent examples are:

(a) **11 cd** ♗g4 12 ♘c3 ♗b4 13 a3 (Berkovich–Zaitsev, Moscow Ch. 1983) ♗xc3 14 bc ♘a5 Suetin.

(b) **11 ♘xd4** ♘xd4 12 cd ♗e6 13 ♘c3 ♕d7 14 a4 c6 15 ab cb 16 ♗d2 a5 17 ♗c2 ♘c7 18 ♘e2 a4 19 ♘g3 f5 20 ef ♗xf6=/± (½-½, 47) Ochoa de Echaguen–Seitaj, Thessaloniki Ol. 1988.

11 ♘xd4!?

This leads to great complications which appear to favour Black. If 11 cd ♗g4 (or 11 ... ♘a5 12 ♗c2 f6 13 ef ♗xf6! Szily–Szabo, Budapest 1952) 12 ♗e3 (12 ♘c3 ♗xf3! 13 gf ♘xc3 14 bc ♕d7± or 14 ... f5!? Tal and Gutman) ♘a5 13 ♗c2 f5 14 ♗d3 ♘c4 15 ♗c1 c5 16 ♗e2 cd 17 ♘xd4 ♗c5 18 ♘c3 ♘xf2 19 ♔xf2 ♕b6 20 ♗e3 (Kuzmin–Nunn, Budapest Tungsram 1978) ♘xe3! 21 ♔xe3 ♗xd4+ 22 ♕xd4 f4+ ∓∓.

11 ... ♘xe5!

12 f3

Not 12 ♘c6? ♘xc6 13 ♗xd5
♘xf2! nor 12 ♘xb5?! ♗b7 13
♘d4 c5 14 ♘f5 ♗f5∓ Tal.

12 ...   c5
13   fe

13 ♗f4?! ♗f6! 14 ♗xe5 (14 fe
cd 15 ♗xe5 ♗xe5 16 cd ♕b6∓)
♗xe5 15 ♘c6 ♗xh2+ 16 ♔xh2
♕h4+ 17 ♔g1 ♕f2+ 18 ♔h2
♕g3+ 19 ♔g1 ♘g5! (threat ...
♘h3+) 20 ♔h1 ♕h4+ 21 ♔g1
♘h3+! 22 gh ♗xh3 23 ♘e7+
♔h8 24 ♖e2 ♖ae8 25 ♕e1
♕g5+ 26 ♔h2 ♖xe7 27 ♔xh3
♖e6! 28 ♖xe6 fe 29 ♕g3
♕c1!∓∓ Kruppa–Vladimirov,
Frunze 1988.

13   ...   cd
14   ♗xd5

If **14 ♕xd4 ♕c7!** (threat ...
♗c5; if 15 ♗f4 ♘f3+)∓ (Vladimirov) or **14 cd ♗g4** 15 ♕d2
♘c4∓ (*ECO*) or **14 ed!?** ♗d6 15
♗f4 ♖e8! 16 cd ♘d3! 17 ♖xe8+
♕xe8 18 ♕xd3 ♕e1+ 19 ♕f1
♕xf1+ 20 ♔xf1 ♗xf4 21 ♘c3
♗xh2∓ (Hegde–Lukacs, Kolha-
pur 1987).

14   ...   dc
15   ♗xa8?!

15 ♘xc3 (*MCO*) is best met by
15 ... ♗b7 (Nunn).

15   ...   ♗c5+
16   ♔h1

So far Neikirkh–Zinn, DDR
1966. Zinn later demonstrated a
missed forced win by 16 ... ♘d3

17 ♕e2 ♗g4 18 ♕f1 ♕h4 19
♘xc3 ♘f2+ 20 ♔g1 ♗e2! (threat
... ♘g4+).

C

9   ed   ♘xd5 *(101)*
Still by far the most popular
sequence.

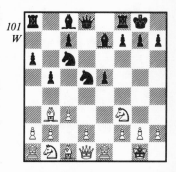

101
W

From the diagram:

C1   10 d3
C2   10 d4
C3   10 a4

10 h3?! ♗b7 11 ♘xe5 ♘xe5 12
♖xe5 ♗d6?! (12 ... ♘f4! is more
convincing) 13 ♖xd5 ♗xd5 14
♗xd5 ♖b8 15 d4 ♖e8 16 ♗e3
♕h4 17 ♕g4? (17 ♘d2!)
♖xe3!∓∓ Hamoda–Brown,
World Junior Ch. 1984.

C1

10   d3
This is inconsistent with 9 ed.
Black has several options.

10   ...   ♗b7
(a) **10 ... ♗g4!?** 11 ♕e2 (11

♘bd2? ♞f4) 11 ... ♖b8! (Not 11
... ♕d6 12 h3!± Tal, nor 11 ...
♗f6 12 ♕e4 ♗e6 13 ♘bd2±
Lutikov–Spassky, USSR Teams
Ch. 1966) 12 ♕e4 ♞f6! with good
counterplay e.g. 13 ♕xc6? ♖b6
14 ♘xe5 ♗d6! Yudovich.

(b) **10 ... ♕d6!?** 11 ♘bd2 ♗b7
12 ♘e4 ♕d7 13 ♗g5 ♖ad8 14 d4
f6 15 ♗h4 ed 16 ♘xd4 ♘e5 17
♗g3 c5∓ (Chaumont–Hebden,
Dinard 1986).

11 ♘xe5 ♘xe5
12 ♖xe5 ♕d7

This position is very similar to
the 11 ... ♗b7 Marshall (Chapter
14, C) except that White's d-pawn
is on d3 instead of d4. Black has
good counterplay according to
ECO. Two games by Zsuzsa Polgar demonstrate this: 13 ♕f3 (13
♘d2 ♞f4) ♖ad8 14 ♘d2 c5 and
now:

(a) **15 ♘e4 c4!?** 16 dc ♞f6 17
♗e3 ♘xe4 18 ♖xe4 ♕d3 19 ♖d4
♗xf3 20 ♖xd3 ♖xd3 21 gf= ♗f6
22 ♔g2 ♖d7 23 cb ab 24 f4 ½-½
(Spassky–Polgar, Cannes 1987).

(b) **15 ♕f5 ♕xf5** (15 ... ♗f6 16
♕xd7 ♖xd7 17 ♖e1 ♞f4 18 ♘e4
♗xe4! 19 de ♘d3 20 ♖d1 c4 21
♗c2 ♖fd8= Polgar) 16 ♖xf5
♞f6 (16 ... g6!? 17 ♖e5 ♗f6 18
♖e1 ♞f4 19 ♘e4 ♗xe4 20 de
♘d3 with compensation—Polgar) 17 ♗c2 ♘d7! 18 ♘f1 g6 19
♖f4 f5 20 d4 c4 21 a4?! (21 d5!=)
♖a8 22 ♗d2 ♖fe8 23 b3 ♗g5 24
h4?! ♗xf4 25 ♗xf4 ♗e4 26 ♗d1?

(time trouble; 26 ♗xe4! is the best
chance) ♘b6 27 ♘d2 ♗d5 and
Black cashed in her advantage as
follows: 28 bc ♘xc4 29 ♘xc4 bc
(29 ... ♖e1+?? 30 ♔h2 bc 31
♗f3!±±) 30 ♗e5 ♖a7 31 a5
♖b7 32 ♔h2 ♖b2 33 ♔g3 ♖e7
34 ♗a4 ♖d2 35 f3 ♖b7 36 ♗f4
♖e2 37 h5? gh 38 ♖h1 ♖g7+ 39
♔h4 ♖exg2 40 ♖e1 ♗xf3 41
♔h3 ♖a2 42 ♗d1 ♗g4+ 43
♗xg4 ♖xg4 44 ♖f1 ♖xa5 45
♗e5 f4 46 ♖f2 ♖a1 47 ♖d2 ♖b1
48 ♔h2 f3 49 d5 ♖g2+ 0–1,
London–Polgar, New York Open
1987.

C2

10 d4?!(*102*)

This was first played in 1901 in
a game that Marshall was perhaps
unaware of.

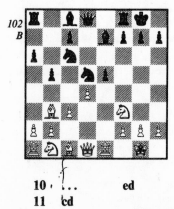

10 ... ed
11 cd

Black also has no problems
after 11 ♘xd4 ♘xd4 12 ♕xd4
♗b7 13 ♘d2 (13 ♗c2 ♗d6 14
♘d2 ♞f4 15 ♘f3 c5 16 ♕d1

♛f6∓) Kaliwoda–Trajkovic, corr. 1963) c5 14 ♕e4 ♝f6 15 ♘f3 ♖e8! 16 ♕xe8+ ♕xe8 17 ♖xe8+ ♖xe8 18 ♝d2 c4 19 ♝c2 b4! Rautio–Oim, corr. 1966.

11 ...   ♝g4

(a) **11 ... ♘b6** (followed by ... ♝g4) is also good (Keres).

(b) **11 ... ♝b4** 12 ♝d2 ♝g4 13 ♘c3 ♘f6 14 ♝e3 ♝xf3 15 gf ♕d7 16 d5 ♘e7 17 ♝g5 ♕h3 18 ♝xf6 featured in two historic encounters:

(b1) **18 ... ♝d6** 19 f4 ♝xf4 20 f3 ♕xh2+ 21 ♔f1 ♘f5 22 ♘e4 gf 23 ♕d3 ♔h8 24 ♕c3 ♖g8 25 ♕xf6+ ♖g7 0–1, Sittenfeld–Soldatenkov, Paris 1901.

(b2) **18 ... gf** 19 ♕d4 ♝d6 20 ♕g4+ ♕xg4 21 fg ♘g6 (0–1, 84) Morrison–Marshall, New York 1918.

12   ♘c3   ♘b6

Or 12 ... ♘f6 13 ♝e3 ♘a5 14 ♝c2 ♘c4 15 ♝c1 ♖c8 16 h3 ♝h5 17 g4 ♝g6 18 ♝xg6 hg 19 ♘e5 ♝b4!± Simagin–Lilienthal, Pärnu 1947.

13   ♝e3   ♘c4
14   ♖c1   ♘b4±

Levenfish–Nezhmetdinov (USSR 1950).

C3

10   a4*(103)*

This leads to positions which can, less frequently in practice, also arise via the 8 a4 Anti-Marshall. White's plan, whatever the move order, is to induce ... d5

with its implications of open piece play, but on his terms: an early start to queenside play and (usually) no immediate acceptance of the black e-pawn.

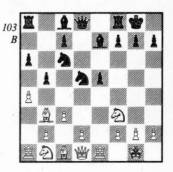

103
B

10   ...   ♝b7

ECO mentions no other move, but **10 ... b4!?** is also possible (with a position that can arise via 8 a4 b4 9 c3 d5 10 ed ♘xd5).

After 11 ♘xe5 ♘xe5 12 ♖xe5 Black has tried:

(a) **12 ... ♘f6** 13 d4 ♝d6 14 ♖e2 ♖b8 (unclear) 15 c4 ♘h5 16 ♘d2 ♘f4 17 ♖e3 c5 18 d5 ♕g5 19 ♖g3 ♕e5 20 ♖e3 ♘e2+ 21 ♔f1 ♕xh2∓ (Kremenetsky–Zaitsev, USSR 1983).

(b) **12 ... c6** 13 c4!? (13 d4 ♝d6 14 ♖e1 ♕h4 15 g3 ♕h3 16 ♝c4! M. Winter) ♝d6 14 ♖e1 ♘f6 15 d4 ♘g4 16 h3 ♕h4 17 ♕f3 ♘xf2 18 ♝d2 ♝g4 19 ♕xf2 ♝h2+ 20 ♔f1 ♝g3 21 ♝g5± Vennix–Leusink, corr. 1987.

10 ... ♖b8 11 ab ab is dealt with in Chapter 17, B1, since it is really the main line of 8 a4 ♖b8 whereas these pseudo-Marshalls are minor sidelines to 8 a4 ♗b7 or 8 ... b4.

11 ab

(a) **11 ♘xe5?** ♘xe5 12 ♖xe5 ♘f4∓ (Ellrich–Brinckmann, Bad Meinberg 1960).

(b) **11 d3?!** ♗f6 12 ♘bd2 ♘f4 13 ♘e4 ♘xd3 14 ♘xf6+ gf 15 ♗h6 (Ishenko) ♘xe1 16 ♕xe1 ♕d3! 17 ♗xf8 (17 ♖d1 ♕g6 18 ♗xf8 ♘d4!∓ — Vitomskis) ♖xf8 18 ♖d1 ♕f5∓ — Tal.

11 ... ab
12 ♖xa8 ♗xa8
13 d3

This is the only move to be tried in master play of late. White adopts a waiting stance hoping to probe for weaknesses in Black's pawn structure. Others:

(a) **13 ♘xe5?** ♘xe5 14 ♖xe5 ♘f4 is an 11 ... ♗b7 Marshall gone badly wrong for White, e.g. 15 d4 (15 g3? ♘h3+ 16 ♔f1 ♕d3+ ∓∓ Pulkis–Zhuravlev, Latvia 1970) ♘xg2 16 ♕g4 ♘h4 17 d5 ♗f6 18 ♗g5? ♗xg4∓∓ Cherchem–Santamaria, Thessaloniki Ol. 1988.

(b) **13 d4** ed 14 ♘xd4 ♘xd4 15 ♕xd4 ♗d6 (15 ... ♗f6 16 ♕d3 ♖e8 unclear; Fulton–Eltaher, Dubai Ol. 1986) 16 ♗c2 (16 ♘d2 c5∓; Wikman–Jovcic, corr. 1957) c5 17 ♕g4 ♖e8 18 ♖xe8+ ♕xe8

19 ♕e4! ♘f6∓ Beninsh–Elburg, corr. 1988–89.

(c) **13 ♘a3!?** when:

(c1) **13 ... ♕d7?** 14 ♘xb5 ♘f4 15 d4 ♘xg2 16 ♔xg2 ♘xd4 17 ♘xd4! ♕g4+ 18 ♔f1 ed 19 ♘xe7 ♗f3 20 ♕d4± ± M. Winter.

(c2) **13 ... ♗xa3** 14 ba ♕d6 15 ♕e2 (15 c4 bc 16 ♗xc4 ♘f4 17 d3 ♘xg2!∓, Noone–Harding, Dublin 1978; 15 ♕e2 ♘f4 16 ♕xb5 ♘d3) h6 16 d4 ed 17 cd ♘f6= Korensky–Krogius, Sochi 1973.

(c3) **13 ... ♘a5** 14 ♗a2 (14 ♘xe5? ♘xb3 15 ♕xb3 ♘f4 16 f3 ♗d6∓ — *ECO*) e4 15 ♘e5 (Balashov–Tseitlin, USSR Ch. 1970) 15 ... ♗xa3 16 ba ♕h4= *ECO*.

13 ... ♗f6
14 ♘a3

(a) **14 ♕c2** g5!? 15 d4 ed 16 ♕f5 ♘ce7 17 ♕g4 ♘g6 18 cd ♘df4 19 ♗xf4 gf 20 ♘c3 ♗xf3 21 ♕xf3 ♕xd4 22 ♘xb5?? ♕b4 0–1, Campora–Djuric, New York Open 1987.

(b) **14 ♗e3** ♘xe3 15 ♖xe3 ♖e8 16 ♘bd2 ♘a5 17 ♖a2 c5 18 ♕e2 ♕d6 19 ♘e4 ♗xe4 20 ♖xe4 ♘c6 21 g4 h6 22 d4 cd 23 cd ♖e7 24 de ♘xe5 (Martinez–Ebeling, Mexico City 1981) ½–½.

14 ... b4
15 ♘c4 bc

16 ♘cxe5 ♘xe5 17 ♘xe5 ♕d6 18 d4 cb 19 ♗xb2 ♖b8 20 ♗c1 (Krum Georgiev–Kiril Georgiev, St John Open 1988) ½–½.

16 Steiner Variation: 9 . . . e4

1 e4 e5 2 ♘f3 ♘c6 3 ♗b5 a6 4
♗a4 ♘f6 5 0–0 ♗e7 6 ♖e1 b5 7
♗b3 0–0 8 c3 d5
    9 ed   **e4**(*104*)

This variation is generally
named after Herman Steiner
(1948 US Champion) who introduced it into international chess
in 1930, but it was originally
played by Marshall himself in
1926.

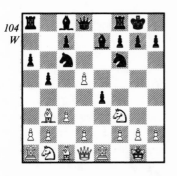

104
W

The Steiner Variation is a
happy hunting-ground for analysts of gambit variations who
enjoy sacrificing other people's
pawns and pieces for dubious
compensation. Occasionally they
may be rewarded with a spectacu-
lar winning line for Black but
most masters believe that White
can repulse the attack. The main
thing for White is to know the
main line and thus avoid traps
and nasty surprises.

Most experience with 9 . . . e4
has been in postal tournaments
and internal USSR events. The
main development of the variation in the past decade was a
major *Shakhmatny Bulletin* article
by Krogius and Matsukevich (6/
1987). Therefore we have con-
siderably reduced the space given
to this variation compared with
previous books because of the un-
likelihood of 9 . . . e4 ever enjoy-
ing a serious revival.
    10 dc

10 ♘g5?! plays into Black's
hands after 10 . . . ♗g4! viz.:
  (a) **11 f3?** ef 12 gf?! (12 ♘xf3?!
♘a5! 13 ♗c2 ♖e8∓) ♘xd5 13
♘xh7 ♗d6! 14 ♗xd5 (14 ♘xf8
♕h4!) ♗xh2+ 15 ♔xh2 ♕h4+

16 ♔g1 ♕g3+ 17 ♔h1 (Pulevic–Zhuravlev, Kalinin 1954) ♗xh7! 18 fg ♖h8 19 ♗g2 (19 ♗xf7? g6!) ♗g8+ 20 ♔g1 ♖h2 21 ♕f3 (21 ♖e2 ♘e5 22 ♖f2 ♘xg4 23 ♕f3 ♖h1+) ♖xg2+ 22 ♕xg2 ♕xe1+ 23 ♕f1 ♖e8∓∓ Gutman and Vitomskis, 1973.

(b) 11 ♕c2 ♘e5 12 ♘xe4 (12 d4 ed 13 ♕d2 ♗c5!) ♘xe4 13 ♕xe4 ♗d6 14 f4 (14 d4 f5 15 ♕e3 f4! 16 ♕e4 ♗f5 17 ♕e2 f3 18 ♕f1 ♘g4 19 g3 ♘xh2! 0–1 Strukov–Balitschev corr. 1988–89; 15 ♕c2 ♘f3+! 16 gf ♕h4! 17 ♖e5 ♗h3!∓∓) ♘g6! 15 d4 (15 f5 ♕h4 16 h3 ♕g3 17 hg ♘f4!∓∓) ♕d7 16 ♖f1 ♖ae8∓ —Gutman and Vitomskis.

10 ... ef

This is the main crossroads of the variation:

A 11 ♕xf3
B 11 d4!

A

11 ♕xf3

White ambitiously seeks both to complete his development and to avoid the weakening of his kingside pawns, but Black obtains at least equal chances by moving swiftly to challenge the e-file. White must beware of back rank mates and other tricks.

11 ... ♗g4
12 ♕g3

However, 12 ♕f4!? (12 ♕e3?? ♖e8) ♖e8 13 ♖e3 ♗d6 14 ♕d4! ♗f5 15 h3 ♘e4 16 d3 ♘c5 is unclear, e.g. 17 ♘d2 (17 ♗c2?? ♘e6) ♘xd3 18 ♘f1 ♘e5 (18 ... ♘xc1? 19 ♖xc1 ♕g5 20 ♖ce1 ♖ed8 21 ♕d5! and 22 ♘g3) 19 ♖g3 ♗g6? (19 ... ♘g6! and if 20 ♗g5?! ♕c8) 20 ♗d5 ♘c4? 21 ♗xf7+! ♔xf7 22 ♕d5+ ♖e6 23 ♖f3+ ♔e7 24 ♗g5+ ♖f6 25 ♖e1+ ♔f8 26 ♖xf6+ ±± Airapetian–Rositsan, Erevan 1981.

After 12 ♕g3 Black has:

A1 12 ... ♗d6!
A2 12 ... ♖e8

A1

12 ... ♗d6
13 f4

Or 13 ♕h4?! ♖e8 (13 ... ♗f4?! 14 d4 ♖e8 15 f3! or 14 ... g5 15 ♕h6 ♖e8 16 ♖xe8+! ♕xe8 17 ♗d2 ♕e7 18 h3± Krogius and Matsukevich) 14 f3 (14 ♖xe8+ ♕xe8 15 f3 ♕e2!∓∓) ♗f5 (14 ... ♗xh2+?! 15 ♔xh2 ♕d6+ 16 ♕g3! or 15 ... ♗xf3 16 ♖xe8+) 15 d4! ♗xh2+ 16 ♔xh2 ♘g4+ 17 ♔g3 ♕xh4+ 18 ♔xh4 ♖xe1 19 fg ♖xc1 20 gf (Fischer–Bernstein, USA Ch. 1959–60) ♔f8! when Black has good compensation after 21 f6 gf 22 a4 ba 23 ♗xa4 ♖e8 (Krogius and Matsukevich) or 21 a4 (21 d5 ♔e7 or 21 ♔g3 ♖b8!) ba 22 ♗c4 (or 22 ♗xa4 ♖e8! with fair chances) ♖b8 23 ♗d3 ♖d1 24 ♗c2 ♖h1+

25 ♔g3 ♖xb2∓ Gutman and
Vitomskis.

13 ...   ♖e8!
14 d4   ♘h5

Normal, but 14 ... ♖xe1+!?
15 ♕xe1 ♕f8!? (15 ... ♕e8 16
♕f2= Popov) 16 ♕f2 ♖e8 17
♘d2 (Simagin) ♗xf4! 18 ♕xf4
♖e1+ 19 ♔f2 ♕e7 20 ♘f1 ♗h5
21 ♘e3 ♖h1! 22 g4 ♘xg4+ 23
♘xg4 ♕e1+ ∓∓ (Popov) re-
quires practical tests.

15 ♖xe8+   ♕xe8
16 ♕f2

16 ♕h4?! permits the invasion
16 ... ♗xf4 17 ♗xf4 ♘xf4 18
♘d2 ♕e3+ 19 ♔h1 ♘d3 (Miz-
kevich–Pullianin, corr. 1966).

16 ...   ♕xc6
17 h3   ♗e6
18 ♗e3

Or 18 g4!? (18 ♗d1 ♘f6 19 ♗f3
♗d5=) ♘f6 19 ♗xe6 fe 20 ♕g2
♘d5 21 ♘d2 ♗xf4 22 ♘e4 e5
(Hakanen–Erstrin, corr. 1958–61)
23 ♗xf4 ef 24 ♕f3= Estrin.

18 ...   ♖e8
19 ♘d2   ♗d5

Simplest, with an edge in a
drawish situation. 19 ... ♗xb3!?
20 ab g5! is unclear after **21 ♘f1**
(21 fg? ♗g3 22 ♕e2 ♘f4∓∓ or
21 ♘f3 gf 22 ♗d2 ♘g3 23 ♖e1
f6!∓ Gutman and Vitomskis)
♗xf4!? (21 ... gf 22 ♗d2 ♘g3=
Archives) 22 ♖e1 ♗xe3 23 ♖xe3
♖xe3 24 ♘xe3 ♘f4 Bogatyrev–
Larssan, corr. 1962.

20 ♗xd5   ♕xd5
21 g4

Not 21 a4? (or 21 ♘f1 ♖e6!)
g5! ∓ Nedeljkovic–Djurasevic,
Yugoslavia 1959.

21 ...   ♘f6

22 b3 ♘c4 23 ♘xe4 ♕xe4 24
♖e1 ♕d3! 25 ♗d2 ♖xe1+ 26
♕xe1 ♔f8∓ Gutman and
Vitomskis.

A2

12 ...   ♖e8(*105*)

This is a trappy but less forcing
move. It is unlikely that Black can
find a more favourable outcome
than after 12 ... ♗d6 and he is
running some risk in the lines that
do not transpose.

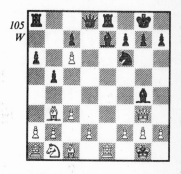

105
W

13 f3!?

An improvement for White in
this line is crucial to the reassess-
ment of 12 ... ♖e8. Others are
not dangerous:

(a) **13 ♖e3?** (13 ♕h4? ♗c5!)
♗d6 14 ♕h4 ♗f4 15 ♖xe8+? (15
d4) ♕xe8 16 f3 ♕e2! 17 c4 (17 fg

g5!) b4! 18 g3 ♕e1+ 19 ♔g2
♗xf3+! 0–1, Levchenkov–Sako-
vich, Riga Ch. 1972.

(b) **13 f4** ♗d6 14 ♖xe8+ (14 d4
see A1; 14 ♖e5?! ♗xe5! 15 fe
♘h5! 16 ♕e3!? ♗e6 17 ♗d1 ♕h4
18 d4 ♗d5 with good compensation—Krogius and Matsukevich)
♕xe8 15 d4 ♕xc6 16 ♘d2? (16 h3
♗f5 17 ♘d2 ♖e8 18 ♕f2 ♗d3
with compensation) ♖e8 17 h3
♖e2! 18 ♘f1 (18 hg ♗xf4!) ♗f5
19 ♘e3 ♘h5 20 ♕g5 ♘xf4! 21
♕d8+ ♗f8 22 ♗d5 ♕g6 23 ♕h4
♘xd5 0–1, Preibsch–Pötzsch,
corr. 1959.

(c) **13 d4** ♗d6 14 ♖xe8+!? (14
f4 see A1; 14 ♖e5? ♗xe5 15 de
♗d1!∓∓) ♕xe8 15 ♕e3 (15 f4?!
see previous note) ♕xc6 16 f3
(Black gets good compensation
after 16 ♕d3 ♖e8 17 ♗e3 ♗f3
[17 ... ♗h5!?] 18 gf! ♕xf3 19
♘d2 ♕h3 [19 ... ♕g4+!?] 20
♘f1 ♘g4 21 ♘f5 ♔h8! threatening ... g6—Tal) ♖e8 17 ♕f2
when:

(c1) **17 ... ♗f5!?** (Pötzsch) 18
♗g5 ♗d3 19 ♘d2 ♖e2 20 ♕h4
♕e8 21 ♘f1 c5 22 ♗xf6 gf 23
♕xf6 ♗e7 24 ♕f4 c4 25 ♘g3
♖e6 26 ♕d2± Kopel–Armas,
corr. 1982; Black's initiative is
gradually weakening.

(c2) **17 ... ♖e7!** 18 ♗g5! (18 fg?
♘xg4 19 ♕f1 ♗xh2+ 20 ♔h1
♗g3 21 ♗d2 ♕g6∓∓ or 18 ♗d2
♕e8 19 ♗d1 ♗f5 20 ♘a3 ♗f4 21

♖c1 ♖e1+∓∓) ♕e8 19 ♘d2
(19 ♘a3? ♖e2!∓∓) ♖e2! 20 ♕f1
(20 ♕h4? h6 21 ♗xf6 ♕e3+ 22
♔h1 [22 ♔f1 g5!] ♗h3!∓∓
Kuszko–Baran, Katowice 1972 or
21 ♗xh6 gh 22 ♕xf6 ♕e3+ 23
♔h1 ♗h5∓∓ or 21 fg hg 22
♕xg5 ♘h7!∓∓ Krogius and
Matsukevich) ♗h3! 21 gh h6! (21
... ♘h5 22 ♘e4! ♕xe4 23
♗xf7+!) when:

(c21) Black retains chances
after Tal and Gutman's line **22
♗xf7+** ♔xf7 23 ♘e4 ♗xh2+ 24
♔h1 ♖xb2.

(c22) After **22 ♗h4** ♕e3+ 23
♗f2 Krogius and Matsukevich
suggest 23 ... ♕xd2! (threatening
... ♗xh2+ and ... ♘h5; 23 ...
♗xh2+ 24 ♔g2 ♕xd2 25 ♖e1
♖xe1 26 ♕xe1 ♕xe1 27 ♗xe1±)
24 ♖e1 ♖xe1 25 ♕xe1 ♕xb2
unclear. An early draw seems
likely.

13 ...   ♕d3!
14 fg   ♗c5+
15 ♖e3

The only move. 15 ♔h1
♖xe1+ 16 ♕xe1 ♖e8 17 ♕d1
♘xg4 Krogius and Matsukevich.

15 ...   ♖ad8!

(a) **15 ... ♖xe3?!** 16 de ♖e8
(Ed. Lasker–Marshall, Chicago
1926) 17 ♘a3! ♗xa3 18 ba ♕xc3
19 ♖b1 ♘e4 (19 ... ♕d3 20 ♖b2
♕c3 21 ♖c2) 20 ♗b2 ♘xg3 (20
... ♕d3 21 ♕e1) 21 ♗xc3 ♘e2+
22 ♔f2 ♘xc3 23 ♖c1± (end-

game) Krogius and Matsukevich.

(b) **15 . . . ♘d5!?** (15 . . . ♘e4? 16 ♕e1 ♖ad8 17 ♔h1!±±) 16 ♘a3! (16 ♕f3? ♘xe3 17 de ♖e6!∓; Polugayevsky–Ivashin, Kuibyshev 1975) 16 . . . ♘xe3 17 de ♗xa3 18 ba ♖e4 (18 . . . ♖e6 19 e4! Yudovich) 19 ♕f2 ♖ae8 20 ♗c2 ♕xc3 21 ♖b1 ♖xg4 22 ♗b2 ♕xc6± (Krogius and Matsukevich): material is about equal, but the white bishops are clearly more active than the black rooks.

16   ♘a3!?

If 16 ♕f3 (16 ♕e1? ♘xg4) ♖e7! (16 . . . ♖d6?! 17 ♘a3 threat ♗c2) 17 h3 (17 ♘a3 ♘e4 18 ♗c2 ♘xd2 19 ♗xd3 ♘xf3+ 20 gf ♖xd3∓; 17 ♔h1? ♘xg4) ♘e4 18 ♕f4 ♘xd2 19 ♗xd2 ♖xe3 20 ♔h1 ♖xh3+ ∓∓ Sevkeira–Iten, Tyrol 1977.

16   . . .   ♘e4
17   ♕f3!

A saving resource. Not 17 ♗c2 (or 17 ♕e1 ♘xd2! 18 ♗xd2 ♕xd2∓∓) ♕xd2! 18 ♗xd2 ♘xg3 19 ♗c1 ♖xe3 20 hg ♖e2+ 21 ♔h2 ♗xa3 0–1, Pavlovichev–Yablonsky, Moscow 1968.

17   . . .   ♘xd2
18   ♗xd2   ♕xd2

19 ♗xf7+ ♔h8 20 ♗xe8 ♖xe8 (White can counterattack after 20 . . . ♗xe3+ 21 ♔h1 ♖xe8 22 ♕f7) 21 ♔f1 (21 ♖f1 h6∓) 21 . . . ♖xe3 (21 . . . ♖f8? 22 ♕xf8+ ♗xf8 23 ♖e2 ♕d5 24 ♘c2±) 22

♕d1 ♖d3! 23 ♕xd2 ♖xd2=
Krogius and Matsukevich.

Thus we come to the end of the 11 ♕xf3 variations which, by and large, offer Black very good chances and provide excellent scope for home analysis. However, White can spoil most of the fun by playing instead:

B

11   d4! *(106)*

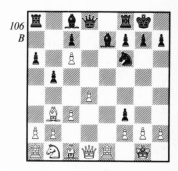

106
B

White avoids time-wasting Q moves, prepares the development of his Q-side and reduces the scope of Black's pieces.

B1   11 . . . ♗g4?!
B2   11 . . . ♗d6?!
B3   11 . . . fg

11 . . . ♖e8!? 12 ♗g5 fg (12 . . . ♗g4 13 h3 ♗h5 14 g4 ♗g6 15 ♕f3± Krogius and Matsukevich) 13 ♕f3 (for *ECO*'s 13 ♕e2!? see note (a) to the next diagram) ♗d6 14 ♘d2 or 13 . . . ♗g4 14 ♕xg2 looks±.

B1

 11 **...**   **Bg4?!**
 12 **gf**

This gives active piece play at the cost of damaged pawns. White can also consider 12 h3!? (12 Bg5 see B31; 12 g3 Re8!? 13 Nd2/Bf4 Bd6 or 13 Bg5 h6—Krogius and Matsukevich) Bh5 13 g4 Nxg4 (13 ... Bg6 14 Qxf3 Bd6 15 Be3±) 14 hg Bxg4 15 Qd2! h6 (15 ... Re8 16 Qf4 Bd6 17 Bxf7+ or 15... Bd6 16 Qg5) 16 Qf4 h5 17 Qe5 Bh4 18 Bf4 Re8 19 Qxe8+ Qxe8 20 Rxe8+ Rxe8 21 Na3±± Zilberstein–Philippe, Euro. Club Ch. Final 1974.

 12 **...**   **Bh5**

Or 12 ... Bh3 13 Bf4 Nh5 14 Bg3 Bd6 15 Nd2 Bf4 16 Kh1 Kh8 17 Ne4± Neber–Haller, corr. 1966.

 13 **Bf4!±**

White prevents ... Qd6 and prepares a barrier on the e-file, e.g. 13 ... Bd6 14 Be5 (or 14 Bg3 Nd5!? 15 Bxd5 Bxg3 16 hg Qxd5 17 Re5! O'Kelly–Rohacek, Trencianske Teplice 1949) Qc8 15 Nd2 Qh3 16 Re3 Rad8 17 Qf1 Qh5 18 Qg2 (Kovalev–Baleyev, RSFSR 1956) h6!? 19 Rc1!

B2

 11 **...**   **Bd6?!**
 12 **Bg5!?**

This works tactically but 12 Qxf3 should leave Black without compensation: 12 ... Re8 (or 12 ... Bg4 13 Qd3! Re8 14 Be3± Klovan–Estrin, Moscow 1958) 13 Bd2! Bg4 (13 ... Rxe1+ 14 Rxe1 Qe7 15 Nd2 Bg4 16 Qe3 Qf8 17 f3±) 14 Qd3 Rxe1+ 15 Rxe1 Qe8 16 Nd2 Qxc6 17 f3 Bh5 18 Bh4! Bg6 19 Qf1 ± Haller–Dal, corr. 1970.

 12 **...**   **Bxh2+!?**

12 ... h6 13 Bxf6 Qxf6 14 Qxf3 Qg5 15 g3± Prusz–Pötzsch, corr. 1961.

 13 **Kxh2**   **Ng4+**
 14 **Kg1**   **Qxg5**
 15 **Qxf3**   **h5!?**

Estrin's attempt to revive the line since 15 ... Nf6 16 Qe3±, 15 ... Qh4? 16 Qxf7+!, 15 ... Be6 d5 Bf5 17 Nd2 Rae8 18 Nf1± (Pötzsch) and 15 ... Bf5 16 Nd2 Rae8 17 Nf1 h5 (Kofman–Kopayev, Kiev 1948) 18 Ne3 (Gutman and Vitomskis) do not scare White.

 16 **Na3!**   **Bf5**
 17 **Nc2**   **Rae8**

18 Ne3! (18 d5? Bxc2 19 Bxc2 Qd2∓∓) Be4 19 Qg3 Bxc6 20 Qxc7!± e.g. 20 ... Nxe3 (20 ... Bf3 21 Qg3 or 20 ... Rxe3 21 fe Bxg2 [21 ... Qh4 22 Re2!] 22 Qf4! Qg6 23 Kxg2±± Shevtsov–Morozov, corr. 1959) 21 Qxc6 Rc8 22 Qf3 Ng4 23 a4!± Gutman and Vitomskis.

B3

 11 **...**   **fg***(107)*

The capture on g2 spells the end of back rank tricks but it does at least weaken White's king position. If Black could exchange his pawn on g2 for the one at c6 and bring some pieces to bear on the kingside he could be all right, but experience and analysis show that this is probably impossible.

107
W

From the diagram:

B31 12 ♗g5
B32 12 ♕f3!

(a) **12 ♕e2!?** (*ECO*) is untested: 12 ... ♗d6 (12 ... ♖e8 13 ♗g5 ♗g4 14 f3 ♗h3! is also critical) 13 ♗g5 h6 14 ♗h4 (14 ♗xf6 ♕xf6 15 ♘d2? ♗xh2+!) ♗g5 15 ♗g3 ♖e8 16 ♗e5 ♗xe5 17 de ♘g4 when Krogius and Matsukevich say: 'Notwithstanding the obvious weakness of his kingside, Black possesses definite counterchances'.

(b) **12 ♗f4** is unclear after 12 ... ♗g4! (12 ... ♖e8 13 ♕f3 ♗g4

14 ♕xg2 ♗d6!? Krogius and Matsukevich) 13 ♕d3 ♘h5 14 ♗e5 ♗d6 15 ♘d2 ♔h8 (15 ... ♘f4? 16 ♕g3! ♗xe5 17 ♕xg4!±) 16 ♗c2 f5 17 ♘f3 ♘f4 18 ♕e3 ♘h3+ 19 ♔xg2 (Gufeld–Chikovani, Tbilisi 1961) 19 ... f4! 20 ♕d3 (20 ♕d2 ♗xf3+! 21 ♔xf3 ♕h4) ♖f5! Gutman and Vitomskis.

B31
    12 ♗g5   ♗g4
If 12 ... ♘d5!? (12 ... ♕d6? 13 ♕f3 ♗g4 14 ♗f4 ♕f6 15 ♘d2± Gipslis–Witkowski, Riga 1959) 13 ♗xe7 ♘xe7 14 ♕f3 ♕d6 15 d5 ♘g6 (Botterill) 16 ♘d2 ♘e5 17 ♕g3!± Krogius and Matsukevich.
    13 ♕d3   ♖e8
(a) **13 ... ♘d5?** 14 ♗xe7 ♘xe7 15 ♕e4 ♗e6 16 ♗xe6 fe 17 ♕xe6 ♖f7 18 ♘d2 ♘g6 19 ♖e4 ♔f8 20 ♕h3 ♕f6 21 ♕xg2± Oim–Nash, corr. 1973–75.

(b) **13 ... ♗h5** 14 ♕h3! ♗g6 15 ♘d2 ♖e8 16 ♘f3 h6 (16 ... ♘e4? 17 ♖xe4! ♗xe4 18 ♗xf7+!± or 16 ... a5 17 a3 ♕d6 18 ♘e5±) 17 ♘e5! ♔h7 18 ♗xf7±± Krogius and Matsukevich.
    14 ♘d2   ♘h5
(a) **14 ... ♕c8** 15 ♗c2 ♗h5 16 ♗xf6 ♗g6 17 ♗xe7! ♗xd3 18 ♗xd3± Shakarov–Bakarzhinsky, Donetsk 1964.
(b) **14 ... ♘d5!?** 15 ♘f3 (15 ♗xe7 ♖xe7 16 ♖xe7 ♘xe7 17

♛e4 ♝f5 18 ♛f3± Browne–Bisguier, USA Ch. 1975) e.g. **15 ...** ♝xg5 16 ♜xe8 ♛xe8 17 ♘xg5 or **15 ...** ♝xf3 16 ♝xe7 ♜xe7 17 ♛xf3± Krogius and Matsukevich.

15 ♜xe7!?

White's advantage is tiny after 15 ♘f3 ♝f6 16 ♜e5 ♛d6 17 ♛e4 ♜xe5 18 ♛xg4 ♜xg5 19 ♘xg5 ♝xg5 20 ♛xh5 ♛g6 21 ♛xg6 hg 22 ♚xg2 (½–½, 29) Strand–Dalko, corr 1963–64.

15 ... ♜xe7

Now the question is whether 16 h3 (16 ♝xe7 ♛xe7 17 ♛e3 ♜e8 18 ♜e1 ♚f8 19 ♛xe7+ ♜xe7 20 ♜xe7 ♚xe7 21 ♘e4 ♝e2!= Euwe) ♝e6! (16 ... ♝e2? 17 ♛f5!) 17 ♛e3!? (Lepeshkin) gives White a significant advantage. If it does, 12 ♝g5 may be as good as the next variation.

B32

12 ♛f3! *(108)*

This is generally considered White's strongest line against the Steiner Variation. He will soon hold an extra pawn with freer development, making it hard for Black to find compensation.

12 ... ♝e6!?

A 1970s suggestion, offering a second pawn, which still lacks practical tests at a high level. Others have been refuted:

(a) **12 ...** ♜e8?! 13 ♝g5 a5 (13 ... ♝d6 14 ♘d2±) 14 a3 ♝g4 15

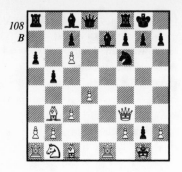

108 B

♛xg2 ♝f5 16 ♘d2± Vasyukov–Tolush, Moscow 1961.

(b) **12 ...** ♝g4 13 ♛xg2 allows the ♛ to defend c6 and attack on the kingside without being vulnerable. White can then develop normally:

(b1) **13 ...** ♛d6!? (13 ... ♝d6 14 ♝g5 ♜e8 15 ♘d2±) 14 ♝g5 ♝f5 15 ♘d2 a5 (15 ... h6? 15 ♝xh6 ♘g4 17 ♝e3± Schabo–Koskinen, corr.) 16 a4 b4 17 ♜e5! ♝g6 (17 ... ♝e6? 18 ♝h6 ♘e8 19 ♘e4) 18 ♘c4±.

(b2) **13 ...** ♜e8 14 ♝g5 ♝f5 15 ♘d2 ♘h5 (15 ... ♛d6 16 ♜e2 ♝f8 17 ♜ae1 ♜xe2 18 ♜xe2 ♘h5 19 ♜e5± Angelov–Herling, corr. 1963) 16 ♜e5! ♝xg5 17 ♜xf5 ♘f4 18 ♝xf7+ ♚h8 19 ♝xe8 ♛xe8 20 ♛e4± ± Pribylov–Kantorovich, Moscow 1962.

(c) **12 ...** ♘g4?! 13 ♝f4 ♚h8 (13 ... ♝d6 14 h3 ♛h4 15 ♝xd6 cd 16 ♛xf7+!) 14 ♘d2! g5 15 ♝g3 f5 16 h3! f4 17 hg fg 18 ♛xg3

♗d6 19 ♕xg2 ♖f4 20 ♗e6!± Gutman and Vitomskis.

(d) **12 ... a5?!** (12 ... h6 13 ♕xg2 ♔h8 14 ♔h1± or 12 ... ♗d6? 13 ♗g5!) 13 ♗g5! a4 14 ♗c2 ♗e6 15 ♘d2 ♗d5 16 ♕d3 g6 17 ♖xe7! ♕xe7 18 ♕xb5±± Gutman and Vitomskis.

13 ♗f4!

If 13 ♗xe6 fe Black has counterplay in the f-file, e.g. 14 ♕h3 (14 ♗g5 ♘d5= while 14 ♘d2 ♘d5 15 ♕g4 ♖f6! and 14 ♖xe6 ♘d5 15 ♕e4 ♗d6 or 15 ♕xg2 ♗h4 [e.g. 16 ♗h6 ♖f7 17 ♘d2 ♔h8 18 ♖e5 gh 19 ♖xd5 ♕g8 20 ♘e4 ♗xf2+ ∓∓ Ady–Baker, Barnsdale 1989] give the initiative to Black) ♘d5! (14 ... ♗d6 15 ♗g5) 15 ♕xe6+ ♔h8 16 ♖e2 (or 16 ♖e4 ♗h4) ♗g5 17 ♗xg5 ♕xg5.

13 ...   ♘d5

If 13 ... ♗d5 14 ♗xd5 ♘xd5 (14 ... ♕xd5?! 15 ♘d2 or 15 ♕xd5 ♘xd5 16 ♗xc7!± Gutman and Vitomskis) 15 ♗g3± e.g. 15 ... f5 16 ♗e5 ♘b6 17 ♘d2 and ♕xg2 staying a pawn ahead.

14 ♗g3   a5
15 ♘d2!   a4
16 ♗c2!

± (Suetin).

17 Anti-Marshall: 8 a4 Introduction and 8 ... ♖b8

1 e4 e5 2 ♘f3 ♘c6 3 ♗b5 a6 4 ♗a4 ♘f6 5 0-0 ♗e7 6 ♖e1 b5 7 ♗b3 0-0

8   a4(*109*)

The tactical complexity and depth of theoretical investigation of the Marshall are strong motives for White to avoid 8 c3. With 8 a4, the move most often chosen for this purpose, White prepares the development or exchange of his queen's rook, his major problem piece in the Marshall, and so deters ... d5 in most lines.

109
B

Black has two satisfactory re-plies to 8 a4, which lead to interesting middlegames giving chances to both players. These are the very thoroughly investigated 8 ... ♗b7 (Chapters 19–20) and the interesting alternative 8 ... b4 (Chapter 18).

In this chapter we look only at inferior choices for Black from the diagram:

A   8 ... d5?!
B   8 ... ♖b8

8 ... ba? 9 ♗xa4 ♗b7 10 ♘c3 d6 11 ♗xc6 ♗xc6 12 d4± Matanovic–Puc, Yugoslav Ch. 1957.

A

8   ...   d5?!

The move White thought he had prevented! In principle, Black should not rush this central advance with the queen's wing unstable.

9   ed

This is possibly the least good option. White can consider:

(a) **9 ♗xd5** (*Archives*, 1968) 9 ... ♘xd5 10 ed ♕xd5 (10 ... ♘d4

11 ♘xe5±) 11 ♘c3 followed by 12 ab after the queen moves. Or if 9 ... ♗b7 10 ♘xe5 ♘xe5 11 ♗xb7 ♖a7 (*MCO*) 12 d4! ♖xb7 (12 ... ♘c4 13 ♗c6) 13 de ♕xd1 14 ♖xd1 ♘xe4 15 ab ab 16 ♗e3± *TDH*.

(b) **9 ab!?** also comes into consideration: 9 ... ♘d4 (9 ... de 10 bc ef 11 ♕xf3±) 10 ♗xd5 (or 10 ♘xd4 ed 11 e5 but not 10 ♘xe5? ♘xb3 11 cb de) ♘xf3+ (10 ... ♘xd5 11 ♘xd4±) 11 ♕xf3 ♘xd5 12 ed ♗b7 13 c4 ab 14 ♖xa8 ♕xa8 15 d3.

    9 ...   ♘d4
    10 ♘xe5?!
Probably giving Black more play than he deserves. Gipslis suggested 10 ♘xd4 ed 11 ab.

    10 ...   ♗b7
    11 ♘c6
Not 11 ♗a2 ♘xd5 12 c3 ♘f4! 13 cd ♘xg2 with unfavourable complications (Tsarev–Martoinov, USSR 1968).

    11 ...   ♘xc6
    12 dc   ♗xc6
    13 d4
It is hard to see any compensation for Black (Habel–Konietzka, corr. 1968).

B
    8 ...   ♖b8
This cedes control of the a-file without any positional compensation. Black intends to play ... d5 anyway.

    9 ab
It is illogical to defer opening the a-file.

    9 ...   ab
Now:

B1 10 d4
B2 10 c3

Both **10 d3** d6 11 ♘bd2 ♘d7 12 c3 ♗f6 13 ♘f1 b4= (Benko–Bilek, Hungarian Ch. 1955) and **10 ♘c3** ♘d4 11 ♘xd4 ed 12 ♘d5 ♘xd5 13 ♗xd5 c6= (Karakalajic–Ciric, Yugoslav Ch. 1958) enable Black's rook move to have some value.

B1
    10 d4
A logical move recommended in *Chess Archives*, 1954. Black cannot reply 10 ... d6, along the lines of Chapter 21, because of 11 d5.

    10 ...   ♘xd4!?
Necessary in view of 10 ... ed 11 e5 ♘g4 (11 ... ♘e8 12 ♗d5!±) 12 h3 ♘h6 13 ♗xh6 gh 14 ♘xd4 ♘xd4 15 ♕xd4 ♖b6 (Ader–Pauk, Chile Ch. 1960) 16 ♘c3!±.

    11 ♘xd4
11 ♗xf7+? (by analogy with Chapter 21, A1) fails because after 11 ... ♖xf7 12 ♘xe5 ♘e6 13 ♘xf7 ♔xf7 14 e5 ♘e8 15 ♕f3+ ♔g8 Black's rook is not hanging on a8. But after the more positional text move, the relative pos-

ition of the rooks should favour White on the queenside.

11 ... ed

12 e5 ♘e8

The only example of this line is inconclusive: 13 c3!? dc 14 ♘xc3 (with compensation according to *ECO*) d6 15 ♕f3 de 16 ♖xe5 b4 17 ♘e4 (17 ♘d5 ♗d6) ♗f6 = Rietz–Leisebein, corr. 1986.

B2

10 c3 d5!?

Marshall players will naturally want to try this rather than 10 ... d6, which gives a position more usually resulting from 7 ... d6 8 c3 0-0 9 a4 ♖b8 10 ab ab (*ECO* C90). One recent example went 11 d4 (11 h3 ♗b7 12 d4 ♖a8 13 ♖xa8 ♕xa8 14 ♗g5 h6 15 ♗xf6 ♗xf6 16 d5± Gipslis–Holmov, USSR Ch. 1965) ed 12 cd ♗g4 (with an inferior form of Chapter 21, B) 13 ♗e3 (13 ♘c3 and 13 h3 are also good) d5 14 e5 ♘e4 15 h3 ♗h5 16 ♘c3 ♗b4 17 ♕c1 ♘a5 18 ♗a2 ♘c4 19 ♗xc4 bc 20 ♘d2 ♘xd2 21 ♕xd2 ♗g6 22 ♗g5± (1–0, 43) Zapata–Agdestein, Thessaloniki Ol. 1988.

11 ed ♘xd5

11 ... e4? 12 dc ef 13 d4± *ECO*.

12 ♘xe5 ♘xe5

13 ♖xe5(*110*)

13 ... ♘f6

This is a version of Chapter 13 with the inclusion of two moves

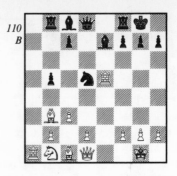

each on the queenside which may benefit Black since the rook on b8 may support ... ♗b7 at key moments while its white counterpart has no immediate function.

On the other hand 13 ... c6?! is liable to lead to lines where the white rook (normally only activated by 18 a4 etc.) is already able to strike behind Black's lines. After 14 d4 ♗d6 15 ♖e1:

(a) The only line of independent significance is **15 ... ♖b7** 16 ♘d2 ♖e7 (Haag–Kurtes, Budapest 1966) 17 ♘e4!±.

(b) **15 ... ♕h4** 16 g3 ♕h3 17 ♕d3?! (better 17 ♗e3, when White is a tempo ahead of Spassky's Variation, or maybe 17 ♖e4!?) ♗f5 18 ♕f1 ♕h5 19 ♗e3 ♗h3 20 ♗d1 ♕f5 21 ♕e2 ♖be8 with compensation (H. Schmid–Litkiewicz, corr. 1967).

14 d4 ♗d6

15 ♖e2

15 ♖e1 ♘g4 16 h3 ♕h4 17 ♕f3 ♘xf2! 18 ♗d2 (18 ♕xf2??

♗h2+! 19 ♔f1 ♗g3∓∓; 18
♖e2 ♘g4! 19 g3 ♗b7) ♗b7! illus-
trates the important difference
mentioned above (compare
Chapter 13, B112):
(a) **19 d5?** ♗c5! 20 ♔h2 ♗c8!
21 ♘a3 ♖b6 22 d6 ♗xd6 23 ♔g1
♘xh3+ 24 gh ♗c5+ 25 ♔h2
♖f6 26 ♖e4 ♖xf3 27 ♖xh4
♖f2+ 28 ♔g3 ♖xd2∓∓ Rip-
per–Leisebein, corr. 1985.
(b) **19 ♕xf2** ♗h2+! 20 ♔f1
♗g3 21 ♕g1 (21 ♕f5! g6 22 ♕g4
♕f6∓∓ or 21 ♕e2? ♖be8 22
♕xe8 ♕f6∓∓) ♖be8! 22 ♖e3
(22 ♖xe8? ♖xe8 and 23 ...
♕f6∓∓) ♖e6! 23 d5 (23 ♗xe6?
fe∓∓) ♖f6+ 24 ♖f3 ♖xf3+ 25
gf ♖e8 26 ♘a3 ♗c8 27 ♗e3 ♗f5!
(27 ... ♗h3 28 ♔e2 ♗f4 29 ♘c2
♗f5 30 ♔d1!± Leisebein) 28
♘c2 (28 ♗c2? ♗h3 29 ♔e2 ♗f4)
♗d3+ (not 28 ... ♗f4? 29
♗d2!±±) ½–½ (29 ♔g2 ♗f5 30
♔f1 ♗d3=) Preussner–Leisebein, corr. 1985. Black followed
Vukcevic–Minic, but could not
win because of back row threats
created by the white rook.
15 ... ♘h5
Compare variation B2 in
Chapter 13. Others:
(a) **15 ... b4** 16 ♘d2 ♖b5 17
♘f1 bc 18 bc ♘d5 19 ♗xd5
♖xd5 20 ♗a3± Tseshkovsky–
Zaitsev, USSR Ch. 1969.
(b) **15 ... ♘g4** 16 h3 ♕h4 17
♘d2 ♗b7 18 ♘f1± Matanovic,

ECO (by analogy with Chapter
13).
16 ♗e3
Or 16 ♕d3 (16 ♘d2 ♘f4 17
♖e3 ♕g5 18 ♖g3 ♕e7= by analogy) ♕h4 17 g3 ♕h3 18 ♗d5 (18
♕e4? ♗b7 19 ♗d5? ♘f6 20 ♕g2
[20 ♕d3 ♖be8 or 20 ♕f3 ♘g4]
♕h5!∓) ♗f5 19 ♕e3 ♘f6 (the
rook is not *en prise* in this variation) 20 ♗g2 ♕h5 threatening
... ♘g4 and ... ♖e8—Dun-
haupt.
16 ... ♗g4!?
Not known in the Chapter 13
line. *NIC Yearbook 3* gives 16 ...
♗b7! 17 ♘d2 ♔h8 18 d5 (18 ♘f1
f5) ♘f6 (18 ... f5 19 ♘f3 f4 20
♗d4) 19 c4 bc 20 ♘xc4 ♗d5= by
analogy, but this needs more
detailed examination, especially
of 18 ♖e1!?
17 f3±
Now the only practical example
went 17 ... ♕h4 (17 ... ♗d7 18
♘d2 ♔h8 19 d5± *YB3*) 18 g3 (18
fg ♗xh2+ 19 ♔f1 ♘g3+ [Dun-
haupt] 20 ♔e1 ♘xe2 21 ♔xe2
♕g4+ 22 ♔f1 ♕h4 unclear—
YB3; 18 h3 ♗xh3 19 gh ♕xh3
and if 20 ♖g2 ♖be8 Dunhaupt)
♘xg3 (18 ... ♗xg3 19 fg! ♕xg4
20 hg ♕xg3+ 21 ♔f1 ♕h3+ 22
♔e1±± *YB3*) 19 ♖g2! ♗h3 20
♗f2!±± ♖xg2 21 ♔xg2 ♘f5 22
♗xh4 ♘e3+ 23 ♔g1 ♘xd1 24
♗xd1 ♖a8 25 ♘a3 b4 26 cb
♖fb8 27 ♖b1 ♖xb4 28 ♘c2 ♖b3

29 ♘e1 ♖b5 30 ♗e2 ♖ba5 31 ♘c2 ♗xh2+ (better 31 ... f5) 32 ♔xh2 ♖h5 33 ♔g3 g5 34 ♗xg5 ♖xg5+ 35 ♔f2 ♖e8 36 ♘e3 ♖h5 37 ♘g4 ♔f8 38 ♖c1 ♖e7 39 ♖c2 ♖h1 40 ♗f1 ♖h5 41 ♗g2 ♖b5 42 ♘e5 ♖b6 43 f4 ♔g7 44 ♘c6 ♖e6 45 d5 ♖f6 46 ♔e3 ♖h6

(46 ... h5 47 ♘d4 h4 48 ♖c7! ♖b2 49 ♗e4 h3 50 ♘f5± ± Dunhaupt) 47 ♘d4 ♖h2 48 ♔f3 ♖b4 49 ♘f5+ ♔g6 50 ♘e3 ♖b3 51 ♖c3 ♖xb2 52 ♔g3 ♖h5 53 ♗f3 1–0, Dunhaupt–Lehikoinen, corr. 1984.

18   Anti-Marshall: 8 a4 b4

1 e4 e5 2 ♘f3 ♘c6 3 ♗b5 a6 4 ♗a4 ♘f6 5 0-0 ♗e7 6 ♖e1 b5 7 ♗b3 0-0

      8   a4   b4(*111*)

This is a major line and is probably not worse than 8 ... ♗b7. It leads to active counter-play with the b-pawn a distinct thorn in White's flesh. 8 ... b4 has the advantage for Black of being less expected and less fully analysed and a player who does good homework can expect rewards since there are several relatively unexplored lines.

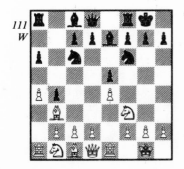

111
W

White can reply:

A   **9 a5**
B   **9 c3**
C   **9 d3**
D   **9 d4**

If 9 ♗d5 (*Archives* 1954) ♗b7 10 d3 (10 ♘xe5 ♘xd5 11 ed ♘xe5 12 ♖xe5 ♗f6 is very good for Black) may be met by the safe **10 ... d6** or the speculative **10 ... ♘xd5** 11 ed ♘d4 12 ♖xe5 ♘xf3+ 13 ♕xf3 ♗f6 and ... ♖e8 with some play for the ♙ — Nunn.

A

      9   a5

A double-edged move, aiming at later attacks on the potentially weak black a-pawn.

Now Black has tried:

A1   **9 ... d5!?**
A2   **9 ... d6**

(a) **9 ... ♖b8!?** (threatening ... ♖b5 and ... ♘xa5) 10 d4 d6 (10 ... ed 11 ♘xd4 ♘xd4 12 ♕xd4 c5

13 ♕d3 d6 14 ♗f4 followed by ♘bd2 exposes the weak black queenside pawns) 11 d5 ♘a7 when:

(a1) **12 ♗e3 ♘b5 13 ♖a4** (13 c4?! bc 14 bc ♘xe4 15 c4 ♘bc3 16 ♘xc3 ♘xc3 17 ♕c2 ♘e4 Nunn) 13 ... ♘g4!? 14 ♗d2 ♘d4 15 ♘xd4 ed 16 h3 ♘e5 (Plachetka–Tseshkovsky, Dubna 1976) 17 ♖xb4 ♖xb4 18 ♗xb4 c5 19 ♗d2± Plachetka.

(a2) **12 ♘bd2** c6 13 dc ♘xc6 14 ♘c4 ♖b5 (14 ... ♗e6!± ; 14 ... ♘xe4 15 ♕d5! ♗b7 [15 ... ♘c5 16 ♕xc6 ♗b7 17 ♕b6±] 16 ♖xe4 ♘d4 17 ♖xd4 ♗xd5 18 ♖xd5±) 15 ♗e3! d5 16 ♘xce5 ♘xe5 17 ♘xe5 de (17 ... ♗d6 18 ♘c6! ♗xh2+ 19 ♔xh2 ♕c7+ 20 e5 ♘g4+ 21 ♔g1 ♕xc6 22 ♗a4±±) 18 ♕xd8 ♗xd8 19 ♘c6 ♗b7 20 ♘xd8 ♖xd8 21 ♗b6± ♖c8 22 ♖ad1 ♖g5 23 h4! ♖h5 24 ♗d8 ♗d5? 25 g4!±± ♗xb3 26 gh ♗xc2 27 ♖c1 ♖c6 28 ♗xf6 gf 29 ♖e3 f5 30 b3 f4 31 ♖e2 ♗d3 32 ♖xc6 ♗xe2 33 ♖b6 f3 34 ♔h2 e3 35 ♔g3 ef 36 ♔xf2 ♔f8 37 ♖xb4 ♔e7 38 ♖b6 1–0 Nunn–I. Ivanov, Brighton 1983.

(b) 9 ... ♗b7 10 d3 when **10 ... d5!?** 11 ed ♘d4 might be explored. Also **10 ... d6** 11 ♘bd2 ♖b8!? (11 ... ♘d7 12 ♘f1 ♘c5 13 ♗d5 ♘d4 14 ♗xb7 ♘xb7 15 ♘e3 ♘c5 16 ♘xd4 ed 17 ♘d5± Dely–Osz-

vath, Hungary 1966) could be tried, e.g. 12 ♘c4 ♘d4 13 ♘xd4 ed 14 ♗g5 ♘d7 15 ♗xe7 ♕xe7 16 ♘d2 ♘c5 17 ♗c4 ♗c8 18 e5 ♗e6= Liang–Lechtynsky, Dubai Ol. 1986.

A1

9 ... d5!?

This is critical because, if playable, it would enable Black to avoid many of the lines in this chapter.

10 ed e4!?

Nunn says that 10 ... ♘xd5 is interesting because taking the pawn looks more dangerous than a normal Marshall:

(a) 11 ♘xe5?! ♘xe5 12 ♖xe5 ♘f6!? (other moves should be investigated) 13 d4 ♗d6 14 ♖e1 (for 14 ♖e2!? compare Chapter 13, B2) 14 ... ♘g4 15 h3 ♕h4 when Black may have more chances than usual because the d-pawn is not protected by a pawn on c3.

(b) But after 11 ♗a4! Black has nothing better than 11 ... ♗b7 and the hope that his two bishops will give him something for the ♙ —Nunn.

The text move was suggested by Plachetka in *Informator* 21. By analogy with Chapter 16, one would expect this to be a bad move but here too a4–a5 is a less useful move for White than c2–c3.

11 dc ef
12 d4!? fg

Now the usual ♕f3 is unavailable, but Suetin suggested 13 c4!? The one example is inconclusive: 13 ♗g5 ♘d5 (13 ... ♖e8!? Suetin) 14 ♗xe7 ♘xe7 15 d5 ♘g6 16 ♘d2?! (better 16 ♔xg2 Suetin) ♘f4 17 ♖e3 (17 ♕f3?+ ♘h3+ 18 ♔xg2 ♕g5+ ∓ ∓) ♕g5 18 ♖g3 ♕e5 19 ♘c4 ♕e4 20 f3 ♕f5? (according to Suetin, Black could seek a promising endgame by 20 ... ♕xd5 21 ♕xd5 ♘xd5; also worthy of consideration were 20 ... ♕e2!?, 20 ... ♕e8 or the complicated line 20 ... ♕e7 21 d6! cd 22 ♕xd6 ♘e2+ 23 ♔g2 ♕xd6 24 ♘xd6 ♘xg3 25 hg ♖a7 26 ♖e1 ♖c7) 21 ♕d2! ♖d8 22 ♖e1 ♗e6 23 ♕d4! g5?! (23 ... ♘g6 24 ♘e3 ±) 24 ♘e3 ♕g6 25 h4! 1–0 (25 ... h6 26 hg hg 27 ♕xf4 gf 28 ♖xg6+ fg 29 de ± ±) Suetin–Zaitsev, Moscow Ch. 1983.

This game is very hard to assess and it is probably impossible to give a reliable opinion without further practical tests.

A2

9 ... d6(*112*)

Clearly the soundest move, this was Karpov's choice, and it brings about the diagram position which may also arise via 7 ... d6 8 a4 b4 9 a5 0-0.

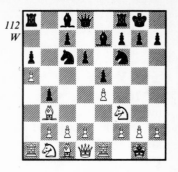

112
W

From the diagram:

A21 10 d3
A22 10 c3

(a) **10 h3** ♗e6 11 d4 ♘xd4 12 ♘xd4 ed 13 ♕xd4 c5 14 ♕d3 d5 15 ed ♘xd5 16 ♘d2 ♘c7 = Hjartarson–Smyslov, Copenhagen 1985.

(b) **10 d4!?** when:

(b1) **10 ... ♗g4** (for 10 ... ♖b8 see 9 ... ♖b8) 11 de (11 c3? bc 12 bc ♖b8 13 ♗c2 ed 14 cd ♘b4∓) ♘xe5 12 ♘bd2 ♘fd7 (12 ... ♕c8!?) 13 h3 ♗h5 14 g4 ♗g6 15 ♘xe5 (15 ♘h2 ♗g5∓) de 16 ♗d5 ♖b8 17 ♘f3! (threat ♗c6; 17 ♘c4? ♗c5= Nunn–Korchnoi, Zurich 1984) ♗d6 18 ♗g5 ♗e7 19 ♗e3 ♗d6± (20 ♗a7 ♖a8! unclear)—Nunn.

(b2) **10 ... ♘xd4** 11 ♘xd4 ed 12 ♕xd4 ♖b8! 13 ♗g5 (13 ♘d2 ♘d7=) h6 14 ♗h4 ♘g4! 15 ♗xe7 ♕xe7 16 ♘d2 ♗e6= Klinger–Hort, Biel 1986.

A21

10 d3

No clearly equalizing line has yet been established here but active play should serve Black well.

10 ... ♖b8

(a) **10 ... ♗e6** (10 ... ♗b7 see 9 ... ♗b7) 11 ♗xe6 (11 ♘bd2 ♗xb3 12 ♘xb3 ♖e8 13 d4 ed 14 ♘fxd4 ♘xd4 15 ♘xd4 ♗f8 16 ♘c6 ♕d7 17 ♘xb4 ♕b5 18 c3 ♘xe4 unclear; Szabo–Unzicker, Bern 1987) fe 12 ♘bd2 ♘d7 13 c3 ♗f6 14 ♕a4 bc (Parma–Sanguinetti, Mar del Plata 1962) 15 ♕xc6 cd 16 ♗xd2 ♘c5 17 ♖a3± Barden, *ECO*.

(b) **10 ... ♗g4!?** seems playable: 11 ♗e3 ♗e6 12 ♘bd2 (12 ♗xe6 fe 13 ♘bd2 d5 threatening ... d4) ♘g4 13 ♘c4 ♘xe3 14 ♘xe3 ♖b8 15 ♘d5 ♗g4 16 ♗c4 ♗xf3 (16 ... ♔h8 17 c3 bc 18 bc f5 19 ♗xa6 fe 20 de ♗xf3 21 gf ♗h4 with compensation; Malaniuk–Podgayets, Harkov 1985) 17 ♕xf3 ♘d4 18 ♕d1 c6 19 ♘b6 ♕e8 20 c3 (20 ♗xa6 b3 21 cb ♗d8 with queenside initiative) bc 21 bc ♘b5 22 ♕g4 ♖b7 23 ♖ac1 ♗d8 24 ♗xb5 cb 25 ♘d5 ♕e6= (½-½, 41) Malaniuk–Smagin, Minsk 1985.

11 ♘bd2

Black has nothing to fear from **11 c3** bc (11 ... ♗g4!? TDH) 12 bc ♘a7= (Karpov) or **11 ♗c4** ♗e6 12 ♘bd2 ♘d7 (drawn here in Tseshkovsky–Kuzmin, Sochi 1976).

11 ... ♔h8

Black plays on the kingside since 11 ... ♘d7 12 ♗a4! (12 ♗d5?! ♘xa5! 13 ♖xa5 c6∓ Kuzmin–Smyslov, USSR 1975) is awkward: 12 ... ♘d4 (12 ... ♗b7 13 ♘b3 idea d4±) 13 ♘xd4 ed 14 ♘f3 c5 (14 ... ♗f6 15 ♗f4 ♘c5 16 e5±) 15 ♗f4 ♗b7 16 ♗xd7 ♕xd7 17 ♘d2± Savon.

12 c3 ♘h5!?

13 d4 ♗f6

14 d5 (14 ♘xe5 de 15 d5 ♘f4 with compensation) ♘e7 15 ♘f1 c6 16 cb cd unclear. Kapengut–I. Ivanov, Chelyabinsk 1975, continued 17 ed ♖xb4 18 ♗d2 ♖b5 19 ♗c4 ♖xb2 20 ♗c3 ♖b8 21 ♘xe5 ♘f4 22 ♘c6 ♘xc6 23 ♗xf6 ♕xf6 24 dc ♖b2 25 ♕f3 ♘h3+! 26 ♔h1 ♘xf2+ 27 ♔g1 ♕d4 28 ♘e3 ♖d2 29 ♖ab1 ♘g4 30 ♖b8 h5 31 ♗xa6 ♖f2∓∓.

A22

10 c3(113)

One of the main lines of the 8 a4 b4 variation.

10 ... ♖b8!

Here 10 ... ♗g4, 10 ... ♗e6?, 10 ... ♗b7 and 10 ... bc have all been found wanting. It is better to see if White intends d4, e.g. 10 ... h6!? 11 d4 bc 12 bc ed 13 cd d5! 14 e5 ♘e4 15 ♖e3! unclear (Malaniuk–Timoshchenko, Harkov 1985).

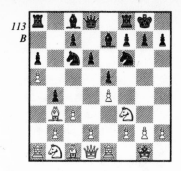

11 &c4!?

This move, avoiding b-file tactics, may be the only White try for an advantage.

11 d3 is equal (A21, note to White's 11th) while **11 d4?!** looks too sharp: 11 ... bc 12 bc ed 13 cd (13 ♘xd4? ♘xd4 14 cd c5 15 dc dc 16 ♕c2 ♘g4 17 &f4 ♖xb3 18 ♕xb3 ♕xd4 19 ♖a2 &e6∓; Kavalek–Lutikov, Beverwijk 1967) d5 14 e5 ♘e4 15 &a3 (15 ♖e3!?) ♘b4 16 &c2 &f5 17 ♖e2 c5∓ (Klovan–Mileika, USSR 1966).

11 ... bc

(a) An interesting Marshall lookalike is **11 ... d5** 12 ed ♘xd5 13 ♘xe5 ♘xe5 14 ♖xe5 &b7 15 d4 &f6 16 ♖e1 c5 with compensation for the pawn, e.g. 17 dc (17 &e3 ♖e8!? [or 17 ... bc 18 bc ♖c8 unclear] 18 dc bc 19 bc ♘xe3 20 ♕xd8 ♖bxd8 21 fe ♖c8∓ Klovan) bc 18 bc ♘xc3 19 ♕xd8 ♖fxd8 20 &b2 ♘e2+ 21 &xe2 &xb2 22 ♖a4 &c6 23 ♖c4 &b5

24 ♖e4 &c6 (24 ... f5!?∓) 25 ♖c4 &b5 ½-½ (A. Ivanov–Klovan, Kostroma 1985).

(b) **11 ... h6** 12 h3 ♘h7 13 ♕e2 ♘g5 14 ♘xg5 &xg5 15 ♔h1 (Moors–Hessenbruch, Bundesliga BRD 1985) ♔h8!? intending ... f5.

(c) **11 ... &b7** 12 d3 (12 ♕e2 ♖a8 13 d3 d5 14 &b3 d4= Bertok–Forintos, Yugoslavia–Hungary 1962) h6 (12 ... d5 13 ed ♘xd5 14 ♕b3 bc 15 bc ♘f4 16 &xf4 ef 17 ♕d1± Gipslis–Sakharov, USSR Ch. 1963) 13 ♘bd2 ♘h7!? (13 ... ♖e8 Mestel) 14 d4 bc 15 bc &f6 (15 ... ed 16 cd &f6 17 &b2±) 16 d5 ♘e7 17 &f1 ♘g5 (Mestel–Rubinetti, Lucerne 1985) 18 c4± Mestel.

(d) **11 ... ♘a7** 12 d4 (12 ♕e2 &b7 13 d4 &xe4 14 de de 15 ♘bd2 &xf3 16 ♘xf3 c4 17 ♘g5 bc 18 bc ♘b5= Ruderfer–Kirpichnikov, USSR 1967) bc (12 ... ed 13 cd± or 12 ... ♘xe4 13 ♖xe4 d5 14 &xd5 ♕xd5 15 ♖xe5 ♕d8 16 ♖e1±) 13 ♘xc3± *ECO*.

12 dc

12 ♘xc3 (12 bc? ♘xa5) &g4 13 h3 &xf3 14 ♕xf3 ♘d4 15 ♕d1 c6 16 ♘e2 ♘b5 17 d3 d5= Tal–Smyslov, USSR Team Ch. 1966.

12 ... ♘a7

Or 12 ... &b7 13 ♘bd2 (13 ♕d3 ♕c8) ♕c8 (13 ... ♘a7 below; 13 ... ♕d7 14 ♘f1 ♘d8!? or 14 ... &d8!? intending ♘e7—

Spraggett) 14 ♘f1 ♘d8 15 ♘g3 ♖e8 (15 ... ♘e6 16 b4 ♖d8 17 ♕b3 c6 18 ♗f1! and ♘d2–c4± Polugayevsky; 15 ... g6!? Spraggett) 16 ♕a4! ♘e6 17 ♕a2 c6 (17 ... ♗f8 intending ... g6, ... ♗g7 Spraggett) 18 ♗b3!± (½–½, 41) Spraggett–Nunn, Wijk aan Zee 1985).

13 ♗f1!?

If 13 ♘bd2 Karpov's suggestion **13 ... ♘b5!?** will probably transpose to the text.

Instead **13 ... ♗b7?!** 14 ♕c2 is ± despite the eventual result of the game: 14 ... ♘b5 15 ♘f1 ♗c6 16 ♘g3 ♗d7 17 h3 ♕c8 18 ♗d3 ♗e6 19 ♗e3 c5 20 ♘d2 ♕c6 21 ♘c4 ♘d7 22 ♖ad1 ♔h8! 23 ♕e2 ♖fe8 24 f4 ef 25 ♗xf4 ♗f6 26 ♘h5 ♗e5 27 ♕f2 f6 28 ♗c1 ♕c7!? 29 ♖f1 ♖e7 30 ♕h4 ♗xc4!? 31 ♗xc4 ♕xa5! 32 ♖f5 ♕d8 unclear, although White went wrong and failed to justify his pawn sacrifices (Nunn–Karpov, Amsterdam 1985).

13 ... ♘b5

14 ♘bd2 ♘d7?! 15 ♕c2 ♘c5 16 b4 ♘e6 17 ♘c4 g6 18 ♗h6 ♘g7 19 ♖ad1± Gipslis–Nikitin, USSR 1970. Karpov presumably prepared an improvement on this game, maybe 14 ... ♗d7 15 ♘c4 (15 ♕c2 ♘h5) ♗c6 16 ♕c2 ♕c8 intending ... ♕b7 or ... ♘h5, ... ♔h8, ... f5.

B

9 c3

Instead of 'isolating' the advanced b-pawn by a5, White challenges it and also prepares d4.

9 ... d6*(114)*

9 ... d5!? again comes into consideration, but unlike A1 White does have d4 under control. So after 10 ed (10 d4?! compare Chapter 15, C2.) Black should transpose to Chapter 15, C3, by 10 ... ♘xd5 since after 10 ... e4 11 dc ef 12 d4 fg the inclusion of 8 a4 b4 is unlikely to alter the Chapter 16 assessment of ±.

Nevertheless it may be worth searching for any significant differences, e.g. 13 ♗g5 (13 ♕f3!?) ♖e8? (critical tries are 13 ... ♖b8!? or 13 ... ♗g4 or 13 ... ♘d5—Pliester) 14 ♕f3 ♗g4 15 ♕xg2 ♗f5 16 ♘d2 bc 17 bc ♖b8 18 ♖e5!±± ♗g6 19 ♖ae1 ♔f8 20 h4 ♘g8 21 ♕f3 f6 22 h5 ♗xh5 23 ♕xh5 ♖xb3 24 ♘xb3 fe 25 ♘c5 1–0, Yudasin–Plachetka, Trnava 1985.

114
W

The diagram can also arise via 7 ... d6 8 c3 0-0 9 a4 b4.

10 d4

Although this is the most consistent follow-up to 9 c3, 10 a5 (line A22) is probably wiser. White has also tried 10 d3 (C, note b to White's 10th) and 10 h3 ♖b8 11 d4 bc 12 bc ed 13 ♘xd4 ♘xd4 14 cd d5 15 ed ♗b7 16 ♗g5 ♗xd5= (Stein–Tal, Moscow 1967).

10 ... bc

Another sound line is 10 ... ed 11 ♘xd4 (11 cd?! ♗g4 12 ♗e3 ♘a5 13 ♗c2 c5 14 b3 ♘d7 15 ♘bd2 ♗f6 16 ♕b1 h6 17 ♖a2 ♘c6∓; Levenfish–Keres, Leningrad–Moscow 1939) ♗d7 12 cb ♘xb4 13 ♘c3 ♖b8= Pachman.

11 bc

Or 11 de when:

(a) **11 ... cb** 12 ♗xb2 de (12 ... ♘xe5 13 ♘d4± Levenfish) 13 ♘xe5 ♘xe5 (13 ... ♕xd1 14 ♖xd1 ♘xe5 15 ♗xe5±) 14 ♗xe5 ♗b4!= Polugayevsky.

(b) **11 ... ♘xe5** 12 ♘xe5 de 13 ♘xc3 ♖b8 (13 ... a5 14 ♘d5 ♘xd5 15 ♗xd5 ♖a6 16 ♗d2± Keres) 14 ♘d5 ♘xd5 15 ♗xd5 ♗b7= *ECO*.

11 ... ♗g4

Black is clearly more active than in the analogous line of Chapter 21, B. Also playable is 11 ... ed 12 cd d5 e.g. 13 ♘e5 ♘b4 14 ed ♗b7 15 ♘c3 ♘bxd5= Jackson–Levin, Ventnor 1943.

12 ♗e3

Others favour Black to some extent, e.g. 12 a5?! ed 13 cd d5 14 e5 ♘e4 15 ♗a3 ♗xa3 16 ♖xa3 ♘g5 (Nezhmetdinov–Furman, USSR 1948) or 12 d5 ♘a5 13 ♗c2 c6 14 dc ♕c7 15 ♕d3 ♕xc6 16 ♘bd2 ♖ac8∓ (Romanovsky–Botvinnik, USSR 1927) or 12 ♗d5 ♘xd5 13 ed ♘a5 14 de de 15 ♖xe5 c6 16 ♗a3 ♗f6 17 ♖e1 ♖e8∓ I. Rabinovich.

12 ... ed
13 cd d5

14 e5 ♘e4 15 ♘bd2 (15 h3 ♗h5 16 ♘bd2 ♗b4∓ Tolush–Furman, USSR Ch. 1958) ♘xd2 16 ♕xd2 ♗b4 17 ♕c2 ♗xf3 18 gf ♗e1 19 ♕c6 with chances for both sides (Spassky–Kolarov, Varna 1958).

C

9 d3

Quiet but not easy to meet adequately.

9 ... d6*(115)*

Not 9 ... ♗b7 10 ♘bd2 (10 a5 see A) d6 (10 ... d5?! 11 ed ♘xd5 12 ♘c4 f6 13 d4! ♘xd4 14 ♘xd4 ed 15 ♘a5!±± Meulders–Ludvigsson, Groningen jr 1971) 11 ♘c4 ♘d7 12 c3 a5 13 ♗e3± Matanovic–Saren, Helsinki 1972.

The diagram can also arise via 7 ... d6 8 a4 b4 9 d3 0-0.

10 ♘bd2

For 10 a5 see A21. White has also tried:

115
W

(a) **10 h3** ♖b8 11 ♘bd2 ♘a5 12 ♗a2 c5 13 ♘c4 ♘xc4 14 ♗xc4 a5 15 ♗d2 ♘d7 16 c3 ♗f6 17 ♗b5 ♗b7= Valkesalmi–Westerinen, Finnish Ch. 1986.

(b) **10 c3** ♖b8 11 ♘bd2 (11 a5 see A22 with 11 d3) ♘a5 12 ♗c2 c5 13 d4 ♕c7 14 d5 (14 de de 15 cb cb= Stean–Plachetka, Moscow 1977; 14 cb ♖xb4=) ♗d7 15 c4 g6 16 b3 ♘h5 17 ♘f1 ♗b7 18 ♗h6 ♘g7 19 h4 ♘d8 20 h5 ♗g4 21 ♘1h2 ♕c8= Kotronias–Muco, Thessaloniki Ol. 1988.

10 ... ♖b8

(a) **10 ... ♗g4** 11 h3 ♗h5 12 c3 ♖b8 13 ♗c4 ♕c8 14 a5 ♖d8 15 ♘f1 bc 16 bc d5 17 ed ♘xd5 18 ♗d2 f6 19 ♘g3 ♗f7 20 ♕a4 ♕b7 unclear (½–½, 83) Short–Timman, Amsterdam 1983.

(b) **10 ... ♘a5** 11 ♗a2 ♗e6 (11 ... c5 12 ♘c4 ♘xc4 13 ♗xc4 ♘e6 14 ♘bd2± Ivkov–Damjanovic, Yugoslavia 1966) 12 ♗xe6!? fe 13 c3 (intending d4) *ECO.*

(c) **10 ... ♗e6** 11 a5 ♖b8 12 ♗c4 ♕c8 13 ♘f1 ♗xc4 14 dc

♕e6 15 ♘e3 ♗d8 16 ♘d5± Fuchs–Spassky, Sochi 1966.

11 ♘c4

11 c3 (11 a5 see A21) ♘a5 12 ♗a2 ♗g4 13 ♘c4 ♘xc4 14 ♗xc4 bc 15 bc a5 16 h3 ♗h5 17 ♗a3 c6 18 d4 ed 19 cd ♖e8= Ostojic–Zaitsev, Polanica Zdroj 1970.

11 ... ♗e6

Or 11 ... ♗g4 (11 ... ♘d7?! 12 ♗e3 ♗f6 13 c3± *ECO*) 12 ♗e3 (12 ♘e3 ♗xf3 13 ♕xf3 ♘d4 14 ♕d1 ♘xb3 15 cb ♘d7= Klovan–Zaitsev, USSR 1969) ♘d7 13 ♘4d2 ♘a5 14 ♗a2 c5 15 ♘c4 ♗e6= Ivkov–Reshevsky, Santa Monica 1966.

12 c3

12 h3 ♘d7 13 ♗e3 ♗f6 14 d4= Minic–Spassky, Belgrade 1964.

12 ... ♘d7
13 ♗e3 bc

13 ... ♗f6?! 14 d4 ed 15 cd d5 16 ♘cd2± Ivkov–Geller, Yugoslavia–USSR 1964.

14 bc ♗f6=

(Keres). Not now 15 d4? ♖xb3 16 ♕xb3 ♘a5.

D

9 d4 d6
10 de*(116)*

This direct central treatment probably has been the most popular answer to 8 ... b4 in recent years.

After 10 h3 (10 c3 see B) Black has two simple equalizing lines:

(a) **10 ... ♗b7** 11 c3 bc (11 ... ed 12 cd d5 13 e5 ♘e4 14 a5

♘a7= R. Garcia–Najdorf, Buenos Aires 1968) 12 ♘xc3 ♖b8 13 ♗c4 ♘xd4 ½–½ (Balashov–Geller, USSR Ch. 1985).

(b) **10 ... ♘xd4** 11 ♘xd4 ed 12 ♕xd4 c5 13 ♕d3 ♗b7 14 ♘d2 ♖e8 15 ♘f3 (Romanovsky–C. Torre, Moscow 1925) d5= Belavenets.

(c) **10 ... ed** 11 ♘xd4 ♘a5!? (11 ... ♘xd4 see b) is more ambitious: 12 ♗a2 (12 c3 bc 13 ♗d5?! cb 14 ♗xb2 ♘xd5 15 ed ♗d7 16 ♗c3 ♘b7∓ Kotronias–Hjartarson, Thessaloniki Ol. 1988) c5 13 ♘f3 ♗b7 14 ♘bd2 ♕c7 15 c3 bc 16 bc ♘d7 17 ♘c4 ♘xc4 18 ♗xc4 ♘b6 19 ♗b3 ♗f6 20 ♗f4 ♖ad8 21 a5 ♘c8 22 ♕d3 ♘a7 23 ♕c4 ♘b5 24 ♖e3 ♖de8 25 ♖d1± ♗xc3?! 26 ♗a4 ♗xa5 27 ♗xb5 ab 28 ♕xb5 ♗c6 29 ♕b3 ♕b7 (29 ... ♖d8 30 ♖3d3 ♗xe4 31 ♗xd6 ♕c6 32 ♘e5) 30 ♗xd6 ♗xe4 31 ♕a3 ♗c2 32 ♖c1 ♗b4 33 ♕b2 ♖xe3 34 ♗xf8± Balashov–Simagin, Moscow Ch. 1982.

116
B

From the diagram:
D1 10 ... ♘xe5
D2 10 ... dxe5

D1

10 ...   ♘xe5
11 ♘xe5

Maintaining the tension leads to rich and unclear middle games:

(a) **11 ♘bd2** ♗b7!? (11 ... ♗g4 Kupreichik; 11 ... ♘xf3+ 12 ♕xf3 ♗b7 13 ♘f1 d5= Pachman) 12 ♘xe5 de 13 ♕f3 (13 ♕e2!?) ♔h8! (threat ♘xe4) 14 g4!? ♗c5 (14 ... g6!?) 15 ♘c4 ♘xe4!? with enormous complications (1–0, 41 after Black missed drawing chances) Ehlvest–Kupreichik, USSR Ch. 1987.

(b) **11 ♗f4!?** ♘g6 (11 ... ♗g4 12 ♗xe5 ♗xf3 13 ♕xf3 de 14 ♖d1 ♕b8 15 ♘d2± Kiarner–Vark, Estonian Ch. 1964) 12 ♗g3 ♗b7 13 ♘bd2 ♘h5 (or 13 ... ♕d7 14 ♘d4 d5 15 e5 ♘e8 unclear; Dubinin–Tolush, USSR 1947) 14 ♘c4 ♘xg3 15 hg a5 16 ♘d4 ♗f6 17 ♘f5 ♘e5 18 ♖b1 g6 19 ♘xe5 ♗xe5 20 ♘e3 h5 21 ♗d5 c6 22 ♗b3 ♕f6 23 ♘c4 ♗a6 24 ♘xa5 h4 25 ♕f3 hg 26 ♕xf6 ♗xf6 27 ♘xc6 ♗b7 28 e5 ♗h4 29 fg ♗xg3 30 ♖e3 ♗f4 31 ♖f3 de 32 ♗d5 ♗xc6 33 ♗xc6 ♖ac8 34 ♗e4 f5 35 ♗d5+ ♔g7 36 c4 g5 37 a5 e4∓ (0–1, 56) Klovan–Moskovich, Riga 1984.

11 ...   de
12 ♗g5!

(a) 12 Qxd8 Rxd8 13 Nd2 (13 Bg5!?) Bc5 14 h3 (14 Bc4 Bb7 15 Bd3 Ba7 intending ... Nd7–c5=; 14 Nc4? Nxe4 15 Be3 Bxe3 16 Rxe3 Nc5 17 Nxe5 Nxb3 18 Rxb3 c5 ∓; Hlousek–Tseitlin, Olomouc 1977) Bb7 15 Bc4 a5 16 Bd3 Ba6 17 Bxa6 Rxa6 18 Nc4 Bd4 19 Be3 Rc6= Jansa–Tseitlin, Kragujevac 1974.

(b) 12 Qf3?! (12 Qe2 Bc5 13 Bg5 Bg4 14 Qc4 Qd4 15 Qxd4 Bxd4 16 c3= Furman–Klovan, USSR Ch 1975) Bb7 (12 ... Be6 13 Nd2 Bc5 14 h3 ± Vasiukov–Zaitsev, Moscow 1983) 13 Nd2 a5 (13 ... Qe8 14 Nf1 ± Zaitsev) 14 Nf1? Kh8! 15 Rd1 Qe8 16 Ng3 Nxe4!∓∓ Kir. Georgiev–Velimirovic, Vrsac 1987.

12 ...   Nd7

12 ... Bb7!? gives good chances of drawing, e.g. 13 Nd2 h6 14 Bxf6 Bxf6 15 Nc4 Qxd1 16 Raxd1 Rfd8 17 f3 Bc6! 18 Kf1 Kf8 19 Na5 Rd1 20 Rxd1 Be8 21 Bd5 Rd8 22 Nb7 Rb8 23 Nc5 a5 24 Bc4 Rd8! 25 Rxd8?! Bxd8= Kupreichik–Malich, 2nd Telex-Olympiad Final 1982.

13   Bd5!?

13 Be3 a5 14 Nd2 Bb7 15 Qh5 Bf6= Weinstein–Pinter, Budapest 1976.

13 ...   Rb8

14 Be3 [threat Ba7] Nb6 (14

... Bb7 15 Bxb7 Rxb7 16 Nbd2 idea Nb3±) 15 Bb3 (15 Bxb6 Rxb6 16 Nd2 Rg6 unclear) a5 (15 ... Qxd1 16 Rxd1 a5 17 Nd2 Ba6 18 Nf3±) 16 Nd2 Ba6 17 Qh5!± Bf6 18 Nf3 Qe7 19 Rad1 g6 20 Qh6 Bg7 21 Bg5 Bxh6 22 Bxe7 Rfe8 23 Bc5 Kg7 24 h4 Bc8 25 Bxb6 cb 25 Rd6 Rb7 27 Bc4 Rc7 28 b3 Bd7 29 Rxb6 Bxa4 30 Ra6 Rxc4 31 bc Bxc2 32 Rxa5 b3 33 Rb5 f6 34 Ra1 Kg8 35 c5 Rd8 36 Ra7 Bf8 37 c6 Bxe4 38 c7 Rc8 39 Nd2 Bc6 40 Rb6 Bc5 41 Rb8 1–0 Kupreichik–Tseshkovsky, USSR Ch. 1987.

D2

10 ...   de

11   Nbd2!

Or 11 Qxd8 Rxd8 12 Bg5 (12 Nbd2 h6 13 Nc4 ½–½; Nunn–Spassky, Zurich 1984) when:

(a) 12 ... Bb7 13 Nbd2 h6 14 Bxf6 (14 Bh4? g5 15 Bg3 g4∓∓) 14 ... Bxf6 15 Bd5 (with the idea Nc4±) Na5 16 Bxb7 Nxb7 17 Nc4 Re8 (Sax–A. Rodriguez, Lucerne Ol. 1982) 18 Ne3 Be7! 19 Nxe5 Bd6 20 Nd3 Rxe4± Rodriguez.

(b) 12 ... h6 13 Bxf6 gf (the e-pawn is weak after 13 ... Bxf6? e.g. 14 Bd5 Bd7 15 Nbd2 Re8 16 Nb3 Rad8 17 Nc5 Nb8 18 h3 Bc8 19 Rad1 Rd6 20 Nd2 c6 21 Bb3 Red8 22 Nd3 Rd4 23 Nf3 R4d6 24 Ra1± Vasiukov–

Imanaliev, Frunze 1983) 14 ♗d5
♗d7 15 ♘bd2 ♖ab8 16 ♘b3
♗d6 17 ♘h4 ♘a7 18 ♗c4 ♖a8
(Vasiukov–Simagin, Moscow Ch.
1982) 19 ♗xa6±.

11 ... ♗b7

Or 11 ... ♗c5 (11 ... ♗g4 12
h3±) 12 h3 (12 ♕e2 ♕e7 13 a5
♖d8 14 ♗c4 ♘d4 15 ♘xd4 ♗xd4
16 ♘b3 ♗b7= Ivanovic–
Spassky, Bugojno 1982) h6 13 a5
♗b7 14 ♗c4 ♗a7 15 c3 ♕e7 16
♕e2 ♘h5 17 ♘b3 ♕f6 18 ♗d5±
Jansa–Hardicsay, Budapest 1978.

12 ♕e2 ♘d4!?

12 ... a5!? may be better. If 12
... ♘a5 13 ♘xe5 ♘xb3 14 ♘xb3!
(14 c6 ♖e8 with compensation)
♗xe4 (14 ... ♘xe4 15 ♘a5± ±)
15 ♗g5± Tukmakov.

13 ♕c4!?

If 13 ♘xd4 ♕xd4= but now
White may keep an edge:

(a) **13 ... a5!?** 14 ♘xd4 (14
♘xe5? ♗a6∓ ∓) 14 ... ♕xd4 (14
... ed unclear) 15 ♕xd4 (15
♕xc7? ♗c5 with an attack) ed 16
♗c4± Tukmakov.

(b) **13 ... ♗d6!?** 14 ♘xd4 (14
a5? c5!) ed 15 e5?! (15 h3!? or 15
a5!? Tukmakov) ♘g4! 16 ♕xd4
(16 ed? ♕h4) ♘xe5 17 ♖xe5
♗xe5 18 ♕xe5 ♖e8 19 ♕g3??
(the critical line is 19 ♕h5 ♖e1+
20 ♘f1 ♕d7 21 ♗c4 ♖ae8 22 b3
♖8e5 with compensation—Tukmakov) ♖e1+ 0–1, (mate in two)
Kupreichik–Geller, USSR Ch.
1985.

19 Anti-Marshall: 8 a4 ♗b7 Main Line (10 ♘c3, 12 ♘e2)

1 e4 e5 2 ♘f3 ♘c6 3 ♗b5 a6 4 ♗a4 ♘f6 5 0-0 ♗e7 6 ♖e1 b5 7 ♗b3 0-0

8	a4	♗b7
9	d3	d6
10	♘c3	♘a5
11	♗a2	b4
12	♘e2	(117)

It is an indication of the enormous development of this variation within the past decade that the second (1981) edition of *ECO* devotes just one row (C88/14) to this position, which is one of the most critical arising from 7 ... 0-0 and which now requires a major chapter for its thorough exposition. *New In Chess Yearbook 7* contains a great deal of study material on this line (up to 1987) but A. C. van der Tak's analysis fails to include some important sub-variations, notably D2.

The clash of ideas is here at its keenest. Black has in recent years radically revised his plans, following some disillusionment with the ♙ sacrifice ideas which used to be recommended. White will combine traditional kingside pressure with refutation of any over-optimism by his opponent on the queenside, but Black should find clearer ways to equality (or better) than after 7 ... d6 etc. Indeed an element of bluff is at work: 7 ... 0-0 'threatens' the Marshall and may induce replies other than 8 c3 even if Black had no intention of gambitting his d-pawn.

From the diagram:

A	12 ... b3?!
B	12 ... d5?!
C	12 ... ♖b8
D	12 ... c5!

(a) **12 ... ♘d7?!** 13 ♘g3 ♗f6 14 c3 bc 15 bc c5 16 ♘f5 ♕c7 17 ♘g5 h6 18 ♕h5 hg 19 ♖e3 g4 20 ♖g3 c4 21 ♘h6+ 1–0 Klovan–Ozolins, Riga 1984.

(b) **12 ... ♘h5?!** 13 c3 bc (13 ... c5 see D2 below) 14 ♘xc3 (14 bc ♔h8 15 g4!? unclear; Enklaar–Schneider, Eksjo 1975) ♘f6 15 d4 ♘c6 16 de de 17 ♗g5 ♘b4 18 ♗c4 h6 19 ♗h4 ♘d7 20 ♗g3 ♗f6 21 a5± (1–0, 65) Yudasin–Hjartarson, Leningrad 1984.

(c) **12 ... ♖e8?!** 13 ♘g3 ♗f8 14 c3 bc 15 bc h6 16 ♗d2 ♖b8 17 d4 c5 18 ♖b1± Browne–Harandi, Manila 1976.

A

| **12 ...** | **b3?!** |

This sacrifice, to devalue White's pawns and open the b-file, recurs in different forms in this chapter. Although its worth in any context is now doubtful, here it definitely is premature and White has at least two favourable replies.

13 cb

(a) 13 ♗d2!? ba 14 ♗xa5 ♘h5 15 ♘g3 ♘f4 (Liberzon–Obukhovsky, USSR 1971) 16 d4!± Yudovich or 16 ♘f5!? (Van der Tak).

(b) 13 ♗xb3 ♘xb3 14 cb c5 15 ♗d2 (15 ♘c3!? ♖b8 16 ♘d2 ♘e8 17 ♘c4 f5 unclear; Tseshkovsky–Seredenko, Aktiubinsk 1985) a5 16 ♗c3 ♗c8? 17 ♘d2 ♗e6 18 ♘c4 ♘h5 19 ♖f1 ♕c7 20 ♕d2 ♗d8 21 f4± (Thipsay–Reika, Biel 1986) is a good example of how Black can end up with nothing for the ♙, but it is less clear after 16 ... ♘e8! aiming for a rapid ... f5.

| **13 ...** | **c5** |

Or 13 ... ♘c6 (13 ... d5!? 14 ed see B) 14 ♗d2 a5 15 ♘g3 ♖e8 16 ♖c1 ♗f8?! (16 ... d5!? van der Tak) 17 b4! ♘xb4 18 ♗xb4 ab 19 ♘g5 ♖e7 20 d4± Timman–Riemersma, Dutch Ch. 1987.

14 b4

14 ♘g3 (14 ♘d2!? to hold the ♙) transposes to a sideline of D11 considered satisfactory for Black.

| **14 ...** | **cxb4** |
| **15** | **♘g3** |

15 ♗d2 d5 (15 ... ♘c6 16 ♘g3 ♗c8 17 ♖c1 ♕b6 18 ♗e3 ♕b7 19 h3 ♖b8 20 d4 b3 21 ♗b1± Oll–Guliev, USSR 1983; 15 ... b3? 16 ♗xa5 ♕a5 17 ♗xb3—van der Tak) 16 ♘g3 de 17 de ♗c5 18 ♘c1 ♕b6 19 ♕e2± Gipslis–Cuellar, Sousse 1967.

| **16 ...** | **♖b8** |

15 ... ♗c8 16 d4 ♗g4 (16 ... ♘c6 17 h3 h6 18 ♗e3 ♗d7 19 ♖c1 ♖c8 20 ♗c4! ed 21 ♘xd4 ♘xd4 22 ♗xd4 a5 23 ♕b3 ♘e8 24 ♗b5!± Parma–Medina, Malaga 1973) 17 de! (17 h3 ♗xf3= Lukin–Zakharov, USSR Cup 1973) ♗xf3 18 ♕xd3 de 19 ♘f5± Gheorghiu.

16   d4! ±

The older 16 ♗d2 is less clear since instead of 16 ... ♘c6 (or 16 ... ♘d7 17 ♗xb4 ♘c5 18 ♘f5± Tal–Sygulski, Yurmala 1987) 17 ♖c1 d5?! 18 ♘f5!± (Gipslis–Pogats, Budapest 1964) Black can play 16 ... ♗c8 (16 ... b3!? 17 ♗b1 g6!? unclear—van der Tak) 17 h3 h6 18 ♖c1 ♖e8 19 ♘f1 ♗f8 20 ♘e3 ♗e6 21 ♘c4 ♘xc4 22 ♗xc4 ♗xc4 ½–½ (Parma–Ivanovic, Yugoslav Ch. 1982).

16   ...   ♘c6
17   ♘f5   ♗c8

18 ♗g5 ♗xf5 19 ef h6 20 ♗h4 e4!? 21 ♗xf6 ♗xf6 22 ♖xe4 ♕b6 23 ♖c1 b3!? 24 ♗xb3 ♘a5 25 ♗d5 ♕xb2 26 g4 (Klovan–Maseyev, corr. 1971). Despite gallant efforts at active counterplay, Black obtained no genuine compensation and was squashed.

B
12   ...   d5?!

Pachman's idea, closely allied strategically to the previous variation, is also reckoned to be unsound.

13   ed   b3(118)

13 ... ♗xd5 is inadequate after 14 ♗xd5 (14 ♘xe5 ♗xa2 15 ♖xa2 ♕d5 16 ♘c4 ♘xc4 17 ♘f4 ♕f5 18 ♖xe7 ♖ae8! Matulovic–Tseshkovsky, Zagreb 1975) ♕xd5 15 c4! (Balashov) ♕c5 (15 ... bc 16 ♘xc3 or 15 ... ♕d6 16 ♘g3 ♘c6 17 ♘f5 ♕e6 18 ♘xe7+

♕xe7 19 ♘xe5! Holmov) 16 ♘g3 ♘c6 17 ♘f5 e4 18 de ♕xc4 19 b3 ♕e6 20 ♕c2 ♘a5? (20 ... ♖fe8 21 ♘g5 ♕d7 22 e5±) 21 ♘g5 1–0 (21 ... ♕d7 22 ♖d1 ♕e8 23 e5 h6 24 ef ♗xf6 25 ♘xh6+ ± ±) Holmov–Zhukhovitsky, Smolensk 1986.

118
W

14   ♗d2!

Accepting the second ♗ is risky in view of 14 cb ♘xd5 15 ♘c3 (15 ♘xe5!? ♗b4! unclear—Keres) ♘b4! 16 ♘xe5 c5 17 ♗e3 ♕c7 18 ♘c4 ♖ad8 19 ♗f4! ♕xf4 20 ♘xa5 ♗a8! (20 ... ♕c7 = Endzelins–Heemsoth, corr. 1976) 21 ♖xe7 ♕g5 22 ♖e4 f5 23 f4 ♕g6 24 ♖e2 ♘xd3 25 ♕f1 ♖d4! with a very strong attack (Heemsoth).

14   ...   ba

14 ... ♕xd5 15 ♘c3 ♕c6 16 cb ♖ad8 17 ♖xe5 ♗b4 18 ♕e2± Gipslis–Ghitescu,   Kecskemet 1968.

15   ♗xa5   ♕xd5
16   ♗xc7!

This simplifies to a position where Black has given away one ♙ too many. If 16 ♗d2 e4 (16 ... ♘g4 17 h3 f5 18 ♘c3 ♕c6 19 ♕e2 ♗c5 20 ♗e3± Arnlind–Schütt, corr. 1976) 17 ♘c3 ♕f5 18 ♘h4 ♕e5 19 ♖xa2 ♗d6 with compensation (Lukin–Fedorov, Leningrad Ch. 1975).

16 ...   ♕c5
17 ♗xe5   ♗xf3
18 ♗xf6 ♗xf6 19 gf ♗xb2 20 ♖xa2 ♖ab8 21 ♕d2 ♗e5 22 d4 ♕c4 23 ♖a3 ♗d6 24 ♕d3 ♕c7 25 ♖b3! ♖bc8 26 ♖c3 ♕a5 27 ♖a1 ♖ce8 28 ♘g3 ♖e6 29 ♖b3 ♖fe8 30 c4 h5 31 c5 ♗xg3 32 hg h4 33 ♕c3 ♕d8 34 g4±± Klinger–Djuric, Szirak 1985.

C

12 ...   ♖b8(*119*)
Now we start to examine the critical modern variations. This rook move usually occurs sooner or later, aiming for counterplay on the b-file, but its timing is important. Playing it at once, as Hebden prefers, avoids variation D2 but the indications are that it is better deferred for a move or two, although there are many transpositional possibilities.

13 ♘d2
After 13 ♘g3! (not 13 c3 b3! Psakhis) Black can transpose to D12 by **13 ... c5!** while **13 ... b3?!** 14 cb c5 15 b4!? cb is A. Against the alternative 13 ... ♗c8 (aiming

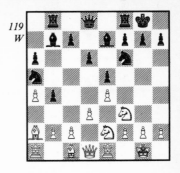

for D13) White need not spend a tempo on h3–h3 but can play 14 d4! e.g. 14 ... ed (14 ... ♘c6 15 c3 bc 16 bc ♗g4 17 ♗e3 ed 18 cd ♘b4 19 ♗b1± Yudasin–Agapov, USSR 1984) 15 ♘xd4 ♖e8 (15 ... g6!? 16 ♘f3 c5 17 ♗h6 ♖e8 18 e5!? de 19 ♘xe5 b3 unclear; Reyes–Gavrilakis, Thessaloniki Ol. 1988) 16 ♗f4 ♖b6 17 h3 ♘c6 18 c3 bc 19 bc ♗d7 20 ♘f3 h6 21 a5 ♖b5 22 ♗c4 ♖xa5 23 ♕b3± Jansa–Skembris, Vrnjacka Banja 1983.

13 ...   c5
14 ♘c4   ♘xc4
15 ♗xc4
White's typical exchange manoeuvre has clarified the light squares, making it hard for Black to break through on the queenside, but it costs time and enables simplification to occur. Two examples:
(a) **15 ... ♘d7** 16 ♘g3 ♘b6 17 ♗b3 ♗g5 18 ♗xg5 ♕xg5 19 a5 ♘c8 20 ♘f5 g6 21 ♖e3 ♔h8 22

♖g3 ♕f6 23 ♘h6 (threat ♖f3) ♕g7 24 ♕d2!? (24 ♘f5 ♕f6=) ♘e7 25 ♕g5 f6 26 ♕h4 f5 27 ♗e6 ♕f6 28 ♕xf6+ ♖xf6 29 ef ♘xf5 30 ♘f7+ ♖xf7 (30 ... ♔g7? 31 ♗xf5 ♖xf5 32 ♘xd6) 31 ♗xf7 ♘xg3 32 hg d5= (½-½, 65) Kupreichik–Razuvayev, Moscow 1987.

(b) 15 ... ♘e8 16 c3 (16 ♘g3 see D122) 16 ... bc 17 bc ♘c7 18 f4 ♗f6 19 fe ♗xe5 20 ♗f4 a5 21 ♗xe5 de 22 ♘g3 ♗a6 23 ♗xa6 ♘xa6 24 ♘f5 ♘c7 25 ♖b1 ♖xb1 26 ♕xb1 ♘e6 with a slight Black initiative (½-½, 48) Kupreichik–Hebden, Malmo 1988.

D

12 ... c5! *(120)*

Necessary sooner or later, this move keeps more options open.

120
W

From the diagram:

D1 13 ♘g3
D2 13 c3

The first of these has been the most popular in the 1980s; the second is tricky and may make a come-back. Others:

(a) **13 ♗d2!?** ♗c8 (13 ... ♖b8!? 14 ♘g3 see D12; 13 ... ♖e8 14 ♘g3 g6! 15 ♘f1 ♗f8= Kasparov/Keene) 14 ♘g3 ♗e6 15 ♘g5 (15 ♗xe6 fe 16 c3 bc 17 bc ♖b8= Kurajica–Jansa, Titovo Uzice 1978) ♗xa2 16 ♖xa2 g6 17 ♘f3 ♕c7= Ivanovic–Ivkov, Skopje 1976.

(b) **13 ♗g5** ♘h5! 14 ♗xe7 ♕xe7 15 ♘d2 ♗c8 (15 ... ♔h8!? intending ... f5 with the attack— Parma) 16 ♘c4 ♘xc4 17 ♗xc4 ♗e6 18 ♘g3 ♘f4 19 ♘h5 ♗xc4 20 dc ♘e6 21 ♘g3 draw (Karpov–Tal, Tilburg 1980).

D1

13 ♘g3

The most popular choice in recent years:

D11 13 ... b3!?
D12 13 ... ♖b8
D13 13 ... ♗c8

Or 13 ... ♖e8!? 14 ♘g5 d5 (14 ... ♖f8!?) 15 ed b3 (15 ... ♘xd5? 16 ♕h5±) 16 cb ♘xd5 17 ♖xe5!? f6 18 ♘e6 ♕d7 19 ♖e1 ♗d6 (19 ... ♘b4!? 20 ♕g4 ♗f8 21 ♘h5 ♔h8 22 ♗d2 ♗c8 23 ♘hf4 unclear—Pliester) 20 b4! cb 21 ♘d4 ♔h8 22 ♘e4± Kosten–M. Pavlovic, Geneva Open 1986.

D11

13 ... b3!?

This move is an improved form of line A, aiming at control over b4 and d4. 13 ... b3 used to get a ! from theory but Nunn warns against it as White can accept the sacrifice: 'A subsequent ♘d2–c4 shields the extra ♙ from attack, whereupon White may become active on the kingside with f4. ... Why should White return the ♙ with b4?' he asks.

14 ♗xb3!

It is better to exchange the ♗ since 14 cb?! ♘c6 leaves it hemmed in: 15 ♘f5?! (15 ♘d2!?; 15 b4 ♘xb4 16 ♗c4 a5 17 ♘f5 ♘e8 = Ciric–Jansa, Vrnjacka Banja 1975) 15 ... ♘b4 16 ♗b1 (16 ♗g5 ♗c8 17 ♘xe7+ ♕xe7 18 ♗b1 h6 19 ♗d2 ♖b8 20 h3 ♗e6 and ♗xb3; Timmerman–van der Zwan, corr. 1983) a5 17 ♗g5 ♗c8 18 ♘xe7+ ♕xe7 19 ♘d2 h6 20 ♗e3 g5!∓ (Klovan–Spassky, USSR Ch. 1963).

14 ... ♘xb3

15 cb(121)

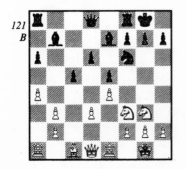

121
B

15 ... a5!

As suggested by Jansa 'though White can continue ♘d2–c4 and a later f4'. Many sources say the position is now equal, because a draw was agreed here in Karpov–Tukmakov, USSR Ch. 1983. Clearly more play is possible, but top GMs have not been involved and as yet there is no clear model for White.

White retains more chances after:

(a) 15 ... ♘d7 16 b4! cb 17 d4 a5 (or 17 ... ♖e8 18 d5 ♘c5 19 ♗e3 ♖c8 20 ♖c1 ♗f6 21 b3 g6 22 ♗xc5± Klovan–Venailainen, corr. 1971–74) 18 b3 ♖e8 19 ♖a2 ♖c8 20 ♖d2 ed (Matulovic–Jansa, Kapfenberg 1970) 21 ♗b2!±.

(b) 15 ... ♖e8 16 ♗d2 a5 17 ♘f5 ♗f8 18 ♗c3 ♘d7 19 ♘e3 ♘b8 20 ♘d2 ♘c6 21 ♘dc4± Chandler–Thipsay, British Ch. 1984.

(c) 15 ... ♗c8 16 b4!? (16 ♘d2!?; 16 ♗d2 ♖b8 17 ♗c3 ♖b7 18 ♘d2 ♗g4 19 f3 ♗e6 20 ♘c4 ♘e8 21 ♘f1 ♗g5 22 ♘a5 ♖b6 23 ♘c4 ½–½; Tukmakov–Geller, Moscow 1985) cb 17 d4 ed (17 ... ♕c7 18 b3! and ♗b2) 18 ♘xd4 ♗g4 19 f3 ♗e6 20 ♘gf5 ♖c8 21 ♗g5 ♔h8 22 ♖c1 ♕d7 23 ♕d2 b3 24 h3 ♖xc1 25 ♖xc1± Matulovic–Djuric, Vinkovci 1986.

16 ♗d2

Following Pachman's suggestion intending ♗c3 and ♘f3–d2–c4 putting the black pawns under fire.

Van der Tak considers White's best treatment may be 16 ♘f5!? (16 ♗e3 should be met by 16 ... ♘d7 and ♘d7–b8–c6) ♗c8 17 ♘e3!? (17 ♘xe7+ ♕xe7 18 ♕c2 ♗e6 19 ♘d2 ♖fb8 20 ♘c4 ♗xc4 21 bc ♘d7= Veröci–Hund, Thessaloniki Ol. 1984) e.g. 17 ... ♘d7 18 ♘d2 ♘b8 19 ♘dc4 ♘c6 20 ♘d5 ♗e6 21 f4 f6 22 ♗d2 (Ghinda–Vlahos, Iraklion tt 1985) but after 22 ... ♖f7! (intending ... ♗f8) the position is not very different from the main example below.

16 ... ♘d7

It is important for Black to switch this ♘ to the queenside rapidly and not dither as in 16 ... ♗c8 17 ♗c3 g6 18 ♘d2 ♘d7 19 ♘c4 ♘b8 20 ♖f1 ♗g5 21 ♘e2 ♗h6 22 f4 f6 23 ♗d2 ♘c6 24 ♘c3 ♘b4 25 ♘d5!± Klovan–Goldin, Gomel 1983.

17 ♗c3

Or 17 ♘f5 ♘b8 18 ♗c3 ♘c6 19 ♘d2 ♗c8 20 ♘xe7+ ♕xe7 21 ♘c4 ♗e6 (21 ... f5!? van der Tak) 22 ♕d2 ♖fb8 (Elburg–Van der Zwan, corr. 1984–85) 23 ♘xa5 ♘xa5 24 ♗xa5 ♗xb3= van der Tak.

17 ... ♘b8
18 ♘d2 ♘c6

19 ♘c4 ♗c8 20 ♖f1 (20 f4!? ef!? 21 ♘h5 g5!? and if 22 g3?! fg 23 ♘xg3 ♗f6∓ van der Tak–Sande, corr. 1982–83) ♗e6 21 f4 f6 22 ♘f5 ♖f7 23 ♘fe3 ♗f8 24 f5 ♗d7 25 ♘d5 ♗e8 26 ♖f3 ♖b7 27 g4 ♔h8 28 ♔h1 ♗f7 29 ♖g3 ♘e7 30 ♘ce3 ♘xd5 31 ♘xd5 ♗xd5 32 ed ♗e7 33 ♖h3 ♕g8 34 ♕f3 ♖xb3= Anand–Bryson, Thessaloniki Ol. 1984.

D12

13 ... ♖b8(122)

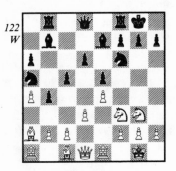

From the diagram:

D121 14 ♘f5
D122 14 ♘d2

14 ♗d2!? is sometimes tried:
(a) **14 ... ♗c8** when:
(a1) **15 ♕e2** (15 h3 see D131; 15 c3!? b3! unclear) ♘c6 16 h3 (Djurasevic–Averbakh, Yugoslavia–USSR 1959) ♗e6! with a somewhat improved form of D131 for Black.

(a2) **15 ♘f1!?** ♗e6 16 ♗xe6 fe
17 ♘e3 h6 18 ♘c4! ♘xc4 19 dc
♕e8 20 b3 (after 20 g3 [Kurajica–
P. Littlewood, Borovo 1980]
Black should play similarly with
20 . . . g5! 21 ♕e2 ♔g7 etc.) g5 21
♕e2 ♕g6 22 ♖ad1 ♖f7 23 ♕d3
g4 24 ♘h4 ♕h5 25 g3 ♘h7 26
♘g2 ♖bf8∓ Oll–Razuvayev,
Moscow 1983.

(b) Alternatives are **14 . . .**
♗c6!? 15 ♘f5 c4 16 ♘3h4 ♖e8 17
♘xe7+?! ♕xe7 18 ♘f5 ♕e6!
(Chandler–Sarapu, New Zealand
1983) and **14 . . . ♘e8** 15 ♘f5 ♗f6
16 h3 ♘c7 17 ♘e3 ♔h8 18 ♕c1
g6 (intending . . . ♗g7 and . . . f5)
19 ♘c4± J. Delaney–Hebden,
London (Lloyds Bank) 1987.

D121

14 ♘f5 ♗c8

14 . . . b3 is probably premature: 15 ♗xb3 (15 cb!? ♘c6 16 b4
Keene) 15 . . . ♘xb3 16 cb ♗c8 17
♘e3 ♗e6 18 ♖a3 ♘g4 19 ♘c4 f5
20 ♕e2 unclear (Spassky–Karpov, London 1982).

15 ♘3h4!?

Malaniuk suggested 15 ♘e3!?
as Black need not fear 15 ♘xe7+
♕xe7 16 ♘d2 (16 ♗g5 b3 17
♗xb3 ♘xb3 18 cb ♗g4 19 ♖e3
h6 20 ♗xf6 ♕xf6 21 ♕c2 ♗xf3
22 ♖xf3 ♕e6 23 ♕c4 ♕c8 24
♖c1 a5 25 ♕d5 ♕e6 26 ♕xe6
fe∓ Westerinen–Timoshchenko,
Helsinki 1986) ♗e6 17 ♘c4 ♘xc4
18 ♗xc4 a5 19 ♗xe6 fe 20 ♗d2

h6 21 c3 ♖f7= Short–Holmov,
Erevan 1984.

15 . . . b3!?

With the ♘ offside at h4 this
looks more justifiable than usual.
Black can also consider 15 . . .
♘e8 (15 . . . ♗e6!? Kuzmin) 16
♘xe7+ ♕xe7 17 ♘f5!? (17 g3 b3
18 cb ♘c6= Kupreichik–Razuvayev, Minsk 1985) ♗xf5 18 ef
♕d7 19 g4 b3 20 cb!? (Prasad–
Pein, London 1986) ♘c6 unclear.

16 cb

16 ♗d2 bc 17 ♕xc2 ♖e8! 18
♖e3!? ♗e6 19 ♗c4 ♘b3! 20
♗xb3 ♗xb3 21 ♕c1 ♗f8 22 ♖f3
♘d7 23 ♖g3 ♔h8 24 ♘f3
(Kupreichik–Malaniuk, Erevan
1984) f6!?± Malaniuk.

16 . . . ♗e6
17 b4 cb

18 d4 b3 19 ♗b1 ♘e8 about=
e.g. 20 ♘xe7+ ♕xe7 21 ♘f5
♗xf5 22 ef ♘f6 23 ♗g5 h6 24
♗h4 ♖b4 25 ♕d2 ♖fb8 26 de de
27 ♗g3 ♘c6 28 ♗d3 ♕d6 29
♕c3 ♖d4 draw (Balashov–Razuvayev, USSR Ch. 1985).

D122

14 ♘d2

This looks best, to keep control
of the light squares.

14 . . . ♗c8

Black can also try the immediate 14 . . . ♘e8!? (14 . . . ♘d7
15 ♘f5± Klovan–Dorfman,
USSR 1st League 1975; 15 ♘c4
♘xc4 16 ♗xc4 see C) 15 ♘c4 (15

c3 bc 16 bc ♗c8 17 ♘f3 ♘f6 18
♗e3 g6= Gipslis–Ivkov, Zagreb
1965) ♘xc4 16 ♗xc4 ♘c7 17 ♘f5
♗f6 18 f4 ♘e6 19 ♕g4 ♔h8 20 fe
♗xe5 21 ♖e3 ♕g5 22 ♕d1 g6 23
♖f3 ♕h5 24 ♘g3 ♕h4 25 ♕f1
♘d4 26 ♖f2 f5! (26 ... ♗xg3? 27
hg ♕xg3 28 ♗f4) with a kingside
initiative, e.g. 27 c3 ♘c6 28 ♗d2
bc 29 bc ♘a5 30 ♗e6 f4 31 ♘e2 f3
32 ♘g3 ♕e7 33 ♗a2 fg 34 ♕xg2
c4 35 dc ♗xg3 36 hg ♗xe4∓ ($\frac{1}{2}$-
$\frac{1}{2}$, 56) Abramovic–Hebden, London 1988.

15   ♘c4
15 h3! is D132.

15   ...   ♘xc4

(a) **15 ... ♘c6** 16 ♘e3 (16 c3
♗e6 17 f4 ef 18 ♗xf4 ♖b7 19
♘f5 ♗xf5 20 ef d5= Kupreichik–
Kuzmin, USSR 1987) ♗e6 17
♗c4 a5 18 ♘gf5 g6 19 ♘xe7+
♘xe7 20 c3 ♔g7 21 ♗b5 ♗d7 22
♗xd7 ♕xd7 23 ♘c4 ♘c6 24 f4
♖fe8 25 ♖f1 ♕e6 26 f5± Cs.
Horvath–P. Lukacs, Debreçen
1988.

(b) **15 ... ♗e6** (15 ... ♗g4 16
f3 ♗e6= Geller) 16 ♘xa5 ♕xa5
17 ♗c4 ♘e8 18 ♕f3 ♗xc4 19 dc
♕d8 20 ♘f5 ♗g5= Balashov–
Harandi, Manila 1976.

16   ♗xc4   ♘e8!
17   f4   ef
18   ♗xf4   ♗f6

19 ♖b1 (19 ♕c1?! ♘c7 20 ♘f1
♘e6 21 ♗g3 h5∓ Tal–Kuzmin,
Tallinn 1985) ♘c7 20 ♘h5

♗d4+ 21 ♗e3 ♗e5 22 ♘f4 ♘e6
23 ♘xe6 ♗xe6 24 ♗xe6 fe=
A. Sokolov–Balashov, Moscow
1987.

D13

13   ...   ♗c8(123)
Relocating the ♗, which has
served its purpose on b7, has
become the normal plan in the
past decade, but the cost of two
moves makes one wonder whether
8 ... b4 is not best after all.

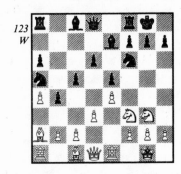

123
W

14   h3!
White has tried many moves,
but only this is really current.

(a) **14 ♗d2!?** ♖b8 (14 ...
♗e6!?) is note a at the start of
D12; then 15 h3 is D131.

(b) **14 ♗g5 b3** (14 ... ♖b8!?) 15
♗xb3 ♘xb3 16 cb ♖b8 17 ♗d2
♗e6 unclear (Plachetka–Sygulski,
Warsaw 1983).

(c) **14 ♘d2 ♗g4!** 15 f3 ♗e6 16
♘c4 ♘xc4 (16 ... b3!? Lau-Lin
Ta, Thessaloniki Ol. 1984; van der
Tak prefers White after 16 ...

♘c6 17 f4 ef 18 ♗xf4 d5 19 ♘xe5 ♘xe5 20 ♗xe5 [drawn in Matulovic–Balashov, Yugoslavia–USSR 1979] de 21 ♗xe6 fe 22 ♘xe4 ♕d5 23 ♘d2) 17 ♗xc4 ♕d7 (17 ... ♘e8!?) 18 f4 ef 19 ♗xf4 d5 with good play for Black, e.g. 20 ♗a2 ♖ad8 21 ♗e5 c4 22 ed ♕xd5 23 d4 ♘g4 24 ♕f3 ♘xe5 25 ♕xd5 ♖xd5 26 ♖xe5 ♖xe5 27 de ♖d8 28 ♘e4 b3 29 cb cb 30 ♗b1 ♖d1+ ∓∓ Peters–Pinter, Hastings 1980–81.

(d) **14 c3 ♖b8** (14 ... ♘c6!? van der Tak; 14 ... bc?! 15 bc± Balashov–Pinter, Helsinki 1983) 15 d4 (15 ♘d2 ♗e6 16 ♗xe6 fe 17 ♘f3 ♘d7 18 d4 ed 19 cd c4 20 d5 e5 21 ♗e3 ♘b3∓ Thipsay–Torre, Thessaloniki Ol. 1984) b3 16 ♗b1 ♕c7 17 ♗d3 ed 18 cd c4 19 ♗f1 c3 20 ♗d3 ♘c4 21 ♕e2 cb 22 ♗xb2 ♘xb2 23 ♕xb2 unclear (½–½, 72) Grunfeld–Kosashvili, Holon 1986–87.

14 ... ♖b8!

Nunn recommends this as the precise moment to move the ♖.

14 ... ♗e6 accepts a doubled pawn to open the f-file and keep the white ♘ out of f5 temporarily, but Black cannot equalize, e.g. 15 ♗xe6 fe 16 c3 (or 16 ♗e3 ♕d7 17 c3 bc 18 bc ♖ab8 transposing) bc (16 ... ♖b8 17 cb ♖xb4 18 ♗d2 ♖xb2 19 ♗c3 ♖b7 20 ♘g5 ♕b6 21 ♘xe6 ♖fb8 22 ♘f5± W. Watson–Tseshkovsky, Moscow II

1985) 17 bc ♖b8 (17 ... ♘d7 18 d4 ed 19 cd [Jansa–Grigorov, Prague 1985] ♖b8!? Pliester) 18 ♗e3 ♕d7 19 ♕c2 ♖b7 20 ♖ab1 ♖fb8 21 d4 ♖xb1 (21 ... ed 22 cd cd 23 ♗xd4 ♘b3 24 ♗xf6 ♗xf6 25 ♖bd1± Chandler-Thipsay, Commonwealth Ch., London 1985) 22 ♖xb1 ♖xb1+ 23 ♕xb1 ed 24 cd cd 25 ♗xd4! ♘c6 26 ♕d3 ♘b4 27 ♕b3 ♘c6 (Chandler–Tal, World–USSR 1984) 28 ♗c3! with lasting pressure—Tal.

After 14 ... ♖b8:

D131 15 ♗d2
D132 15 ♘d2!?

D131

15 ♗d2 ♗e6!?

(a) Nunn believes 'that some interesting plans for Black have yet to be tried in this type of position' e.g. 15 ... ♘d7 and ... ♘b6 ... ♗d7 with a siege of the weak a-pawn.

(b) 15 ... ♘e8 (15 ... ♕c7 16 ♕e2 ♘c6 17 ♖f1 ♗e6 18 ♗xe6 draw; Balashov–Razuvayev, USSR Ch. 1983) 16 ♘f1 (16 ♘f5 ♗e6=) ♘c7 17 ♘e3 ♗e6 18 ♗xe6 ♘xe6 19 g3 g6 20 c3 (Iversland–Sande, corr. 1983) bc 21 bc c4 22 dc ♕c8 23 ♘d5 ♖e8±/= Nunn.

16 ♗xe6

16 ♘f5 ♘e8 17 g4 ♗xa2 18 ♖xa2 g6!? 19 ♘h6+ ♔g7 20

♖a1 ♘c7 21 ♔h2 ♘e6=
Vasiukov–Tseshkovsky,   USSR
1985.

16 ...   fe

17   ♗e3

(a) **17 c3!?** bc 18 bc ♘d7 19 ♗e3
d5 20 ed ed 21 c4 e4 22 de d4 23
♗c1 ♘xc4 24 e5 (Jansa–Maksi-
movic, Nis 1983) 24 ... ♕c7!?∓.

(b) **17 ♘g5** ♕d7 18 f4 ef 19
♗xf4 ♘c6 20 ♖f1!? (20 ♘f3
♘g4! 21 ♘e2 ♘ge5 22 ♘xe5 de
23 ♗e3 ♗h4!= Tal–Zakharov,
USSR Ch. 1976) ♖be8 21 ♕d2
♗d8 22 ♔h1 ♗c7 23 ♖ae1 ♖e7
24 e5± Kuzmichev–Borisenko,
Yurmala 1975.

17 ...   ♘d7

White is better after **17 ... ♘c6**
18 c3 bc 19 bc d5 20 ed ed 21
♘f5± (Kupreichik–Psakhis,
USSR Ch. 1980–81) or **17 ...**
♕e8 18 c3 bc 19 bc ♘h5 20 ♘xh5
♕xh5 21 ♖b1 ♕g6 22 ♖xb8
♖xb8 23 d4± Kavalek–Bala-
shov, Buenos Aires Ol. 1980.

18 c3   bc

19 bc   d5!?

unclear.

20 ♕c2 ♕c7 21 ed ed 22 c4 e4
(22 ... d4 23 ♗d2 ♘c6 24
♘h2±) 23 de d4 24 ♗d2 ♖xf3!
25 gf ♘e5 26 ♔g2 ♘axc4 with
interesting compensation for the
exchange: 27 f4 (27 ♗f4!? ♕c6 28
♘f5 ♗f8 29 ♖ab1 ♖e8 unclear—
Tseshkovsky) ♖b2 28 ♕c1 ♖xd2
29 fe ♘e3+ 30 ♔g1 (30 ♔f3 ♖c2

31 ♕b1 ♗h4! 32 fe d3! unclear)
♖c2 31 ♕b1 ♕xe5! 32 ♖e2 ♖xe2
33 ♘xe2 (Kupreichik–Tseshkovsky, USSR Ch. 1980–81)
d3!∓ Tseshkovsky.

D132

15   ♘d2!? *(124)*

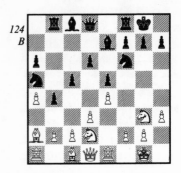

15 ...   ♗e6!

White has some chance of advantage after **15 ... ♘e8** (15 ...
g6 16 ♘c4 ♘c6 17 f4 ef 18
♗xf4± Kuporosov) 16 ♘c4
♘xc4 17 ♗xc4 ♗g5 (17 ... ♘c7!?
Chandler) 18 c3 ♘c7 (18 ...
♗xc1 19 ♖xc1 bc 20 bc ♘c7 21
♖b1 ♗d7 22 ♕c2 g6? [22 ...
♕g5!? Busch] 23 ♖xb8 ♕xb8 24
♖b1 ♗xa4?! 25 ♗xf7+ ± Nunn–
Fahnenschmidt, Bundesliga BRD
1985–86) 19 d4 ♗e6! 20 ♕e2! bc
21 bc ed 22 cd cd 23 ♗xa6 ♘xa6
24 ♗xg5 ♕xg5 25 ♕xa6 h5!
unclear (Chandler–Tal, Naestved
1985).

16   ♘c4   ♘c6

Seeking complexity. Black can also consider:

(a) the simpler **16 ... ♘xc4** 17 ♗xc4 ♗xc4 (17 ... a5!? Chandler) 18 dc ♘e8 19 ♘f5 ♗f6 20 ♗e3 g6 21 ♘h6+ ♔h8 (Thipsay–Tseshovsky, Calcutta 1986) when White's doubled c-pawn balanced Black's backward d-pawn.

(b) **16 ... ♖e8?!** 17 ♗d2 ♘c6 (17 ... ♘xc4 18 ♗xc4 ♗xc4 19 dc± Geller) 18 c3 d5 19 ed ♘xd5 20 a5! (Geller–P. Littlewood, Plovdiv 1983) ♘c7!? Geller.

17 f4!?

17 ♗d2 (17 c3!? Busch) ♘e8 18 ♘e3 ♗xa2 19 ♖xa2 g6 20 c3 ♗g5 21 ♘d5 ♗xd2 22 ♕xd2 ♘c7 23 ♘xc7 ♕xc7 24 ♘f5 ♘e7 25 ♘xe7+ ♕xe7 26 d4 cd 27 cd ♖fc8∓ (0–1, 75) Jansa–Nunn, Bundesliga BRD 1989.

17 ... ef
18 ♗xf4 ♘e8!?

(a) **18 ... ♖c8!?** 19 ♘f5 (19 ♘e3 d5 20 e5 ♘e8 and 19 ♔h1 d5 20 ♘e5 ♘xe5 21 ♗xe5 ♕d7 are unclear—Kuporosov) 19 ... ♗xf5 20 ef d5 21 ♘e3 h6! 22 ♗g3 ♖e8= (23 ♔h1 ♕d7 24 ♕f3 ♘d4 25 ♕f2 c4 26 c3 ♘b3! or 23 ♗h4 ♕d7! 24 ♕f3?! ♘d4 25 ♕g3 ♘h5!) Yudasin–Kuporosov, USSR 1985.

(b) **18 ... ♖b7** 19 ♔h1 d5 20 ♘e5 ♕c8? (20 ... ♘xe5!? 21 ♗xe5 de 22 ♗xe6 fe 23 ♘xe4

♕d5! unclear—Chandler) 21 ed ♘xd5 22 ♘xc6 ♕xc6 23 ♕f3± Chandler–Ornstein, Thessaloniki Ol. 1984.

19 ♘f5 ♗f6!?
20 ♖f1

Not 20 ♘fxd6? ♘xd6 21 ♘xd6 ♗xb2 nor 21 ♗xd6 ♗xc4∓, while if 20 ♘cxd6?! ♗e5!? Black has compensation.

20 ... ♗xf5

Maybe 20 ... ♘e5!? Busch.

21 ef d5!?
22 ♗xb8

(a) **22 ... dc?!** 23 ♗g3?! (costs a tempo; 23 ♗f4±) b3 24 c6 cd 25 ♖c1 ♘d6! 26 ♗b1? (26 ♕xd3 ♗d4+ 27 ♔h1 ♘b4 28 ♕b1 ♘xa2 29 ♕xa2 ♘e4 30 ♗e1 unclear) ♘e4 27 ♗f4 ♘b4? (27 ... ♕d4+ 28 ♔h2 ♘e5!) 28 ♖c4 ♗d4+ 29 ♔h2 g5 30 fg fg 31 ♖xb4 ♖xf4 32 ♖xf4 ♕d6 33 g3 ♘xg3 34 ♖bxd4 cd 35 ♔xg3 1–0 Chandler–Herbrechtsmeier, Bundesliga BRD 1986.

(b) **22 ... ♕xb8!** (C. D. Meyer) and Black probably has good compensation for the exchange, e.g.:

(b1) 23 ♘e3 ♗xb2 24 ♖b1 (24 ♘xd5 ♗xa1 25 ♕xa1 ♘d4 unclear—Busch) ♗d4 25 ♕f3 (25 ♖f3!?) ♕e5 26 ♖be1 ♗c3 unclear.

(b) 23 ♘d2 ♗xb2 24 ♖b1 ♗d4+ 25 ♔h1 ♘f6 26 ♘f3 ♘h5! (26 ... ♗e3 27 ♕e2! idea 28 g4±)

27 ♘xd4 ♘g3+ 28 ♔g1 ♘xd4
unclear—Busch.

Nunn says that Chandler–
Herbrechtsmeier 'was unclear'
while Thipsay–Tseshkovsky and
Yudasin–Kuporosov 'provide
viable alternatives'. He concludes
that 'the lines with 12 ... c5 13
♘g3 don't seem to promise too
much for White ... he has to find
three improvements before 13
♘g3 would look good. Therefore
13 c3 may be critical'.

D2

13   c3(125)

Fighting for the centre.

From the diagram:

D21   13 ... c4
D22   13 ... bc!

(a) 13 ... ♘h5 (13 ... ♖e8 14
♘g3 bc 15 bc see note a to diagram 126) 14 cb cb 15 ♗d2! d5 16
ed ♗xd5 17 ♗xd5 ♕xd5 18
♘g3!± Gipslis–Savon, 34 USSR
Ch. 1966–67.

(b) **13 ... ♖b8!?** 14 cb cb 15
♘g3 b3!? (15 ... g6 16 d4 ♘d7
unclear—Psakhis) 16 ♗b1 d5!? 17
♘xe5?! (after 17 ed! ♗xd5 18
♘xe5 it is hard to see Black's
compensation) de 18 d4!? (18 de
♗b4 19 ♖f1 ♖e8) ♗b4 19 ♗g5!?
(19 ♖e2 ♖e8! threat ... ♖xe5)
♗xe1 20 ♘h5 (Kupreichik–Psakhis, Erevan 1982) ♕c8! 21 ♗xf6
♕f5∓ Psakhis.

D21

13 ...   c4
14 c6!

(a) **14 dc** (14 ♗xc4? ♗xc4 15 dc
♘xe4 16 cb ♕b6) b3! 15 ♗xb3
♘xb3 (15 ... ♕b6 16 ♗c2 ♗xe4!
[Psakhis] 17 ♘g3 or 17 ♘g5!?
unclear) 16 ♕xb3 ♗xe4 17 ♘g3
♗xf3 18 gf ♕c8 19 ♔g2 ♖b8 20
♕a2 ♘d7 21 b3 ♖e8 22 ♕c2±
(but draw to clinch first prize)
Karpov–Nunn, London 1984.

(b) **14 ♘g3** cd 15 ♕xd3 (15
♗g5 h6 16 ♗xf6 ♗xf6 17 ♖e3 bc
18 bc ♕c7 19 ♖xd3= Karpov–
Geller, 41 USSR Ch. 1971) b3! 16
♗b1 ♘d7 (16 ... ♖e8?! 17 ♘f5
♗f8 18 ♗g5 h6 19 ♗xf6 ♕xf6 20
♘e3± Psakhis–Hebden, Chicago
1983; 16 ... g6!? 17 h3 ♖e8 18
♕e2= Tseshkovsky) 17 ♗e3
g6= Liberzon–Jansa, Luhacovice
1971.

14 ...   cd
15 ♘c3   ♘c6

16 ♗d5!? (16 ♘d5 ♘xd5 17
♗xd5 ♖b8 18 ♗d2 ♘xb4

unclear—Kupreichik) ♖b8! 17 b5
(17 ♗xc6 ♗xc6 18 ♕xd3 ♖xb4
19 ♕xa6 ♗xe4 20 ♘xe4 ♘xe4 21
♕c6 unclear) ab (17 ... ♘b4
unclear) 18 ab ♘b4 19 ♗xb7
♖xb7 20 ♖a4! d5 21 ed (21
♘xe5!? de 22 ♘c6 ♘xc6 23 bc
♖c7 24 ♖c4!±) e4 22 ♘e5 (22
♘g5!?) ♘fxd5 23 ♘xe4 (23
♖xe4±) ♖xb5 24 ♘c3±
Kupreichik–Psakhis, USSR Ch.
Minsk 1987.

D22

13 ... bc!
14 bc*(126)*

126
B

14 ... c4!

(a) 14 ... ♖e8 (14 ... ♕c7!?
Matanovic; 14 ... ♖b8?! 15 ♘g3
♗c8 16 d4± Fuchs–Westerinen,
Leningrad 1967) 15 ♘g3 ♗f8 16
♗g5 (16 ♖b1 ♖b8 17 ♗g5! h6 18
♗xf6± Browne–Planinc, Wijk
aan Zee 1974) c4 17 ♘f5 h6 18
♗xf6 ♕xf6 19 ♘e3 cd 20 ♕xd3
♗c6 21 ♘d5 ♖ec8 22 ♘d2 ♖a7
23 ♗xc6 ♖xc6 24 ♘d5 ♕d8 25

♖eb1± Ehlvest–Pavlovic, Erevan 1988.

(b) 14 ... ♘h5 15 ♘g3 ♘xg3
16 hg ♖e8 17 ♘h2 ♗f8 18 ♘g4
♖b8 19 ♘e3 ♕d7 20 ♗d2 ♗c6
21 ♗d5 ♗xd5 22 ♘xd5 c4 23
♗e3 ♕c6 24 ♕c2 f5 25 ♘b4 ♕c8
26 dc ♕xc4 27 ♕a2 fe 28 ♕xc4+
♘xc4 29 ♘xa6 ♖b7 30 ♘b4 ♖a8
31 ♗c1 e3 32 ♗xe3 ♘xe3 33 fe
♖ba7 34 ♘d5 ♖xa4 35 ♖xa4
♖xa4 36 e4± (1–0, 71) Kupreichik–Ehlvest, Moscow 1987.

15 ♘g3 ♘d7

Both authors agree this is
probably the best of a wide selection, unless White can find an
early improvement on our model
game. Others:

(a) 15 ... ♕c7?! (15 ... ♖e8 16
♘f5 ♗f8 17 ♗g5± Lukacs and
Hazai) 16 ♘f5 ♖fe8 17 ♗g5
♖ad8 18 ♘xe7+! ♕xe7 19
♗xc4! ♘xc4 20 dc ♖c8 21 ♘d2
a5 22 ♖b1! ♗a6 (Ehlvest–Nunn,
Thessaloniki Ol. 1988) 23 ♖b6!
♗xc4 24 ♘xc4 ♖xc4 25 ♖xd6
♖xc3 26 h3±.

(b) 15 ... cd 16 ♕xd3 ♗c8!
(several games showed 16 ...
♘d7 to be worse) 17 ♗g5 (17
♗a3 ♕c7! 18 ♘d2 ♗e6! 19 ♘f5
♗xf5 20 ef d5!= Lukacs) ♗e6 (17
... ♘b7 18 ♘d2 ♘c5 19 ♕c2
[Ljubojevic–Karpov, London
1982] ♗e6!? Matanovic) 18 ♘f5
(18 ♘h4 g6) ♗xf5 19 ef ♘b7 20
♗xf6 ♗xf6 21 ♗d5 ♘c5 22 ♕c2

♖c8 23 ♘d2 e4!= Adorjan–Lukacs, Hungary 1978.

(c) **15 ... d5?!** 16 ♘xe5 de 17 d4 ♗d6 18 ♗g5 ♖e8 19 ♘g4 ♗e7 20 ♘f5± Ehlvest–Djuric, Tallinn 1986.

(d) 'Perhaps even **15 ... g6!?** is playable' Nunn says; 'weakening f7 looks very risky, but I cannot see a concrete way for White to exploit this.'

16 ♗a3

If 16 ♘f5 ♘c5! or 16 d4 g6! Lukacs and Hazai.

| **16** | **...** | **g6** |
| **17** | **d4** | **♕c7!?** |

After 17 ... ed?! 18 ♕xd4 ♕c7 19 ♖ad1± (Kupreichik–Psakhis, Minsk 1982) Black soon had to give up his d-pawn but managed to reach a drawn ending.

| **18** | **♖c1** | **♖fe8** |
| **19** | **♗b4** | **♖ac8** |

Black has promising compensation, e.g. 20 ♘d2? d5!∓ 21 ed ♗xd5 22 de ♗g5! 23 ♘ge4 ♗xe4 24 ♖xe4 ♘xe5 25 ♖c2 ♖cd8 (White is in a tangle.) 26 ♕e1

♖e6 27 h4 (precipitates complications) ♘d3 28 ♕e2 ♖xe4 29 ♘xe4 ♗xh4 30 ♗xa5 ♕xa5 31 ♗xc4 ♘e5 32 ♗b3 ♔g7 (Material is level but Black is still better coordinated) 33 g3 ♗e7 34 ♘d2 ♖d7 35 ♔g2 h5 36 ♕e4 ♘g4 37 ♘f3 ♗c5 38 ♕c6 ♖c7 39 ♕d5 ♕b6 40 ♘d4 ♘f6 41 ♕a8 ♗xd4 42 cd ♖d7 43 ♕f3 ♕xd4 44 ♖c4 ♕e5 45 ♕c3 ♕xc3 46 ♖xc3 ♘e4 (∓) 47 ♖c6 ♖d2 48 ♖c2 a5 49 ♖xd2 ♘xd2 50 ♗d5 f5 51 f3 ♔f6 52 ♔f2 ♘b1 53 ♔e3 ♘c3 54 ♗c6 f4+! 55 gf h4∓∓ (0–1, 81) Kupreichik–Rodriguez, Minsk 1982.

Conclusion

Black has more than held his own during an intensive debate on these lines during the 1980s; he has more prospects of playing for a win than after 7 ... d6. In the next chapter we look at the less frequently played lines arising from 8 a4 ♗b7.

20 Anti-Marshall: 8 a4 ♗b7 Lesser Lines

1 e4 e5 2 ♘f3 ♘c6 3 ♗b5 a6 4 ♗a4 ♘f6 5 0-0 ♗e7 6 ♖e1 b5 7 ♗b3 0-0

    8   a4   ♗b7(*127*)

This has long been considered best play for both sides when White wants to avoid the Marshall. In this chapter we look at divergences from the principal sequence discussed in Chapter 19.

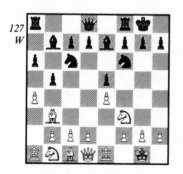

127
W

Now there are two main moves and some occasionally played alternatives:

A 9 ♘c3
B 9 d3

(a) After **9 c3** Marshall players will surely choose 9 ... d5! which transposes to Chapter 15, C3 with 10 ed ♘xd5 or 10 ab ab 11 ♖xa8 ♗xa8 12 ed ♘xd5. The timid but playable 9 ... d6 transposes to the closed Spanish line 7 ... d6 8(9) c3 0-0 9(8) a4 ♗b7 which is outside the scope of this book.

(b) **9 ab** ab became obsolete because it prematurely releases the tension: 10 ♖xa8 ♕xa8! (10 ... ♗xa8 11 d3 d6 12 c3±) 11 c3 (11 ♘c3 ♘d4!? Barden; 11 d3 d6 12 ♘c3 b4 13 ♘d5 ♘xd5 14 ♗xd5 ♘a5!=) d6 12 d3 ♘a5 13 ♗c2 c5 14 ♘bd2 g6 15 ♘f1 ♖e8 16 ♘g3 ♗f8= Scherbakov–Borisenko, USSR Ch. 1955.

A

    9   ♘c3

There has been a small revival of this move in recent years. By attacking the b-pawn White provokes a reaction before Black has had time to protect his e-pawn by ... d6.

    9   ...   ♘d4

If 9 ... b4!? (or 9 ... ♘a5?! 10 ♗a2 b4 11 ♘d5 transposing) 10 ♘d5 ♘a5?! (better 10 ... d6 11 a5 ♘d4!? or 11 c3 a5 12 d4 h6= or 10 ... ♘xd5 11 ed ♘d4) 11 ♗a2!? (11 ♘xf6+ ♗xf6 12 ♗a2 d5!= Guzel–Stupica, Tuzla 1959; 11 ♘xe7+!? ♕xe7 12 d3 van der Tak) then:

(a) 11 ... b3 12 ♘xf6+ ♗xf6 13 cb ♘c6 (13 ... d5 14 ed e4 15 ♖xe4 ♗xd5 16 ♖e3 ♖b8 17 d4 c5 18 dc ♗xb3 19 ♕xd8 ♖fxd8 20 ♗d2± Gipslis–Suetin, Leningrad 1971; 13 ... c5 14 b4! cb 15 d4! d6 16 ♗d2±) 14 d4! d6 (14 ... ed 15 e5 idea ♘d4±) 15 d5 ♘b4 16 ♗b1 a5 17 ♗d2 c5 18 dc ♗xc6 (18 ... ♘xc6 19 ♗c3) 19 ♗xb4! ab 20 ♗d3 ♕d7 21 ♗c4± Barbero–Hazai, Vinkovci 1986.

(b) 11 ... ♘xd5 12 ed! (12 ♗xd5 c6 13 ♗a2 d6 14 d4 ♕c7 15 c3 bc 16 bc c5 17 de de 18 ♗d5 ♖ad8∓ Alvir–van der Sterren, Dieren 1986) d6 13 d4± Barbero.

10 ab!?

(a) 10 ♗a2 (10 ♘xe5? b4) 10 ... b4 11 ♘xd4 ed 12 ♘d5 ♘xd5 13 ♗xd5 (13 ed= Botvinnik) ♗xd5 14 ed d3! 15 ♖e3 ♗c5 16 ♖d3 ♖e8! 17 ♖f3 ♕e7 18 ♕f1 ♕e4∓ Botvinnik–Bondarevsky, Absolute Ch. of USSR 1941.

(b) 10 ♘xd4 ed 11 ♘d5 ♘xd5 12 ed (12 ♗xd5 ♗xd5 13 ed d3! 14 ab! ♗c5 15 ♖xa6 ♕h4! 16 ♖f1 ♖ab8 with compensation;

Fucak–Steinberg, Yugoslavia–USSR 1968) d3!? 13 ♕f3 ♗c5 14 ♕xd3 ♕f6 15 ♕f1 ♖fe8 16 ♖d1 ♖e4 17 c3 ba 18 ♗a2 ♖ae8 19 d4 ♗d6 20 ♗e3 ♕g6 21 g3 f5 22 ♕g2 ♕f7 23 c4 f4 with an enduring initiative for the ♙ (Hennigan–Pein, British Ch. 1987).

10 ... ♘xb3
11 cb ab
12 ♖xa8 ♕xa8
13 d3 d6!

13 ... b4 14 ♘e2 d6 15 ♘g3 g6 (15 ... ♗c8!?± van der Tak) 16 ♗g5 ♖e8 17 ♕d2 c5 18 h3 (with initiative) ♕a2 19 ♕c2 ♗c8 20 ♘d2 ♘d5 21 ♗h6! ♘c7 22 f4 ♗f6 23 f5± Otovic–Kanjo, corr. 1984.

14 ♘xb5 ♖b8

With compensation for the ♙. A possibly superior alternative is 14 ... ♕a5!? intending 15 ... ♗a6 and 16 ... ♖b8= Minic.

15 ♘c3 ♗c8
16 ♗g5

16 d4 ♗g4 17 de de 18 h3 (Zagorovsky–Nyman, 6th Corr. World Ch. 1968–71) ♗xf3 19 ♕xf3 ♖xb3 20 ♕f5 ♗d6=.

16 ... ♗e6
17 d4 ♗xb3

18 ♕d2 ed 19 ♘xd4 ♗e6 20 h3 (Chandler–Fernandez, Yurmala 1983) ♗d7=.

B
9 d3*(128)*

This is the beginning of the

'main' Anti-Marshall and in practice 7 ... 0-0 often leads to this position.

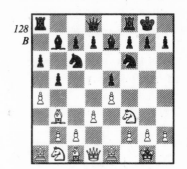

128
B

From the diagram only two moves really matter. Although several others have been tried from time to time, there have been no significant developments in recent years:

B1 9 ... ♖e8!?
B2 9 ... d6 (Introduction and Lesser Lines)

(a) **9 ... b4** is a minor line in Chapter 18.
(b) **9 ... d5?!** is just wishful thinking. After 10 ed ♘d4 (10 ... ♘xd5 11 ♘xe5± Tal) 11 c4! Black has tried:
(b1) **11 ... ♘xb3** 12 ♕xb3 ♖b8 13 ab ab 14 ♕d1! ♘d7 15 ♘c3 c6 16 dc ♗xc6 17 cb ♗b7 (17 ... ♗xb5 18 d4±±) and now 18 ♗e3 (18 d4? ♗xf3 Tal–Kuzmin, USSR 1972) f5 19 ♕b3+ ♔h8 20 ♘d5±± Tal.

(b2) **11 ... ♖b8** 12 ♘xd4 ed 13 ab ab 14 ♗f4 ♗d6 15 ♗xd6 ♕xd6 16 ♘d2 ♕b4 17 ♖c1 c5 18 dc ♗xc6 19 cb ♕xb5 20 ♗c4± (but ½–½, 88) Howell–J. Knox, British Ch. 1988.

(c) **9 ... ♘d4?!** 10 ♘xd4 ed 11 c3 dc 12 ♘xc3 b4 13 ♘e2 c5 (13 ... a5 14 ♗g5 ♘g4 15 ♗f4 ♗h4 16 ♕f3± Djurasevic–Beltram, Oberhausen 1961) 14 ♘g3 d5 15 e5 ♘e8 16 ♘f5 g6 17 ♘h6+ ♔g7 18 ♕f3± Arnlind–J. Steiner, corr. 1973.

(d) **9 ... ♘a5!?** 10 ♗a2 (10 ♘xe5? ♗xb3 11 cb d5!∓) d6 11 ♗d2!? (11 ♘c3 see Chapter 19) ♘c6! 12 ♘c3 (12 ♘a3!?) ♘a7 13 d4 (13 b4!?) ed 14 ♘xd4 when *ECO*'s ± is questionable. Keres–Ivkov, USSR–Yugoslavia 1956, went 14 ... b4 (eventually drawn) while Kauranen–Sanakoyev, 6th World Corr. Ch. 1968–71, was also inconclusive after 14 ... ba.
B1
  9 ...   ♖e8!?
Envisaging a rapid ... d5 without loss of tempo. This has been a major variation in the past decade but the consensus seems to be that White has now found the answer.
  10   ♘c3
(a) **10 ♘g5!?** (crude and ineffective) d5 11 ed ♘d4 (cf the Fritz Variation of the Two Knights Defence) 12 ♗a2 (12 d6?? ♘xb3 13 de ♕d5∓∓) ♘xd5 13 ♘f3 (13

♖xe5?! ♗xg5! 14 ♗xg5 ♛d7 15
♖xe8+ ♖xe8 16 ♘d2 ♘b4∓ 17
♗b1 ♘e2+ 18 ♔f1 ♗xg2+ 19
♔xg2 ♛g4+ 20 ♔h1 ♘g3+ 0–1
Zapata–Nunn, Dubai Ol. 1986)
♘b4 14 ♘xd4 ed! (14 ... ♘xa2 15
♘f5 ♘xc1 16 ♘xe7+ ♖xe7 17
♛xc1 ♖e6 ½–½, Tal–Planinc,
Moscow 1975) 15 ♗b3 ♗d6∓
Nunn.

(b) **10 c3!?** d6 11 ♘bd2 (11 ♘g5
♖f8 12 f4 ef 13 ♗xf4 ♘e5=)
♘a5 (11 ... ♗f8 12 ♘f1 g6 is also
playable) 12 ♗a2 (12 ♗c2 c5=)
c5 13 ♘f1 c4!? (13 ... ♘c6 14
♘e3±; 13 ... h6 14 ♘e3 ♗f8 15
b4 cb 16 cb ♘c6 17 ♘d5±) 14
♗g5 h6 15 ♗xf6 ♗xf6 16 ♘e3
♖c8 17 ab ab 18 dc ♘xc4 19
♗xc4 bc 20 ♘d2 ♗g5! 21 ♘exc4
d5 22 ♘a5 ♗a8 unclear (0–1, 43)
Klinger–Nunn, Biel 1986.

(c) **10 ♗d2** b4 (or 10 ... ♗f8 11
ab ab 12 ♖xa8 ♗xa8 13 ♘c3
♘a5 14 ♗a2 b4 15 ♘g5 b3! 16 cb
♗b4 with compensation; Parma–
Planinc,   Ljubljana/Portoroz
1973) 11 ♗g5 (11 a5! d5!? with
counterplay) ♘a5! 12 ♗a2 d5! 13
♘bd2 (Ghinda–Pein, Netanya
Open 1987) 13 ... de (Ghinda).

(d) Zapata has done well with
10 ♗g5!? e.g. 10 ... d6 (10 ... h6
11 ♗xf6 ♗xf6 12 ♘c3 ♘d4 13
♘xd4 ed 14 ♘d5± or 10 ...
♘d4?! 11 ♘xd4 ed 12 ♘d2 d6 13
c3!± Zapata–Riemersma, Dieren
1987) 11 ♘c3 b4 12 ♘e2 h6 (12

... ♘a5 13 ♗a2 c5 14 ♘g3±
Zapata: 13 ... ♘h5!?) 13 ♗xf6
♗xf6 14 a5! ♘e7 (14 ... ♖b8!?)
15 ♘g3 c5 16 c3 (16 ♛b1!? threat
♛a2xf7) bc 17 bc ♖b8 18 ♛c2 g6
19 ♛a2± Zapata–Am. Rodri-
guez, Subotica 1987.

(e) **10 ab** ab 11 ♖xa8 ♛xa8 12
♘c3 b4 13 ♘d5 ♘xd5 14 ♗xd5
d6 15 ♗d2 ♘a5 (15 ... ♘d8!? 16
♗b3 c5 van der Sterren) 16 ♗xb4
(16 ♗a2 c5 threat ... b3) ♗xd5
17 ed ♛xd5 18 c4 ♛a8 19 ♗c3 c5
20 ♘d2 ♘c6= Short–P. Nikolic,
Wijk aan Zee 1986.

(f) **10 ♘bd2** ♗f8 11 ♘g5 d5 12
ed ♘d4 13 ♗a2 (13 d6? ♘xb3 14
dc? ♛d5) h6 (safer 13 ... ♗xd5
14 ♗xd5 ♛xd5= Elburg–Ziese,
corr. 1987–88) 14 ♘f3 ♘xd5 15
♖xe5 ♖xe5 16 ♘xe5 ♗d6 17
♘ef3!? (17 ♘df3 van Oirschot)
♛f6 18 ♘e4 ♘xf3+ 19 ♛xf3
♛xf3 20 gf ♖e8! 21 ab (21
♗xh6!? ♘b4 unclear) ab 22 ♗xd5
♗xd5 23 ♗e3 ♖e6 24 ♘xd6
♖xd6 ½–½ (Di Bucchianico–Van
Oirschot, corr. 1985–86).

10 ...   b4
Dubious alternatives are **10 ...
♘a5?!** 11 ♗a2 b4 (Razuvayev) 12
♘xe5!± and **10 ... ♘d4?!**
(Rumens) 11 ♘xe5 ♘xb3 12 cb
d5!? 13 ab!

11   ♘d5
11 ♘e2?! d5 12 ed ♘a5!? (or 12
... ♘xd5 13 ♘g3 ♗f8 14 ♘g5
f6∓ Rechlis–N. Nikolic, Gausdal

jr 1986) 13 c4 bc 14 ♘xc3 ♘xb3 15 ♕xb3 ♖b8! 16 ♕c4 ♘xd5 17 ♘xe5 ♗f6 18 d4 ♖e6 19 a5 ♗a8 20 ♘xd5 ♕xd5 21 ♕xd5 ♗xd5 with compensation for the ♙ (Fishbein–Morovic, New York Open 1987).

11 ...   ♘a5
12   ♘xe7+
12 ♗a2 b3 13 ♘xf6+ ♗xf6 14 cb c5 15 b4 cb 16 ♗d2 ♘c6 17 ♗d5± (Timman) is an alternative.

12 ...   ♕xe7
13   ♗a2   d5?!
To settle for 13 ... d6± (having conceded the ♗ pair for nothing) would be an admission of failure. 13 ... ♖b8!? is also unconvincing: 14 ♘h4 (14 ♗g5!? h6 15 ♗h4 g5? 16 ♘xg5! Harding) d5 15 ♗g5 h6 16 ♘f5 ♕e6 17 ♗h4 b3 (Przewoznik–Blatny, Poznan 1986) 18 ♗xb3 ♘xb3 19 cb de 20 de ♗xe4 21 ♘xg7! ♔xg7 22 ♗xf6+ ♔xf6 23 ♖xe4 ♖xb3 (23 ... ♕xb3 24 ♕h5) 24 ♖c1± Nunn.

14   ♗g5!
14 ed ♕d6 gives Black good play:
(a) 15 c4?! bc 16 bc ♗xd5 17 ♗a3 (17 ♗g5?! ♗xa2 18 ♖xa2 ♘d5 19 ♖c2 c5∓ Short–P. Nikolic, Naestved 1985) c5 18 ♕e2 (Ghinda–van der Sterren, Dortmund Open 1986) ♖ab8!∓ van der Sterren.

(b) 15 ♗d2 ♗xd5 16 ♗xd5 ♘xd5 17 ♕e2 (17 ♘g5 h6 18 ♘e4 ♕g6 19 ♕f3 ♖ad8 20 ♘g3 ♘c6∓; Buelen–Dam, Amsterdam Open 1977) c5 18 ♘g5 ♕g6 19 ♕f3 ♖ad8 20 h4 ♘c6 21 h5 ♕f6 22 ♕e4 g6 23 ♕c4 ♘d4= (0–1, 38) Adams–Conquest, British Ch. 1988.
(c) 15 ♘d2!? ♗xd5 16 ♗xd5 ♕xd5 (16 ... ♘xd5 17 ♘c4!) 17 b3 ♘c6 18 ♗b2 ♘d4= van der Sterren.

14 ...   de
15   de   ♖ad8
16   ♕e2±
16 ... h6 17 ♗h4 b3 (17 ... g5? 18 ♘xg5 hg 19 ♗xg5 ♖d6 20 ♕f3± intending ♕g3–h4) 18 ♗xf6 (18 cb? g5) ♕xf6 19 ♗xb3 ♘xb3 20 cb ♕b6 21 ♕c4 ♗c8 22 a5 ♕b7 23 ♖ac1 ♗e6 24 ♕xc7± ♕xc7 25 ♖xc7 ♖b8!? 26 ♘xe5 ♖xb3 27 ♖e2 ♖b5 28 ♘c6 ♗c4 29 ♖d2 ♖xe4 30 f3 ♖e1+ 31 ♔f2 ♖f1+ 32 ♔e3 ♖e1+ 33 ♔f4 ♗e6 34 ♖a7 h5 35 h4 g5+ 36 hg ♖f5+ 37 ♔g3 ♖xg5+ 38 ♔f2 ♖c1 39 ♖xa6 ♔g7 40 ♖b6 ♗c4 41 b4 ♖a1 42 ♘d4 ♗f1 43 g4 hg 44 fg ♔h7 (44 ... ♖xg4 45 ♘f5+ ♔h7 46 ♔f3 threat ♖h3+, ♘e3) 45 ♔g3 ♖a3+ 46 ♔f4 ♖g6 47 ♖h2+ ♗h3 48 ♖xg6 ♔xg6 49 ♖f2 ♖a4 50 ♘c6 f5 51 g5 ♔g7 52 ♖d2 ♗f1 53 ♔xf5 ♗b5 54 ♖d7+ ♔f8 55 ♖d8+ ♔g7 56 ♖d7+ ♔f8 57

♖c7 ♗xc6 58 ♖xc6 ♖xb4 59 a6 1–0 Hübner–Zsuzsa Polgar, Biel 1987.

Nunn has played 9 ... ♖e8 a few times, but has given it up because of this game and it does seem suddenly to have vanished, so perhaps others too have failed to find any way to make this playable.

B2

9 ...   d6(129)

This position sometimes arises via 7 ... d6 8 a4 ♗b7 9 d3 0-0.

129
W

From the diagram:

B21   10 c3
B22   10 ♗d2
B23   10 ♘c3! (Minor Lines)

(a) **10 ab** ab 11 ♖xa8 ♕xa8 12 c3 d5 see Chapter 15, C3.

(b) **10 ♘bd2 ♘d7!** 11 c3 ♗f6 (or 11 ... ♘c5 12 ab ab 13 ♖xa8 ♕xa8 14 ♗c2 ♘f6 15 ♘f1 d5= Dely–Malich, Budapest 1965) 12 ♗c2 ♘e7 13 d4 c5 14 ♘f1=

Janosevic–Bisguier, Birmingham 1975.

(c) **10 ♗g5 ♘d7!** 11 ♗e3 ♘a5 12 ♗a2 c5 13 c3 ♘b6 14 b4 ♘c6 15 a5 ♘d7 16 ♗d5 ♕c7 17 ♕b3 ♘f6 18 ♘bd2 ♖ac8= Kupreichik–Dorfman, USSR Cup 1978.

B21

10 c3

Grandmaster Sax has had some success with this tricky move.

10 ...   ♘a5!?

10 ... ♖e8! is Klinger–Nunn in B1. Others:

(a) **10 ... ♘d7** 11 ♗e3!? (11 ♗c2 ♗f6 12 ♘a3 ♘b6! 13 ab ab 14 b4 ♘e7= Hübner–Kuzmin, Leningrad 1973; 11 ab ab 12 ♖xa8 ♗xa8 13 ♘bd2 ♗f6!? 14 ♖b1 ♘e7= *ECO*) ♘a5 12 ♗a2 c5 13 ♘a3 b4 14 cb cb 15 ♘c4 ♘xc4 16 ♗xc4 ♔h8?! (16 ... a5!?) 17 a5 f5 18 ♗d2 ♘c5 19 ♗xb4 fe 20 de ♗xe4 21 ♗d5± Sax–Hebden, Hastings 1983–84.

(b) **10 ... h6** 11 ♘bd2 ♖e8 12 ♘f1 ♗f8 13 ♘g3 ♘a5 (13 ... d5? 14 ed ♘xd5 15 d4± Kubler–Kranzl, corr. 1977–78) 14 ♗c2 c5 15 ♗d2 ♘c6= Sax–Djuric, Szirak 1985.

(c) **10 ... b4!?** 11 ♘bd2 d5 12 ♕c2 ♖b8 13 ♗a2 a5 unclear (Dely–Plachetka, Kecskemet 1975).

11 ♗c2!   c5
12 ♘bd2   ♕c7

If 12 ... ♘c6 (Jansa) 13 ♘f1 d5

14 ed ♕xd5 15 ♗b3 ♕d6 16 ♘g3
g6 17 ♗h6 ♖e8 18 ♘g5 ♘d8 19
ab ab 20 ♖xa8 ♗xa8 21 ♘3e4
♘xe4 22 ♘xe4 ♕c6 23 c4± Sax.
    13 ♘f1 ♘c6
  (a) **13 ... ♖ad8?!** (13 ... ♖fd8
Sax) 14 ab! ab 15 d4 cd 16 cd d5
17 ed e4 18 ♘g5 ♖xd5 19 ♘e4
♖fd8 20 ♕e2!± Sax–Geller,
Linares 1983.
  (b) **13 ... ♖fe8** 14 ♘e3 ♖ad8
15 ♘f5 ♗c8 16 ♘xe7+ ♕xe7 17
♗g5 ♖fe8 18 h3 h6 19 ♗h4±
Biyiasas–Hebden, Hastings 1977–
78.
    14 ♘g3
Or 14 ♗g5!? ♘d8 15 ♘g3 ♘e6
16 ♗d2 ♖fe8 17 ♘g5 ♘f8 18
♘f5 ♘g6 19 ♘xe7+ ± Scriba–
Piskov, corr. 1958.
    14 ... ♖ac8
    15 ♘f5 ♗d8
16 ab ab 17 ♗b3 (17 h3!?) 17
... ♘e7!= Liberzon–Dake, Lone
Pine 1975.
B22
    10 ♗d2(130)
This move of Geller's used to
be one of the critical lines and still
requires care. White prevents the
... ♘a5 manoeuvre but can have
difficulty developing his ♘b1.
    10 ... b4!?
  (a) **10 ... ♕d7** (the safe alternative) when:
  (a1) **11 ♘a3!?** (11 h3 ♘d8 12 c4
♘e6 13 ab ab 14 ♖xa8 ♖xa8=
Kuzmin–Lombardy, Reykjavik

1978) ♘d4 12 ♘xd4 ed 13 c3 dc
14 bc c5 15 f3 ♗c6 16 d4 ba 17
♗c2 cd 18 cd unclear (Mukhin–
Zhidkov, USSR 1979).
  (a2) **11 ♘c3 ♘d8!** (11 ... ♘d4
12 ♘xd4 ed 13 ♘e2 c5 14 ♘g3 d5
15 e5! ♘e8 16 ab ab 17 ♖xa8
♗xa8 18 c3 dc 19 bc was± in
many games from the 1960s; 11
... ♘a5 12 ♗a2 c5!? *ECO*) 12 ab
ab 13 ♖xa8 ♗xa8 14 d4 ♘c6 15
de ♘xe5! 16 ♘xe5 de 17 ♗g5
(Pritchett–Pfleger, Ybbs 1968)
♕xd1 18 ♖xd1 b4= Pritchett.
  (b) The other possibly playable
line is **10 ... ♘d7** (10 ... ♖b8?! 11
ab ab 12 ♘c3 ♗c8 13 h3 ♗e6 14
♘d5 ♕d7 15 ♖a6± Rechlis–
Lev, Beersheva 1988; 10 ... ♘d4
11 ♘xd4 ed 12 ab ab 13 ♖xa8
♗xa8 14 c3 dc 15 ♘xc3 ♕d7 16
♖e2± Matulovic–Gasic, Sarajevo 1966; 10 ... ♘b8 11 ab ab 12
♖xa8 and 13 ♘c3 is also±) 11
♘c3 ♘c5! (11 ... ♘d4 12 ♘xd4
ed 13 ♘e2 and 11 ... ba 12 ♗xa4
♘c5 13 ♗xc6 ♗xc6 14 d4± also

stem from Matulovic) 12 ♗d5 b4 13 ♘e2 ♗f6! 14 ♗e3 ♘e7 15 ♗c4 (15 ♗xb7!? Jansa) ♘e6 16 ♘g3 ♘g6 17 c3 (17 d4!?± Pachman) bc 18 bc d5!= Geller–Tal, Havana 1963.

11 c3

(a) **11 ♗g5** when:

(a1) **11 ... ♘d7** 12 ♗xe7 ♕xe7!? (*ECO* has 12 ... ♘xe7 13 ♘bd2 a5 14 d4 ed 15 ♘xd4 ♘c5 16 ♕f3 ♘g6= Matulovic–Jansa, Siegen Ol. 1970, but 17 ♗d5 was±) 13 ♘bd2 ♘a5 14 ♗a2 c5 15 c3 ♔h8 16 cb cb 17 d4 ed 18 ♘xd4 ♘c5 19 ♘c4 ♘xc4 20 ♗xc4 ♕f6 21 f3 (Matulovic–Hübner, Palma 1970) a5= or 21 ... d5!? 22 ed (22 e5? ♕b6) ♖ad8 23 ♗b3 ♕d6 Wade.

(a2) **11 ... ♘a5!?** 12 ♗a2 c5 (or 12 ... h6 13 ♗h3 c5= Haag–Pinter, Budapest 1976) 13 ♘bd2 ♘d7 14 ♗xe7 ♕xe7 15 ♘c4 ♘xc4 16 ♗xc4 ♘b6= Timoshchenko–Geller, USSR Ch. 1978.

(b) **11 a5** when:

(b1) **11 ... ♖b8** 12 c3 d5 13 ed ♘xd5 14 ♘xe5 ♘xe5 15 ♖xe5 ♗f6 16 ♖e1 c5 17 ♗c4 ♕d7 with compensation (Tseitlin–Tukmakov, USSR Spartakiad 1975).

(b2) **11 ... d5!?** 12 ♗g5 de 13 de ♘xe4 (13 ... ♕xd1 14 ♖xd1 ♘xe4 15 ♗xe7 ♘xe7 16 ♘xe5 ♘c5 17 ♘d2 ♖ad8 18 ♗c4 ♗d5 19 ♗f1± Kuzmin–Hardicsay,

Budapest 1978) 14 ♗xe7 ♘xe7 15 ♘xe5 ♘g6 16 ♕xd8 ♖axd8 17 ♘d3 ♘g5! 18 ♘d2 (18 ♘xb4 ♘h4) ♖d4 19 ♖e3 ♖fd8 20 ♖ae1 ♔f8 21 ♗a4 ♘e6 22 ♘b3 ♖g4 23 f3 ♖g5 24 g3 c6 25 ♔f2 h5 and Black had sufficient counterplay (Kuzmin–Psakhis, USSR Ch. 1981).

11 ... d5!?

The move Black would like to play; this used to be the main line but its soundness has recently been put in question. Alternatives:

(a) **11 ... bc** is clearer but less ambitious; the critical reply is 12 bc! (12 ♘xc3 ♘a5 13 d4 ♘xb3 14 ♕xb3 ♖b8 15 ♕c2 d5 16 ed ed 17 ♘xd4 ♘xd5 18 ♘f5 ♗f6= Matulovic–Reshevsky, Maribor 1967) ♘a5 13 ♗a2 c5 14 ♘a3 ♗c6 (14 ... ♕c7! 15 ♘c4 ♘xc4 16 ♗xc4 ♘d7!= e.g. 17 ♖b1 ♘b6 18 ♗a2 ♗c6 19 a5 ♘d7∓; 14 ... ♗c8 15 h3 ♖b8 16 ♘c4±) 15 ♘c4 ♖b8 16 ♕c2 ♘xc4 17 ♗xc4 a5 18 ♖eb1 ♘d7 19 ♗b5± ♗e8 20 c4 f5? 21 ♗xa5!± Liberzon–P. Littlewood, Hastings 1980–81.

(b) **11 ... ♖b8** needs more tests: 12 ♗g5 bc 13 bc ♘a5 14 ♗a2 (14 ♗c2!? Vasiukov) ♘d7 15 ♗e3 (15 ♗xe7 is harmless) ♔h8 (15 ... c5!? is promising, intending ... ♘b6 and ... ♗c6) 16

♘bd2 f5 17 ef ♖xf5 (Vasiukov–Geller, USSR Ch. 1980–81) 18 ♗e6!? ♖f8 19 ♘e4± (19 ... d5? 20 ♘eg5 e4? 21 de de 22 ♗xd7± ±) Vasiukov.

12 cb

12 ed?! ♘xd5 13 ♘xe5 ♘xe5 14 ♖xe5 ♗f6 15 ♖e1 (15 ♗xd5 ♗xd5 16 ♖e1 ♕d7 and ... ♖e8∓) c5! 16 a5 (16 ♕c2? ♕d6? 17 ♗e3 ♗e5 18 h3 ♘xe3∓) Ivkov–Smejkal, Prague 1970) ♕d6 17 d4 cd 18 cb ♘xb4∓ (Ljubojevic–Smejkal, Amsterdam 1975).

12 ... de

12 ... ♖e8?! 13 ♘c3 ♘xb4 14 ♘xe5 ♗d6 (14 ... ♗c5 15 ♗f4±) 15 d4 c5 is probably refuted by 16 ♘xf7! (16 ♗g5 cd 17 ♘g4 ♗e7! 18 ♗xf6 ♗xf6 unclear; Geller–Jansa, Budapest 1970) ♔xf7 17 e5 ♘d3! (17 ... c4 18 ♗c2± or 17 ... cd 18 ef ♕xf6 19 ♘e4 ♕g6 20 ♘xd6 ♕xd6 21 ♕h5+ ♔f8 22 ♕xh7± ±) 18 ef! ♕xf6 19 ♕h5+! ♔f8 20 ♖f1 c4 21 ♗c2! (21 ♕xh7 ♔e7! 22 ♕h3 ♖h8 23 ♕e3+ ♔d7 24 g3 ♖ae8 with a counterattack) ♕xd4 22 ♕xh7 ♔f7 23 ♘e2! ♕f6 (Hobusch–van der Heijden, corr. 1986) 24 ♗xd3! ♖h8 25 ♕g6+ ♕xg6 26 ♗xg6+ ♔xg6 27 h3± van der Heijden.

13 de ♘xb4

13 ... ♘d4!? deserves another try: 14 ♘xd4 (14 ♘xe5 ♘xb3 15 ♕xb3 ♘xe4 16 ♖d1 ♗d6 17 ♗e3 ♕e7 with good play; 14 ♗a2! ♘xe4 15 ♘xe5 unclear) ♕xd4 (14 ... ed!?) 15 ♗c3 ♕xd1 16 ♖xd1 ♘xe4 17 ♗xe5 ♗xb4 18 ♘c3 ♗d6 19 ♗xd6 ♘xd6 20 ♘d5 ♗xd5 21 ♗xd5 ♖ab8 22 ♖ac1 ♖fc8 23 b3 ♔f8 24 ♖c6± King–Hebden, London 1988.

14 ♘xe5 ♘xe4

14 ... ♗xe4 15 ♘c3± Jansa.

15 ♕f3

Not 15 ♘xf7?! ♖xf7 16 ♕f3 ♗d5= Jansa.

15 ... ♘d6

15 ... ♘xd2? 16 ♗xf7+ ♔h8 (16 ... ♖xf7 17 ♕xf7+ ♔h8 18 ♘xd2) fails to 17 ♕h5! (Jansa) whereas *ECO*'s 17 ♘g6+ can be met by 17 ... hg 18 ♕h3+ ♗h4.

16 ♘xf7!?

The critical line is 16 ♕e2 ♘d5 17 ♘c3 (± Jansa) ♘xc3 18 ♗xc3 ♗f6 19 ♖ad1 ♕c8 planning ... ♕f5.

16 ... ♘xf7

17 ♕xb7 ♘d3

18 ♖f1 (18 ♖e3?! ♗c5!) ♖b8 19 ♕d5 ♕xd5 20 ♗xd5 ♖xb2 21 ♗c3 ♖b6= 22 a5 ♖d6 23 ♗c4 ♖fd8 24 ♖d1 ♔f8 25 ♘d2 ♖c6 26 ♗xf7 ♔xf7 27 ♘e4 ♘c5 ½–½ (Rogulj–Djuric, Slavonska Pozega 1985).

B23

10 ♘c3*(131)*

131
B

This is by far the most frequently played move and the main line arising from it is in a separate chapter. Here we consider only offshoots from it:

10 ... b4!?

(a) **10 ... ♘a5!** 11 ♗a2! (11 ab?! ♘xb3 12 cb ab 13 ♖xa8 ♕xa8 transposes to A; 13 ... ♗xa8!? 14 ♘xb5 d5! Barden) b4 12 ♘e2 see Chapter 19.

(b) **10 ... ♘d4!?** 11 ♘xd4 ed 12 ♘e2 c5 13 ♘g3 d5 (13 ... g6 14 c3 dc 15 bc ♕d7 16 d4± Gipslis–Faibisovich, USSR Cup 1970) 14 ab! ab 15 ♖xa8 ♗xa8 16 e5 ♘e8 17 c3 dc 18 bc f5 19 d4 c4 20 ♗c2 g6 21 ♗h6 ♘g7 22 ♕b1 ♗c6 23 ♘e2!± Matulovic–Donchev, Kastel Stari 1988.

11 ♘d5!?

This attempt to prove ... b4 premature does not give White a clear advantage. After 11 ♘e2 Black can transpose to Chapter 19 by **11 ... ♘a5** 12 ♗a2 or try **11**

... **♖b8!?** (not 11 ... d5?! 12 ed ♘xd5 13 ♘g3 ♗f6!±) 12 a5 ♗c8 13 ♘g3 ♗e6 14 ♗c4 ♕c8 15 h3 ♖e8 16 ♗e3 ♗f8 17 ♘d2 ♘d7 18 c3 ♗xc4 ½–½ (Hjartarson–Hort, Reykjavik 1985).

11 ... ♘xd5

Or 11 ... ♘a5 (11 ... ♖b8 12 ♘xe7+ ♕xe7 13 c3± *ECO*) 12 ♘xe7+ ♕xe7 13 ♗a2 c5 14 ♗g5 h6 15 ♗h4 ♗c8 16 ♘d2 (Short–Westerinen, Brighton 1983) ♗e6!? van der Tak.

12 ♗xd5 ♖b8!

Not 12 ... ♘a5?! (12 ... ♕c8 13 c3 bc 14 bc ♘d8 15 d4± Keres–Shishov, Vilnius 1958) 13 ♗xb7 ♘xb7 14 c3 (14 d4 ♗f6 15 de de 16 ♗e3± Puc–Mihaljcisin, Yugoslav Ch. 1961) c5 (14 ... bc 15 bc ♗f6 16 ♖b1 ♘a5 17 d4 ♖e8 18 ♕c2± Matulovic–Flear, Belgrade 1985) 15 cb cb 16 ♕b3 ♘c5 17 ♕d5 ♕e8 (17 ... ♕d7 18 ♗e3±) 18 b3 ♖c8 19 ♗e3 ♕c6 20 ♕xc6 ♖xc6 21 ♖ac1 ♖fc8 22 ♗xc5 ♖xc5 23 ♖c4± Ljubojevic–Hübner, Tilburg 1985.

13 ♗d2

13 c3 ♕d7 14 ♗e3 bc 15 bc ♘a5 16 ♗xb7 ♖xb7= e.g. 17 d4!? ed 18 ♘xd4!? ♗f6 19 ♘f5 ♕e6! (19 ... ♗xc3?! 20 ♗d4! ♗xe1? 21 ♕g4±±) 20 ♗d4 ♖fb8 21 ♕d3 g6 22 ♗xf6 ♕xf6 23 ♘h6+ ♔g7 24 ♘g4 ♕e6 25 h3 h5 26 ♘h2 ♘b3 27 ♖a3 ♘c5

28 ♕d4+ ♔g8 29 c4 ♖b4∓
(Velickovic–Smejkal, Vrsac
1981).

13 ... ♗f6

(a) 13 ... ♕d7 14 c3 bc 15
♗xc3 (15 bc!?) ♗f6 ½–½ (Oll–
Veingold, Yurmala 1983).

(b) 13 ... ♔h8 14 c3 bc 15 bc
♘a5 16 ♖b1 c6 17 ♗a2 ♕c7 18

♕c2 c5 19 ♗d5 ♗xd5 20 ed c4 21
♖xb8 ♖xb8 22 d4± (Ljubojevic–
Panno, Madrid 1973).

14 c3 bc
15 bc ♘a5

16 ♖b1 c6 17 ♗a2 c5 18 ♕c2
♕c7 19 ♗g5 (19 ♗d5? c4∓
Hulak–Velimirovic, Osijek 1978)
♗xg5 20 ♘xg5= *ECO*.

21 Anti-Marshall: 8 d4

1 e4 e5 2 ♘f3 ♘c6 3 ♗b5 a6 4
♗a4 ♘f6 5 0-0 ♗e7 6 ♖e1 b5 7
♗b3 0-0

    8   d4*(132)*

This is the most interesting
anti-Marshall (apart from 8 a4)
since Black has two reasonable
alternatives:

A 8 ... ♘xd4!?
B 8 ... d6

8 ... ed?! 9 e5 ♘e8 10 ♗d5! (10
♘xd4 ♘xd4 11 ♕xd4 see A1) 10
... ♖b8 gives White an unusually
favourable form of the 6 d4 attack
after 11 ♗f4 (or 11 ♗xc6 dc 12

♘xd4 ♕d7/♖b8 13 ♗e3 c5 14
♘b3) ♔h8 12 ♘xd4 ♘xd4 13
♕xd4 d6 14 ♘c3 de 15 ♗xe5 ♗f6
16 ♕c5 ♘d6 17 ♗xf6± Olsson–
Puig, Varna Ol. 1962.

A

    8 ...   ♘xd4!?
A direct challenge for the initiative. White must choose between
offering a risky gambit himself or
accepting a probably sound one
by Black:

A1 9 ♘xd4
A2 9 ♗xf7+!?

A1

    9   ♘xd4   ed
    10 e5
Not 10 ♕xd4?? c5∓∓ while 10
c3?! dc 11 ♘xc3 is premature
since Black's development is
undisturbed.

    10 ...   ♘e8
    11 c3!?
11 ♕xd4 seems innocuous after
11 ... ♗b7 12 c3 (12 ♕g4 c5 13 c3
d5=) d6 13 ♗f4 de 14 ♗xe5=
(L. Steiner–Marshall, USA 1929)

but 11 ... c5!? is risky, e.g. 12 ♕e4
♘c7!? (12 ... ♖b8 13 ♗d5 ♘c7
Kondratiev) 13 c4! (13 c3 d5! 14
ed ♗xd6= Georgiev) bc 14 ♗c2!
g6 15 ♘c3 ♖b8 16 ♗a4! (16
♖d1!?) ♖b6 (van der Wiel–Kir.
Georgiev, Wijk aan Zee 1988) 17
♖d1 ♖e6! 18 ♗f4±.

11 ...   dc

Declining by 11 ... d6 may be
playable with 12 cd (12 ♕f3
♖b8!) de 13 ♕f3 ♖b8 14 de and
now 14 ... c5 (Vogt).

12 ♘1xc3   ♗b7

If 12 ... d6!? 13 ♕f3 (or 13 ♗f4
de 14 ♗xe5 ♕xd1 15 ♖axd1 with
compensation for the ♙ —Vogt)
♗e6 (13 ... ♖b8?! 14 ♗f4 ♗b7
15 ♗d5 ♗xd5 16 ♘xd5 de 17
♗xe5 ♗d6 18 ♖ad1 ♔h8 19
♘e7!± Vogt–Goldberg, DDR
Ch. 1986) then:

(a) White can either simplify by
14 ♗xe6 fe 15 ♕g4 ♕d7 16 ed=
Vogt,

(b) or try the speculative **14
♘d5!?** ♖c8 (14 ... ♗xd5 15
♗xd5 ♖b8 16 ♗f4 de 17 ♗xe5
♗f6 18 ♖ad1 ♘d6 19 ♗c6 ♖b6
20 b3 with compensation—Vogt)
15 ♗f4 ♗g5 16 ♖ad1 ♔h8 17
♗g3 c6 18 ed!? ♗xd5 19 ♗xd5 cd
20 ♕xd5 ♖c2 21 d7 ♘c7 22 ♗xc7
♖xc7 23 ♕d6 ♖a7 24 ♕xf8+
♕xf8 25 ♖e8 ♖a8 ½–½ (26 d8(♕)
♕xe8 27 ♕xg5=) Tseshkovsky–
Malaniuk, USSR Ch. 1987.

13 ♗f4!?

Kondratiev's move, which
needs tests. White's compensation
seemed inadequate after 13 ♘d5
(or 13 ♕d3 c5 14 ♗d5 ♗xd5 15
♘xd5 ♘c7 16 ♘b6 ♖a7 17 ♗e3
d5 18 ed ♘e6! Romanishin–
Tseshkovsky, USSR Cup 1978)
♗xd5 14 ♕xd5 ♔h8 15 a4 c6 16
♕e4 f5 17 ef ♗xf6 18 ♗c2 g6 19
♖a3 ♘g7 20 ♕g4 ♖e8 21 ♖d1
♖e6 22 h4 ♕e8 (Sznapik–Pytel,
Polanica Zdroj 1984).

A2

9   ♗xf7+!?   ♖xf7

9 ... ♔xf7 10 ♘xe5+ transposes but White is certain of some
advantage after 9 ... ♔h8?! 10
♘xe5 c5!? 11 c3! (Neikirkh) e.g.
11 ... d6 12 cd de 13 de ♕xd1 14
♖xd1 ♖xf7 15 ef ♗xf6 16 e5±
Tseshkovsky–Tseitlin,   USSR
1978.

10   ♘xe5   ♖f8

The only move. 10 ... ♘c6? 11
♘xf7 ♔xf7 12 e5 ♘g8 (12 ...
♘e8 13 ♕d5+ ♔f8 14 ♖e3!)
loses to 13 ♕h5+ then ♕f5+
and ♕xh7 followed by ♕f5+
♕g6+ and ♖e3 (Nunn) or 10 ...
♘e6? 11 ♘xf7 ♔xf7 12 e5 ♗b7
(12 ... ♘e8 13 ♕f3+) 13 ef ♗xf6
14 ♘c3±± Penrose–A. R. B.
Thomas, British Ch. 1961.

11   ♕xd4 *(133)*

11 ...   c5!

If 11 ... ♗b7 12 ♘c3 ♕e8 (12
... c5 see below; 12 ... b4? 13
♘d5 ♘xd5 14 ed ♗f6 15 d6!±

133
B

Gulko–Ivanov, USSR 1st League 1975) 13 ♗g5 (or 13 ♘d3!? with the idea ♗f4–g3± Chiburdanidze and Gufeld) b4! 14 ♘e2! ♘xe4 15 ♗xe7 ♕xe7 16 ♘g3 ♘xg3 17 hg ♕f6 18 ♖e2± *ECO*.

12 ♕d1

(a) **12 ♕d2 ♕c7** 13 ♘f3 ♗b7 14 ♘c3 ♖ae8 15 e5 b4 16 ef bc 17 bc ♗f6∓ (Vogt–A. Goldberg, DDR 1986).

(b) **12 ♕d3 ♗b7** (12 ... ♕c7 13 ♘f3 ♗b7 14 ♗g5 c4 15 ♕d1 ♗c5 16 ♗xf6 ♖xf6 17 ♘c3± Vitolins–Ozolins, Latvian Ch. 1985) 13 ♘c3 (13 ♗g5 ♘xe4! or 13 ♘f3 c4 14 ♕d4 ♕c7) ♕c7 14 ♘f3 c4 15 ♕d4?! (15 ♕d1 b4 16 ♘d5 ♘xd5 17 ed ♗d6 and ... ♖f5) ♗c5 16 ♕d2 ♘g4 17 ♘d1 ♖ae8 18 h3 ♖xf3! 19 hg ♖ef8 20 gf ♕g3+∓∓ Ekblom–Oikamo, corr. 1962.

12 ... ♗b7!

Keres' suggestion; now White will probably have to play ♘g4 instead of the preferred retreat ♘f3. Instead if 12 ... ♕c7 then 13 ♘f3! (13 ♘g4 ♘xg4 14 ♕xg4 d5 15 ♕h5 de 16 ♘c3 ♖f5= Smejkal–Zaitsev, USSR 1970) ♗b7 14 ♗g5 is strong (e.g. 14 ... ♖ae8 15 ♘c3 ♔h8 16 e5 ♘g4 17 ♗xe7 ♖xe7 18 ♘d5 ♗xd5 19 ♕xd5 ♖fe8 20 ♕d6!± Bielczyk–Borkowski, Polish Ch. 1975).

13 ♘c3   ♕c7

Or 13 ... b4 14 ♘d5 ♘xd5 15 ed ♗f6 16 ♕d3 ♗xe5 17 ♖xe5 ♕f6 18 ♕g3 ♖ae8 19 ♗f4 d6 20 ♖xe8 ♖xe8 21 c3 bc 22 bc ♕f5 (22 ... ♗xd5!?±) 23 c4 ♕e4 24 ♕e3 ♔f7 25 ♖c1 ♕g6 26 ♕g3 a5 27 ♕xg6+ hg 28 ♗xd6± Howell–Blatny, European Junior Ch. 1985–86.

14 ♘g4

Now Black has enough for the ♙, but if 14 ♘f3 b4 15 ♘d5 ♘xd5 16 ed ♗d6 creates the threat of ... ♖f5 which is not so easy to meet—Nunn.

14 ...   ♘xg4

This leads to a balanced situation. 14 ... ♖ae8!? is worth a try, e.g. 15 ♘xf6+ ♗xf6 16 ♘d5 ♕e5 17 c4? bc 18 ♘b6 ♗h4 19 g3 ♕f6 20 f3 ♕xb6 21 gh ♕g6+ 22 ♔h1 ♖xf3! 23 ♕xf3 ♖xe4 24 ♗e3 ♗c6 25 h5 ♖g4 26 ♖f1 ♕f6 0–1, Carton–Crawley, London (GLC II) 1986.

15 ♕xg4   ♗d6
16 ♕h3   ♖ae8
17 ♗g5 ♗e5 18 ♖ad1 d6 19

♗h4 ♕f7 20 ♕d3 b4 21 ♘d5
♗xb2= e.g. 22 f3 ♗d4+ 23 ♗f2
♗xd5 24 ed ♕xd5 25 ♖xe8 ♖xe8
26 ♗xd4 cd 27 ♕b3 ♕xb3 28 ab
♖e2 29 ♖xd4 a5 30 ♖d5 ♖xc2
31 ♖xa5 ♖b2 32 ♖d5 ♖xb3 33
♖xd6 ♖c3 34 ♖b6 b3 35 h4
♖c1+ 36 ♔h2 ♖b1 37 ♖b7 g6
38 ♔g3 h6 39 ♔f4 b2 40 ♔g3
♔f8 41 ♔f2 ♔e8 42 ♖b6 ♔d7 43
♖b3 ♔c6 44 ♖b8 ½-½ (Rantanen–J. Pinter, Helsinki 1983).

B

8 ... d6

In discussing this, preference
has been given to the most critical
lines and examples from grandmaster play of the 1980s, since an
exhaustive treatment would
occupy a disproportionate per-
centage of the book.

9 c3

(a) **9 d5!?** ♘a5 10 c4 c6!? (10 ...
♗b7 11 cb ab 12 ♗c2 c6 13 dc
♘xc6 14 ♘c3± Vitolins–I. Ivanov, USSR 1982) 11 dc ♗e6 12
♘a3 ♕b6 13 cb ♘xb3 14 ab ab 15
♗g5 ♕xc6 16 ♕d3 ♖ab8 17 ♘c2
♕c5 unclear (Vitolins–Shulman,
USSR 1982).

(b) **9 h3?** ♘xd4! 10 ♘xd4 ed 11
c3 ♗b7∓ (Foguelman–Wade,
Buenos Aires 1960).

9 ... ♗g4! *(134)*

Other ninth moves allow White
comfortable advantage.

This variation also arises via 7
... d6 8 c3 0-0 but White generally

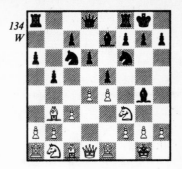

prefers 9 h3 to allowing this pin.
After 9 ... ♗g4 White can choose
between several moves, but only
two are current in grandmaster
play:

B1 10 d5
B2 10 ♗e3

(a) **10 h3** ♗xf3 when:

(a) **11 ♕xf3?!** ed 12 ♕d1 dc 13
♘xc3 ♘a5 14 ♗c2 is obsolete
because of 14 ... ♖e8 (or 14 ...
c5 15 ♘e2 ♘c6 16 ♘g3 ♘d4 17
♗e3 ♘xc2 18 ♕xc2 ♖e8∓ ECO)
15 f4 b4! 16 ♘d5 ♘xd5 17 ♕xd5
c6 18 ♕d3 g6 19 ♔h1 ♗f8 20 ♖f1
(Bronstein–Keres, Budapest
1960) d5! 21 e5 ♘c4 22 b3 ♘a3 23
♗xa3 ba∓ Botvinnik.

(b) **11 gf** ♘a5 and now:

(b1) **12 ♗c2** ♘h5 13 f4 ♘xf4 14
♗xf4 ef 15 ♕f3 (15 ♘d2 c5 16
♘f3 ♗g5∓ ECO; 15 ♕g4 ♕c8)
c5 16 dc ♘c4 17 ♕xf4 ♗g5∓
Hansson–F. Olafsson, Reykjavik
Open 1984.

(b2) **12 f4** ♘xb3 13 ab c6 14 fe

(14 d5 ♞d7 15 f5 ♝g5 16 ♞d2
♞f6 17 ♕f3 a5 18 ♔h1 ♔h8 19 c4
b4 20 ♞f1 ♝xc1 21 ♖exc1 ♞d7
22 ♖a2 ♞b6 23 ♖ca1 a4!∓
McKerracher–Bryson, corr.
1978–79) de 15 d5 ♞e8 16 f4
♝d6∓ (Padevsky–Blatny, Reykjavik 1957).

(b) **10 a3!?** (*ECO*) ♝xf3 11 gf
♞a5 12 ♝a2 c5 remains untested.

(c) **10 ♕d3** ♝xf3 11 gf ♞a5 12
f4 (or 12 ♝c2 c5 13 f4 cd 14 cd
♞c6 15 ♝e3 ♞b4 16 ♕d2 d5!? 17
de ♞xe4 18 ♝xe4 de∓ Heile-
mann–J. Steiner, corr. 1973–76)
♞xb3 13 ab ♞d7 14 ♞a3 ed 15 cd
c5 16 d5 (16 ♞c2!?= *ECO*) ♝f6
17 ♞c2 ♖e8∓ Tolush–Bronstein,
USSR Ch. 1958.

(d) **10 a4 ♕d7!** (10 ... ♕b8 is
also about=) 11 ab (11 d5 ♞a5
12 ♝c2 c6 is similar to main line
B1) ab 12 ♝xf7+?! (12 ♖xa8
♖xa8 13 ♞a3 ♖b8=) ♔xf7 13
♕b3+ d5! 14 ♖xa8 ♖xa8 15
♞g5+ (15 ♞xe5+ ♞xe5 16 de
♞xe4! 17 ♖xe4 ♖a1 18 ♖f4+
♔g8 19 ♕c2 ♝g5∓∓ Mesing–
Kovacs, Kikinda 1976) ♔g8 16
♞d2 ed∓∓ Panchenko–Suetin,
Dubna 1979.

B1

    10   d5   ♞a5
    11   ♝c2(*135*)

If 11 h3 ♞xb3 12 ab ♝d7! 13 c4
c6 14 dc (14 ♞xe5?! de 15 d6
♝e6=) ♝xc6 15 ♞c3 b4 16 ♞d5

♞xd5= Suetin–Kondratiev, Olomouc 1975.

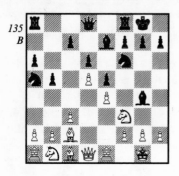

135
B

This variation has enjoyed a
major revival since the mid-1970s
with the introduction of several
new ideas. Black can find more
counterplay than is usual in the
closed Spanish since he can attack
the advanced d-pawn and open
the c-file, but he must beware of
long-term strategic disadvan-
tages.

From the diagram:

B11   11 ... c6
B12   11 ... ♕c8

(a) **11 ... c5?!** gives White the
promising extra options, after 12
h3! (12 dc is B11; 12 ♞bd2!? g6!?
Yudasin–Balashov, USSR Ch.
1986 or 12 ... ♕c7!? unclear)
♝d7 (12 ... ♝c8!? Suetin), of
playing a tempo up on the closed
Spanish (13 ♞bd2± Halifman–
Lev, Euro. Junior Ch. Groningen

1985–86) or taking the two bishops by 13 ♘xe5 de 14 d6 ♗e6 15 de ♕xe7 16 ♘d2 ♖fd8 17 ♕f3± Timman–Ree, Dutch Ch. 1978.

(b) **11 ... ♘c4** (11 ... ♕d7 12 h3 ♗h5 13 ♘bd2 c6 14 b4 ♘b7 15 ♘f1± *ECO* or 11 ... ♘e8?! 12 h3 ♗d7 13 ♘bd2 g6 14 a4 ♘g7 15 b4 ♘b7 16 c4 ba 17 ♗xa4 f5?! 18 ♗c6!± Semashev–Luk, Mogilev 1985) 12 h3 ♗d7 13 a4 ♘b6 14 a5 ♘c8 15 b3± Sax–Gligoric, Osijek 1978.

B11
11 ...   c6
The traditional and most direct way for Black to handle the variation, seeking counterplay down the c-file.

12 h3!
This is almost invariably chosen now because each possible reply involves a drawback. By postponing the capture on c6, White prevents the black ♗ finding a good home on e6. In the past this variation has been underestimated; in fact it can be hard for Black to equalize.

12 dc was once customary, but 12 ... ♕c7! (12 ... ♘xc6 13 ♗g5!±) gives Black a comfortable game after 13 ♘bd2 (13 h3 ♗e6 usually transposes; 13 ♗g5 ♘c4!) ♕xc6 (Alekhine's 13 ... ♖fd8 is unclear; 13 ... ♘xc6!? 14

♘f1 b4! 15 ♗d2 d5= Boleslavsky–Nei, USSR 1968) 14 ♘f1 (14 h3 ♗e6 15 ♘g5!? ♗c8 16 ♘f1 ♘c4 17 a4 h6= Tringov–Sokolov, Belgrade 1967) ♘c4 15 h3 (15 ♘g3 ♘d7! 16 ♘f5 ♗xf5 17 ef d5 18 ♘d2 ♖fd8!∓ Cuadrado–Purdy, 1st Corr. World Ch. 1950–52) ♗e6 16 ♘g3 (16 a4 h6= Ostojic–Sokolov, Belgrade 1967) g6 17 b3 (17 a4 ♖fd8 18 ♕c2 ♘a5= Padevsky–Yudovich, Moscow 1962) ♘b6 18 ♗d2 ♖fe8 Salov–Bykhovsky, Moscow 1986.

After 12 h3:

B111	12 ...	♗d7?!
B112	12 ...	♗h5?!
B113	12 ...	♗xf3
B114	12 ...	♗c8

B111
12 ...   ♗d7?!
This concedes the ♗ pair.

13 ♘xe5!
ECO mentions 13 dc!? but compared with B12 below, Black saves a tempo as he need not move his ♕.

13 ...   de
14 d6   ♗xd6
14 ... ♗e6 15 de ♕xe7 16 ♕f3 ♖fd8 (16 ... ♘d7 17 ♘d2 f6 18 ♘f1 ♕f7 19 b3 ♖fd8 20 ♘e3 ♘b6 21 ♘f5± Moscovich–Hualpa, Cordoba 1986) 17 ♕g3 ♘d7 18 b3 (18 ♘d2!? threat ♘f1–e3) c5 (18 ... f6!? Bellin) 19 ♘d2

b4 20 cb cb 21 ♘f3 ♖ac8 22 ♗h6 f6 23 ♖acl± Vasiukov–Romanishin, USSR Ch. 1974.

15 ♕xd6   ♘c4

15 ... ♕b8 16 ♕d3 ♗e6 17 ♕f3 (17 ♘d2 c5 18 ♕g3 ♘h5 19 ♕f3 ♘f4 20 ♘f1 f6 21 ♘e3 ♕b7 22 ♕g3 ♖ad8 23 ♘f5± Klundt–Laven, Bundesliga BRD 1985) ♘d7 18 ♘d2 ♕c7 19 ♘f1± Vasiukov–Ostojic, Reykjavik 1968.

16 ♕d3!?

16 ♕d1 ♗e6 17 b3 ♘b6 18 ♗g5 ♕xd1 19 ♖xd1± Tseshkovsky–Smyslov, Lvov 1978.

16 ...   ♗e6

17 ♕g3   ♘d7

18 b3 ♘cb6 19 ♘d2 a5 20 ♘f3 f6 21 ♘h4 a4 22 ♘f5! ♗xf5 (or 22 ... g6 23 ♗h6 ♖f7 24 ♖ed1 threat ♖d6±) 23 ef ♕c7 (23 ... ab 24 ♗h6!) 24 ♗h6 ♖f7 25 ♖ad1!± Halifman–Nenashev, Tashkent 1987.

B112

12 ...   ♗h5?! *(136)*

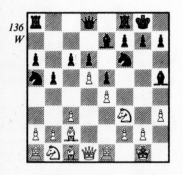

136
W

13 dc   ♕c7

The problem here is that the ♗ cannot contribute much on the kingside. Also after 13 ... ♘xc6 14 ♗g5! ♕b6 15 ♘bd2 ♖ad8 16 ♗b3 ♘d7 17 ♗e3 ♕c7 18 ♘f1 ♘a5 19 ♘g3 ♗g6 20 a4 White takes the initiative on the far wing (Belyavsky–Kuzmin, USSR Ch. 1978).

14 ♘bd2

Again 14 ♗g5 comes into consideration: 14 ... ♕xc6 (14 ... ♘xc6 15 ♘bd2 ♖fd8 16 ♗b3± *ECO*) 15 ♘bd2 ♖ad8? 16 a4 ♘b7 17 ab ab 18 ♖a7 ♖a8 19 ♖xa8 ♖xa8 20 ♗b3± Howell–Waddingham, British Ch. 1985.

14 ...   ♘xc6

If 14 ... ♕xc6 15 ♘f1 ♘c4 (15 ... ♖fe8 16 ♘g3 ♗g6 17 ♘h4 ♗f8 18 a4!±) 16 ♘g3 ♗g6 17 ♘h4 ♖ae8 18 ♘gf5± *ECO* or 14 ... ♖ad8? 15 ♕e2 ♘xc6 (Taulbut–Biyiasas, Hastings 1978–79) 16 a4± Bellin.

15 ♘f1

Chasing the ♗ is weakening: 15 g4?! ♗g6 16 ♘f1 d5 17 ed ♖ad8∓ (M. Mikhalchishin–B. Lengyel, Prague 1979).

15 ...   ♖ad8

16 ♘g3!

If 16 ♘e3 d5! frees Black's game, e.g. 17 ♘xd5 ♘xd5 18 ed f5! 19 ♕e2 e4 20 dc ♗c5 21 ♗g5 (21 ♗e3 ef 22 gf ♖de8 with compensation; Gufeld–Schneider, Jurmala 1978) ♗xf3 22 ♕f1 (not

22 gf? ♕g3+ nor 22 ♗b3+ ♔h8
23 ♗xd8 ♖xd8 24 ♕f1 ♖d2 25 gf
♗xf2+ ∓ Wagner–Perecz, Dortmund 1978) ♖de8 23 a4 ♕e5 with
good compensation (Kuzmin–
Lukacs, Budapest 1978).

16	...	♗g6
17	♘h4	**d5**

18 ♘xg6 hg 19 ed ♘xd5 20 ♕f3
♘f4 21 ♗e4 ♘a5 22 ♗xf4 ef 23
♘e2± Vasiukov–Bukhtin, USSR
1972.

B113

12	...	♗xf3

The obvious objection to this
move (used to good effect by
Akiba Rubinstein) is its surrender
of the ♗ pair and with it the
potential control of the light
squares. Black avoids the tempo
loss involved in retreats and sad-
dles White with a weak d-pawn,
but 12 h3 has enjoyed a revival
since it became understood that
this ♟ may be sacrificed.

13	♕xf3	**cd**
14	**ed**(*137*)	

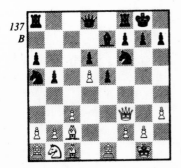

137
B

The asymmetric pawn structure
is an important factor here. Black
has the potential to mobilize his
kingside majority but must
reckon with problems when
White opens up the queenside: the
pawn at b5 can become a serious
weakness. Concrete variations are
very important for the assessment
of the position.

14	...	♘c4

Other moves might be recon-
sidered:

(a) **14 ... ♖c8** when:

(a1) **15 ♘d2** (15 b4 ♘c4∓
Szabo–Lengyel, Solingen 1968) g6
(15 ... ♘c4 note to Black's 15th;
15 ... b4?! 16 ♗f5! bc? 17 ♗xc8
cd 18 ♗xd2 ♘c4 19 ♗f5 ♘xd2 20
♕c3± ± Bellin) 16 b4! (16 ♗d3
♘h5 17 a4 f5∓ Stein–Geller, Kislovodsk 1966) ♘c4 17 ♘xc4
♖xc4 18 ♗d2 ♘h5 19 ♗d3 ♖c7
20 a4± Tseshkovsky–Belyavsky,
Ashkabad 1978.

(a2) **15 b3!** g6 (15 ... ♘b7 16
b4! g6 17 ♗h6± Tal; 15 ...
♕c7!?) 16 ♗h6 ♖e8 17 ♘d2 ♕c7
18 ♖e3± Vasiukov–Vogt, Cienfuegos 1975.

(b) **14 ... ♕c7** 15 ♘d2 (15 b3
g6 16 ♗h6 ♖fc8 unclear—*ECO*,
or 16 ♘d2 ♖ac8 17 ♗b2 ♘h5
unclear; Vogt–Pinter, Kecskemet
1977) g6 (15 ... b4 16 ♘e4!±
Belyavsky–Razuvayev, Frunze
1979) 16 b4!? (16 ♘f1 Vogt) ♘b7?
(16 ... ♘c4 17 ♘xc4 ♕xc4 18
♗d2 unclear—Vogt) 17 ♘f1 ♘h5

18 g4 ♘g7 19 ♗h6 a5 (Vogt–Lukacs, Kecskemet 1977) 20 ♖ec1 and ♗d3± Vogt.

15 ♘d2!

15 a4 ♘b6 (15 ... g6!? 16 ♖d1!? Djuric, or 16 ♗d3 ♕d7 17 ♕e2 ♕b7 18 ♖d1 ♘b6 19 ab ab 20 ♘a3 b4 21 cb ♖b8 with compensation; Benjamin–Short, match 1983) 16 ♖d1 ♕c7 (or 16 ... ♘xa4!? Ostojic–Donner, Havana 1968) 17 ab ab 18 ♘a3 b4 19 cb ♖xa3 20 ♗xh7+ ♔xh7 21 ba unclear (Bronstein–Geller, Teesside 1975).

15 ... ♘b6

Recent praxis has almost exclusively involved this move, which avoids the risks of 15 ... ♖c8 16 ♘f1 (Kmoch suggested 16 ♘xc4 with the idea **16 ... bc** 17 ♗a4 or **16 ... ♖xc4** 17 a4) g6 17 ♗h6! (17 ♘g3 ♘e8∓ Yates–Rubinstein, Hastings 1922) ♖e8 18 a4! ♘xb2 19 ab ab 20 ♘g3 b4 21 c4! ♘xc4 22 ♗a4 ♘a3 unclear (Razuvayev–Vasiukov, USSR 1978).

16 ♘f1

White offers a sound positional sacrifice of his d-pawn (not 16 ♗b3 ♘fd7!? intending ... ♘c5, ... f5 *ECO*).

Now:

B1131 16 ... ♘e8
B1132 16 ... ♘bxd5

Or variations on a theme:

(a) **16 ... ♘fd7** 17 ♘g3 g6 18 ♗h6 ♖e8 19 ♘f5!? ♘c5 20 ♘xe7+ ♕xe7 21 ♖ad1 ♖ac8 (Lemachko–Akhmilovskaya, match 1977) 22 ♕g3 with the idea f4± Gufeld.

(b) **16 ... ♖c8!?** 17 ♘g3 g6 18 ♗h6 ♖e8 (Vasquez–Hase, Buenos Aires Ol. 1978) 19 a4!? b4 20 a5 ♘bxd5 21 ♗b3 (21 ♗a4 bc unclear) ♘c7 22 ♖ad1± Kovacevic.

(c) **16 ... ♕c7!?** (could be critical) 17 ♘g3 g6 18 ♗h6 ♖fc8 19 ♖ad1 (19 a4!? *ECO*) ♘fd7 20 ♘f5 ♗f8 unclear, e.g. 21 ♖e4 ♕d8 (21 ... ♘f6 22 ♖h4 with the attack) 22 ♖g4 ♖c4!∓ (½–½, 38) Timman–Hübner, Wijk aan Zee 1979.

(d) **16 ... g6!?** 17 ♗h6 ♖e8 18 ♘e3?! (18 a4± A. Mikhalchishin) ♔h8!∓ (Belyavsky–Ljubojevic, Linares 1988).

B1131

16 ... ♘e8

Black declines the ♗ and prepares kingside expansion. But the plan fails to equalize.

17 a4

17 g4!? may be playable: 17 ... g6 (17 ... ♗g5?? 18 ♕f5) 18 ♗h6 (18 ♘g3? ♗g5!∓ A. Mikhalchishin–Zakharov, USSR 1976) ♘g7 19 ♘g3 (Vogt–Franzen, Stary Smokovec 1979) since *ECO*'s∓ assessment of 19 ... ♗g5 is hard

to accept after 20 ♗xg5 ♕xg5 21 ♘e4 (Vogt).

17 ...   ♘xa4

17 ... ♘c7!? (*ECO*) 18 a5!? ♘d7 (with the idea ... ♘c5; not 18 ... ♘bxd5? 19 ♗e4) may be playable but others favour White: 17 ... g6 (17 ... ba see below) 18 ab ab 19 ♗h6 ♘g7 20 ♗d3 (20 ♕e2!? or 20 ♕d3!? Tal) b4 21 cb ♖xa1 22 ♖xa1 ♗g5 23 ♗xg5 ♕xg5 24 ♖a7 ♕f4 25 ♕xf4 ef 26 b5!± Adorjan–Gligoric, Osijek 1978.

18   ♗xa4   ba
19   ♘e3

Or 19 ♖xa4!? (19 ♖e4 f5!? Mikhalchishin) f5 20 c4 ♕c8!? 21 ♗d2 ♘f6 22 ♘g3 g6 23 ♖ea1 ♘d7 24 ♕e2 ♘b6 25 ♖b4± Gufeld–Tseitlin, USSR 1976.

19   ...   g6
29   ♘c4   f5
21   ♖xa4   ♘c7

Black's counterattack fails after 21 ... f4 22 ♘a5 ♕d7 23 ♘c6 ♗f6 24 ♗d2 ♘g7 25 ♖ae1 ♕f5 26 ♕e4! ♕h5 27 b4! (Szewczyk–Kaliwoda, corr. 1977–80).

22   ♘a5±

With the idea ♘c6 and ♗e3 (Romanishin and Mikhalchishin). Also possible is 22 ♘e3 (Antoshin) but not 22 ♗h6? ♖f7 23 ♗e3 ♕e8 24 ♖a5 ♖b8! 25 ♗b6 (25 b4 ♖b5!) ♘a8 26 ♗a7 ♖b7 27 ♗e3 ♘c7 28 ♘xe5!? de 29 d6 e4 30 ♕d1 ♗d8!= (½–½, 41)

Romanishin–Karpov, USSR Ch. 1976.

B1132

16   ...   ♘bxd5*(138)*

Accepting is probably no worse than declining (but not 16 ... ♘fxd5?? 17 ♗e4).

17   ♘g3   ♘c7

17 ... g6!? (*ECO*) 18 a4 gives White compensation for the ♙ says Mikhalchishin. If 17 ... ♖e8? 18 ♘f5 ♗f8 19 ♗g5! h6 20 ♗d2 ♕d7 21 ♖ad1± Gufeld–Klovan, USSR 1979.

18   ♘f5

18 a4 should transpose after 18 ... b4 (or 18 ... ba) 19 ♘f5 ♘e6 but 19 cb ♖b8 20 ♗d2 ♘e6 21 ♘f5 g6 22 ♘xe7+ ♕xe7 23 ♗c3 ♖fc8 is unclear—Kovacevic.

18   ...   ♘e6
19   a4   ba

19 ... b4!? needs more tests: 20 ♕b7 (20 ♗b3!? *ECO*) ♖e8 21 ♘xe7+ (21 ♕xb4 a5!? Kovacevic; 21 ... ♗f8 22 a5 ♖b8 23 ♕h4

g6 24 ♘h6+ ♗xh6 25 ♕xh6
♕c7= Kurajica–Smejkal, Titovo
Uzice 1978) ♕xe7 22 ♕xb4 ♕c7
(22 ... a5!= Kovacevic) 23 ♕h4
d5 24 ♕g3 ♘c5 25 ♗h6 g6 26
♕f3 ♖e6 27 ♖ad1 ♖ae8 28 b4
♘ce4 29 ♖c1 ♘d6 30 ♗b3 ♘f5
31 ♗g5 ♘e4∓ (L. Bronstein–Servat, Buenos Aires 1988).

20 ♖xa4!

If 20 ♗xa4!? g6 21 ♘xe7+
♕xe7 Black's chances are not
worse: 22 ♗c6 ♖ab8 23 ♖xa6 e4
24 ♕e2 (24 ♗xe4 ♘c5 25 ♗g5
♘xa6 26 ♗xf6 ♕e6 27 ♕f4 d5 28
♗xd5 ♕xe1+ 29 ♔h2 ♖b6 ∓∓
Djuric) ♘c5 25 ♖a3 ♖fc8 26
♗b5 ♕e5 unclear (Shamkovich–
Djuric, Toronto 1983).

20 ... g6
21 ♘xe7+ ♕xe7

22 ♗h6 ♖fc8 23 ♖ea1
(Gufeld–Gavashelishvili, USSR
1977); White regains his material
and retains a positional advantage, although the game eventually ended in a draw, which
makes the line unattractive for
Black unless 19 ... b4 is good.

B114

12 ... ♗c8(139)

A flexible move, ready to
regroup the ♗. The loss of time is
a less serious matter than the strategic concessions of the previous
lines. Either this or the very similar B12 is probably Black's best
choice.

13 dc

13 b3!? led to weird sacrifices in
Speelman–Hodgson, Bath 1987:
13 ... ♕c7 (13 ... cd!? 14 ed
♗b7!? 15 c4 bc 16 b4 ♘xd5 17 ba
♕xa5 unclear) 14 c4 bc 15 b4
♘b7 16 dc ♘d8 17 ♘c3 ♘xc6 18
a3 ♗e6 (Black seems OK here) 19
♗g5 h6 20 ♗e3 ♖fd8 21 ♘d5
♗xd5 22 ed ♘a7 23 ♘h4 ♘b5 24
♘f5 ♘c3 25 ♕f3 ♘cxd5 26
♘xh6+ ♔f8 27 ♗g5 gh 28
♗xh6+ ♔e8 29 ♗a4+ ♖d7 30
♖ad1 ♘b6 (unclear, but 1–0, 55).

13 ... ♕c7

13 ... ♘xc6 14 ♘bd2 ♗b7 15
♘f1 ♘b8 16 ♘g3 ♖e8 17 a4±
Nunn–Godoy, Haifa Ol. 1976.

14 ♘bd2

(a) 14 a4 ♕xc6 (or 14 ... ♗e6
15 ab ab 16 ♘g5 ♕xc6 17 ♘xe6
fe 18 ♘d2 ♖fc8 19 ♗d3 ♕b7
with active play in Schranz–Hardicsay, Hungary 1978; not 14 ...
b4 15 cb ♘xc6 16 b5!± Malaniuk) 15 ♘a3 (15 ♘bd2! below)
♘c4 (or 15 ... ♗e6 16 ♘g5 ♗d7

17 b4 ♘c4 18 ♕e2 h6 19 ♘f3 ♖fc8!∓ van der Wiel–Timman, Amsterdam 1988) 16 ♗d3 ♘xa3 17 ♖xa3 ♗e6 18 ♕e2 ba 19 ♗c2 ♖fc8 20 ♖xa4 h6 21 ♗d2 ♕b5 22 b3 ♕xe2 23 ♖xe2 a5= Ljubojevic–Short, Amsterdam 1988.

(b) 14 ♗g5?! ♘c4 (14 ... h6!?) 15 ♘bd2?! (safer 15 b3 and 16 ♕d3) 15 ... ♘xb2 16 ♕c1 ♘a4! 17 ♗xa4 ba 18 ♕a3 ♗e6 and ... ♖fc8 (Hazai).

14 ...   ♕xc6
15 ♘f1

15 a4 is possibly more dangerous: 15 ... ♗e6 (15 ... ♗b7 16 ♗d3! ♘c4 17 ♕e2 ♘xd2 18 ♗xd2 ba 19 ♕d1 ♘d7 20 ♗e3 ♘b6 21 ♗xb6± B. Ivanovic–Hjartarson, Belgrade 1987) 16 ♘g5 ♗d7 17 ♗d3 h6 18 ♘gf3 ♘b7 19 ♗c2 ♖fc8 20 ♕e2 ♘c5 21 a5 ♘a4 22 ♘h4 ♕c7 23 ♘b1 ♕xa5 24 b3 ♘xc3 25 ♖xa5 ♘xe2+ 26 ♖xe2 ♘xe4 27 ♘f3 ♘c5 (Lederman–Lev, Beersheva 1988) 28 ♖a1 unclear.

15 ...   ♘c4
(a) White has so far found nothing against 15 ... ♗e6 (or 15 ... ♗b7 16 ♘g3 g6 17 ♗g5 ♘c4 18 b3 ♘b6 19 ♖c1! ♘bd7 20 c4! ♕b6 unclear; Vogt–Smagin, Dresden 1985) 16 ♘g3 g6 (or 16 ... ♖fe8 17 ♕e2 ♗f8 18 ♘g5 ♗c8! 19 ♘h5 ♘d7= Tseshkovsky) 17 ♗h6 (17 a4!?) ♖fc8! 18 ♘g5 ♗f8 19 ♗xf8 ♖xf8 20

♕c1 ♗d7!= Ligterink–Timman, Amsterdam 1978.

(b) Not 15 ... h6?! 16 ♘g3 ♖e8 (16 ... ♘c4 17 ♘h4 ♖e8 18 ♘hf5 ♗f8 19 ♕f3± Sax–Perenyi, Hungarian Ch. 1977) 17 ♘h4!± Halifman–Petran, Euro. Club Final, Rotterdam 1988.

16 ♘g3
16 a4 transposes; not 16 b3?! ♘b6 17 ♗d2 ♕b7 18 ♖c1 a5∓ Penrose–Wade, England 1958.

16 ...   ♖e8
17 a4

17 ♕e2 ♗b7! 18 ♘f5 ♗f8 with the idea ... d5 unclear (*ECO*); not 17 ♘f5?! ♗f8 18 ♖b1 (18 ♗g5? ♗xf5! 19 ef ♘xb2 20 ♕c1 ♘c4 21 ♗xf6 gf) h6 19 ♘h2 ♗xf5 20 ef d5!∓ Hazai.

17 ...   ♗b7
(a) 17 ... g6!? is worth further investigation, e.g. 18 b3?! ♘b6 19 a5 ♘bd7 20 ♗d2 ♗f8 21 ♖c1 ♗b7 22 b4 d5! 23 ♗g5 ♗g7 24 ♕d2 ♖ac8 25 ed ♕xc3 26 ♕xc3 ♖xc3 27 ♘xe5 ♖xe5 28 ♖xe5 ♘xe5 29 ♗xf6 ♗xd5! 30 ♗xg7 ♔xg7 31 ♘e2 ♖c4∓ (Halifman–Kozlov, Riga 1988).

(b) 17 ... ♗f8 18 b3!? ♘b6 19 a5 ♘bd7 20 ♗d2 ♗b7 21 b4 h6 22 ♖c1 ♖ad8 23 c4 unclear; Nunn–Littlewood, London 1978.

18 ♗d3   ♗f8
19 ♕e2   d5!=
20 ab ab 21 ♖xa8 ♗xa8 22 ed ♘xd5 23 ♘f5 e4!∓ 24 ♗xe4

♘xc3 25 bc ♖xe4 26 ♕xe4 ♕xe4 27 ♖xe4 ♗xe4 28 ♘5d4 b4 29 ♘d2! ♘xd2 30 ♗xd2 bc 31 ♗xc3 ½-½ (Timman–Spassky, Montreal 1979).

B12

    11 ...   **♕c8**(*140*)

This refines the preceding strategy. By freeing d8 for the ♗e7, Black enables the other ♗ to retreat safely to d7.

140
W

    12 h3

12 a4!? c6 13 ♗g5 (Tseshkovsky–Romanishin, match 1979) has not been repeated; Black can consider **13 ... cd!?** (Parma) or **13 ... ♗xf3!?** 14 ♕xf3 (14 gf!?) ♘xd5 15 ed ♗xg5 16 ♕h5 h6.

    12 ...   **♗d7**
    13 ♘bd2   **c6**
    14 dc   **♕xc6**

Compared with B114, the equalizing lines involving ... ♗b7

are unavailable; on the other hand, the rooks are already linked.

After other recaptures the ♕ looks misplaced:

(a) **14 ... ♗xc6** 15 b4! (15 ♘f1 ♘c4 16 ♘g3 g6 17 ♘h2 ♘e8 18 a4 ♘g7 19 b3 ♘b6 20 a5 ♘d7 21 b4 ♘f6= Halifman–Razuvayev, Minsk 1985) ♘b7 (15 ... ♘c4 16 ♘xc4 bc 17 ♗g5 with the idea 18 ♘d2±) 16 ♘f1 ♘d8 17 ♘g3 ♘e6 18 ♗b3 (18 ♘f5 ♕c7 19 ♗b3 ♖fe8 20 ♘g5 ♗f8 unclear— Belyavsky) ♖d8 (18 ... ♕b7!?) 19 ♕e2 ♖a7 20 ♘g5 d5 21 ♘xe6 ♕xe6 22 ♗g5 h6 23 ♗xf6 ♗xf6 24 ♖ad1 ♖ad7 25 ♖d3 ♕e8 26 ♘h5 ♕e7 (26 ... ♗g5!?) 27 ♕g4? (27 ♘xf6+ ♕xf6 28 ed or maybe 27 ed±) de 28 ♖g3 ♖d3 29 ♖ee3 ♖xe3 30 fe ♔h8∓∓ Halifman–Belyavsky, USSR Ch. 1988.

(b) **14 ... ♘xc6?!** 15 ♘f1 h6 (15 ... ♗e6 16 ♘e3 ♕d7 17 ♘g5± Belyavsky) 16 ♘e3 ♖d8 17 ♘h2 ♗e6 18 ♘d5± Ciocaltea–Belyavsky, Bucharest 1980.

    15 ♘f1   **♖fe8**

Or 15 ... ♘c4 (15 ... ♗e6! see B114; 15 ... ♖fc8!? 16 ♘e3 ♖ab8 17 a3 ♘c4 unclear in Halifman–Dorfman, Minsk 1986) 16 a4 when:

(a) **16 ... ♘b6!?** 17 a5 ♘a4 18 ♘e3 ♘c5 (18 ... ♖fe8 19 ♘f5 ♗xf5 20 ef ♘c5 21 ♗g5± Halif-

man–Timoshchenko, USSR
1987) 19 ♘f5 ♗xf5 20 ef ♖ab8!
(threat ... b4) 21 ♗g5 b4 22 ♘h2!
unclear (Halifman–Goldin, Vilnius 1988).
   (b) **16...** ♖ac8 17 ♘g3 b4?! (17
... g6 unclear—Halifman) 18 b3
♘a3 19 c4! ♘xc2 20 ♕xc2±
Halifman–Balashov, Sverdlovsk
1987.

16   ♘g3   ♘c4
If 16 ... h6 17 ♘h4 (17 a4!?
♕c7 18 ♕e2 ♗f8 19 ab ab 20
♗d3 ♖ab8 21 ♘d2 b4 22 c4±
Klundt–Krallman, Bundesliga
BRD 1986–87) ♖ad8 18 ♘hf5
♗f8 19 a4 ♘b7 20 ♕f3 d5 21 ab
ab 22 ed ♘xd5 23 ♗b3?! (23 ♗e4)
♘f4!= Timman–Scheeren, Netherlands 1983.

17   b3
A *YB1* suggestion after 17
♘f5?! ♗xf5 18 ef ♗f8 19 a4
♖ab8 20 ♖a2 h6 21 ab! ab 22
♘h2   d5 (Ligterink–Smejkal,
Amsterdam 1979).

17 ...   ♘b6
18   ♗b2   ♗f8
19 ♕d2 g6 20 ♖ad1 ♖ad8
unclear   (Martens–Shvidler,
Amsterdam Open 1988).

B2
10   ♗e3 *(141)*
This move, less forcing but
maintaining the central tension,
has been popular recently.

10 ...   ed

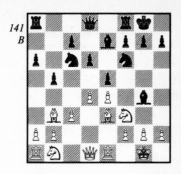

141
B

This is normal. A summary of
alternatives:
   (a) **10 ... d5!?** (10 ... ♘xe4?! 11
♗d5 ♕d7 12 ♗xe4 d5 13
♗xh7+! ♚xh7 14 de ♕f5 15
♘d4!± or 14 ... ♕e6 15 ♗d4±
ECO) 11 ed ed (11 ... ♘xd5 12 de
♘xe3 13 ♖xe3 ♗c5 14 ♖e1 ♕b8
15 ♘bd2 ♕b6 16 ♕e2 ♖ae8 17
♕f1± Razuvayev) 12 ♗xd4 (12
cd ♘a5 13 ♗c2 ♘xd5= or 12
♗g5 ♘xd5! 13 ♗xd5 ♕xd5 14
♗xe7 ♗xf3 15 ♕xf3 ♕xf3 16 gf
♖fe8∓ J. Toth–Perenyi, Hungary 1977) ♘xd4 13 cd (13 ♕xd4
♗xf3 14 gf ♘d7 15 ♘d2 ♗c5 16
♕g4 f5 17 ♕g2 ♗d6 with compensation—Razuvayev) ♗b4 (13
... ♖e8!? with the idea ... ♗d6)
14 ♘c3 ♗xc3 15 bc ♘xd5 16
♕d3± van der Wiel–P. Nikolic,
Novi Sad 1982.
   (b) **10 ...** ♘a5!? 11 de! ♗xf3 (11
... de!? 12 ♕xd8 ♖ad8 13 ♘xe5
♗d6 unclear; Mitchell–Madsen,
1st corr. World Ch. 1950–53) 12

♕xf3 de 13 ♗c2 ♘c4 14 ♗c1 c6
(14 … ♗c5!? Hulak–Sampouw,
Indonesia 1982) 15 b3 ♘b6 16
♘d2 a5 17 ♘f1 ♘fd7 18 ♘e3
(Kasparov–Litvinov, USSR 1978)
g6!? ± *ECO*.

(c) **10 … ♗h5 11 ♘bd2** (11
h3!? ♗g6 12 ♘bd2 ed 13 ♘xd4
♘a5 14 ♗c2 c5 15 ♘4f3± Panchenko–Zaitsev, Sochi 1977) d5
12 ed ♘xd5 13 de ♘xe5 14 ♗g5
♘d3 15 ♗xd5 ♗xg5 16 ♗xa8
♘xe1 17 ♕xe1 ♗xd2 =
Chandler–Romanishin, Leningrad 1987.

11 cd
Now:

B21 11 … d5!?
B22 11 … ♘a5

B21

11 … d5!?
12 e5

12 ed? ♘xd5 13 ♘c3 ♘xe3 14
fe ♘a5 15 ♗c2 c5∓ Smyslov–
Savon, Lvov 1978.

12 … ♘e4
13 h3

13 ♘bd2 (13 ♘c3 ♗b4 14 ♖c1
♘e7 unclear; Yates–Bogoljubow,
London 1922) ♘xd2 14 ♕xd2
♗xf3 15 gf (15 ♖ec1? ♗b4 16
♕c2 ♘xd4 17 ♗xd4 ♕g5∓∓)
♗b4 16 ♕c2 ♘a5! 17 ♗d2 (17
♖fc1!?=) ♗xd2 18 ♕xd2 ♘xb3
19 ab ♕d7∓ Arnason–Torre,
Sochi 1980.

13 … ♗h5

14 g4

A more testing line may be 14
♘c3!? ♗xc3 (14 … ♗b4!?) 15 bc
♘a5 (15 … ♗g6 16 ♕d2 h6 [16
… ♘a5 17 ♗g5±] 17 e6! ±
Haba–Tolnai, Debreçen 1988) 16
♗c2 ♘c4 (16 … ♗g6!?) 17 g4!
♗g6 18 ♗f5! a5 (18 … ♘xe3! 19
♖xe3 ♗g5 20 ♘xg5 ♕xg5 21
♕f3 c6±) 19 ♗f4! b4 20 h4!±
Sznapik–van der Sterren, Copenhagen 1984.

14 … ♗g6
15 ♘h2 a5

15 … ♗b4!? is also very sharp,
e.g. 16 f3 (16 ♖e2 f5 17 f3 unclear;
Yudasin–Tseshkovsky, USSR
Ch. 1981) ♘g5 (16 … ♗xe1 17
♕xe1 ♘g5 18 ♘c3 ♘e6 19 ♖d1!
♘a5! unclear—Timman; 16 …
♕h4? 17 ♖e2 ♘e7 18 ♕c1! ±
van der Wiel–Timman, Arnhem
1983) 17 ♖f1 ♘e6 18 ♘c3 ♗xc3
19 bc ♘a5 20 f4 ♗e4 21 ♘f3 g6
22 ♘d2 ♗d3 23 f5! ♗xf1 24 ♕xf1
♘xb3! 25 ab ♕h4! 26 ♔h2 (26
♘f3 ♕g3+ 27 ♔h1 ♘f4 28 ♖a2
♘d3! 29 ♖g2 ♕xh3+ 30 ♔g1
♘e1!) ♘g5 27 f6 a5 28 ♘f3
♘xf3+ 29 ♗xf3 h5 30 ♖g1 a4!
unclear (Lobron–Greenfeld,
Beersheva 1985).

16 a4!?

16 a3 (16 ♘d2?! a4 17 ♗c2
♘b4 18 ♗b1 a3∓ or 16 f3?! a4 17
♗xd5 ♕xd5 18 fe ♕xe4 19 ♘c3
♕d3∓ Aseyev) a4 17 ♗c2 (17
♗a2 b4!) ♘g5!? (17 … f5!?) 18

♔g2 (18 f4 ♘xh3+ 19 ♔g2 ♗xc2 20 ♕xc2 ♘xf4+ 21 ♗xf4 ♘xd4) ♘e6 (with the idea ... ♘a5, ... c5∓) 19 ♗f5 ♘a5 20 ♘d2 c5∓ (Kindermann–Shvidler, Beersheva 1985).

16 ... ba

17 ♗xa4 ♘b4 (Halifman–Aseyev, USSR 1983) 18 f3 ♘g5 19 f4 (19 h4!? Nunn) ♘xh3+ 20 ♔g2 ♘xf4+! 21 ♗xf4 ♘d3 22 ♖f1 ♘xb2 (Aseyev) when Black's pawns, greater coordination and safer ♔ may outweigh the ♘. It is not really possible to give a definite verdict on such a complex line without more tests.

B22

11 ...   ♘a5
12   ♗c2(*142*)

142
B

From the diagram:

B221   12 ... ♘c4
B222   12 ... c5!

B221

12 ...   ♘c4

This variation is suspect; the ♘ ends up on b6 whereas it should

be on c6; a timely d5 is probably good for White.

13   ♗c1   c5
14   b3!   ♘b6!

If 14 ... ♘a5 (heading for c6) 15 d5! (15 ♗b2 cd! 16 ♗xd4 ♖c8! unclear; Krum Georgiev–Ermenkov, Prague 1985) ♘d7 (15 ... ♘xe4? 16 ♖xe4 ♗xf3 17 ♕xf3 ♗f6 18 ♘c3 b4 19 ♗b2± Fischer) 16 ♘bd2 ♗f6 17 ♖b1 ♗c3 (17 ... ♘e5 18 h3± or 17 ... ♖c8 18 h3 ♗h5 19 g4 ♗g6 20 ♘f1 ♗c3 21 ♖e3 b4 22 ♘g3 c4 23 ♖xc3!? bc 24 b4 with compensation; Nunn–Neunhoffer, Bundesliga BRD 1985–86) 18 ♖e3± (Marjanovic–Ivkov, Yugoslavia 1988) or 18 h3 ♗xf3 19 ♕xf3 b4!? (19 ... ♕f6 20 ♕g3± or 20 ♕d3± *ECO*) 20 ♖d1 ♖e8 21 ♘f1 ♕f6 22 ♕xf6 ♘xf6 23 f3 g6 24 ♗f4 ♘b7 25 ♘d2± Bronstein–Smyslov, Petropolis 1973.

15   ♘bd2

Or 15 dc!? (15 ♗b2 cd 16 ♗xd4 ♘fd7=) dc 16 ♘bd2 ♘fd7 (16 ... ♕c7 17 ♕e2 ♗h5 18 ♗b2) ♗b2 ♖e8 18 e5 ♘f8 19 ♕e2 ♗h5 20 a4 ba 21 ba ♗g6 22 ♗e4± Kindermann–Thipsay, Thessaloniki Ol. 1984.

15 ...   ♘fd7

Not 15 ... d5? 16 e5 ♘e8 17 dc ♗xc5 18 ♗xh7+ ±± nor 15 ... cd 16 h3 ♗h5 17 g4±; 15 ... ♖c8 16 h3 ♗h5 17 d5!±.

16   h3

Another treatment is 16 ♗b2 ♖e8!? (16 . . . ♖c8 17 h3 ♗h5 see next note) 17 a4!? (17 dc van der Wiel) ba 18 ba ♖b8 19 ♕c1! d5! 20 a5 ♘c4 (20 . . . ♗xf3!? 21 ab ♗g5! unclear) 21 ♘xc4 dc 22 ♗a4! ♗xf3 23 gf cd 24 ♗xd4 ♗d6 25 f4 ♖e6 26 e5 ♕h4 27 ♖e3 ♗c5 28 ♗xc5 ♘xc5 29 ♕xc4 (van der Wiel–Rivas, Marbella 1982) ♖g6+!? 30 ♖g3 ♘e6 31 ♗c2 ♖g4 32 ♕xa6 ♘xf4 (unclear—van der Wiel) 33 ♕f1±.

16   ...   ♗h5
17   d5!?

This is more promising than the normal 17 ♗b2 (17 g4 ♗g6 18 d5 ♗f6 19 ♖b1 h5 unclear) ♖c8 18 ♖c1 cd 19 ♗xd4 ♗f6 (Klovan–Geller, USSR Ch. 1975) 20 ♗xf6 ♕xf6 21 ♗b1 = Gufeld.

17   ...   ♗f6

18 ♖b1 ♗c3 (18 . . . ♘e5 19 g4 ♘xf3+ 20 ♘xf3 ♗g6 21 ♗f4± or 21 ♔g2± Yudasin) 19 ♖e3 b4 20 g4 ♗g6 21 ♘f1 h5?! (21 . . . ♖e8 22 ♔g2 and ♘g3±) 22 ♔g2 hg 23 hg ♘f6 24 ♘g5! ♖e8 25 f4!± Yudasin–Timoshchenko, USSR Ch. 1981.

B222

12   ...   c5! *(143)*

This should give clear-cut equality since now d4–d5 would permit the offside ♘ to reach e5 via c4 without losing time.

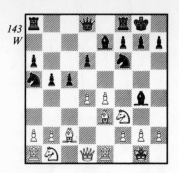

143
W

13   dc

(a) **13 ♘bd2** cd 14 ♗xd4 ♘c6 15 ♗e3 (15 ♘b3 ♘xd4 16 ♘bxd4 ♕b6 17 ♕d2 ♘d7 = *ECO*) d5 when:

(a1) **16 h3** ♗h5 (16 . . . ♗xf3 17 ♕xf3 d4 18 ♗g5 ♘b4 = Todorcevic) 17 g4!? (17 ed ♘b4 18 ♗g5 ♖a7 19 ♗b3 ♘fxd5 = Unzicker–Keres, match 1950) ♗g6 (17 . . . d4!? Byrne) 18 e5 ♘e4 = *ECO*.

(a2) **16 ♗g5** (16 ed ♘xd5 17 ♕b1 ♘f6 18 ♗e4 = *ECO*) ♗xf3 17 ♘xf3 de 18 ♗xe4 ♘xe4 19 ♗xe7 (19 ♕xd8 =) ♕xe7 20 ♕d5 ♖fe8 21 ♕xc6 ♖ac8 22 ♕xa6? (22 ♕d5 =) ♕c5 23 ♖e2 ♘xf2! ∓∓ Mrdja–Torre, Lugano 1984 (24 ♖xf2? ♖a8 25 ♕b7 ♖a7; 24 b4 ♘h3+).

(b) Black has nothing to fear from **13 h3** (13 e5 de 14 de ♘d5 15 ♕d3 g6 = *ECO*; 13 ♘c3 ♘c4 14 dc dc 15 e5 ♕xd1 16 ♖axd1 ♘d7

17 h3 ♘xe3 18 ♖xe3 ♗e6∓
Stoltz–Keres, Sweden–USSR
1954) cd (13 ... ♗h5!?) 14 ♗xd4
♗xf3 15 ♕xf3 ♘c6= or 15 ...
♖c8=.

13 ... dc

13 ... ♘c4!? 14 cd ♗xd6 is a
fascinating new ♙ offer: 15 ♘bd2
(15 ♗d4 ♗xf3 16 ♕xf3 ♗xh2+
regains the ♙ or 15 ♗c1 ♕c7 16
h3 ♖ad8 with compensation)
♕c7 16 h3 ♗xf3 17 ♘xf3 ♘xb2
18 ♕e2 ♘c4 19 ♗g5 ♘d7 20
♗b3 ♘de5 21 ♘xe5 ♗xe5 22
♖ac1 ♖ac8 23 ♖c2 ♗h2+ 24
♔h1 ♗f4 25 ♗xf4 ♕xf4 26 ♖ec1
♖fe8 27 ♗xc4 bc 28 ♖xc4
♕xc1+ 29 ♖xc1 ♖xc1+ 30
♔h2 ♖c6 31 ♕d2 g6 32 f4 ♖ce6
33 e5 ♖b8 34 ♕c3 h5= (½–½, 53)
Tal–Belyavsky, Moscow 1988.

14 ♘bd2!

14 ♕e2 (14 ♘c3 ♘c4 15 e5
♕xd1 16 ♖axd1 ♗xf3 17 ef
♗xd1 18 fe ♗xc2 19 ef(♕)+
♖xf8 20 ♗xc5 ♖c8! 21 ♘d5
♔h8= Belyavsky–Zaitsev, Minsk
1983) ♘c4! 15 ♘c3 ♘d7! 16 a4!?
(16 ♘d5 ♗f6∓ Rantanen–Keres,
Tallinn 1975) ♘de5! 17 ♗f4 (17
ab ab 18 ♘xb5 ♖xa1 19 ♖xa1
♘xb2∓ Kavalek) ♗d6 18 ♖ed1?
(18 ♗g3) b4!∓ (Hartmann–
Kavalek, BRD 1983).

14 ... ♘d7

Or 14 ... ♘c6!? (14 ... ♖e8 15
♕b1 ♘d7 see below) 15 ♖c1 (15

h3 etc. see below; 15 ♕b1 ♕c7 16
h3 ♗h5 17 ♘h4 ♗d6! 18 ♘f1
♗g6= Vasiukov–Klovan, USSR
Ch. 1973) ♘b4 (15 ... ♘e5!?
Gulko; 15 ... c4 16 h3 ♗h5 17 g4
♗g6 18 ♘h4 ♘b4 Nikitin) 16
♗b1 ♖c8 17 h3 ♗e6 18 ♘b3
♕b6 19 ♘g5 ♖fd8 20 ♕f3 ♘d7
21 e5 g6 22 ♕g3 (Gulko–Portisch,
Niksic 1978) ♘d5!? unclear—
Gulko.

15 ♕b1!

(a) 15 ♗f4 ♘c6 (15 ... ♕b6 16
e5 ♖ad8 unclear; Gulko–Geller,
USSR Ch. 1985) 16 h3 ♗e6!? 17
♕e2 (17 e5!? c4 18 ♕e2 ♘c5 19
♖ad1 ♘d3 20 ♗xd3 cd 21 ♕e4
♕d7= De Boer–Lengyel, Copenhagen 1984) ♖c8 (17 ... ♘b4!? 18
♗b1 c4 intending ... ♘c5) 18 a3
c4 (18 ... ♗f6!? with the idea 19
e5? ♘dxe5!) 19 ♖ad1 (Ljubojevic–Trois, Riga 1979) ♕a5!?
intending ... c3—Knezevic.

(b) 15 h3 ♗h5 when:

(b1) 16 g4!? ♗g6 17 ♘h2 is
complicated: 17 ... ♕c7 (or 17 ...
♘c6 18 f4 f6 19 ♘df3 ♘b4! 20
♗b1 c4 21 a3 ♘d3! unclear;
Bengtsson–Schneider, Swedish
Ch. 1985) 18 f4 f6 19 ♘df3 c4 20
♘h4 ♖ad8!? 21 ♕e2 ♘c6 22
♘xg6 hg 23 b3 ♗c5! 24 ♕f2 ♘b4
25 ♖ec1 g5!∓, e.g. 26 bc bc 27 f5
♗xe3 28 ♕xe3 ♘e5 29 ♗b1
♘ed3 30 ♗xd3 ♖xd3 31 ♕e2
♖g3+ 32 ♔h1 ♘d3 33 ♖f1 ♖b8

0–1 (34 ♖ab1 ♖xb1 35 ♖xb1 ♕e5 36 ♖f1 c3) Stern–Penrose, corr. 1986.

(b2) 16 ♖c1 (16 b3 ♗f6! 17 ♖b1 ♗c3= or 16 ♗f4 c4!? with the idea ... ♘c5 unclear—*ECO*) ♖c8 17 ♗b1 ♖e8 18 b3 c4! 19 bc ♗a3!? (19 ... bc unclear or 19 ... ♗xf3 20 gf± Dorfman) 20 ♖c3 ♕e7! 21 ♖d3 ♘e5 22 ♖d5 ♘axc4 23 ♗d4 ♘xd2 24 ♖xe5 ♘xf3+ 25 gf ♕h4∓∓ Prokopp–Giesbergen, corr. 1976.

15 ...   ♖e8
16 e5   ♘f8

A relatively new line; White combines threats on the kingside with an attempt to dominate the light squares.

17 ♗f5

After 17 h3! (17 a4!? *YB2*) ♗h5 18 ♗f5 ♗g6 19 ♕e4 ♗xf5 20 ♕xf5 ♕d5 White has the extra move h3 but its significance is slight: 21 b3 (21 h4 see below) ♘c6 22 ♘e4 ♖ad8 23 ♖ac1 ♘e6 24 ♖e2 g6 25 ♘f6+ ♗xf6 26 ♕xf6 ♘cd4 27 ♘xd4 ♘xd4 28 ♗xd4 cd 29 ♖d1 ♖e6= Chandler–Hodgson, Bath 1987.

17 ...   ♗xf5
18 ♕xf5   ♕d5!

Or 18 ... ♕c8?! 19 ♕h5 ♕e6 (19... ♕c6 20 ♖ac1 ± Matsukevich; if 20 e6 ♕xe6! 21 ♗xc5 ♕g6! Panchenko–Kuzmin, USSR 1988) 20 ♘e4 ♖ac8 21 ♗g5!±

(1–0, 36) Marjanovic–Abramovic, Yugoslav Ch. 1984.

19 h4!?

(a) 19 ♖ed1 (better 19 ♖ad1) ♖ad8 20 ♕c2 ♘c6 21 ♘b3? ♘b4 22 ♕b1 ♕xd1+ 23 ♕xd1 ♖xd1+ 24 ♖xd1 c4 25 ♘bd4 ♘xa2 26 ♘c6 c3 27 bc ♘xc3 28 ♖d3 ♘a4∓∓ Mortensen–Hjartarson, Gausdal 1987.

(b) 19 b3!? (Not 19 ♘e4?! ♗c4 20 b3 ♘xe3 21 ♖xe3 c4 22 h4 cb∓ Marjanovic–Smejkal, Novi Sad 1984) c4?! (19 ... ♘c6 as in Chandler–Hodgson) 20 ♖ed1 ♕b7 21 bc ♘xc4 22 ♘xc4 bc 23 ♕c2 ♕c7 24 ♖ac1 ♖ec8 25 ♖d4 ♗a3 26 ♖b1± Barle–P. Nikolic, Yugoslavia 1985.

19 ...   ♘c6!=

Black's position should be comfortable.

Not 19 ... ♘c4?! 20 ♘xc4 ♕xc4 21 h5 h6 22 b3 ♕e6 23 ♕f4 ♖ad8 24 ♖ed1 ♖d5 25 ♖xd5 ♕xd5 26 ♖c1 ♘d7 27 ♕g3 ♔h8 28 ♗d2 ♕d3 29 ♗c3± (1–0, 51) Chandler–Hawelko, Dubai Ol. 1986.

Conclusion

Marshall players will be tempted to try 8 ... ♘xd4 to avoid transposing into the thoroughly-explored territory that follows after the usual (and certainly playable) 8 ... d6.

22 Other Anti-Marshalls

1 e4 e5 2 ♘f3 ♘c6 3 ♗b5 a6 4
♗a4 ♘f6 5 0-0 ♗e7 6 ♖e1 b5 7
♗b3 0-0 *(144)*

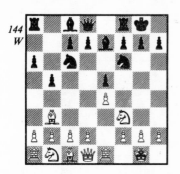

Finally, we discuss miscellaneous 8th moves sometimes used to avoid the Marshall. The first two of these are the most important by far and often transpose to each other or to 7 ... d6 lines:

A   8 d3
B   8 h3
C   8 a3

Three rarities:
(a) **8 ♗d5** ♘xd5 (8 ... ♗b7!?) 9 ed ♘b4 10 ♘c3 (10 ♖xe5 d6=)
♗b7 11 ♘xe5 (11 ♖xe5 ♗f6∓ Johnson–H. Steiner, USA Ch. 1929) d6 12 ♘g4 f5 13 ♘e3 f4 14 a3 fe 15 de ♗h4 16 ♖f1 ♗xf2+! 17 ♖xf2 ♖xf2 18 ♔xf2 ♕f6+ 19 ♔e2 (19 ♔g1 ♖f8) ♕g6∓∓ Black–Marshall, New York 1918.

(b) **8 c4!?** (worth more examination) d6 (8 ... bc 9 ♗xc4 ♘xe4= Ornstein) 9 ♘c3?! (9 cb Ornstein) ♗g4 10 cb ♘d4 11 ba ♕d7 (unclear; 11 ... ♘h5! Ornstein) 12 ♗c4 ♗xf3 13 gf ♘h5 14 ♗f1 f5? 15 ♘b5 fe 16 ♘xd4 ed 17 ♖xe4 ♗f6 18 b4± (1–0, 34) Shirazi–Ornstein, New York Open 1987.

(c) **8 ♘c3!?** d6 (8 ... ♗b7 could lead to an Anti-Marshall after 9 d3 d6 10 a4) 9 ♘d5 ♘a5 10 d4 (if 10 ♘xe7+ ♕xe7 11 d4 ♗g4!= or 11 d3 ♘xb3 12 ab c5 13 ♗g5 h6= Klaman–Spassky, USSR Ch. 1957) ♘xd5 (or 10 ... ♘xb3 11 ab ♘xd5 12 ed f6= Puc–Damjanovic, Yugoslavia 1956) 11 ed ♗b7 12 de de 13 ♘xe5 (13 ♖xe5!? ♗d6 14 ♖g5 c5 15 c4!? unclear; Jamieson–Hebden, Commonwealth Ch. London 1985) ♘xb3 14 ab ♕xd5 15 ♕xd5 ♗xd5 16 ♘g6 hg 17 ♖xe7= Savon–Tal, USSR Ch. 1974.

A

8 d3

'A modest but by no means harmless move'—Karpov.

A1 8 ... ♗b7!?
A2 8 ... d6

A1

8 ... ♗b7!?

Black intends to play ... d5 without losing a tempo, but he leaves his e-pawn attacked for the moment and White may also save time by avoiding c2–c3. Experience seems to show that the move is over-optimistic although it may be a good practical choice against inferior opposition.

9 ♘bd2!*(145)*

9 h3: see variation B. 9 a4 is the main line of 8 a4.

An alternative is **9 c3** when:

(a) **9 ... h6!?** (9 ... d6 see A2, note to Black's 9th, while 9 ... d5!? 10 ed ♘xd5 is Chapter 15, C1) 10 ♘bd2 ♖e8 (10 ... d5?!) is akin to the Smyslov Variation, e.g. 11 d4 (11 h3 ♗f8 12 ♘f1 ♘a5 13 ♗c2 d5 14 ed ♕xd5∓ Zhukhovitsky–Geller, USSR 1970) ♗f8 12 a3 (12 d5?! ♘a5 13 ♗c2 c6∓ Unzicker–Planinc, Ljubljana 1969) d6 (12 ... d5?! 13 ed ♘xd5 14 de ♘f4 15 ♖e4!± Lutikov–

Planinc, Skopje 1969) 13 ♗a2 (13 ♗c2 d5 unclear) a5= Parma, *ECO*.

(b) **9 ... ♖e8!?** (trying to do without ... h6 is a common Spanish theme nowadays) 10 ♘g5 (10 ♘bd2 see note to White's 10th below) ♖f8 (10 ... d5? 11 ed ♘xd5 12 ♕f3 ♗xg5 13 ♗xd5± ± or 11 ... ♘a5 12 d6 ♘xb3 13 ♕xb3! Serper) 11 f4!? d6 12 a4 ♘a5 13 ♗a2 c5 14 ♘a3 b4 15 fe! de 16 ♘c4 ♘xc4 17 ♗xc4 h6 18 ♘f3 ♘d7 19 ♖f1? (19 a5!±) a5 unclear (Serper–Malaniuk, Tashkent 1987).

145
B

9 ♘bd2 introduces a tempo struggle. If Black uses a Smyslov-type formation with ... d6 and ... h6 then White may gain a move by avoiding h3. Also, Black might be tempted by White's seemingly quiet moves to sharpen the struggle in dubious ways.

9 ... ♖e8!

If 9 ... h6 (not 9 ... d5? 10 ed

♘xd5 11 ♘xe5 ♘xe5 12 ♖xe5 ♘f4 13 ♘f3 ♘xg2?! 14 ♔xg2 ♗d6 15 ♗f4±) 10 ♘f1 ♖e8 11 ♘e3! (11 ♘g3 ♗f8 and ... d5) ♗f8 12 ♗d2± because the Black ♘ is denied a5, an attack by a4 is possible and in the meantime White can prepare d3–d4 (Karpov).

Karpov–Geller, USSR Ch. 1983, continued 12 ... d6 13 a4 ♘d7 (safer 13 ... g6 or 13 ... ♘e7 with the idea ... ♘g6 aiming for f4—Karpov) 14 c3 ♘e7 15 ♕b1! ♘c5 16 ♗c2 d5?! (16 ... ♘xa4 17 ♗xa4 ba 18 ♖xa4 ♕d7 19 ♕c2±) 17 ed ♘xd5 18 ♘g4 ♘f4 (18 ... ♕d6 19 ab ab 20 ♖xa8 ♗xa8 21 d4± or 18 ... ♘xa4 19 ♘gxe5 or 18 ... f6 19 d4) 19 ♗xf4 (19 ♘gxe5? ♘xg2! 20 ♔xg2 ♕f6) ef 20 ♘ge5 ♗d6 21 d4 ♗xe5?! (better 21 ... ♗xf3 22 ♘xf3 ♘e6) 22 ♘xe5± ♕g5 23 f3 ♖ad8 24 ab ab 25 ♖a7! ♗d5 (25 ... f6 26 ♖xb7! fe [26... ♘xb7 27 ♕a2+] 27 ♖xc7 ed 28 cd ♘e6 29 ♗b3± ±) 26 ♖xc7 ♘a6 27 ♖a7 ♘c5 28 ♗h7+ ♔f8 29 b4 ♘a4 30 ♕d3 ♗c4 31 ♕xc4! 1–0.

10   ♘f1

Or 10 c3 (10 ♘g5?! d5 11 ed ♘d4 Rogers and Hjorth) 10 ... d5?! (10 ... d6 is A2, note a to Black's 9th) 11 ed! ♘xd5 12 ♘xe5 ♘xe5 13 ♖xe5 ♕d7? (13 ... ♘f4 14 ♖f5 ♘xg2 15 ♗xf7+ ♔h8 16 ♕h5!) 14 ♕f3 c6 (14 ... ♖ad8 15

c4± ±) 15 ♘e4! ♖ad8 (15 ... f6 16 ♖h5±) 16 ♗e3 ♕c7? 17 ♕g3!± ±   Arnason–Hjorth, Dubai Ol. 1986.

10   ...   ♗f8

10 ... h6 transposes to Karpov–Geller above.

However, 10 ... d5!? (or 10 ... a5!? 11 a4 b4 12 ♘e3 h6 13 ♘f5 ♗f8 14 ♘3h4!? d5 15 ed ♘d4 16 ♘xd4 ed 17 ♖xe8 ♕xe8 18 ♘f3± Kuczynski–Przewoznik, Polish Ch. 1987) 11 ed ♘d4 is worth another try: 12 ♖xe5 (12 ♘xe5 ♗d6) ♘xb3 13 ab ♘xd5 14 ♘g3 (14 ♗d2!?) ♕d7 15 ♗d2 ♗f6 16 ♖xe8+ ♖xe8 = Dunne–Harding, Dublin 1976.

11   a4

Rogers and Hjorth suggested 11 ♗g5 h6 12 ♗h4 in *YB6*.

11   ...   ♘a5
12   ♗a2   ba

13 ♗d2 c5 14 ♘e3 ♘c6 15 ♘g5± ♖e6 16 ♘xe6 de 17 ♗c4 ♘a5 18 ♖xa4 ♘xc4 19 ♘xc4 ♘d7 20 ♗c3 ♕c7 21 ♕a1 f6 22 ♕a2 ♖e8 23 ♖a1 ♔f7 24 ♖b1 ♖b8 (Nunn–Lemachko, Lugano Open 1984) 25 ♗a5± ±.

A2

8   ...   d6

Now the e-pawn is protected and a heavyweight middlegame is in prospect.

9   c3*(146)*

This position can also arise via 7 ... d6 8 c3 0-0 9 d3 (*ECO* C90/

11–17). Since it is really part of the Closed Spanish, we give just the main line and recent examples.

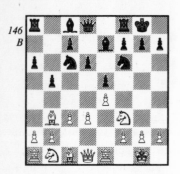

9 ... ♞a5

ECO also gives 9 ... ♝e6 leading to equality but this is suspect since the most recent example dates from 1964. Recent tries to avoid the main line are:

(a) **9 ... ♝b7** 10 ♞bd2 (10 a4 see Chapter 21) ♜e8!? 11 ♞g5 ♜f8 12 ♞gf3 ♜e8 13 ♞f1 ♝f8 14 ♝g5 h6 15 ♝h4 ♝e7 16 ♞e3 ♞h7 17 ♞f5 ♝xh4 18 ♞3xh4 ♛f6 19 ♜e3 ♞g5 20 ♜g3 ♞a5 21 ♝c2 ♝c8 22 ♛h5 d5 unclear (0–1, 49) Serper–Naumkin, Vilnius 1988.

(b) **9 ... h6** 10 ♞bd2 ♜e8 11 a4 (*ECO* gives 11 ♞f1 ♝f8± after 12 ♞e3 or 12 ♞g3 but it is arguable whether White has any real advantage) ♝d7 12 ♞f1 ♞a5 13 ♝c2 c5 14 ab ab 15 ♞g3 ♝f8 16 h3 b4 17 cb cb 18 ♝d2 ♛b6 19 ♝a4 ♞c6 20 ♝e3 ♛b7 21 ♞h4

d5∓ Kosten–Kupreichik, Esbjerg 1988.

10 ♝c2 c5
11 ♞bd2 ♜e8

(a) **11 ... ♞c6** 12 a4 (12 ♞f1 ♜e8!? below; *ECO* also gives 12 ... ♛c7, which is probably inferior, and 12 ... ♞d7 13 ♞g3 ♞b6 14 h3 ♜e8 15 ♛e2 g6 16 ♝h6 ♝f6 17 ♜ad1 a5= Matulovic–Ivkov, Yugoslav Ch. 1955.) ♝e6 13 ♞f1 ♛c7 14 ♛e2 ♞d7 15 ♞e3 ♞b6 (Ilin-Genevsky–Rabinovich, USSR Ch. 1934) 16 ab ab 17 ♝d2= *ECO*.

(b) **11 ... ♞d7** 12 ♞f1 (12 a4 b4 13 cb cb 14 b3 ♞c5 15 ♝b2 ♝f6 16 d4 ed 17 ♞xd4 ♜e8 unclear; van der Sterren–Scheeren, Amsterdam 1977) ♝f6 13 ♞e3 ♞b6 14 h3 ♞c6 15 ♞h2 (15 ♞g4!? *ECO*) g6 16 ♝b3 ♝e6 17 ♞eg4 ♝g7= Lutikov–Averbakh, USSR Ch. 1961.

(c) **11 ... ♛c7** 12 ♞f1 ♜e8 13 ♞e3 ♝f8?! (better 13 ... ♝b7) 14 ♝d2!? c4 (14 ... ♝b7 15 b4 and ♝b3; 14 ... ♞c6 15 ♞d5!±) 15 d4 ♝d7 (15 ... ed 16 cd ♞xe4? 17 ♞d5±±) 16 b4!± (1–0, 70) Smirin–Malaniuk, USSR Ch. 1988.

12 ♞f1

As usual in such positions from the Spanish, 12 ♞g5 leads only to a repetition of position since after 12 ... ♜f8 White has nothing better than 13 ♞f3 etc.

12 ...   ♘c6

Perhaps not best:

(a) **12 ... h6!?** 13 ♘g3 (13 a4 b4 14 cb cb 15 ♘e3 ♗f8 16 d4 ♕b6 unclear; Nezhmetdinov–Zagorovsky, USSR 1963) ♗f8 14 h3 ♗b7 15 d4 (15 b4 cb 16 cb ♘c6 17 a3 a5!) cd 16 cd ed 17 ♘xd4 ♖c8 18 b3?! (18 ♗f4 or 18 ♗d2 ♘c4 19 ♗e3 Keene) d5 19 e5 ♘e4 20 ♗b2 (20 ♘xe4 de 21 ♗xe4 ♗b4 22 ♗xb7 ♘xb7 23 ♖xe4 ♗c3 24 ♖b1 ♘c5∓∓) ♖xe5 21 f3 ♖g5 22 ♘f1? (22 ♘h1! ♘f6 23 ♕d3 fights on) ♖xg2+! 0–1 (23 ♔xg2 ♕g5+ 24 ♔h1 ♘f2+ or 24 ♔h2 ♗d6+) Short–Hebden, Hastings 1983–84.

(b) **12 ... ♗f8** 13 ♗g5 (13 ♘e3 ♗b7 and 13 a4 b4 offer White no advantage according to *ECO*) h6 14 ♗h4 g5!? (14 ... g6 15 d4 cd 16 cd ed 17 ♘xd4 ♗g7 unclear; Najdorf–Eliskases, Torremolinos 1961) 15 ♗g3 ♘h5 16 ♘e3 ♘f4 17 d4 ♗g7 18 d5 ♗d7 19 ♘d2 ♘b7 20 ♘f5 ♗xf5 21 ef c4= Mokry–Lin, Dubai Ol. 1986.

13   ♗g5

Apparently a new move. *ECO*'s main line runs 13 ♘e3 (13 ♕e2 d5, 13 h3 ♕c7 and 13 a4 all lead to= says *ECO*) ♗f8 14 a4 ♗b7 15 h3 ♕c7 16 ♘f5 ♘e7 17 ♘3h4 ♘g6= Ivkov–Filip, Zagreb 1955.

13 ...   ♗e6
14 ♘e3   ♘g4

15 ♗xe3 ♘xe3 16 ♗xd8 ♘xd1

17 ♗c7 (17 ♖exd1!? ♖exd8 18 ♘g5 ♗d7 19 a4± Tal) ♘xb2 18 ♖eb1 ♖ec8 19 ♗xd6 ♘xd3 20 ♗xd3 ♖d8 21 a4 ♖xd6 22 ab ♖xd3 23 bc f6 24 c7 ♖c8 25 ♖xa6 ♔f7 26 ♖c6 ♖xc7 27 h4 ♗d7 28 ♖b8 ♔e7 29 h5 c4 (29 ... h6!? 30 ♘h4 ♗xc6 31 ♖xc8 ♔d7 32 ♖g8 ♔xc7 33 ♖xg7+ ♔b6 34 f3 unclear—Tal) 30 ♔h2 ♖c1 31 ♖xc8 ♗xc8 32 ♘d2 ♔d7 33 h6 gh 34 ♖xc4 ♖xc4 35 ♘xc4 ♔xc7 36 ♘e3 ♗c6 37 ♔g3 ♔c5 38 ♘d5 ½–½ (Ljubojevic–Tal, Reykjavik 1987).

B

8   h3*(147)*

Unlike other eighth moves which are played to avoid the Marshall altogether, this is a specific Anti-Marshall designed to invite but refute 8 ... d5. White can develop his knight at c3 and Black's ... ♕h4 will not win a tempo.

147
B

8 ...   ♗b7

8 ... d6 9 c3 is a main line

closed Spanish, outside the scope of this book.

The main point of 8 h3 is that after 8 ... d5!? 9 ed ♘xd5 10 ♘xe5 ♘xe5 11 ♖xe5 White has options involving ♘c3. However, Black's gambit is perhaps not as obviously bad as once thought.

A recent example is 11 ... ♘f4 (11 ... ♗b7 12 ♘c3 ♘f4 13 d4 ♘xg2? 14 ♗d5 ♗xd5 15 ♖xd5± ± Bronstein; 11 ... c6 12 d4 ♗d6 13 ♖e1 ♕h4 14 ♕f3 and ♘c3) 12 d4 ♘g6 13 ♖e1 ♔h8!? 14 c3 ♗b7 15 ♘d2 ♘h4 16 g3 ♘g6 17 ♘f3 ♕d7 18 h4 ♗d6 19 ♘g5 h6 20 ♕h5 ♕f5 21 ♖e2 ♕d7 22 ♗d2 ♕c6 23 d5 ♕d7 unclear; White now sacrificed unsoundly by 24 ♖e6?! fe 25 ♕xg6 hg 26 ♕h5+ ♔g8 27 de ♕e7 28 ♗xg5 ♖f6 29 ♖e1 ♖af8 30 f4 g6 31 ♕h6 c5 32 ♗c2 ♕g7 33 ♕xg7+ ♔xg7 34 ♗xf6+ ♔xf6 (0–1, 60) Perenyi–Blatny, Leipzig 1988.

9 d3

This position is important as it also often arises via 8 d3 ♗b7 9 h3. Other moves are no problem to Black:

(a) **9 c3** d5! 10 ed (10 d4 ed 11 e5 ♘e4 12 cd ♘a5 13 ♗c2 f5 14 ef ♗xf6 is fine for Black) ♘xd5 when 11 d4! ed 12 cd ♗f6 13 ♘c3= (in several games) not 11 d3 (11 ♘xe5? ♘xe5 12 ♖xe5 ♘f4) ♕d6 12 ♘bd2 ♖ad8 13

♘c4 ♕g6 14 ♘g3 ♗c5∓ (Fischer–Szabo, Portoroz 1958).

(b) **9 ♘c3** d6 10 ♘d5 ♘a5 11 ♘xe7+ ♕xe7 12 d3 ♘xb3 13 ab ♘d7 (13 ... ♖e8 Gheorghiu–Kavalek, Amsterdam 1975) 14 ♕d2 c5= Taimanov–Lilienthal, Moscow 1948.

9 ... d6

Black has two ways to avoid this line. Both are worth more examination but are probably much riskier:

(a) **9 ... ♖e8** 10 c3 (10 ♘g5!? ♖f8 or 10 ... d5!?) ♗f8 (10 ... h6 see note b) 11 ♘bd2 d5!? (11 ... d6 12 ♘f1 ♘a5 and ... c5 Akopian) 12 ed! (12 ♕e2!? Akopian) ♘xd5 13 d4± and now:

(a1) **13 ... ♕d6!** 14 ♘e4 (If 14 c4 ♘f4 and chasing the queen only helps Black after 15 d5 ♘d4 16 ♘e4 ♕g6 17 ♘h4 ♕h5 18 ♗xf4 ♕xd1 19 ♖axd1 ♘xb3 20 ab ef 21 c5 ♖ad8 22 b4 ♖e5— Djuric) ♕d7 15 a4 ba 16 ♗xa4 ed 17 ♘xd4 ♘b6 18 ♗f4 (18 ♗xc6 ♗xc6 19 ♘xc6 ♖xe4∓ Djuric) ♘xa4 19 ♕xa4 ♕d5 20 ♘f3 ♖e7 21 ♗g5 ♖e6 22 c4 (22 ♖ad1 ♕f5 23 ♘h4 ♖xe4 24 ♕xc6 ♖xe1+ 25 ♖xe1 ♕xf2+ ∓) ♕d7 23 ♖ad1 ♕e8 Black plus: two bishops (0–1, 36) S. Perenyi–S. Djuric, Saint John Open 1988.

(a2) **13 ... ♘f4** 14 ♘e4! ♘a5 (Akopian–Blatny, World Junior

Ch. Adelaide 1988) 15 ♘eg5!
♘xb3 16 ♕xb3 ♗d5 17 ♕c2 ±
Akopian.

(b) 9 ... h6!? when:

(b1) 10 ♘bd2 ♖e8 11 c3 ♗f8 12
♘f1 (12 ♘h2 ♘a5 13 ♗c2 d5 14
♘g4 c5 Ljubojevic–Geller, London 1982) ♘a5 (12 ... d5?! 13 ed
♘xd5 [Pritchett–Motwani, British Ch. 1987] 14 d4! e4 15
♘3d2± Hazai, *YB10*) 13 ♗c2
c5!? (13 ... d5 14 ♕e2= *ECO*) 14
♘g3 d5 Hazai.

(b2) 10 ♘c3! d6 11 a4 ♘a5 12
♗a2 b4 13 ♘e2 c5 14 c3 bc? (14
... c4 15 ♘g3 b3 16 ♗b1 ± Balashov; 14 ... ♖b8 intending ... b3
Georgadze) 15 bc c4 16 ♘g3 cd 17
♕xd3 (1–0, 30) Balashov–Geller,
USSR Ch. 1983.

(b3) 10 a4!? ♖e8 11 ♘c3 b4 12
♘d5 or 10 ... d6 11 ♘c3 ♘a5 12
♗a2 b4 13 ♘e2 (compare
Chapter 19) Hazai.

10	c3	♘a5
11	♗c2	c5
12	♘bd2	

A version of the Zaitsev variation has arisen (7 ... d6 8 c3 0–0 9
h3 ♗b7!? with 10 d3 instead of the
critical 10 d4). *ECO* considers this
line in both C88/4 and C92/25
giving different continuations!
The position is roughly equal but
White's slow build-up should not
be underestimated.

| 12 | ... | ♖e8 |

Both 12 ... ♕c7 13 ♘f1 ♖fe8
and 12 ... ♘c6 13 ♘f1 ♖e8 (not
13 ... d5?! 14 ed ♕xd5 15 ♗b3
♕d6 16 ♘g3±) are dealt with
below.

| 13 | ♘f1 | ♘c6 |

(a) 13 ... h6 14 ♘g3 ♗f8 15
d4!? (15 ♘h2 d5 16 ♘h5 ♘h7 17
♕g4 ♖e6 18 f4 Ljubojevic–Sax,
Hilversum 1973) cd 16 cd ed 17
♘xd4 ♖c8 18 b3 d5? 19 e5 ♘e4
20 ♘xe4 de 21 ♗xe4 ♗b4 22
♕g4! ♕xd4 23 ♗xh6 g6 24 ♖ad1
♕b6 25 ♗xb7 ♗xe1 26 ♗xc8
♕xf2+ 27 ♔h2 ♖xe5 28 ♗xa6
♗c3 29 ♕c8+ ♔h7 30 ♕xc3 1–0
Psakhis–Pavlovic, Erevan 1988.

(b) 13 ... ♕c7 14 ♘g3 (14 ♘e3
g6 15 b4 cb 16 cb ♘c6= Spassky–
Szabo, Budapest 1959) d5?!
(better 14 ... ♖ad8 15 ♕e2 d5 16
ed ♖xd5 17 ♗g5 g6! Tal–Geller,
Kislovodsk 1966) 15 ed ♗xd5 16
♘xe5 ♗d6 17 d4 ♗xe5 18 de
♖xe5 19 ♖xe5 ♕xe5 20 ♘e3
♗c6 21 b4 cb 22 cb ♘c4 23 ♗d4
♕d5 24 f3 ♕e6 25 ♘f5 ♘d6 26
♘xg7! ♔xg7 27 ♕d2 ♘de8 28
♖e1 ♕d5 29 ♗e4 1–0 Psakhis–
Malaniuk, USSR Ch. 1987.

| 14 | ♘g3 | |

14 a4 h6 15 ♘g3 ♗f8 16 ab ab
17 ♖xa8 ♗xa8 18 ♘h2 ♗b7 19
♘g4 ♗c8 20 ♗b3 ♘xg4 ½–½
(Kosten–Nunn, Geneva 1987).

| 14 | ... | g6 |

Or 14 ... ♗f8 15 d4 (15 ♘f5!?

h6 16 g4± Ciocaltea–Hennings, Bucharest 1971) cd 16 cd ♖c8 17 d5! ♘b4 18 ♗b1 ♕c7 19 ♗g5 (Timoshchenko–I. Ivanov, USSR Otborochny 1975) ♘d7= Tseitlin.

15	**♘h2**	**d5**
16	**♘g4**	**♘xg4**

17 ♕xg4 ♗c8 18 ♘f5 unclear (Pachman–Geller, Stockholm 1952).

C

8 a3*(148)*

Suetin's patent, envisaging bishop retreats to a2. Nobody else seems to have much enthusiasm for it although it had a brief vogue in the mid-1970s.

148
B

8	**...**	**d6**

With a line usually arising from 7 ... d6 8 a3 0-0 9 c3. Black can avoid this at some risk:

(a) 8 ... ♗b7 9 d3 h6 (9 ... d5!? Suetin; 9 ... d6 below) 10 ♘bd2 (10 ♘c3!? Suetin) ♖e8 11 ♘f1 ♗f8 12 ♘g3 d5! 13 ♗d2 ♕d7 14

♕e2 (Suetin–Plachetka, Dubna 1979) ♖ad8 unclear.

(b) 8 ... d5!? 9 ed ♘xd5 10 ♘xe5 (10 ♗xd5 ♕xd5 11 ♘c3± Gufeld) ♘xe5 11 ♖xe5 c6 12 d4 ♗d6 13 ♖e1 (13 ♖e4!? Suetin) ♕h4 14 g3 ♕h3 with compensation (Suetin–Lukovnikov, USSR 1978).

9	**c3**	**♘a5**

(a) 9 ... ♘d7 10 d4 ♗f6 11 ♗e3 (11 d5 ♘e7=) ♖b8 12 ♘bd2 ♘b6 13 ♖c1 ♗g4 14 d5 (14 h3!? Gligoric) ♘a5 15 ♗a2 ♘ac4 (Suetin–Gligoric, Havana 1969) 16 ♘xc4 (16 ♗xb6!? Gligoric) ♘xc4 17 ♗xc4 bc= *ECO*.

(b) 9 ... ♗e6 10 d4 ♗xb3 (10 ... ♗g4!? is like Chapter 21; Suetin–Simagin, Moscow Ch. 1982) 11 ♕xb3 d5!? (11 ... ♕b8 12 ♗g5 ♕b6 13 ♕d1 ♖fe8 14 h3 ♖ad8 15 d5 ♘b8 16 ♘bd2 ♘bd7 17 c4± Suetin–Zakharov, USSR 1979) 12 ed ♘a5 13 ♕c2 ed 14 cd ♘xd5 15 ♘c3 ♖e8 16 ♗g5!?± Suetin–Lukacs, Leipzig 1986.

10 ♗a2

10 ♗c2 c5 11 d4 (11 b4!? Gufeld) ♕c7 (11 ... cd 12 cd ♘c6 13 h3 ♗b7 14 ♘c3 ♖c8= Minic–Majstorovic, Cacak 1969) 12 b4 (12 ♘bd2!? *ECO*) cb 13 cb ♘c4 14 ♘bd2 ♘xd2 15 ♘xd2 ♗g4 16 f3 ♖ac8 17 ♖a2 ♗e6 18 d5 ♗d7= Suetin–Lengyel, Sarajevo 1965.

19	**...**	**c5**

11 d3

Or 11 d4 ♕c7 12 ♘bd2 ♘c6 13 d5 ♘d8 14 ♘f1 ♘e8 = Tikhomirov–Manteifel, corr. 1968.

11 ... h6

12 ♘bd2 ♗e6 =

Kotov's improvement on 12 ... ♖e8 13 b4 ♘c6 14 ♘f1 ♗f8 15 ♘e3 ♗e6 16 ♘d5± a5 17 a4! (1–0, 38) Malevinsky–Ivanov, USSR 1977.

Index of Variations

1 e4 e5 2 ♘f3 ♘c6 3 ♗b5 a6 4 ♗a4 ♘f6 5 0-0 ♗e7 6 ♖e1 b5 7 ♗b3 0-0

13 ♖e1 ♕h4 14 g3 ♕h3 **5–71**
15 ♗xd5 63
15 ♖e4 g5 **66–71**
  16 ♕f1 67
  16 ♕f3! 68
15 ♗e3 **5–61**
  15 ... ♗f5 59
  15 ... ♖e8 60
15 ... ♗g4 16 ♕d3 **5–57**
  16 ... f5 53
  16 .., ♘xe3 56
16 ... ♖ae8 17 ♘d2 **5–52**
17 ..., f5 18 f4 ♔h8 19 ♗xd5 cd 20 ♕f1 ♕h5 21 a4 **42–52**
  21 ... ba 46
  21 ... g5 48
17 ... ♖e6 **5–41**
18 ♗xd5 cd 19 ♕f1 ♕h5 20 a4 **31–4**
  20 ... ba 33
  20 ... f5 34
18 ♗d1 35
18 ♕f1 37
18 c4 ♗f4 **37–41**
  19 cd 38
  19 ♕f1 39
18 a4 **5–30**
18 ... ba 25
18 ... ♕h5 19 ab ab **27–30**
  20 ♘f1 27
  20 ♕f1 29
18 ... f5 19 ♕f1 ♕h5 20 f4 ba **5–23**
  21 ♗xd5 8
  21 ♖xa4 **11–23**
    21 ... ♔h8 11
    21 ... ♖fe8 12
    21 ... ♖b8 22 ♗xd5 cd 13
      23 ♕g2 14
      23 ♖xa6 ♖be8 16
        24 ♕g2 17